To become a god
Cosmology, Sacrifice, and Self-Divinization in Early China

Harvard-Yenching Institute
Monographs Series 57

To become a god

Cosmology, Sacrifice, and Self-Divinization in Early China

Michael J. Puett

Published by the Harvard University Asia Center for the
Harvard-Yenching Institute
Distributed by Harvard University Press
Cambridge, Massachusetts, and London, England, 2002

Printed in the United States of America

The Harvard-Yenching Institute, founded in 1928 and headquartered at Harvard University, is a foundation dedicated to the advancement of higher education in the humanities and social sciences in East and Southeast Asia. The Institute supports advanced research at Harvard by faculty members of certain Asian universities and doctoral studies at Harvard and other universities by junior faculty at the same universities. It also supports East Asian studies at Harvard through contributions to the Harvard-Yenching Library and publication of the *Harvard Journal of Asiatic Studies* and books on premodern East Asian history and literature.

Library of Congress Cataloging-in-Publication Data

Puett, Michael J., 1964–

To become a god : cosmology, sacrifice, and self-divinization in early China / Michael J. Puett.

p. cm. -- (Harvard-Yenching Institute monograph series ; 57)

Includes bibliographic references and index.

ISBN 0-674-00959-2 (cloth : alk. paper) -- ISBN 0-674-01643-2 (pbk. : alk. paper)

1. God--Proof, Cosmological. 2. Divinization--China. 3. I. Title: Cosmology, sacrifice, and self-divinization in early China. II. Title. III. Series.

BT100.P9 2002

299'.51--dc 21   2002017257

Index by Mary Mortensen

☯ Printed on acid-free paper

First paperback edition 2004

Last number below indicates year of this printing

12 11 10 09 08 07 06 05 04

For God doth know that in the day ye eat therof, then your eyes shall be opened, and ye shall be as gods.

—*The Bible*, Genesis 3, King James version

Emperors and kings,
are but obeyed in their several provinces,
Nor can they raise the wind or rend the clouds;
But in his dominion that exceeds in this
Stretcheth as far as doth the mind of man.
A sound magician is a mighty god:
Here, Faustus, try thy brains to gain a deity.

—Christopher Marlowe, *The Tragedy
of Doctor Faustus*, lines 60–66

Who was it who first
Wrecked the bonds of love
And transformed them into chains?
Which led rebels to make
A mock of their rights
And the heavenly fire and,
Disdaining mortal ways,
Elect presumption,
Striving to become the equals of gods.

—Friedrich Hölderlin, "The Rhine" (Translation by
Richard Sieburth, *Hymns and Fragments*, pp. 73–75)

To David, Mary, Brannon, Connor, and Meg

Acknowledgments

This book is a product of my long-standing interest in three distinct disciplines: anthropology, history, and philosophy. Indeed, three of my scholarly degrees are from these fields (BA's in History and Philosophy, and an MA and a Ph.D. in Anthropology). My strong belief has always been that working across these disciplines can be highly productive—perhaps more from the tensions that arise than from the harmonies. My models have been my teachers: Marshall Sahlins, Anthony C. Yu, Edward Shaughnessy, and Paul Friedrich, each of whose research straddles several disciplines.

I began researching the topics covered in this book as a graduate student at the University of Chicago, but put this research aside when it became necessary to focus on completing my dissertation. The dissertation was subsequently revised and became my first book, *The Ambivalence of Creation: Debates Concerning Innovation and Artifice in Early China* (Stanford University Press, 2001). Much of the research and writing of the present work was undertaken while teaching at Harvard University. Although this book is broader in scope and includes more anthropological and comparative analysis than *Ambivalence of Creation*, the two works are related.

During the decade I have been working on this book, an enormous number of people have played invaluable roles in shaping the project. Foremost among them are my teachers at the University of Chicago: Marshall Sahlins, Anthony C. Yu, Edward Shaughnessy, and Paul Friedrich. I continue to be deeply indebted to each of them, and each remains a constant source of inspiration for me.

I also thank my colleagues at Harvard University, who have provided an exciting intellectual environment over the past seven years. I express my gratitude in particular to Peter Bol, with whom I have had so many stimulating conversations about Chinese intellectual history. Special thanks as well to Wilt Idema, Stephen Owen, and Tu Wei-Ming. I feel myself fortunate to have such intellectually engaged colleagues. My deep appreciation also to Benjamin Schwartz and K. C. Chang, with whom I had many exciting conversations about this book. I have continued my conversations with them in the pages that follow; I deeply regret not being able to hear their replies. Harvard is an emptier place without them.

I also give heartfelt thanks to David Keightley. Even the numerous footnotes and lengthy discussions of his ideas that fill this book do not adequately reveal my debt to David. His ability to link meticulous scholarship, insightful historical analysis, and a provocative use of anthropological theory has long inspired my work. I see this book as being, to a significant degree, part of lengthy and ongoing conversation with David.

The reviewers of an early version of this book for the Harvard University Asia Center, Stephen Durrant and an anonymous reader, helped immeasurably in making this a more coherent and readable work. The remaining errors are my own, but they are probably all places where I failed to address sufficiently the inadequacies the reviewers so expertly pointed out.

Many sections of this book were delivered as conference talks and invited lectures over the past several years, beginning in 1996: several meetings of the Warring States Working Group, organized by E. Bruce Brooks at the University of Massachusetts at Amherst; two Association of Asian Studies meetings (1997 and 1999); the University of Chicago; Stanford University; the University of California at Berkeley; the University of Oregon; the University of Pennsylvania; Grinnell College; Indiana University; the University of Heidelberg; Brown University; Bowdoin College; Princeton University; the University of California at Riverside; and the University of Michigan. I am extremely grateful to the many scholars whose comments on those occasions have been invaluable to the development of the ideas in this book.

E. Bruce Brooks has played a significant role in the field by organizing several Warring States Working Group conferences as well as the Warring

States Working Group e-mail list. My views have benefited immeasurably from the lively and provocative debates he has stimulated.

I am deeply grateful to those many students at Harvard University who had to listen to these ideas about humans and spirits in early China, probably far more than they would have liked, over the years in my seminars and reading groups. I thank them not only for voicing their excellent ideas, comments, and criticisms on those many occasions but also for playing a crucial role in building such a vibrant intellectual community at Harvard. In particular I thank Sarah Allen, Timothy Baker, Anthony Barbieri-Low, Alexander Beecroft, Erica Brindley, Rod Campbell, Jennifer Carpenter, Kang Chan, Jack Chen, Ta-Ko Chen, Stephen Chou, Mary Coker, Wiebke Denecke, Peter Ditmanson, Shari Epstein, Robert Foster, Romain Graziani, Alexander Green, Natasha Heller, Brian Hoffert, Eric Hutton, Jiang Wu, Shiamin Kwa, Vincent Leung, Kit Marlow, Andrew Meyer, David Mozina, Min Byounghee, Anne Ng, Christopher Nugent, Michael Radich, Jeff Richey, Doug Skonicki, Jennie Song, Aaron Stalnaker, David Sundahl, Sung Chia-fu, Nancy Tewkesbury, Cara Tonelli, Julius Tsai, Nicholas Tustin, Honza Vihan, Curie Virág, and Zhou Qin.

I also express my deep appreciation and gratitude to everyone whose friendship has been so important to me throughout this period: D. D. Baron, O. Bradley Bassler, Steve Bokenkamp, E. Bruce and Taeko Brooks, Rob Campany, Eileen Chow, Scott Cook, Mark Csikszentmihalyi, Stephen Durrant, Halvor Eifring, Paul Goldin, Christoph Harbsmeier, P. J. Ivanhoe, David and Vannie Keightley, Barbara Mittler, Krista Ovitz, Willard Peterson, Sarah Queen, Lisa Raphals, Harold Roth, Haun Saussy, Thomas Schmitz, Michael Scott, Laura Skosey, and Tim Weston.

Finally, my deepest gratitude to my family, to whom I owe everything that matters to me in this world.

M. J. P.

Contents

To become a god

Cosmology, Sacrifice, and Self-Divinization in Early China

Introduction

I begin with the origin of the cosmos:

Long ago, in the time before there existed Heaven and Earth, there was only figure
without form. Obscure, dark, vast, and deep—no one knows its gate. There were
two spirits (*shen* 神) born together; they aligned Heaven, they oriented Earth.
So vast—no one knows its end or limit! So overflowing—no one knows where
it stopped! Thereupon, they divided and became yin and yang, separated and became the eight pillars. Hard and soft completed each other, and the myriad things
were thereupon formed. The turbid *qi* 氣 became insects, and the refined *qi* became
humans.[1]

The passage is from the opening of the "Jingshen," chapter seven of the
Huainanzi.[2] It and similar passages are often quoted in the secondary literature as examples of cosmological thinking, of attempts to describe the universe as a spontaneous, self-generating system. Something without form existed in the past and then spontaneously divided into Heaven and Earth,
with the *qi* forming the various objects and beings of the universe.

In referring to cosmogonies like this, Frederick Mote has famously argued: "The genuine Chinese cosmology is that of organismic process, mean-

---

1. *Huainanzi*, "Jingshen," 7.1a.

2. The passage would have been written some time before 139 BC, the probable date when
Liu An gave the work to Emperor Wu of the Han.

ing that all the parts of the entire cosmos belong to one organic whole and that they all interact as participants in one spontaneously self-generating life process."[3] But, if this passage is an attempt to describe the beginnings of a spontaneous universe, then what are we to do with the third sentence: "There were two spirits born together; they aligned Heaven, they oriented Earth"? Why would a universe that is self-generating and spontaneous require two spirits to align and orient it? The spirits themselves may have been born naturally, but their subsequent actions are almost like those of demiurges—figures who actively plan and organize the structure of the cosmos.

Indeed, the words used to describe the actions of the spirits (aligning and orienting: jing ying 經 營) are loaded terms, with strong resonances in the early texts. The terms were commonly used to describe the ways that sages surveyed and organized prior to an act of construction. In the "Shao gao" chapter of the Shangshu, for example, we find: "The Grand Protector arrived in the morning at Luoyang and performed crackmaking about the site. Once he obtained the cracks, he aligned and oriented (jing ying)[the city]."[4] The passage refers to the preparations for the construction of the new capital of the Zhou at the beginning of their dynasty. The Grand Protector, after receiving favorable auguries, aligned the boundaries of the city from which the Zhou could then control the north China plain.

The terms are found as well in the Shijing poem "Lingtai" (Mao #242), which is also quoted in Mencius 1A/2:

> He aligned and commenced the Numinous Tower,
> He aligned it and oriented it.
> The people labored on it,
> In less than a day they completed it.[5]

The figure (understood at least by the time of Mencius to be King Wen) personally aligned and oriented the Numinous Tower prior to the actual work of construction.

In these passages from the Shangshu and Shijing, the words refer to the organizational activities of sages, and in both cases the organizational work involved an attempt to align and orient human structures so as to harmonize them with divine powers. So why would the authors of the Huainanzi pas-

---

3. Mote, Intellectual Foundations of China, p. 15.
4. Shangshu zhengyi, "Shao gao," 15.1b.
5. Shi, #242.

sage utilize such loaded terms to characterize the actions of spirits before the emergence of the cosmos? Why do spirits have to align the cosmos before it is spontaneously formed?

The answer, as I will argue in Chapter 7, has little to do with early Chinese assumptions about the cosmos. Soon after the passage just quoted, the authors of the chapter discuss programs of self-cultivation that enable the adept to become a spirit.[6] Spirits first aligned and oriented the cosmos, and humans can then become spirits and exercise control of the cosmos as well. The opening cosmogony of the chapter, therefore, sets the basis for a series of crucial claims concerning the ability of humans to divinize themselves and thus gain control over natural phenomena. The authors are less interested in positing a spontaneous universe than in asserting the theomorphic powers of human adepts.

A similar concern with humans becoming spirits and thus gaining power over the natural world appears in another chapter of the Huainanzi:

If one climbs twice as high as Kunlun, [the peak] is called the Mountain of Liang-feng. If one ascends it, one will not die. If one climbs twice as high, it is called Xuanpu. If one ascends it, one will become numinous and be able to control the wind and the rain. Twice as high, it stretches up to Heaven. If one climbs it, one will become a spirit. This is called the Realm of the Great God (Di).[7]

The passage describes the process of self-cultivation metaphorically as an act of climbing the peaks above Kunlun Mountain ever higher toward the realm of the Great God. With each step in the process, one gains ever more power over natural phenomena—first achieving immortality and then gaining direct control over the wind and rain. Ultimately, one becomes a spirit and lives with the Great God.

Both Huainanzi passages posit not a spontaneous cosmos but one organized and controlled by spirits. And, in this particular sense, the passages were in the mainstream of the claims made in most texts from early China: as I will argue below, visions of a purely spontaneous cosmos, in which natural phenomena are not under the power of spirits, arose very late in the Warring States period and were never more than a minority opinion. What is noteworthy about these two passages are rather the claims made about the

---

6. Huainanzi, "Jingshen," 7.2b.

7. Huainanzi, "Dixing," 4.3a. See the excellent discussion by John Major in Heaven and Earth in Early Han Thought, pp. 158–61.

ability of humans to divinize themselves. In contrast to the chronologically earlier *Shijing* and *Shangshu*, these segments do not present humans as trying to propitiate or placate divine powers. Indeed, within the cosmology presented in these *Huainanzi* passages, one need not use divination and sacrifice to manipulate the spirits; instead the adept becomes a spirit directly and appropriates their powers.

This book is an attempt to reconstruct the debate within which such claims of the theomorphic potentials of humans were made and within which such claims grew to be increasingly important. I will trace this debate, which ran from the Shang through the Han, analyzing competing arguments concerning the nature of spirits, the proper demarcation (or lack thereof) between humans and spirits, and the types of potency that humans and spirits should be allowed to exercise over the natural world. As I will argue, claims about the nature of the cosmos, and the degree to which it is or is not controlled by willful agents (human or spirit), arose within this debate and can be understood fully only within that context.

In order to analyze this debate in its full complexity, I will discuss the notions and practices of divination and sacrifice during this period and will look in depth at the ways and reasons that these practices were criticized by figures claiming the ability to become, rather than simply manipulate, spirits. And I will also detail the rise of claims that the cosmos is a spontaneous system—claims that arose in opposition both to the sacrificial and divination specialists of the day and to the proponents of the increasingly popular view that humans had theomorphic potentials. In short, I hope to provide a full cultural and intellectual history of the rise of both self-divinization movements and correlative cosmology in early China.

This historical account of the dispute over the relationship between humans and spirits and the natural world will give us a glimpse of a crucial debate in early China, one that had great ramifications for developing notions of human powers, the nature of spirits, and the types of sacrificial practice that should be supported by the state. It will also throw into question numerous long-standing assumptions about early China. The revised picture should shed light on how these aspects of early Chinese religious practice can be understood from a historical perspective and help point to a very different way of thinking about early China from a comparative point of view. In order to outline the implications of the issues to be discussed, I turn to a summary of some of the relevant secondary literature on these issues.

Secondary Scholarship

One of the points I will try to demonstrate in these pages is the degree to which analyses of these issues concerning humans and spirits in early China have been based, implicitly or explicitly, on comparative frameworks and comparative categories that for the most part originated in the fields of sociology, anthropology, and the history of religions. This is true not only for scholars in America and Europe but also for those in China, Taiwan, and Japan. One of my intents here is to tease out these categories (notions such as shamanism, monism, rationality) as well as some of the comparative frameworks (evolutionary, contrastive cosmologies) in which these categories have been employed. In this section, I outline some of the most influential of these comparative categories and frameworks. This will put us in a position to see, as other scholars are discussed in the main part of the book, the degree to which their approaches are based on the categories presented here.

My goal is not to debunk the use of comparative categories or to argue against comparison per se. On the contrary, I, too, will make comparisons, particularly with ancient Greece, and I will be working with a number of anthropological discussions of, for example, kingship, cosmology, and sacrifice. My goal is, rather, to question the types of comparative categories employed thus far and to point toward what I hope are other, more successful approaches.

Perhaps the single most influential figure in the twentieth century to have studied China is Max Weber. The main corpus of Weber's writings consists of comparative analyses of the major civilizations in world history. His guiding concern was the study of rationalism: Why did particular forms of rational activity develop in the West, and why did such activity develop to only limited degrees elsewhere? To undertake this project, Weber made a typology of what he considered the major spheres of society: the economy, society, government, the law, and religion. Since Weber saw each of these spheres as relatively autonomous, he believed they could be studied separately. For Weber, a civilization was the result of the interaction of these spheres.[8] Weber's comparative method consisted of comparing each of these

---

8. Because of the popularity of *The Protestant Ethic and the Spirit of Capitalism*, Weber has incorrectly become associated with the belief that religion determines the degree of rationality that a society achieves. In fact, Weber held no such position. His analysis of Protestantism

spheres across civilizations and the different interactions of these spheres in each society in order to determine the levels of rationality achieved in each civilization and to understand what prevented the full florescence of rationality in non-Western civilizations.

Perhaps Weber's most influential discussion of these issues with respect to China was his contrasting of Confucianism and Protestantism. Weber measured these two religions (in his terminology) according to a universal yardstick of rationalization:

To judge the level of rationalization a religion represents we may use two primary yardsticks which are in many ways inter-related. One is the degree to which the religion has divested itself of magic; the other is the degree to which it has systematically unified the relation between God and the world and therewith its own ethical relationship to the world.[9]

In Weber's view, Protestantism had achieved an extreme form of rationalization in terms of both of these measures. In terms of the first yardstick, Protestant modes of thought "have liquidated magic most completely," leading to a "complete disenchantment of the world" (p. 226). And, in terms of the second, Protestantism precipitated a "tremendous and grandiose tension toward the world" (p. 227).

Confucianism, in contrast, registers far lower on both of these yardsticks. It is characterized by a "toleration of magical and animist conceptions" (p. 196). More specifically, "one may say that every sort of rationalization of the archaic empirical knowledge and craft in China has moved toward a magic image of the world" (p. 196). Instead of rejecting magic altogether, Confucianism converted a magical worldview into a monistic cosmos: "Cosmogonic speculation with the sacred number five operated in terms of five planets, five elements, five organs, etc., macrocosm and microcosm. . . . This Chinese 'universist' philosophy and cosmogony transformed the world into a magic garden" (pp. 199–200). Chinese cosmological thinking, in short, was

---

reflected his claim that it was an important influence on the emergence of capitalism in the West. But he did not hold that religion in general is the only factor that determines rationality. For Weber, a full analysis of any civilization involves the study of the interactions of all these spheres, and a full comparative study involves comparisons of each of these spheres with those found in other civilizations. Religion, then, was only one of many spheres. Thus, although I focus here primarily on Weber's views on Chinese religions, I do so only because of the emphasis of this book.

9. Weber, *The Religion of China*, p. 226 (hereinafter cited in the text).

simply a rationalization of magic into a formal system—for that same reason, it never transcended a magical approach to the world.

Confucianism was also "a rational ethic which reduced tension with the world to an absolute minimum" (p. 227). Indeed, there was no tension at all between the human and the divine spheres: "Completely absent in Confucian ethics was any tension between nature and deity, between ethical demand and human shortcoming, consciousness of sin and need for salvation, conduct on earth and compensation in the beyond, religious duty and sociopolitical reality" (pp. 235–36). Confucianism saw cosmos and society as fully linked, and the ethical imperative was simply to adjust oneself to these cosmic and social spheres:

Confucianism meant adjustment to the world, to its orders and conventions. . . . The cosmic orders of the world were considered fixed and inviolate and the orders of society were but a special case of this. The great spirits of the cosmic orders obviously desired only the happiness of the world and especially the happiness of man. The same applied to the orders of society. The "happy" tranquility of the empire and the equilibrium of the soul should and could be attained only if man fitted himself into the internally harmonious cosmos. (pp. 152–53)

The difference between Protestantism and Confucianism could not be more clear:

From the relation between the supra-mundane God and the creaturally wicked, ethically irrational world there resulted . . . the absolute unholiness of tradition and truly endless task of ethically and rationally subduing and mastering the given world, i.e., rational, objective "progress." Here, the task of the rational transformation of the world stood opposed to the Confucian adjustment to the world. (p. 240)

As a consequence, "the varied conditions which externally favored the origin of capitalism in China did not suffice to create it" (p. 248).

One sees in Weber's argument two concerns that will appear repeatedly throughout twentieth-century discussions of Chinese thought: a concern with comparing China and the West with reference to an evolutionary development of rationality and a concern with comparing China and the West by contrasting their purportedly distinctive cosmologies. At times, as in Weber himself, these two were seen as linked. More often, however, these models came to be presented in opposition to each other. Indeed, these have become two of the basic poles around which scholarship on early Chinese thought and religion has developed. And, intriguingly, although almost all of these sinological studies were written as attempts to defend the Chinese tradition against Weberian critiques, they tend to do so by maintaining one of these two poles of the Weberian framework and simply reversing the valuation given to China.

These poles can be seen in two highly influential studies published in the 1930s: Fung Yu-lan's *A History of Chinese Philosophy*, and Marcel Granet's *La pensée chinoise*. Fung's work was to become one of the most significant studies of the evolution of Chinese philosophy, and Granet's the most important work on early Chinese cosmological thinking. Both were written to defend the Chinese tradition by showing it to be as strong as the Western tradition. But whereas Fung attempted to do so by showing that Chinese philosophy developed through the same evolutionary process as had the Western tradition, Granet defended Chinese thought by arguing that it was based on a cosmology radically different from, but nonetheless as important as, the cosmology that dominated the West. I will discuss each of these works in turn, beginning with Granet.

Granet's main concern in *La pensée chinoise* was to delineate the "governing ideas"[10] of early Chinese thought,[11] and one of his central arguments was that Chinese thought is not "prelogical" or "mystical." On the contrary, once one understands the basic principles that underlie Chinese thought, one can see that it forms a meaningful, coherent system (pp. 28–29).

Intriguingly, Granet's presentation of "Chinese thought" is in its general outlines quite similar to Weber's view of Confucianism, with the crucial difference that what Weber saw as restricting the full development of rationality is the very thing Granet celebrated as part of the genius of Chinese thinking. For example, Granet argued, one finds no "world of transcendent realities outside the human world" (p. 279). Indeed, this claim (made in extremely positive terms) that the Chinese lacked a notion of transcendent principles—one of the characteristics that Weber saw as limiting China—pervades Granet's analysis. According to Granet, the Chinese had no sense of a transcendent Law or God and no notion of abstraction (pp. 476, 479). Indeed, the Chinese assumed a fully monistic cosmos: "Man and nature did not form two separate realms, but one unique society" (p. 25).

---

10. Granet, *La pensée chinoise*, p. 26 (hereinafter cited in the text).

11. I will deal here only briefly with Granet's overall approach. For a more detailed discussion of Granet's work, see Chapters 4 and 6.

To make this argument, Granet worked primarily from those Han texts devoted to building complex correlative systems based on yin-yang, five phases, and microcosmic/macrocosmic relations. However, he read these cosmological notions not as a particular historical development during the Han but as indications of Chinese thinking in general. Indeed, this viewpoint is evident in the organization of the book. The first three quarters are devoted to working out these cosmological systems in detail. Then, in the final quarter of the book, Granet looks at individual thinkers, beginning with Confucius. Each thinker is presented as building on a particular aspect of this "Chinese" cosmology. In other words, instead of presenting cosmology as a late development building on or reacting against earlier figures like Confucius, Granet reads correlative thinking as the guiding principle of all Chinese thought.

Like Granet, Fung Yu-lan was interested in arguing for the value of Chinese thought. But his method of doing so was quite different. Instead of defining a distinct logical system that underlay its seeming strangeness, Fung Yu-lan's main move was to place Chinese thought within the evolutionary framework that dominated contemporary studies of Western philosophy and to read the history of thought in early China in the same terms as was then commonly done for Greece.[12] He presented early Chinese philosophy in terms of a shift from religion to philosophy, from theistic views to rationality, and argued that humanism, rationalism, and naturalism were indigenous to Chinese philosophy and emerged at the same time in China as they purportedly had in ancient Greece. And, although the resulting philosophical tradition in China did not develop in logic and epistemology to the degree found in Greece, it excelled in the study of self-cultivation.[13]

In order to demonstrate this common evolution, Fung Yu-lan began by reconstructing the "primitive" period that China shared with all other civilizations. For Fung, the defining feature of primitive thought was a theistic cosmology: "In the time of primitive man the belief was general, not only in China but in other parts of the world, that natural phenomena and human affairs are all under a divine and supernatural control" (p. 22). In having such a cosmology in the Bronze Age, Fung argued strongly, the Chinese were no different from the Greeks: "The Chinese of that time were superstitious and

---

12. See, e.g., Cornford, *From Religion to Philosophy*.
13. Fung, *A History of Chinese Philosophy*, 1: 1–3 (hereinafter cited in the text).

ignorant; they had religious ideas but no philosophy; so that the religion and spirits which they believed in were exactly like those of the Greeks" (p. 24). Fung reiterated this same point several times, repeatedly emphasizing the degree to which these "superstitions" are common among all early peoples— including, most important, the early Greeks. For example, in discussing the "political and social regulations instituted by Shang Di [the high god],"[14] Fung argued, "The ancient Greeks similarly supposed that the institutions of their city-states had been created by divine beings, a belief probably general among early peoples" (p. 34). This superstitious worldview was replaced by a humanistic one in the Chunqiu period (771–481 bc): "With the coming of the Chunqiu period in China, however, or perhaps even before, there were men who tried to give a human interpretation to the laws and statutes, which they declared were established wholly by human beings for man's own benefit" (p. 34). For Fung, this was part of a crucial shift toward the rise of humanism, naturalism, and "rationalism" (p. 33).

Thus, in Fung's view, the emergence of correlative thinking was a step away from theistic views and a step toward a naturalistic conception:

The attempt to explain the phenomena of the universe through the yin-yang theory, though still primitive, is a step forward compared with explanations based on a Tian [Heaven], a Di, and a multitude of spirits. The "heaven" described in this last quotation [from the *Guoyu*] is a naturalistic one bearing strong resemblance to that of Laozi, and seems to be a forerunner of Daoist philosophy. (p. 35)

Unlike Granet, who presented yin-yang cosmology as based on a distinctively Chinese mode of logic, Fung placed it on an evolutionary scale: although still primitive, it was a step toward a fully rationalistic way of thinking.

The differences between these studies by Granet and Fung, published at almost the same time, exemplify two of the poles of analysis that would dominate twentieth-century studies of Chinese thought. For the first few decades after the publication of these two works, the evolutionary model was more influential, although the past two decades have seen a decided shift toward the cultural-essentialist model. I will continue to follow these arguments in roughly chronological order.

---

14. Here and in all the quotations throughout this book, I have substituted *pinyin* romanizations.

Perhaps the most influential study within the evolutionary framework was undertaken by Karl Jaspers, in *The Origin and Goal of History*. Jaspers's argument was that between roughly 800 and 200 BC, Greece, India, and China all experienced a philosophical revolution that he termed the "Axial Period."[15] For Jaspers, this period was defined by the emergence of transcendence—the point at which man for the first time "experiences absoluteness in the depths of selfhood and in the lucidity of transcendence" (p. 2). It further involved a struggle of "rationality" over myth and an "ethical rebellion" against "the unreal figures of the gods" (p. 17). Like Fung, but very much unlike Granet, the emphasis here is on the universal evolution of consciousness rather than on the growth of different cultural assumptions. Jaspers does admit some cultural differences (for example, he feels that China did not produce a "tragic consciousness"; p. 19), but he views these as irrelevant to a proper understanding of universal history: "Really to visualise the facts of the Axial Period and to make them the basis of our universal conception of history is to gain possession of something *common to all mankind*, beyond all differences of creed" (p. 19). According to Jaspers, China and India underwent the same transcendental breakthrough as Greece. Indeed, this transcendence created a universal form of consciousness. Unlike Weber, then, Jaspers asserts that China did, in this early period, undergo a shift toward transcendence. And also unlike Weber, Jaspers is largely uninterested in culture.

In the China field, the "Axial Period" thesis was adopted most famously by Benjamin Schwartz, who opened his study of Chinese philosophy, *The World of Thought in Ancient China*, with a reference to Jaspers:

I must confess that my own interest in ancient Chinese thought has also been much stimulated by the type of "world-historical" observations which we find in the chapter on the "axial age" in Karl Jaspers' book *The Origin and End of History*. In this small volume Jaspers highlights the fact that in many of the high civilizations of the world—the civilizations of the ancient Near East, Greece, India, and China—we witness over the period of our "first millennium B.C." the emergence of certain "creative minorities" who relate themselves in reflective, critical, and what one might even call "transcendental" ways to the civilizations from which they emerge.[16]

---

15. Jaspers, *The Origin and Goal of History*, p. 1 (hereinafter cited in the text).
16. Schwartz, *The World of Thought in Ancient China*, pp. 2–3.

In an earlier study, Schwartz discussed this notion of transcendence in greater detail:

> If there is nonetheless some common underlying impulse in all these "axial" movements, it might be called the strain towards transcendence. . . . What I refer to here is something close to the etymological meaning of the word—a kind of standing back and looking beyond—a kind of critical, reflective questioning of the actual and a new vision of what lies beyond.[17]

Although Schwartz himself downplayed the evolutionary aspects of Jaspers's argument, he supported the notion that transcendence should be seen as a valid term to compare the changes that occurred in these civilizations in the middle of the first millennium BC.

The next issue for Schwartz was to define the particular types of transcendence that occurred in each major civilization. Unlike Jaspers, then, Schwartz was interested in cultural analysis—in discovering the unique forms of transcendence that arose in each civilization. For China, he argued, the dominant tendency was "to associate the transcendent with the notion of an immanent cosmic and social order." Transcendence, then, occurred in China even within its immanentist cosmology. Thus, Schwartz characterized transcendence in China as being of a "this-worldly" sort.[18]

In making this argument, Schwartz explicitly appealed to Weber. Indeed, Schwartz's consistent move was to largely accept Weber's description of Chinese cosmology but to argue that this cosmology should be considered "rational" and "transcendental." This for Schwartz explains the "rational" cosmology found in texts like the *Shangshu* and *Shijing*, but it is a rationalism based on different principles from those seen in Greece, and thus it did not result in a Weberian "disenchantment of the world":

> To the extent that the word "rationalism" refers to the primacy of the idea of order, we can already speak here of the emergence of a kind of Chinese rationalism. It is, however, a rationalism that is radically different from many varieties of rationalism in ancient Greece. What we have is the image of an all-embracing and inclusive order which neither negates nor reduces to some one ultimate principle that which is presumed to exist. Like the rationalism of bureaucracy, it classifies and subsumes the existent reality. It is a synthetic rather than an analytic conception of order. The

---

17. Schwartz, "The Age of Transcendence," p. 3.
18. Schwartz, "Transcendence in Ancient China," pp. 67, 59–60.

spirits of nature and the ancestral spirits are not banished. Indeed, Chinese thought has never seriously attempted to carry out the "disenchantment" of the world.[19]

Schwartz further contrasted China with other ancient civilizations in terms of one of the basic points emphasized by Weber: the lack in China of a strong tension between the human and divine realms. In other ancient civilizations, most notably Mesopotamia, Egypt, Vedic India, and Greece, the human and divine realms are, according to Schwartz, viewed as contestatory: "On both the human and the divine level, attention is called to those aspects of life in which gods and humans confront each other as somewhat unpredictable individuals and groups rather than in terms of fixed 'role behavior.'"[20] In China, according to Schwartz, one finds a familial order of ancestor worship that led to a philosophical emphasis on a linkage between the divine and the human realms:

Another possible implication of ancestor worship for the religious and even "philosophic" development of China involves the relation between the divine-numinous realm and the human world. The ancestral spirits dwell in the world of the divine or numinous. . . . Thus the line dividing the "divine" from the human is not sharply drawn, and it seems that humans may possess or take on qualities which are truly numinous.[21]

Overall, then, Schwartz accepted much of Weber's framework of comparing civilizations with reference to the notion of rationalization, and he even accepted Weber's basic reading of Chinese culture as being dominated by an immanentist cosmology, a this-worldly orientation, and a lack of a tension between the human and divine realms. The only difference is that Schwartz wanted to follow Jaspers in arguing that China did shift to transcendental thinking in the early period. Schwartz thus maintained a delicate balance between the two paradigms discussed in this chapter. Although clearly working within a Weberian framework, he emphasized that a shift toward transcendence had occurred in China.

However, whereas Schwartz emphasized some degree of similarity between the early Chinese tradition and other early philosophical traditions, the most dominant paradigm over the past two decades has gone in the opposite direction. Several scholars have built on Granet's work to argue that China had a radically different cosmology from that seen in the West.

---

19. Ibid., p. 59.
20. Schwartz, *The World of Thought in Ancient China*, p. 25.
21. Ibid., p. 25.

Indeed, it is not going too far to suggest that, with a few exceptions noted below, the evolutionary framework has largely been rejected in recent scholarship in favor of the cultural-essentialist model that so defined Granet's work. Although many of the supporters of this cultural-essentialist model explicitly claim to be studying the "Axial Age,"[22] they in fact strongly oppose the evolutionary sides of Jaspers's argument.

One of the more influential works based on this approach was roughly contemporary with Jaspers's book: the second volume of Joseph Needham's *Science and Civilisation in China*. Working closely from Granet, whom he quoted frequently,[23] Needham sought to develop an understanding of the fundamental cosmology of the Chinese:

> The key-word in Chinese thought is Order and above all Pattern (and, if I may whisper it for the first time, Organism). The symbolic correlations or correspondences all formed part of one colossal pattern. Things behaved in particular ways not necessarily because of prior actions or impulsions of other things, but because their position in the ever-moving cyclical universe was such that they were endowed with intrinsic natures which made that behaviour inevitable for them. . . . They were thus parts in existential dependence upon the whole world-organism. And they reacted upon one another not so much by mechanical impulsion or causation as by a kind of mysterious resonance.[24]

Within this organismic conception of the world, all things spontaneously harmonize with each other, creating an "ordered harmony of wills without an ordainer."[25] In contrast to a harmony of wills, Needham claimed, European thought is characterized by a "schizophrenia or split-personality. Europeans could only think in terms either of Democritean mechanical materialism or of Platonic theological spiritualism."[26] Just like Weber, Needham argued that China did not possess the radical dualism that was so important for the West. But Needham reversed the formula and clearly sympathized with the Chinese side of the contrast.

Frederick Mote has similarly based his argument on what he calls the general "world view"[27] of early China. Like Granet, Mote begins by describ-

---

22. See, e.g., Hall and Ames, *Anticipating China*, p. xiii; and Graham, *Disputers of the Tao*, p. i.

23. See, among other places, Needham, *Science and Civilisation in China*, 2: 216–17, 280.

24. Ibid., p. 281.

25. Ibid., p. 287.

26. Schwartz, *The World of Thought in Ancient China*, p. 302.

27. Mote, *Intellectual Foundations of China*, p. 16.

ing this worldview and then discusses how the various schools of thought were guided by such a shared cosmology. Mote further builds on Needham to make an argument for the absolute uniqueness of Chinese cosmology:

Needham, analyzing that Chinese model, calls it "an ordered harmony of wills without an ordainer." As he describes the organismic Chinese cosmos, it emerges to our full view as one in striking contrast to all other world conceptions known to human history. It differs from other organismic conceptions, such as classic Greek cosmologies in which a logos or demiurge or otherwise conceived master will external to creation, was regarded as necessary for existence.[28]

If such a cosmology were indeed an assumption in early China, then it would follow that both humans and spirits would be conceptualized as part of a larger monistic system. As Mote argues: "This is an essentially naturalistic conception, in that it describes 'spirit' as having the same qualities and as being subject to the same processes as all other aspects of nature."[29] In contrast to Western conceptions, in other words, humans and gods were seen as similar in nature.

K. C. Chang expanded on these ideas and argued that this difference in the cosmologies of the West and China derived from a different orientation toward shamanism:

Men and gods, animate and inanimate things, the living and dead members of the clans—all of these beings existed in the ancient Chinese world within the same universe, but that universe was layered and subdivided. The most important divisions were the Heaven and the Earth, and the ancient Chinese could be seen as particularly preoccupied with the Heaven and Earth intercommunication. The shamans—religious personnel equipped with the power to fly across the different layers of the universe with the help of the animals and a whole range of rituals and paraphernalia—were chiefly responsible for the Heaven-Earth communication.[30]

As intermediaries who maintain a proper linkage between the human and the divine realms, Chang argued, shamans occupied positions of great importance.[31]

For Chang, China and the West diverged because the Near East experienced what Chang calls a "breakout" from this earlier, shamanistic past,

28. Ibid., p. 15.
29. Ibid., p. 17.
30. K. C. Chang, *The Archaeology of Ancient China*, p. 415.
31. The argument is developed in full in Chang's *Art, Myth, and Ritual*.

whereas China (along with Mesoamerican civilizations) maintained its shamanistic culture. Thus, the West developed, among other things, "a cosmology that emphasized the separate existence of gods," while Chinese culture
was built on an assumption of an "interlinked world continuum." Once again,
Chinese thought is distinguished by a purported assumption of continuity
between the human and divine realms.

Similar arguments, although developed in different ways, underlie the
work of A. C. Graham, one of the most philosophically acute scholars to
study early China. Like Granet, Needham, Mote, and Chang, Graham was
committed to distinguishing Chinese and Western ways of thinking. In a
move reminiscent of Granet, Graham built this contrast on a distinction between analytic thinking (dominant in Western thought) and correlative
thinking (more dominant in China). However, Graham's construction of
this contrast differed in some ways from Granet's.

To begin with, Graham argued that both correlative and analytic thinking are universal modes of thought. Correlative thinking is the precognitive
mode common in most daily life and is the basis for analytical thinking, a
second-order mode.[32] Graham therefore opposed Granet's attempt to read
late Warring States and Han correlative models as representative of a
uniquely Chinese way of thinking. Instead, Graham argued, the attempt by
figures in the third and second centuries BC to build complex, cosmological
systems should be read as simply a particular development of a universal
mode of reasoning: "What Granet saw as the difference between Chinese
and Western thought may nowadays be seen as a transcultural difference between proto-science and modern science. Correlative cosmos-building is
most conveniently approached as merely an exotic example of the correlative
thinking used by everyone, which underlies the operations of language itself."[33] Instead, therefore, of building a contrastive framework between
China and the West on the purported distinctiveness of correlative thinking,
Graham pointed instead to the relative weight that each philosophical tradition placed on correlative and analytic thinking. China embraced correlativity; the West ultimately divorced analytic thinking from correlative thinking and came to value analytical thinking more highly.[34]

---

32. Graham, *Disputers of the Tao*, p. 322.
33. Ibid., p. 320. See also Graham, *Yin-Yang and the Nature of Correlative Thinking*, pp. 8–9.
34. Graham, *Disputers of the Tao*, p. 323.

The consequence of Graham's argument is that Chinese thought is presented as fully distinct from Western thought but based on the same universal types of thinking. Accordingly, although Graham continued to distinguish "China" and the "West," he could argue that the West could learn from and accept fully the traditions of China. The overall argument is thus a variant of the cultural-essentialist paradigm. Graham was committed to a Chinese philosophical tradition based on correlative thinking, but he based it on a universal claim concerning correlative thinking in order to emphasize the general applicability of the Chinese model.

Graham's arguments have been developed in the collaborative work of David Hall and Roger Ames, which represents the most extensive attempt in recent decades to contrast the cultures of early China and the West. Indeed, they describe their work as an attempt to "illumine the contrasting assumptions shaping classical Chinese and Western cultures."[35] And, like Granet, the sympathies of Hall and Ames lie fully with China.

Indeed, Hall and Ames strongly defend Granet's argument that correlative thinking is a defining feature of Chinese thought:

Our view, however, is that Marcel Granet was essentially correct in identifying what we are here calling correlative thinking with a fundamental commitment of the Chinese sensibility. This implies that even among those thinkers such as Confucius and the philosophical Daoists who were not so concerned with physical speculations, the mode of correlative thinking dominates. Our argument here is that Han exercises in correlative thinking are not anomalous, but are rather signal instances of correlative thinking in a tradition replete with such instances. (p. 257)

Like Granet, and unlike Graham, Hall and Ames wish to read the Han correlative texts as representative of all early Chinese thought. Thus, Hall and Ames explicitly critique Jaspers's argument: "If comparative philosophy has anything to say about Chinese culture during the so-called Axial Age, it is certainly this: notions of 'absoluteness,' 'transcendence,' and 'subjectivity' were of doubtful significance" (p. xiii). They also fault Schwartz for following Jaspers in using terms such as "transcendence" and in assuming a commonality among early civilizations (pp. 148, 186–87). But, unlike Weber, Hall and Ames do not criticize China for its lack of transcendence but, like Granet, celebrate it.

---

35. Hall and Ames, *Anticipating China*, p. xviii (hereinafter cited in the text).

In formulating the contrasting assumptions of China and the West, Hall
and Ames invoke a fundamental distinction between what they call "first" and
"second problematic thinking." First problematic thinking, which Hall
and Ames see as dominating Chinese thought, is based on "analogical or
correlative thinking" (p. xvii). "This mode of thinking accepts the priority of
change or process over rest and permanence, presumes no ultimate agency
responsible for the general order of things, and seeks to account for states of
affairs by appeal to correlative procedures rather than by determining agencies or principles" (p. xvii). In contrast to this, Hall and Ames claim, is second problematic thinking, or "causal thinking" (p. xvii)—the mode that has
dominated the West. Among the characteristics of causal thinking is "the
belief that the order of the cosmos is a consequence of some agency of construal . . . [and] the tacit or explicit claim that the states of affairs comprising
'the world' are grounded in, and ultimately determined by, these agencies of
construal" (p. xvii). Theistic systems, therefore, in which divine agencies are
seen as causative forces in shaping the world, are based on a Western, rather
than a Chinese, way of thinking, as would be, of course, any kind of transcendental or foundational thought.

Like Graham, Hall and Ames see each of these ways of thinking as existing to some degree in both Chinese and Western cultures, and they are thus
able to argue that Chinese thought is something that can be fully assimilated
into contemporary Western thinking. But, their sympathies are clearly with
the correlative mode, and they not surprisingly oppose any attempt to present these types on an evolutionary line, with correlative thinking as a more
primitive or lesser stage of consciousness: "Such a claim challenges the viabil-
ity of the Enlightenment reading of cultural development, which argues that
the movement from mythos to logos or 'from religion to philosophy,' or
from analogical to causal thinking, ought to serve as the norm for the civilizing of human experience" (p. xviii). Hall and Ames would thus reject Fung
Yu-lan's "religion to philosophy" argument. Indeed, they would question
Fung's narrative of an evolution in China from theism to humanism and rationalism. For Hall and Ames, all of these are distinctively Western modes
of thinking—not found in the correlative thought of China.

Although the cultural-essentialist model has dominated the study of early
Chinese thought in recent decades, the evolutionist paradigm has recently
been resurrected with great force by Heiner Roetz. Roetz explicitly picks up
on Jaspers's notion of an Axial Period, arguing against Weber that China

did undergo a transcendental breakthrough in the early period.[36] He quotes Schwartz's definition of transcendence for all Axial Period civilizations with approval (p. 273), but, unlike Schwartz, Roetz maintains the evolutionary aspects of Jaspers's argument. Indeed, he explicitly uses Jaspers's framework to reject the culturalist approach: "This should provide us with a universalistic conception of understanding, which avoids the ethnocentric implications or relativistic consequences of recourse to native language and culture specific forms of thought" (p. 23).

In opposition to culturalism, Roetz seeks to provide "a yardstick for measuring and evaluating in its specific variations the cultural evolution of mankind" (p. 30). Clearly, Roetz's image of measuring cultures according to a yardstick of universal development is directly reminiscent (even to the point of using the same metaphor) of the evolutionary sides of Weber's analysis. And, indeed, despite his strong rhetoric, Roetz is strongly indebted to the Weberian paradigm, although Roetz places China higher on the yardstick than did Weber. Roetz's recurrent move is thus to try to show that China did in fact attain the very forms of transcendence and rationality Weber found in the West.

For the purposes of this chapter, the most significant of Roetz's discussions is his explanation of how nature came to be seen as an object of human conquest. Since Weber connected the rise of a "disenchanted" notion of nature in the West to belief in a transcendent god, Roetz needs to explain how this notion could have arisen in a culture without such a belief: "How, unless by means of the concept of an otherworldly god, can nature be 'disenchanted' (Weber) in such a way that it becomes the profane object of systematical transformation and conquest by man?" (p. 21). For Roetz, the shift occurred with the "catastrophe" of the fall of the Western Zhou, which resulted in the "the loss of dignity of Heaven." This "failure of the divine power led man to direct his attention to himself. Religion lost ground to new speculations" (p. 39). Roetz thus offers a variation on the "religion to philosophy" argument: a theistic worldview dominated the early period, but, with the fall of the Western Zhou, theism was destroyed. This led to a de-emphasis on divine powers and a re-emphasis on humans. Roetz thus feels he has proved that, contrary to Weber's view, China did indeed see the rise of ethical rationalization in the early period (p. 274).

---

36. Roetz, *Confucian Ethics of the Axial Age*, p. 23 (hereinafter cited in the text).

But, since Roetz sees this rationalization as necessarily involving the dis-enchantment of nature and the making of nature into a profane object of conquest by man, how does he deal with the emergence of correlative cos-mology—one of the very things that Weber saw as limiting rationalization in China? As Roetz notes, in a reference to Weber, "cosmological, holistic reasoning often counts as an indication that a breakthrough toward enlight-ened thought has not taken place" (pp. 226–27). Roetz's defense of the Chi-nese tradition thus consists of denying the importance of cosmology, and he therefore opposes Granet's attempts to read correlative thinking as domi-nant in early China (p. 227). He argues, for example, that Xunzi's cosmo-logical terminology is simply "rhetoric" (p. 230).

But what about Han texts? Even Roetz cannot deny that cosmology be-comes important in the Han. Perhaps not surprisingly, he has nothing but derision for figures like Dong Zhongshu who embraced correlative cosmol-ogy. For Roetz, Dong Zhongshu "discards the rational view of nature which Zhou philosophy had developed and Xunzi had brought to completion" (p. 231). As a consequence, Dong Zhongshu marks the point at which Confu-cianism returns to "superstition": "Ethically as well as cognitively it [Confu-cianism] falls back on a level which the axial age philosophers had once over-come" (p. 231). Like Weber, Roetz defines correlative cosmology in terms of a lesser form of rationalization—a lower position on the yardstick. The only difference is that since Roetz argues that a transcendental breakthrough oc-curred earlier, he sees the resurgence of correlative thinking as a regression.

Why did the Chinese lapse? Or, when put in terms of the entire history of China, why did China not achieve the full rationalization that Roetz, fol-lowing Weber, thinks occurred in the West? Roetz concludes with an ex-planation of this "discrepancy between the original potential and the actual historical development of China" (p. 275). Ultimately, the problem, as Roetz sees it, is that Confucianism failed to develop because the tension it posited between convention and morality (li and ren) was "not expressed in a tren-chant manner" (p. 277). What is amazing about this argument is how similar it is to Weber's. In essence, Roetz is arguing that the problem with Con-fucianism is that it failed to maintain as extreme a tension between morality and convention as it should have. Moreover, since Roetz agrees that correla-tive cosmology is nonrational, he argues that once correlative cosmology be-comes dominant in the Han, cognition fell to a lower, nontranscendental level. Thus, despite all his discussions of transcendence, Roetz is still committed to claiming the same comparative point we have seen repeatedly (even if valued differently by different thinkers) since Weber: the Chinese tradition failed to achieve the motivating tensions so important to the West.

Method of Analysis

At the center of much of the secondary literature sketched above stand the cosmological texts of the Warring States and Han. The question is how to read these texts. Weber, as well as those who advocated a generally evolutionist framework, present cosmological models as part of an attempt to rationalize an existing magical, theistic, animistic worldview. Correlative cosmology was thus a shift toward rationality and naturalism, even if it unfortunately retained many of the earlier magical notions. In Roetz's variant of this model, rational naturalism (with a cosmological "rhetoric") developed in early China, but then correlative cosmology arose in a throwback to an earlier, nonrational stage of development. However, the emphasis within this paradigm is on the shift from theism to naturalism.

The advocates of the cultural-essentialist model, on the other hand, hold that these cosmological texts are indicative of a set of underlying assumptions in early China. Figures as diverse as Granet, Mote, Chang, Graham, and Hall and Ames hold that even if cosmological systems did not emerge until the third century BC, they are nonetheless representative of a general "Chinese" way of thinking. In this view, theism never existed in China—even in the Bronze Age. According to these interpretations, China and Greece (indeed, all of the West) are distinguished by radically different cosmologies—the Western tradition being defined in terms of (among other things) a disjunction between man and god, and the Chinese assuming an inherent correlation and linkage.

As I will argue below, some of the material on self-divinization may force us to rethink both these frameworks. The complex issues concerning the word spirit (*shen* 神) in early Chinese texts are an example.[37] As I discuss at length in this book, the term is used to describe both spirits who reside

---

37. Willard Peterson ("Making Connections," p. 104) has suggested translating *shen* as "numinosity," a word that does capture the adjectival sense of *shen* quite well. However, the nominal form "numen" works poorly to describe *shen* when it refers to spirits. In this work, I will therefore continue to utilize the common translations of *shen* as "spirits" or "divinities," when used in the nominal form, and "spiritual" and "divine" when used in the adjectival. Such translations allow one to more easily convey the shifts that appear in the early texts.

above and possess direct powers over natural phenomena and refined forms of *qi* within humans.

On the question of how to account for these two meanings of the term *shen*, Hall and Ames have argued that "with the appearance of any given character in the text, the full seamless range of meanings is introduced." Our task as readers is "to reconstitute the several meanings of any term as an integrated whole."[38] This means that we must strive to understand the implications of a worldview in which *shen* can simultaneously contain both meanings:

Shen, for example, is a complex notion, meaning as it does both "human spirituality," and "divinity." *Shen* does not *sometimes* mean "human spirituality," and *sometimes* "divinity." It always means both of these, and moreover, it is our business to try and understand philosophically how it can mean both. What are the implications of this particular range of meanings where humanity and divinity are continuous?[39]

In other words, the dual meaning of the term reveals a way of thinking in which humanity and divinity are continuous, and the job of the analyst is to reconstruct that way of thinking. Their argument continues: "How does this factor into the familiar formula, *tianren heyi*—the continuity between *tian* [Heaven] and the human world?"[40] Or, as they put it elsewhere: "We may wonder what the fact that the single term *shen* can mean both 'divinity' and 'human spirituality' in the classical Chinese language reveals about Chinese religiousness."[41]

In contrast, I argue in the chapters that follow that the term *shen* does *not* mean both "human spirituality" and "divinity." The term *shen* was used exclusively in the Bronze Age to refer to divinities. It was not until the Warring States period that the term came to be applied to substances within humans, and this was part, I will argue, of an attempt to redefine the term for specific purposes. It did not, therefore, represent an assumption that "humanity and divinity are continuous." Rather, it involved a claim to that effect—a claim that was strongly contested throughout the entire early period. I am not sure what the dual meanings of the term would in themselves tell us about "Chinese" religiousness. But if, instead of trying to reconstruct a "Chinese" viewpoint, we see the existence of different meanings as indicative

---

38. Hall and Ames, *Thinking from the Han*, pp. 236–37.
39. Ibid., p. 236.
40. Ibid., p. 237.
41. Hall and Ames, *Anticipating China*, p. 226.

of specific arguments advanced within a particular historical context, then they may reveal a great deal. In other words, instead of trying to "reconstitute the several meanings of any term as an integrated whole," I will work to reconstruct the debate within which these various meanings were developed and contested.

I emphasize this point to underline one of the central dangers of contrastive approaches such as that of Hall and Ames. Building such a contrastive framework requires taking particular texts out of context and reading them as assumptions of the entire cultures being compared. And, in this particular case, restoring that context allows us both to provide a historical account of why such statements were made and to restore the provocative power that such statements would have held at the time. To reduce them to being simply examples of a common Chinese way of thinking makes it impossible for us to recover the cultural potency that such claims possessed.

In short, I want to restore the historical power of such statements by asking Why would humans claim they could become spirits? How were such claims read at the time? And what is the cultural history of such claims—What happened when people said such things, and what happened when others opposed them? As we will see, these questions became major issues of state policy and practice by the early imperial period.

Similarly, an evolutionary perspective on the changing meaning of *shen*—as a shift from a magical to a naturalistic/rationalistic/humanistic worldview—creates problems as well. Unlike a cultural-essentialist approach, the evolutionary perspective recognizes that a significant shift did occur in the perceived relations between humans and spirits over this period. But ignoring the contexts in which specific claims were made in favor of a universal yardstick risks the same kind of misunderstanding as the cultural-essentialist model. Even if one wanted to assert a universal yardstick of rationality, it would be meaningless to assess the rationality or lack thereof of a given text unless one first, at the minimum, ascertained the contemporary meaning of the text.

Moreover, the advocates of this model see the emergence of a correlative cosmology that links humans with divine forces as a development *toward* a fully rationalistic perspective, but one unfortunately too mired in the earlier magical worldview to mark a complete breakthrough toward rationality. Even Roetz, who argues that a transcendental breakthrough did occur in Warring States China, believes that Chinese thinkers failed to develop the kind of tension with the world that occurred in the West. Accordingly, a full development of rationality was hindered. Beyond the obvious dangers of reading another culture according to a universal yardstick of rationality, one of the immediate implications of such an approach is that it binds the analyst to de-emphasizing tensions in the early texts: claims about the continuity between humans and divinities in Warring States texts are explained away as too mired in an earlier magical view of continuity. The analyst is thus committed to finding an assumption of continuity between humans and divinities in the Bronze Age as well, for only in this way can one explain the inability of later thinkers to move further toward a more rational worldview. Like the cultural-essentialist approach, then, the framework again forces the analyst to see a lack of tension between humans and divinities as a guiding theme in early China, even if the analyst does see a shift from an earlier "animistic" or "magical" worldview to a correlative one.

Both frameworks, then, rest on remarkably similar foundations. Both rest on seeing a fundamental dichotomy between China and the West, and both define that difference in very similar ways. Either (in negative terms) China did not manifest the tensions found in the West, or (in positive terms) it maintained a notion of continuity between humans and divine powers lost in the West. The differences simply come down to whether this distinction is worked out on a contrastive model (with China and the West holding opposing assumptions) or on a developmental line (with China and the West occupying different positions on the yardstick).

In contrast to both these frameworks, I will attempt to provide a full historical study of the relations of humans, spirits, and the cosmos from the Bronze Age to the early Han. I will read the texts in question as claims, and my goal will be to reconstruct the contexts in which these claims were meaningful. I will argue that we cannot understand early Chinese cosmology until we understand why certain figures presented cosmological arguments, what they were reacting to, and what impact their claims had at the time. I thus build on the recent, important work of Nathan Sivin, John Henderson, and Wang Aihe to argue for a historical understanding of cosmology.[42]

In short, I am recommending that we dispense with both of the frameworks discussed above—both the contrastive and the evolutionary models.

42. See Sivin, "State, Cosmos, and Body in the Last Three Centuries B.C."; Henderson, *The Development and Decline of Chinese Cosmology*; Wang Aihe, *Cosmology and Political Culture in Early China.*

We should instead work toward a more nuanced approach in which we make no *a priori* assumptions regarding single statements made in single texts and the significance of individual claims. Once this is done, and once we move away from a commitment to seeing a lack of tension between humans and divinities as a guiding theme in early China, we may discover a rich, and perhaps more troubled, world of debate concerning humans, divinities, and sacrificial practice than previous analyses have accustomed us to expect from Chinese texts.

This methodological point is relevant as well to the question of how we should organize the analysis of these texts. As should be clear from the recurrent references in the secondary literature to "schools of thought" in early China—such as Confucianism or Daoism—many scholars have organized their studies in terms of such categories. I would argue, in contrast, that the attempt to categorize texts in terms of schools is usually unhelpful and often misleading: rather, our concern should be to explicate the claims of each text within the debates of the time.[43] Discussion of these claims in terms of a "school" is seldom helpful.[44] Even when dealing with a text that explicitly posits itself within a defined textual tradition, the analyst should seek to understand how such a textual tradition is being posited and what claims are being made through that positing.

All these interpretive strategies—reading in terms of schools, essentialized definitions of culture, evolutionary frameworks—have the consequence of erasing the unique power that particular claims had at the time. My strategy is, instead, to contextualize through a different approach: to ask why statements are made in particular situations, to understand the cultural significance they would have had at the time, and to work out the historical consequences of the ensuing debates.

But my goal is not to discredit the use of comparative terminology by simply pointing out the obvious lack of fit between the indigenous categories

---

43. For an excellent critique of the use of the category "Daoism," see Sivin, "On the Word Taoism as a Source of Perplexity." Sivin makes a related, and equally powerful, critique of the category of "Naturalists"; see "The Myth of the Naturalists," in his *Medicine, Philosophy, and Religion in Ancient China*, pp. 1–33.

44. With the exception of Confucianism and Mohism, many of the "schools" into which early Chinese thought is often categorized first appear in our received texts in the essay "Yaozhi," by Sima Tan (d. 110 BC). As Kidder Smith ("Sima Tan and the Invention of Daoism, 'Legalism,' et cetera") has convincingly shown, many of these "schools" were invented by Sima Tan and are therefore of questionable applicability for discussions of pre-Han texts.

and the comparative terms—a point that could of course be made for any culture. On the contrary, I think comparative work can be very helpful, and I see my work as helping to develop a comparative framework. Ultimately, I hope to show that an alternative form of cultural analysis than has heretofore been practiced with these texts will aid in developing better comparative methodologies. In particular, I will build on a number of recent works in anthropology to argue for a somewhat different approach to the study of early China; in turn, the material on early China may help us to rethink issues in the anthropological literature as well.

Outline

In Chapter 1, I utilize paleographic materials and received texts to discuss the complexities of ritual practices in the Bronze Age dealing with divinities. I analyze changes in notions of the nature of spirits and ancestors, as well as the rituals relating to both groups. I question several of the dominant models for analyzing this material and argue that, contrary to most interpretations, these documents reveal a highly agonistic world, in which divine powers were perceived to be capricious and in which humans were in the position of trying, within their limited abilities, to utilize sacrifices and divinations to understand and influence the spirit world. More specifically, I argue that there is an overriding concern in these materials to anthropomorphize the divine. Building on the work of David Keightley, I trace the attempts, through ritual practices, to make the spirits into ancestors who could then be arranged into a hierarchy and directed to work on behalf of the living to obtain support for the non-ancestral spirits as well.

Chapter 2 focuses on the emergence, during the Warring States period, of numerous attempts to bypass the dominant modes of orientation toward the world of spirits (involving, among other things, divination and sacrifice) through practices of self-cultivation. The advocates of these practices began articulating new definitions of the nature of spirits and of humanity and the relationship between the two. More precisely, these articulations were attempts to reduce the distinction between humans and spirits and to argue that, through proper practices, one can attain powers comparable to those possessed by spirits and that one could dispense with divination and sacrifices. Instead of anthropomorphizing the divine, humans, through self-cultivation, could themselves become ru shen—"like spirits."

I also critique in detail the argument, made for both China and Greece, that such movements—which I refer to as "self-divinization movements"— arose through a re-reading of earlier shamanistic practice. I develop a comparison with early Greece and argue for an approach to analyzing relations between humans and divine powers in early Greece and China different from the ones that have thus far been influential in sinology.

In Chapter 3, I look in detail at the rise of so-called naturalistic philosophy in Mencius and Zhuangzi. I argue against a reading of these texts as representing either an assumption concerning the inherent continuity between humans and Heaven in early China or a shift from an animistic religion to a more rational worldview. On the contrary, as I hope to show, these texts should be read as statements in the contemporary debate over the potentially divine powers of humans, and both texts contain attempts to think through the implications of such claims for the relations of humans and Heaven. If humans can indeed become spirits and can indeed gain divine powers, then should they still accept the commands of a potentially capricious Heaven? Both Zhuangzi and Mencius answer this question in the affirmative, although in different ways. In opposition to the way these figures are usually read, I argue that the texts of Mencius and Zhuangzi reveal the tremendous tensions emerging at this time between Heaven and man.

In Chapter 4, I turn to a study of correlative cosmology. I argue that the emergence of correlative systems in the late Warring States period was directly related to the emergence of much stronger claims of self-divinization. In contrast to the statements in fourth-century BC texts that humans can attain powers comparable to those possessed by spirits, by the third century BC numerous figures began to claim to possess techniques that enable them to become spirits.

In making this argument, I propose an alternative approach to reading early Chinese correlative thinking. If, as discussed above, Granet sought to explicate Chinese correlative thinking through a reconstruction of "Chinese thinking," Graham tried to do so by positing correlative thinking as a universal mode of human thought. They disagree, in other words, on the relationship of early Chinese correlative thinking to contemporary observers: Granet emphasized difference, Graham similarity. But both Granet and Graham hope to explain why cosmology would have seemed natural in early China. And my disagreement with both of their approaches begins here. I argue, building on the points discussed in Chapters 2 and 3, that cosmology was in fact *counterintuitive* in early China. Not only did it arise late (as Graham correctly points out), it arose in direct opposition to the sacrificial practices dominant at the time. Correlative thinking emerged as a language of critique against the dominant notions of the time, and it remained a language of critique and opposition throughout the early imperial period.

To develop this argument, I analyze numerous late Warring States texts in full. I also review the anthropological literature on sacrifice and cosmology that has been so influential in sinological discussions of Chinese correlative thinking and argue that a somewhat different reading of that literature, particularly of Granet and Claude Lévi-Strauss, will allow for an alternative, and in my opinion more convincing, understanding of Chinese correlative thought.

Chapter 5 is a study of the large literature on spirit journeys and ascension from early China. Although this literature has usually been read as a survival of shamanism, I argue in contrast that it makes sense only when placed within the historical contexts sketched in Chapters 2 through 4. In particular, several of the texts represent an attempt to develop self-divinization claims to argue that humans not only can become spirits but also can leave their body altogether and ascend to the heavens. The goal of Chapter 5 is to analyze these claims in depth and see precisely why they were being advanced at the time.

Chapter 6 turns to Qin and early Han court practices. I reconstruct aspects of the sacrificial system and imperial ideology of the Qin and early Han courts and analyze the reasons for the prominence of *fangshi* (masters of formulas) at the courts of the First Emperor and Emperor Wu of the Han. My main interest in this chapter is to investigate the emergence during this period of theomorphic claims of rulership and the resulting debates that arose concerning the emperor's proper relationship to the world of spirits. I reconstruct the historical complexity of these various stances over the course of the Qin and early Han empires to show both the rise of theomorphic forms of rulership and the reaction against it.

I also trace the intensification of efforts by various officials to develop correlative models during this period. I focus in particular on Lu Jia, who strongly advocated following the transmitted texts of the ancient sages. Lu Jia turned to correlative models to critique both the dominant imperial ideology and the various self-divinization claims that were becoming increasingly popular among the early Han elite: by arguing that the cosmos consists of spontaneous processes and patterns, not directed by spirits at all, Lu Jia and others like him could deny the theistic underpinnings of much of early Han elite culture. If spirits do not control natural phenomena, then both the theomorphic pretensions of the emperors and the claims of autonomy made by some practitioners of self-divinization could be opposed.

Chapter 7 is an in-depth study of the cosmologies presented in several chapters of the *Huainanzi*, which build on the ascension and self-divinization literatures to argue for a cosmos populated by theomorphic humans and anthropomorphic gods. I analyze why these cosmologies were being presented and what claims were being made. I also discuss the continuing proliferation of self-divinization movements during the early Han and trace the various appeals that were made for such powers, explicating why they became so prominent during this period.

Chapter 8 studies the shifts in the imperial sacrificial system from the time of Emperor Wu to the late first century BC in response to the contemporary debates over how the system should operate. I analyze Emperor Wu's creation of a new sacrificial system based upon Taiyi (the Great One), as well as Dong Zhongshu's and Sima Qian's critiques of the emperor. I then investigate why, in 31 BC, the imperial court embraced the arguments of the ru-ists, abolished significant portions of its sacrificial system, and put in place a new set of sacrifices to Heaven and Earth. These new sacrifices were based in part on a particular reading of documents concerning the sacrificial system of the Western Zhou. I seek to discern the significance that had come to be associated with these various sacrificial rites and to explain the reasons for this shift in sacrificial practice. I argue that the shift was in part a reaction to the claims of autonomy that had developed in the self-divinization movements. Although these movements had themselves flourished in reaction to the theomorphic presentations of the early Han court, the claims of autonomy that came to be associated with these movements were seen as highly dangerous and ultimately provoked a strong shift in court policies.

The new sacrificial system put in place at the end of the first century BC involved a rejection of any claims to self-divinization or theomorphism on the part of humans. Humans and Heaven were posited as normatively correlated with each other, but they were also distinguished, with each given its proper sphere of activity. Divine kingship was rejected; the ruler was defined as human. Thereafter, self-divinization and ascension came to be associated with millenarian movements opposing the imperial court.

1 *Anthropomorphizing the spirits*
Sacrifice and Divination in
Late Bronze Age China

In both strains of the secondary literature discussed in the Introduction, a common reading of the Chinese Bronze Age prevails: humans and spirits were seen as continuous and were perceived to be harmoniously linked. Moreover, this period is repeatedly seen as the formative era in Chinese history, the period when one first finds the assumption of a continuity between the human and divine realms that, the argument goes, thereafter pervades Chinese history.

Weber saw this as a restricting aspect of Chinese culture, as did Roetz, who argued that it ultimately reversed the transcendental breakthrough of the Axial Age. Most of the scholars we looked at, however, from Chang and Mote to Graham and Schwartz, fully celebrated it. But is it true? Were humans and spirits seen as linked in a harmonious continuum? And is it true that this period marks the beginning of a set of assumptions that (for better or worse) predominated in later Chinese history? In order to explore this question, it will be worthwhile to look anew at some of these materials as well as at some of the secondary literature devoted to the Bronze Age.

The Foundations of Chinese Cosmological
and Bureaucratic Thought

One thinker who has tremendously influenced several recent scholars of the Chinese Bronze Age is Mircea Eliade. It was Eliade who popularized the notion that primitive cultures universally attempt to define a sacred space in which they can link Heaven and Earth: "Mountains are often looked on as the place where sky and earth meet, a 'central point' therefore, the point through which the *Axis Mundi* goes, a region impregnated with the sacred, a spot where one can pass from one cosmic zone to another."[1] Building on Granet, Eliade argued that the Chinese capital was perceived along similar lines—as an *axis mundi*, or a symbolic cosmic mountain: "In China, the capital of the perfect sovereign stood at the exact centre of the universe, that is, at the summit of the cosmic mountain."[2]

Paul Wheatley has extended Eliade's argument to formulate a theory of the origins of urban centers in China. Like Eliade, Wheatley argues that Chinese urban centers not only "in traditional China but also throughout most of the rest of Asia" emerged out of a widespread form of cosmological thinking, which he refers to as "astrobiology." Given this cosmology, the goal of ritual specialists was to "establish an ontological link between the realm of the sacred and the realm of the profane."[3]

For Wheatley, the figure who has most convincingly worked out the ways in which capitals were constructed according to such cosmological models is Eliade:

Throughout the continent of Asia . . . there was thus a tendency for kingdoms, capitals, temples, shrines, and so forth, to be constructed as replicas of the cosmos. Mircea Eliade has illustrated this point with a plethora of examples drawn primarily from the architecture, epigraphy, and literature of the ancient Near East and India, and numerous others could be adduced from Southeast Asia and Nuclear America. In the astrobiological mode of thought, irregularities in the cosmic order could only

---

1. Eliade, *Patterns in Comparative Religion*, pp. 99–100.

2. Ibid., p. 101, referring to Granet, *La pensée chinoise*, p. 324. See also Eliade, *The Sacred and the Profane*, p. 39. Eliade's reference to Granet is slightly misleading. Granet's concern in the passage that Eliade cites is the notion of the ruler as the microcosm of the universe. As Granet argues on the previous page: "he [the king] is the center, the pivot of the world" (*La pensée chinoise*, p. 323). Eliade would have found better support for his argument in Granet's discussion of time and space in Chinese thought (*La pensée chinoise*, pp. 77–99).

3. Wheatley, *The Pivot of the Four Quarters*, pp. 414–16.

be interpreted as misfortunes, so that, if a city were laid out as an *imago mundi* with the cosmogony as paradigmatic model, it became necessary to maintain this parallelism between macrocosmos and microcosmos by participation in the seasonal festivals that constituted man's contribution to the regulation of cyclic time, and by incorporating in the planning a generous amount of symbolism.[4]

The capital thus serves as an *axis mundi*, in the same way as a "shaman's sapling" does.[5]

After describing the "cosmo-magical basis" of urban forms, systematized by Eliade as involving things such as a "parallelism between the macrocosmos and the microcosmos" and necessitating the use of ritual to "maintain the harmony between the world of gods and the world of men," as well as a "participation in the symbolism of the center, as expressed by some form of *axis mundi*,"[6] Wheatley then notes the degree to which Chinese thinking conforms to the Eliadean model:

Indeed, the astrobiological conceptual framework of which these ideas are an expression was structurally conformable to the associative or co-ordinative style of thinking of which the Chinese were perhaps the foremost exponents. In fact, it might even be said that the pre-established harmony of the Chinese universe, which was achieved when all beings spontaneously followed the internal necessities of their own nature, and which led Chinese philosophers to seek reality in relation rather than in substance, represented the most sophisticated expression of astrobiological concepts ever attained by any people.[7]

Not only does China conform to this "traditional"[8] way of thinking, but China is in fact the fullest and most sophisticated expression of it. In this specific sense, Wheatley's argument is quite comparable to Graham's view that China was the civilization that most fully developed the universal mode of correlative thinking.

K. C. Chang has a similar argument, although he builds it on slightly different foundations. In a highly influential article, Chen Mengjia argued that, in the Shang dynasty, kings were shamans.[9] K. C. Chang developed this argument in detail and, as mentioned in the Introduction, saw shamanism as

---

4. Ibid., p. 417.
5. Ibid.
6. Ibid., p. 418.
7. Ibid.
8. Ibid.
9. Chen Mengjia, "Shang dai de shenhua yu wushu."

lying at the heart of Chinese culture.[10] He compiled bodies of evidence that, in his opinion, "point to an ancient Chinese shamanism at the core of ancient Chinese belief and ritual systems, which were preoccupied with the interpenetration of heaven and earth."[11]

Chang did not indicate which scholarly definition of shamanism he had in mind in making these arguments, but he did occasionally refer to Eliade.[12] Moreover, as is apparent from the passage quoted in the preceding paragraph, Chang's interpretation of a shamanistic cosmology is identical to Eliade's. Thus, although Wheatley did not argue that the Shang kings were shamans, Chang's reading of early Chinese culture is quite similar to the one developed by Wheatley.

For Chang, divination—the late Shang ritual about which, because of oracle-bone inscriptions, we know the most—was based in shamanism, as was the *bin* (or "hosting") ritual:

Was Shang divination an act of Shang shamanism? The inscriptions make it clear they were directed to long-departed ancestors, and that the diviner served as an intermediary. The inscriptions often contain the word *bin*, which in later classical texts usually means to receive as a guest or to be a guest. In the oracle bone inscriptions, the word is often placed between the word for king and the name of a specific ancestor or of Di; the Supreme God. A phrase consisting of these elements is sometimes interpreted as "the king receives as a guest a specific ancestor," or "the kings receives as a guest the Supreme God." But more likely it means that the king "called upon" a departed ancestor or God. . . . In any event, there was a Shang ritual that enabled the king and the spirits to be together, presumably brought about by some kind of middleman. The act of divination was intended, similarly, to bring the middleman diviner and the spirits together.[13]

The divination ritual itself involved either the ascent of the shaman to the spirits or the descent of the spirits to the shaman:

The descent of the spirits or the ascent of the shaman or king was achieved in a manner not altogether clear. Music and dance were apparently part of the ceremony. Alcoholic drinks were possibly involved: the Shang were notorious drinkers, and many bronze ritual vessels were designed to serve alcoholic beverages. Did the alco-

---

10. The argument is most fully developed in K. C. Chang, *Art, Myth, and Ritual*, pp. 44–55.
11. K. C. Chang, "Ancient China and Its Anthropological Significance," p. 164.
12. See, e.g., K. C. Chang, "The Animal in Shang and Chou Bronze Art," p. 543.
13. K. C. Chang, *Art, Myth, and Ritual*, p. 54.

hol or other substances bring about a trance, during which the shaman engaged in imagined flight? Possibly, but there is as yet no evidence for this. The role of animals in the ritual art of the Shang may provide significant clues.[14]

Chang builds on his theory of shamanism to provide a reading of the origin of the Chinese state comparable to that given by Wheatley. Chang reads the late Neolithic in China as an "Age of Jade *Cong* [jade tubes], the period when shamanism and politics joined forces."[15] Chang reads these jade tubes as symbols of "the interpenetration of heaven and earth" and as thus representing "a microcosmic *axis mundi*."[16] The Chinese Bronze Age, "the period of the further development of shamanistic politics," followed from this.[17] Thus, like Wheatley, Chang's reading is similarly based on the notion that Chinese civilization developed through ritual specialists who attempted to join Heaven and Earth by building a particular *axis mundi*.

Julia Ching has expanded on this point as well. Chinese civilization, she argues, in part came together because of a common inspiration,

that the human being is open to the divine and the spiritual, attuned to the divine and the spiritual, and desirous of becoming one with the divine and the spiritual. I am here referring to the familiar adage that describes the harmony underlining Chinese thought and civilization: Heaven and humanity are one—*tianran heyi* (literally: Heaven and the human being join as one).[18]

Like Hall and Ames, Ching posits the notion of a continuity between Heaven and man as a basic assumption of Chinese thought. But Ching goes on to claim that the origin of this notion lies in shamanistic experience:

It is an adage that I believe to have originated in that very mystic and ecstatic union between the human being and the possessing deity or spirit. This was the primeval experience, the experience of a shaman. It was never forgotten. It has been celebrated in songs, myths and rituals. It was formulated philosophically as an expression of the continuum between the human being as the microcosm of the universe as macrocosm. And this microcosm-macrocosm correspondence has been basic to most of philosophising in China.[19]

---

14. Ibid., p. 55.
15. K. C. Chang, "An Essay on *Cong*," p. 42.
16. K. C. Chang, "Ancient China and Its Anthropological Significance," p. 158.
17. K. C. Chang, "An Essay on *Cong*," p. 42.
18. Ching, *Mysticism and Kingship in China*, p. xi.
19. Ibid.

The ecstatic experience between the shaman and deity, therefore, provided the primeval experience of Chinese culture, and the correlative cosmology found in later Chinese philosophy was an expression of this experience.

For Ching, this experience is directly comparable to the primeval experiences of oneness that Eliade cites as the root of religious life:

In illo tempore ('Once long ago' or 'At that time'). Thus do the Gospels begin their chapters. Thus does Mircea Eliade describe the primeval, sacred time when humankind had its original experience of oneness with the deity. This was an experience recapitulated in myth and reenacted in ritual. Eliade speaks more of India, and of the Australian aborigines, then he does of Chinese civilisation. But his insight, mutatis mutandis, is reflected in the Chinese experience as well, as I have just described.[20]

A primordial experience of a linkage between humans and deities exists in all humanity, and the distinctiveness of Chinese civilization lies in its remembrance of this experience.

A very different approach to the study of Bronze Age China has been undertaken by David Keightley. Although he occasionally quotes Eliade,[21] Keightley's understanding of the Shang originates in very different intellectual sources. Accordingly, his interpretation differs markedly from those scholars, such as Wheatley, Chang, and Ching, who base their interpretations of the Shang upon Eliade. In particular, Keightley rejects the shamanistic hypothesis.

In contrast to both K. C. Chang and Julia Ching, David Keightley has convincingly questioned the prevalence (or even presence) of shamanism in Bronze Age China.[22] Keightley's argument, based on an exhaustive review of the evidence, is that Chang's theory of the continuing presence of shamanism in the Shang is wrong. To the contrary, Keightley argues, the transition to a state society involved a routinization and control of whatever shamanistic practices might have existed earlier. Shamanism as discussed by figures like Chang would have "flourished at an earlier, pre-agrarian, hunter-gatherer stage of social development." "The rise of agrarian cultures, accordingly, like that of the Late Shang, has been associated with a reduction of the role played by shamans at the state level, or by its reorientation." Keightley's

---

20. Ibid., pp. xi–xii.
21. See, e.g., Keightley, "The Religious Commitment," p. 215n18.
22. Keightley, "Shamanism, Death, and the Ancestors."

critique, therefore, is based on claims concerning what he calls "stages of social development." Since the Late Shang kings were ruling a Bronze Age,
agrarian state, he concludes that "the Late Shang kings were not shamans,"
or "were, at best, 'light' or 'small' shamans, whose involvement in the full
shamanic experience was much reduced from what it might once have been
at an earlier stage of societal development." They were "bureaucratic media-
tors" who had "so routinized and disciplined older forms of religious mediation" that only the "civilized trappings" of an earlier shamanism would still
have existed.[23]

This argument that the Shang state was orderly, bureaucratic, and "civilized" recurs throughout Keightley's article. Thus, he reads the *bin* ritual according to a similar bureaucratic mentality,[24] concluding, in opposition to
Chang, that the ritual was not shamanistic:

> The Shang king was the communicator with the hierarchy of the dead; he attracted
> them to his cult center, in sequence, with rigorously scheduled sacrifices and hosted
> them with ordered groups of rituals; he communicated with them through the
> highly formalized techniques of pyromantic divination; he commissioned inscrip-
> tions, carved into divination bones, that recorded the whole procedure in detail. Or-
> derly divination, the hosting of guests (whether alive or dead), sacrifice—these were
> the ways of civilized men dealing, not with the wild and the unknown, not with ec-
> static inspiration or trance, but, through ritual and schedule, with their own kin.[25]

Both sacrifice and divination are here explicable as expressions of a rational,
bureaucratic, civilized system, rather than of the shamanistic model advanced by Chang.

Keightley's concern with rationalization in the successive stages of social
development reveals a strong Weberian influence. And, like Weber, Keightley is interested in how the religious orientations he finds in the Shang
played out in later Chinese history. So, like Chang, Keightley sees the Shang
as the origin of later Chinese cultural orientations, although he and Chang
read this history very differently. As Keightley argues in his seminal "The
Religious Commitment: Shang Theology and the Genesis of Chinese Political Culture": "It is the argument of this exploratory essay that the secular
values and institutions representing the great tradition of the Zhou and Han
dynasties were characterized to a significant extent by habits of thinking and

23. Ibid., pp. 816–17, 820.
24. Ibid., pp. 808–14. See also Keightley, "The Religious Commitment," p. 218.
25. Keightley, "Shamanism, Death, and the Ancestors," p. 813.

acting that had been sanctified at least a millennium earlier by the religious logic of the Shang theology and cult."[26]

For Keightley, however, what one finds in the Shang is not Chang's shamanism but Weber's vision: "The radical world optimism which Weber identified as a central Confucian value was already present in Shang religious belief."[27] As he elaborates: "In Weberian terms, then, we can refer to the hierarchical, contractual, rational, routinized, mathematical, compartmentalized nature of Shang ancestor worship as bureaucratic."[28] The Shang, then, was the origin of a bureaucratic mentality that Weber—correctly, in Keightley's view—saw as a dominant aspect of later Chinese culture. For Keightley, the oracle-bone inscriptions reveal a bureaucratic mentality that both routinized whatever shamanistic tendencies might have existed in the Neolithic period and initiated the "radical world optimism" that Keightley, following Weber, sees as characterizing later Chinese culture.

Keightley's position leads him to a view of urban genesis somewhat different from that given by Wheatley. He refers quite favorably to Wheatley's emphasis on the importance of religion in the genesis of the Chinese state.[29] But Keightley reads the significance of religion in China differently. If Wheatley is working from Eliade, Keightley is working from Weber. After describing the importance of religion for the Shang state, Keightley continues:

There is nothing uniquely Chinese in this account so far. Religious belief has played similar roles in the genesis of other states. [Keightley provides another reference here to Wheatley.] Significant in the Chinese case, however, were the modes of conceptualization central to the theology. For it is in the logical relationships that Shang theology postulated as basic, and in the emotions associated with those relationships, that we find the characteristic elements which influenced the development of political culture in Zhou and later times. We find, in fact, a paradoxical situation: a Shang state permeated with a commitment to the ancestors, strongly religious in the totality of its demands; and yet we find that the commitment can be characterized as nonreligious, nonmysterious, and—because so explicitly goal directed—rational in its logic. The logic may be characterized, in fact, with appropriate cautions to which I shall return, as "bureaucratic" in Max Weber's sense of the term.[30]

---

26. Keightley, "The Religious Commitment," pp. 211–12.
27. Ibid., p. 216. See also Keightley, "Clean Hands and Shining Helmets," p. 42.
28. Keightley, "The Religious Commitment," p. 216.
29. Ibid., p. 214.
30. Ibid.

If Wheatley (like Chang and Ching in this particular sense) saw the significance of China as lying in its embodiment of, in the fullest sense, a primordial cosmological emphasis on the linkage of the human and sacred realms,
Keightley sees the significance in the peculiar bureaucratic logic of Shang
religion.[31]

However, as we saw in the Introduction, the Weberian reading of Chinese culture does share a number of similarities with the cultural-essentialist
model underlying (in somewhat different ways) Wheatley's and Chang's interpretations. Thus, although Keightley rejects the shamanism hypothesis
for early China and although he does implicitly revise Wheatley's interpretation, he also sees humans and divinities as harmoniously linked in early
China. He explicitly compares this with the situation in early Greece:
"Greek epics also derive much of their complexity and dramatic tension from
the frank recognition that unresolvable conflicts exist in the world. This
fundamental assumption is symbolized in the conflict between the values
and wills of men and gods." According to Keightley, no such discord between gods and men can be found in early China: "There was little discord
between gods and men. . . . The Chinese knew neither a Prometheus nor a
Zeus."[32]

Like Wheatley, Chang, and Ching, therefore, Keightley sees in the Shang
the origins of what he deems to be dominant orientations of Chinese
thought. Moreover, although his reading of these dominant orientations is
based on a Weberian interpretation and although he (very convincingly, in
my opinion) rejects the shamanism hypothesis, he, too, emphasizes a contrast between China and Greece based on the tragic cosmology of the former
and the optimistic cosmology of the latter. Indeed, Keightley's critique of
Chang was aimed almost entirely at pointing out the lack of any evidence for
ecstatic techniques and ascensions. But the most important issue for Chang
was his claim that, in the Shang, humans and gods were linked in harmony—and Keightley, despite his enormous differences from Chang,

---

31. Keightley's argument is foreshadowed in a review of Wheatley's book that Keightley
wrote some five years before the article under discussion. Overall the review is favorable, but
he does argue that the next step in a comparative inquiry should be to stress differences as
well as similarities between China and the rest of the world. See "Religion and the Rise of
Urbanism," p. 529.

32. Keightley, "Clean Hands and Shining Helmets," pp. 41–42.

accepts this as well. As was noted in the Introduction, the Weberian perspective and the cultural-essentialist perspective (Keightley and Chang respectively, in this instance) read early China in similar ways.

Thus, although Chang and Ching emphasize the shamanistic union of human and deity in the oracle bones, and Keightley emphasizes rational, bureaucratic hierarchy, all three agree that Shang divination and sacrifice practices reveal an assumption of harmony between humans and divinities. In what follows, I question parts of this reading. In doing so, I follow David Keightley's research on Shang oracle-bone inscriptions closely and, in particular, build directly on Keightley's arguments concerning what he calls "making the ancestors."[33] But I argue that acceptance of Keightley's arguments opens to question some of the notions of harmony that Keightley himself, as well as so many other scholars, want to read into the Shang.

The Agon of Humans and Spirits in the Late Shang

The main god of the pantheon was Di,[34] who controlled the wind and rain:

Divining: "Crackmaking on *bingyin* [day 3], Zheng divining: This eleventh month, Di will order the rain."[35]

Divining: "This eleventh month, Di will not order the rain." (*Heji* 5,658 正)

Divining: "On the next *guimao* [day 40], Di will order winds." (*Heji* 672 正)

The very existence of these divinations implies that there is no belief here that Di will necessarily give rain when humans need it.

Indeed, Di often created disasters for the king:

Di will make [for] the king misfortune. (*Heji* 14,182)

As did other spirits:

Que divining: "Huan [the Huan River] will make [for] this city misfortune." (*Heji* 7,854)

One of the concerns in divination was thus to discover whether the divine powers intended to send down misfortune:

---

33. David Keightley, "The Making of the Ancestors."
34. For the exact nature of Di, see below, pp. 48–49.
35. Guo and Hu, *Jiaguwen heji* 5,658 正 (hereinafter cited in the text as *Heji*)

Crackmaking on *xinmao*, Nei divining: "The king will have the making of misfortune." (*Heji* 536)

Crackmaking on *xinmao*, Zheng divining: "The king will not have the making of misfortune." (*Heji* 536)

Crackmaking on *wuxu*, Bin divining: "This city will be without the having of misfortune." (*Heji* 7,852)

Divining: "This city will have the sending down of misfortune." (*Heji* 7,852)

A constant give-and-take existed between human actions and divine powers. In a world controlled by spirits, certain human actions were seen as coming into contact with divine powers, and it was thus around these actions that sacrifices, rituals, and divinations came to be associated. The goal of these activities was to influence, mollify, and determine the will of the divine powers, to persuade them to grant assistance, and to prevent them from making disasters.

Take, for example, the issue of making a settlement. Following are a number of inscriptions from Period I:[36]

Divining: "The king will make a settlement, [for if he does] Di will approve." (*Heji* 14,201)

Divining: "The king ought not to make a settlement, [for if he does not] Di will approve." (*Heji* 14,201)

Crackmaking on *renzi*, Zheng divining: "We will make a settlement, [for if we do] Di will not oppose." Approved. Third month. (*Heji* 14,206)

In order to make a settlement, a divination must be performed to determine the will of Di. It seems plausible to hypothesize that founding a settlement involved bringing divinely controlled natural elements into the human realm and required divination to determine if the action would be acceptable to Di. Contrary to Wheatley, the making of a settlement did not involve correlative concerns or a notion of an *axis mundi*. The concerns were based, instead, on a potentially agonistic relationship between humans and Di: Di controlled

---

36. Period I is Dong Zuobin's term for the earliest grouping of oracle-bone inscriptions, dating to the reign of Wu Ding. For convenient summaries of the issues surrounding the periodization of oracle-bone inscriptions, see Keightley, *Sources of Shang History*, pp. 91–133; Shaughnessy, "Recent Approaches to Oracle-Bone Periodization"; and Li Xueqin and Peng Yushang, *Yinxu jiagu fenqi yanjiu*.

the land, and humans had to utilize rituals to make that land available for human use.[37]

Agriculture was another repeated topic of concern in the early portions of the corpus of oracle bones. Like the making of a settlement, the preparation of fields involved a human appropriation of natural elements controlled by divine powers. As we find in two Period I inscriptions:

Command Yin to prepare the great fields.

Ought not command Yin to prepare the great fields. (*Heji* 9,472)

The divinations reflect an attempt to determine whether this act of preparing the fields, of readying them for human appropriation, was acceptable to the divine powers.

Similar concerns underlie the opening of a field for agriculture. The following is a set of inscriptions located on a single scapula. Reading from bottom to top:[38]

On *guihai*, divining: "At PN open the fields."[39]

On *guihai*, divining: "The king will command the Many Yin to open the fields in the west, [for if they do, we] shall receive millet."

On *guihai* divining: "The Many Yin ought not to do [this], [for if they do not, we] shall receive millet."

On *wuchen* divining: "We will pray for millet, [starting] from Shang Jia. We will offer the *liao* [burning sacrifice]."

---

37. Indeed, I would question not only Wheatley's reading of the Shang material but his use of a correlative model to account for the rise of cities in general. As noted above, Wheatley's argument concerning the *axis mundi* was based on the work of Eliade. Eliade in turn based his arguments on the Pan-Babylonian scholars—with the crucial difference that the Pan-Babylonian scholars saw notions of the sacred center as diffused from the Near East, whereas Eliade saw them as a universal aspect of what he called primitive cultures. In other words, the entire notion of an *axis mundi* came originally from the Pan-Babylonian scholars' reading of Near Eastern materials, and Eliade, and later Wheatley, then universalized the notion.

However, the existence of the notion of an *axis mundi* in the Near Eastern materials has been called into question as well. As Jonathan Z. Smith (*To Take Place*, p. 16) has argued: "There is no pattern of the 'Center' in the sense that the Pan-Babylonians and Eliade described it in the Near Eastern materials." Thus, beyond the problems I have raised for Wheatley's reading of Bronze Age China, I would question the entire Eliadean argument on which Wheatley based his comparative analysis.

38. As is common for scapulas. See Keightley, *Sources of Shang History*, p. 52.

39. Here and below, the abbreviation "PN" is used to refer to an unidentified place name.

On *guihai* divining: "We will pray for millet, [starting] from Shang Jia."

On *yichou* divining: "The king will order the opening of the fields at Jing."

"At PN open the fields." (*Heji* 33,209)

Thus, a successful millet harvest depended in part on whether the Many Yin opened the fields in the west: according to the third inscription in the set, they would receive millet only if they did not prepare the western fields. Here again, the human appropriation of a field could potentially upset the divine powers.

Plowing involved similar issues:

Crackmaking on . . . , divining: "The multitudes will do the plowing. There will be no loss. . . ." (*Heji* 8)

As did cutting grasses for hay:

Divining: "Do the grass-cutting [i.e., make hay]. The rain will not . . . ." (*Heji* 13,793)

Moreover, the harvests themselves were controlled by divine powers:

On *guihai*, divining: "The Many Yin ought not undertake the harvesting of the millet." (*Heji* 33,209)

Jiawu, divining: "Today we will *sui* [sacrifice], [for if we do, we] will receive millet [i.e., a good harvest]." (*Heji* 2,124)

The goal of these divinations was thus to determine whether the divine powers would allow humans to appropriate natural resources.

But just as divine actions affect the human realm, so human actions have repercussions in the divine world. I explore this point more fully below; here it is enough to point out that a recurrent concern in the inscriptional material is to determine the proper amount of sacrifices at any given time that will influence the divine powers in a way favorable for human concerns:

The king will set forth jades to Zu Yi, [give] the burnt sacrifice offering of three penned sheep, and cleave three great . . . . This was used. (*Heji* 32,535)

. . . will make the *ding* sacrifice at the two shrines, [for if he does,] the king will receive assistance. (*Heji* 2,345)

Crackmaking on *bingzi*: "In sacrificing [to] Zu Yi, we will offer the *ding* [sacrifice], [for if we do,] the king will receive assistance." (*Heji* 27,226)

The sacrifices are aimed at gaining assistance for the king: making a particular sacrifice, it is hoped, will result in divine aid. The purpose of the divination was thus apparently to determine if a particular sacrifice, offered at a particular time, would indeed have the desired effect.

A similar concern with controlling the divine spirits can be seen in the frequency of exorcism rituals in the inscriptional corpus. If the divinations concerning agriculture and settlements were aimed at making divinely controlled land available for human appropriation, exorcism involved driving the spirits away from the human realm altogether.

Divining: "Make an exorcism [to eliminate] Fu Hao's trouble." (*Heji* 13,646)

At times, this ritual form of controlling and managing the divine forces could encompass large portions of the pantheon:

Crackmaking on *yihai*, Bin divining: "Make the great exorcism [starting] from Shang Jia." (*Heji* 14,860)

There is, thus, in the late Shang, a constant agon between humans and spirits, with spirits controlling natural phenomena and humans attempting to appropriate aspects of the natural world for their own benefit. This results in seemingly endless attempts by humans to placate, coax, and influence the spirits through sacrifice and divination. And the attempt seems often to fail: the spirits are capricious and far more powerful than the rituals humans use to control them.

Placing the Ancestors: The Construction of the Shang Pantheon

The obvious questions, then, are: What precisely are these divine powers, Wherein lies their capriciousness, and How precisely are human rituals supposed to control them?[40] A significant portion—but by no means all—of the pantheon consists of ancestral spirits.

The construction of the pantheon begins with an individual's death:[41]

Crackmaking on *bingshen*, Chu divining: "In making Xiao Si's day, let it be a *gui*." Eighth month. (*Heji* 23,712)[42]

---

40. My understanding of these issues has been helped greatly by Sarah Allan's *The Shape of the Turtle.*

41. My argument here follows the interpretation given by, and set of inscriptions compiled by, Li Xueqin in his "Ping Yinxu buci zongshu."

42. The same divination is found on *Heji* 23,714; *Heji* 23,713 has the same divination, but without the *ri*.

The divination is an attempt to determine the temple name of Xiao Si, as well as the day on which he or she receives cult.[43] And the following inscription reveals that Xiao Si (still being referred to by the name he or she had while alive) is venerated on a *gui* day:

Crackmaking on *renwu*, Da divining: "On the next *giuwei*, offer to Xiao Si three penned sheep and X-sacrifice one ox." (*Heji* 23,719)

Once the day on which the ancestor will receive sacrifices has been determined, the ancestor then receives a temple name based on that day. Thus, for example, Father Yi receives cult on an *yi* day:

Crackmaking on *jiachen* [day 41], Que divining: "On the next *yisi* [day 42], make an offering to Father Yi of penned sheep." Use. (*Heji* 1,402 正)

This pattern holds throughout our sources. The rituals following death, therefore, involved the attempt to make the spirit of the deceased into an ancestor and to place that ancestor within a ritual system designed by the living. As Keightley has brilliantly argued, the Shang were "making" their ancestors.[44] The deceased were given temple names, granted a day on which to receive sacrifices, and placed within the sacrificial cycle. Xiao Si moved from being a dead—and presumably highly powerful and potentially dangerous—spirit to being an ancestor with a defined place. In short, the point of these rituals was to place the deceased in

---

43. I am here following David Keightley's interpretation of temple names. For a brief summary, see his *The Ancestral Landscape*, pp. 33–35. Keightley was reacting against K. C. Chang's argument that the temple name reflected different descent groups within the Shang lineage; see Chang's "T'ien kan: A Key to the History of the Shang."

The evidence given here—clearly demonstrating that the temple names were given posthumously—should be sufficient to disprove the theory that the names represented different descent groups. It should further be mentioned that one of the circumstantial pieces of evidence Chang used in defense of his hypothesis was Dong Zuobin's alternation of Old and New Schools of diviners (for Dong's theory, see his "Yinxu wenzi yibian xu"). Chang argued that this alternation was based on a regular alternation of the kingship between the *yi* and *ding* descent groups. Here too, however, the evidence does not support Chang. Recent scholarship has fairly successfully questioned Dong's reading of alternating Old and New School diviners; see, e.g., Lin Yun, "Xiaotun nandi fajue yu Yinxu jiagu duandai"; Li Xueqin, "Xiaotun nandi jiagu yu jiagu fenqi"; and Qiu Xigui, "Lun Li zu buci de shidai." Chang's theory, therefore, is no longer tenable.

44. Keightley, "The Making of the Ancestors."

the proper hierarchy of sacrifices. And it was a place determined by the living.

The entire pantheon of Shang ancestors was built up through such a process. By adding together the clues from the inscriptional evidence, scholars have been able to work out the entire ancestral hierarchy.[45] Shang Jia was the highest ancestor of the Shang, and Da Yi was Cheng Tang, the founder of the Shang dynasty, according to later accounts from the Zhou. The hierarchy also seems to reflect the power possessed by each ancestor: the older the ancestors, the more power they possessed.

Thus, sufferers of relatively minor things like toothaches, sicknesses, and dreams would divine to recently deceased ancestors to see if the sicknesses in question were caused by curses:

Divining: "It is Father Yi who is cursing Fu Hao." (*Heji* 6,032 正)

Divining: "It is not Father Yi who is cursing Fu Hao." (*Heji* 6,032 正)

Divining: "As for Fu Hao's dream, it is not Father Yi." (*Heji* 201 正)

If such divinations reveal that the problem is indeed a curse from one of the ancestors, then sacrifices would be made to dispel the curse:

Crackmaking on *wuyin* [day 15], Bin divining: "Exorcise Fu Jing to Mother Geng." (*Heji* 2,725)

". . . Mother Geng exorcise Fu Hao's tooth."

"[We] ought not to Mother Geng exorcise."

"Exorcise the misfortune to Father Yi." (*Heji* 2,194)

Crackmaking on *yimao*, Que divining: "Exorcise Fu Hao to Father Yi. Cleave sheep, offer pigs, and make a promissory offering of ten penned sheep." (*Heji* 271)

All these divinations and sacrifices are aimed at the generation immediately above the living.

But, for topics like the harvest, higher ancestors would usually be invoked. The following divination begins with the highest ancestor, Shang Jia:

On *guihai* divining: "We will pray for millet [starting] from Shang Jia." (*Heji* 33,209)

---

45. Much of the crucial work for this was done by Dong Zuobin and published in his "Yinxu wenzi yibian xu." On the hierarchy itself, see the useful summary in Keightley, *The Ancestral Landscape*, pp. 98–103.

Similarly, military campaigns would involve significant portions of the pantheon:

Divining: "This spring the king will not ally with Wang Cheng to attack Xia Wei [for if he does,] the upper and lower [divine powers] will not approve. It will not be we who will be receiving the divine assistance." (*Heji* 6,506)

The ancestors, therefore, appear to grow more powerful the longer they are dead. The generation of ancestors immediately above the living can curse specific individuals with sicknesses, toothaches, and nightmares, whereas the higher powers control phenomena that affect the entire Shang people, such as harvests and military campaigns.

And this hierarchy provides the context for understanding the *bin* ritual—the ritual discussed by both Chang and Keightley. If Chang read the ritual as an example of shamanism, Keightley read it as revealing a proto-bureaucratic sense of hierarchy. Let us look at the evidence:

Ought not entertain. (*Heji* 33,796)

Crackmaking on *wu* . . . Que divining: "We ought not make the entertainment [ritual]." (*Heji* 15,191)

Crackmaking on *yichou*, Que divining: "We ought not perform the entertainment [ritual]." (*Heji* 15,179)

Divining: "Cheng will be a guest to Di." (*Heji* 1,402 正)

Divining: "Da Jia will be a guest to Cheng." (*Heji* 1,402 正)

Divining: "Cheng will not be a guest to Di." (*Heji* 1,402 正)

Divining: "Da Jia will not be a guest to Cheng." (*Heji* 1,402 正)

Crackmaking on *jiachen* [day 41], Que divining: "Xia yi will be a guest to . . . ." (*Heji* 1,402 正)

Divining: "Xia Yi will not be a guest to Cheng." (*Heji* 1,402 正)

Divining: "Da . . . will be a guest to Di." (*Heji* 1,402 正)

Divining: "Xia Yi . . . to Di." (*Heji* 1,402 正)

Divining: "Da Jia will be a guest to Di." (*Heji* 1,402 正)

Divining: "Xia Yi will not be a guest to Di." (*Heji* 1,402 正)

The *bin* ritual involved attempts by one figure to entertain or treat another. The "figures" involved were humans, ancestors, or Di. The crucial point, as Keightley has argued so effectively, is that the figures in question are ar-

ranged hierarchically: humans entertain the most recently deceased ancestors, and the most recently deceased ancestors entertain the still earlier ancestors, who in turn entertain Di.[46]

This hierarchy of ritual action reveals a hierarchy of power, since the recently deceased ancestors were seen as weaker than the older ones, who were
in turn weaker than the nature gods and Di. As Keightley has demonstrated:
"In terms of functions, Di, the Nature Powers, and a few of the Former
Lords, like Huang Yin, tended to affect the dynasty or the country as a
whole, influencing the weather, the crops, and warfare; by contrast, . . . the
ancestors were more directly concerned with the king's personal activities:
his illnesses, his well-being, and the fault-free management of the rituals."[47]
And the hierarchy also reveals a hierarchy of pliability—at least from the
point of view of the living: the more recently deceased ancestors were seen as
more amenable to human ritual promptings. To quote Keightley again:
"The Shang conceived of the Nature and the Ancestral Powers as occupying
a hierarchy of negotiability, with the close ancestors and ancestresses of the
pantheon being most open to this kind of pledging, and the higher Powers,
both ancestral and natural, being less approachable in this way."[48]

The goal of the ritual was thus to prompt the weaker ancestors to host
the more powerful, all the way up to Di. The ritual, then, served two purposes: it maintained the proper hierarchy of the pantheon, and it used the
lower, more pliable ancestors, to mollify the higher, more powerful ancestors—ultimately including even Di.

But then who—or what—is Di? Several scholars have tried to argue that
Di is the supreme ancestor. Robert Eno even argues that Di is in fact a collective name for the entire pantheon of ancestors.[49] But I would argue
against Eno's reading. It is difficult to read the *bin* ritual inscriptions mean-
ingfully if we interpret Di as a collective name. But then the question still
stands: If Di is a singular being, then what is he? The evidence for answering
the question is limited. But it is clear that Di is more powerful than the
other ancestors. He is the most powerful of the gods and controls the wind
and rains. It could be argued that Di is very much like an ancestor: as we

---

46. Keightley, "Shamanism, Death, and the Ancestors," pp. 808–14. See also Hu
Houxuan, "Yin buci zhong de shangdi he wangdi," p. 89.

47. Keightley, "The Making of the Ancestors," p. 9.

48. Ibid., p. 15.

49. Eno, "Was There a High God Ti in Shang Religion?"

have already seen, the more distant ancestors are more powerful. At the same time, however, he is not part of the sacrificial pantheon: he does not have a temple name, and he does not have a designated day in the sacrificial cycle. Indeed, Di never receives sacrifices at all.[50] As the most powerful god, Di seems relatively uncontrollable by human ritual.

The most reasonable hypothesis is that Di was not recognized as part of the Shang ancestral line, and he was probably not an ancestor at all. And this may in part explain the motivation for the *bin* ritual. If the human ability to influence Di directly is limited, humans can nonetheless attempt to influence the lower ancestors, who can influence the higher ancestors, who can in turn influence Di. In other words, they can create a hierarchical chain that ultimately includes Di.

We thus find inscriptions such as:

Crackmaking on *guichou* [day 50], Zheng divining: "We will dwell in this settlement and perform the great entertainment ritual, [for if we do,] Di will approve." Third month. (*Heji* 14,206 正)

Crackmaking on *guichou* [day 50], Zheng divining: "Di will not approve." (*Heji* 14,206 正)

To determine whether Di approves of the Shang's continued dwelling in a particular settlement, a "great entertainment ritual" is offered. The term "great X ritual" is used in Shang inscriptional literature to refer to a ritual encompassing the entire pantheon. The "great exorcism," for example, includes all ancestors, beginning with Shang Jia:

Crackmaking on *yihai*, Bin divining: "Make the great exorcism [starting] from Shang Jia." (*Heji* 14,860)

It is reasonable to conclude, then, that the great entertainment ritual involved the full pantheon, including the entertaining of Di by the higher ancestors. Thus, the way to gain the support of Di for the continued occupation of the settlement was through the *bin* ritual: Di could not be coerced into accepting the Shang order through sacrifices, but the pantheon could be employed to coerce him through the *bin* ritual.

---

50. There are no inscriptions in which Di clearly receives sacrifice. Shima Kunio has attempted to argue that Di did in fact receive sacrifices, but his evidence is unconvincing; see his *Inkyo bokuji kenkyū*, pp. 195–97. For a careful, and convincing, refutation of Shima's argument, see Eno, "Was There a High God Ti in Shang Religion?" pp. 7–8.

These attempts to use the *bin* ritual to create and maintain a proper hierarchy of non-ancestral powers can further be seen in the entertainment of nature spirits such as the sun and the Yellow River:

Crackmaking on *yisi* [day 42]: "The king will entertain Ri [the sun]. (*Heji* 32,181)
He will not entertain the sun." (*Heji* 32,181)

Crackmaking on *xinsi* [day 18], divining: "The king will entertain He [the Yellow River] and offer a *liao* [burnt-offering sacrifice]."[51]

Crackmaking on *renzi* [day 49], Lü divining: "The king will entertain Ri [the sun]. It will not rain." (*Heji* 22,539)

In contrast to the treatment of Di, the king himself can directly entertain these nature powers. But, as we saw with Di, the *bin* ritual appears to connect the non-ancestral divinities with ancestral powers:

Crackmaking on *guiwei* [day 20], Que divining: "On the next *jiashen* [day 21], the king will entertain Shang Jia and Ri." The king prognosticated and said: "It will be an auspicious entertainment ritual." They really were entertained. (*Heji* 1,248 正)

The purpose of the ritual was to entertain Shang Jia, the highest Shang ancestor, alongside the sun. It seems reasonable to conclude, therefore, that natural powers as well were being brought into and harmonized with the ancestral powers. Dead humans are made into ancestors, and non-ancestral powers are then brought into accord with these ancestors. And, in the case of Di, the ancestors themselves are called upon to bring Di into the pantheon.

Transforming the Spirits: Sacrifice in the Shang

So what does this mean for our understanding of the *bin* ritual? I would agree with Keightley that Shang ritual process should not be read as shamanistic. Humans do not ascend to the heavens, nor do the ancestors descend into humans. The ancestors certainly descend to receive their sacrifices, but there is nothing shamanistic about that.

But I would not follow Keightley in reading this as proto-bureaucratic. And my disagreement comes down to a question concerning Keightley's argument about sacrifices in the Shang. For Keightley, "Shang religious practice rested upon the *do ut des* ('I give, in order that thou shouldst give') belief

---

51. Zhongguo shehui kexueyuan, Kaogu yanjiusuo, *Xiaotun nandi jiagu*, 1,116.

that correct ritual procedure by the Shang kings would result in favors conferred by Di."[52] A similar reading of Shang sacrifice underlies Poo Mu-chou's understanding:

In the [Shang] inscriptions one senses that the diviner addressed the deities, or ancestors, as if they were immediately accessible. In fact, since man believed so firmly that the deities and ancestors actually extended care and power to the propitiator directly, the world of extra-human powers in the conception of the Shang diviners should be seen as having been either conterminous with the human world or a continuous extension of it.[53]

The ancestors, deities, and humans are on the same plane, and sacrifice allows for a proper relationship between them: "A person's relationship with the powers, moreover, can be described as *do ut des*."[54] Keightley and (following Keightley) Poo Mu-chou are arguing that insofar as the Shang divinational and sacrificial experts saw humans and divinities as continuous, a simple bureaucratic operation of giving and taking was set up between them: one gives in order to receive. In making this argument, Keightley is reading China according to a sacrificial model proposed by the early theorists of sacrifice—Edward Tylor, Robertson Smith, and, to some extent, Henri Hubert and Marcel Mauss.[55] All these theorists read sacrifice as a gift from human to god. And Weber lies in this tradition as well. Weber reads the sacrificial *do ut des* as a rationalization of magic[56]—just as he reads the this-worldly orientation of later Chinese religion.

In fact, however, Hubert and Mauss's argument contains more than just a discussion of sacrifice as a gift. Indeed, as many have argued,[57] the definitions of sacrifice as a gift that still appear in the work are the weakest parts of the argument. Other parts of Hubert and Mauss's analysis are far more powerful and may prove more helpful for analyzing Shang sacrificial practices than the gift model. The main idea behind their argument is that sacrifice is a transformative act. They read the act as involving a series of trans-

---

52. Keightley, "The Religious Commitment," pp. 214–15.
53. Poo, *In Search of Personal Welfare*, p. 28.
54. Ibid.
55. Tylor, *Primitive Culture*; William Robertson Smith, *Lectures on the Religion of the Semites*; Hubert and Mauss, *Sacrifice*.
56. Weber, *Economy and Society*, 1: 424.
57. See, in particular, the excellent discussion by Valeri, *Kingship and Sacrifice*, pp. 64–66.

formations of sacralization and desacralization between the sacrifier,[58] the victim, and the divine powers involved. Thus, for example, Hubert and Mauss argue that the sacrificial victim is sacralized by the process, as, therefore, is the sacrifier.[59] Sacrifices throughout the world are then read as a series of permutations of this model; Hubert and Mauss focus in particular on which transformations are emphasized and what function these transformations have in the society under discussion. Of particular interest to our current concerns is their description of one aspect of the Vedic soma sacrifice: "Thus not only is it in sacrifice that some gods are born, it is by sacrifice that all sustain their existence. So it has ended by appearing as their essence, their origin, and their creator."[60] In other words, gods as well as the sacrifier can be transformed by sacrifices.

And, in fact, Keightley's argument concerning the "making of ancestors" points precisely to this transformative notion of sacrifice rather than to the bureaucratic *do ut des* framework within which both he and Poo Mu-chou attempt to interpret Shang sacrificial action. The Shang sacrificers were not assuming that human and divine powers were continuous or that the giving of a gift would result in benefits from the gods. They were rather transforming spirits into figures who would operate within a humanly defined hierarchy. In other words, sacrifice did not rest upon the "belief" that correct ritual procedures would result in favors. Rather, it rested on the attempt to *create* a system in which this would be the case.

Thus, when dead beings are given a temple name and placed within the sacrificial hierarchy, they are being formed into ancestors who will, the living hope, act on their behalf. And the *bin* ritual not only maintains this hierarchy but also (again, it is hoped) brings Di into it as well. And all these divine powers are then called on to act on behalf of the living. Perhaps, then, instead of representing a bureaucratic mentality, the ritual involved an attempt to create hierarchy. Hierarchy was not an assumption; it was a goal.

I would argue that the guiding assumption behind Shang sacrificial action is that if left to their own devices, the spirits (Di, nature spirits, and deceased humans) do not act in the best interests of humans. Indeed, the

---

58. The "sacrifier," according to the Hubert/Mauss model, is the "subject to whom the benefits of sacrifice thus accrue, or who undergoes its effects" (Hubert and Mauss, *Sacrifice*, p. 10).

59. Ibid., pp. 19–49.

60. Ibid., pp. 91–92.

assumption seemed to be that spirits were capricious and quite possibly malicious. And they were more powerful than humans: they control natural phenomena, and they have the ability to send disasters.

Accordingly, humans had to, within the limits of their powers, use rituals to place these spirits in a hierarchical system, in which (it was hoped) the spirits would further the interests of the living. The Shang ancestral cult represented an attempt to forge nature spirits and the ghosts of deceased humans into a single, unified system. The deceased humans would become ancestral spirits, defined by their roles in a hierarchy, and both nature spirits and nonrelated yet nonetheless powerful deceased humans would be placed in this hierarchy as well. Moreover, these ancestral spirits would themselves serve to keep the non-ancestral spirits in place.

And, from the evidence in the divinatory material, it is clear that these efforts often failed. Even with the sacrificial system in place, the spirits frequently, at whim, created problems for the living, and the living then had to divine to determine what additional sacrifices would mollify the spirit in question. Spirits, in short, were more powerful than mere human rituals, and Di and the other (natural and ancestral) spirits would frequently act contrary to the interests of humans. Thus, humans were neither collaborating with the spirits nor assuming that their rituals would work. Instead, they were attempting, within their limited powers, to use rituals to create an ordered, helpful pantheon of spirits.

My full argument, then, is that adopting Keightley's insight about "making ancestors" leads to a questioning of Keightley's own Weberian framework. If correct, this would mean that there was no assumption of a harmonious collaboration of man and spirit in the late Shang. The need to make spirits of the deceased into ancestors and to bring nature deities and Di itself into that pantheon shows, among other things, a belief that spirits are *not* inherently inclined to act on behalf of the living. And the divinational record reveals a belief that the ritual system often did not work anyway.

This reading of the inscriptions implies that a this-worldly optimism did not prevail in the Shang and that humans and spirits were not seen as inherently connected. On the contrary: the specific concern of the Shang cult was, in a sense, to anthropomorphize the spirit world: to make the deceased into proper ancestors and to have the ancestors guide the nature spirits and Di. The reigning assumption, then, would appear to be that the relations between humans and spirits were, without this ritual action, agonistic and potentially dangerous; the goal was thus to domesticate the sprits and thereby render them controllable.

A Moral Cosmos? The Zhou Conquest and the Mandate of Heaven

In the mid-eleventh century BC, the Shang fell to the Zhou armies led by King Wu. This would become one of the defining moments in early Chinese history. But was it just a military victory of one state over another, or did it represent a fundamental change in the perceived relations between humans and spirits in early China?

Scholars who emphasize that the Shang was foundational for later Chinese culture argue, not surprisingly, against a fundamental break. (Both Chang and Wheatley, for example, quote from Zhou texts in discussing Shang materials.) But several scholars have tried to argue, on the contrary, that the Zhou conquest does indeed represent a rupture. Indeed, there is a clear pattern: scholars who see a substantial break tend to find in the Western Zhou the very things that Wheatley, Chang, Ching, and Keightley tried (in my opinion unsuccessfully) to find in the Shang: a belief in an inherent and harmonious link between divine powers and humanity. For example, Eno recently described the Shang/Zhou transition in the following terms: "Whereas the Shang king had been merely chief priest to the high gods, the Mandate of Heaven theory made the Zhou king Tian's [Heaven's] executor on earth.[61] Tian and the king were now virtually indistinguishable."[62] In a footnote to this statement, Eno further remarks: "This had not been the case with the Shang. There are inscriptions that portray the Shang high god Di

---

61. Heaven was the high god of the Zhou, just as Di was the high god of the Shang. However, as we shall see, the Zhou presented Heaven and Di as the same deity and used the two terms interchangeably.

Shima Kunio (*Inkyo bokuji kenkyū*, pp. 174–86) and, following him, Robert Eno (*The Confucian Creation of Heaven*, pp. 183–86) have tried to argue that Heaven does in fact appear in the Shang inscriptions, represented by the graph *ding* 丁. I find the argument unpersuasive. The word *ding* simply refers to the *ding* day, and I would read the inscriptions about sacrifices *yu ding* 於 丁 as simply meaning sacrifices "on a *ding* day," or "to *ding* ancestors" (i.e., ancestors sacrificed to on *ding* days), not "to Heaven." As Eno (*The Confucian Creation of Heaven*, p. 186) himself points out: "Criteria for identifying which inscriptions use the graph as a cyclical sign and which as Tian need to be developed, otherwise the argument that all instances of □ in the sense of a deity refer to *ding*-sign kings remains plausible."

62. Eno, *The Confucian Creation of Heaven*, p. 23.

as the potential adversary of the king and the state."[63] The potentially arbitrary aspects of divinity in the Shang are thus replaced by an inherent linkage in the Zhou. Similarly, Lester James Bilsky, in his survey of early Chinese religion, has argued that, in the early Western Zhou: "The gods and spirits were thought of as immortal beings who invariably acted according to the ideals of perfection and who, thus, inhabited a world of ideal perfection."[64] Both Eno and Bilsky, in other words, find in the Western Zhou a linkage between humanity and divinity comparable to that which K. C. Chang and others have found in the Shang.

David Pankenier, in what is perhaps the most fascinating of recent attempts to discuss the Shang-Zhou transition, provides an account that builds on the work of many of the scholars discussed above. Pankenier's stated goal in the essay is to provide "an account of the ancient Chinese politico-religious imagination according to which macrocosmic/microcosmic correspondences legitimated the social order."[65] Pankenier sees the Shang/Zhou transition as a crucial moment in the development of this cosmological view. To make this argument, Pankenier claims that the Shang did *not* think according to such a cosmology. To the contrary, the late Shang—the period covered in the oracle-bone materials—reveals a lack of interest in cosmology and astrology:

The window on the world of the Shang provided by the oracle bone inscriptions, formulaic and limited in scope though they are, seems skewed by the particular preoccupations of late Shang divinatory theology. Cosmology and astrology figure almost incidentally, the natural powers finally not at all, in a magico-religious practice largely devoted during the final decades of the dynasty to the routine observances of the ancestral cult. (p. 174)

In contrast, Pankenier argues, the Zhou developed a view based on the cosmological linking of the king with Heaven.

When put in these terms, the argument seems directly based on the rationalization models discussed in the Introduction—the arguments, found in works from Weber to those committed to a general "religion to philosophy" framework, for a gradual shift in early China from a magical view to a

---

63. Ibid., p. 212*n*25.
64. Bilsky, *The State Religion of Ancient China*, 1: 62.
65. Pankenier, "The Cosmo-Political Background of Heaven's Mandate," p. 122 (hereinafter cited in the text).

rational one. Indeed, Pankenier at one point even describes the Shang/Zhou transition in precisely these terms: "My portrayal of the emergent contrast between late Shang and early Zhou religious dispositions is informed by Clifford Geertz's elaboration (following Max Weber) of the distinction between 'traditional' and 'rationalized' religions" (p. 173n103).

However, Pankenier's overall argument in fact is much closer to those of figures like Wheatley. Pankenier wishes to argue that a form of correlative cosmology, based in astrology, formed in China in the second millennium BC with the emergence of the state. Indeed, he quotes and supports Wheatley's argument on this point (p. 145). Starting well before the Shang, Pankenier argues, kingship was understood as an institution that maintained the proper correlation between the human and natural realms: "The ability to comprehend the celestial motions and to sustain a reciprocal conformity between their regular variations and human activity, that is, the discernment necessary to 'pattern oneself on Heaven,' was a fundamental qualification of kingship" (p. 146).

Pankenier's full argument, therefore, is that the lack of cosmological and astrological thinking distinguishes the late Shang not only from its successors but also from its predecessors: "The late Shang may have represented a significant departure from the norm in significant respects" (p. 175). The theological shift from the Shang to the Zhou was thus not a unilinear evolution from a magical to a rational worldview; rather, the Zhou reverted to a more archaic notion of cosmology:

With regard to the supernatural sanction underpinning the universal kingship the key shift is marked by a deemphasis of legitimacy based on the principle of contiguity, that is, membership in the royal lineage, toward a focus on legitimacy premised on emulating Heaven as the paradigm of order and harmony, an ethos inspired by an archaic, fundamentally metaphorical idea about the congruence obtaining between the supernatural and temporal realms. (pp. 173–74)

Even the ethical aspects of Zhou thought are simply a more articulated aspect of an earlier cosmology:

By attributing human-like personality to Heaven, and by vigorously reviving the conception of phenomenal nature as an index of Heaven's activity, the Zhou Chinese inevitably reimbued nature with an ethical quality. This feeling for the ethical dimension comes most strongly to the fore in the early Zhou texts, but it was by no means a Zhou innovation. (p. 170)

In short, Pankenier sides with Wheatley in arguing for a deep strain of cosmological thinking directly associated with the rise of the state. The Shang
was simply an aberration.

> In view of the evidence of a fundamental consistency between late Zhou cosmologi-
> cal conceptions and their second millennium B.C. antecedents, the Zhou claim to
> have re-established the continuity of a cosmo-political tradition that took its cues
> from Heaven and the natural order now appears well founded. (p. 176)

The Zhou thus represents the consolidation of an earlier archaic tradition
resting on the harmony of man and Heaven.

And this tradition accounts for the optimistic, humanistic disposition of
Chinese thought: "By taking matters into their own hands, so to speak, a
fundamentally optimistic, human-centered disposition began to evolve, bur-
dened though it was by a heavy responsibility to maintain ritual regularity"
(p. 155). Pankenier thus finds in the Western Zhou, as well as earlier in the
Chinese Bronze Age, the same form of this-worldly optimism that Weber
defined as characterizing Chinese culture in general.

But are these scholars right? Are the views of the Western Zhou that different from those of the Shang? Did the Zhou introduce a fundamentally
different (or, in the case of Pankenier, restore a more primordial) way of
conceptualizing the relations of humans, spirits, and the cosmos than that
which existed in the Shang? More pointedly, is it true that such a correlation
of the wills of Heaven, the ancestors, and the king was assumed to exist in
the early and middle Western Zhou—along with an attendant this-worldly
optimism?

The answer to these questions is, in my opinion, no. But before spelling
out my own view, let me provide some of the evidence behind the argument
for a fundamental break in religious beliefs between the Shang and Zhou.

A few years after the conquest, the Duke of Shao, one of King Wu's
brothers, purportedly gave as the reason for the Shang's failure that "they
did not respect their power (de) and thereupon prematurely lost their mandate."[66] The Zhou then received the mandate to rule instead.

A fuller discussion of what this mandate entailed can be seen in the inscription on the Maogong *ding*:

---

66. "Shao gao," *Shangshu*, 15.6a. My translations have been aided by Karlgren, "The Book
of Documents," p. 49; and Nivison, "An Interpretation of the 'Shao gao,'" p. 181.

The king said to the effect: "Father Yin, as for greatly illustrious Wen and Wu, august Heaven was extensively
satisfied with their virtue, and made us, the rulers of Zhou, a counterpart [of himself]. [We] greatly responded to and received the great mandate, and led and embraced
the borderlands which were not coming to court. None was not opened by Wen's and Wu's brilliant glory. It was Heaven that directed
and gathered their mandate, and it was the former officers who yielded to and assisted their rulers, toiling and laboring for the great mandate.
And then august Heaven tirelessly watched over and protected us, the rulers of the Zhou, and greatly strengthened the mandate of which the former kings were the counterpart."[67]

Heaven granted the mandate to the Zhou rulers Wen and Wu, and Wen and Wu then served as the counterpart of Heaven on earth.

At first glance, this appears to be quite different from the Shang material. Throughout the Shang texts there is a strong notion that the world has a proper pattern. However, the evidence clearly reveals this pattern to have been given by humans to the spirits, not the other way around: living humans, through their rituals and particularly through their sacrificial system, place spirits into a hierarchy and thereby attempt to obtain an order favorable to themselves. Spirits do not give this pattern to humans; nor left to their own devices, would the spirits observe such a hierarchy. And, in fact, even with the full sacrificial system in place, spirits are still quite capricious: the rituals do not always work. What appears different about the notion of a mandate is that it explicitly comes from Heaven, and Heaven's support is based on the virtues of the rulers in question rather than on their ritual actions. Humans do not determine the ancestors; rather, they follow Heaven and are rewarded for doing so and punished for not doing so.

Thus, for example, the decision by King Cheng, Wu's son and successor, to found the city of Luoyang is presented in several Western Zhou texts as simply the fulfillment of the wishes of Di. The "Shao gao" chapter of the *Shangshu* quotes the Grand Protector as making precisely this point:

The king should come and continue the [work] of the Di on high, and himself serve in the center of the land.[68]

---

67. Shirakawa, *Kinbun tsūshaku*, 30.181:637. All bronze inscriptions are referenced in terms of this work, henceforth abbreviated as "Sh."
68. "Shao gao," *Shangshu*, 15.5a.

The founding of the city is thus presented as a continuation of the actions of Di (or Heaven), and it serves to center the realm. Contrast this with the inscriptional material discussed above concerning the making of settlements. There, the concern was the human appropriation of land controlled by Di, and the king was attempting to use sacrifices and divination to determine Di's will. Here, Di is the prime mover, directing the king to settle a new city.

Indeed, the entire relationship between ancestors and descendants that prevailed in the late Shang appears to have been turned upside down. Instead of having the kings determine the ancestors, living kings are frequently presented in Western Zhou bronze inscriptions as simply following the models and paradigms of the ancestors. As King Kang states in the *Da Yu ding*:

Now it is that I approach the model and receive from King Wen
upright power. Like King Wen's commanding the two or three officials, now it is
that I command you, Yu,
to assist Rong in respectfully supporting the continuance of the power. (Sh
12.61:647)

King Kang presents himself as following the model of King Wen and receiving the latter's power. Even Kang's act of giving commands is posed as following in the mold of King Wen. Similarly, the king commands Yu to use the same approach of modeling himself on a great ancestor:

The king said: "Ah. I command you, Yu, to model yourself on your inheritance from grandfather Nangong."

Instead of the living making the deceased into proper ancestors, the descendants are here presented as following the deceased. And all are part of Heaven's larger mandate. We find the following on the Lu Bo Dong *gui*, a vessel from the reign of King Mu:

It was the king's first month, with the *chen* at *gengyin* [day 27], the king said to the effect:
"Lu Bo Dong, in planning, starting from your grandfather and father, [your family] has helped
in laboring for the Zhou state and helped in opening up the four quarters. May it be extensive,
Heaven's mandate. In what you have undertaken, you have not failed." (Sh
17.92:211)

Post-conquest military endeavors were also presented as a carrying out of Heaven's mandate. For example, in the Ban *gui*, King Mu is presented as ordering the Duke of Mao to attack the eastern states. After the attack, the Duke is recorded as saying:

The Duke [of Mao] announced his service
to above: "It is that the people did not come (to court). In[69] norms they darkened[70] Heaven's
mandate." (Sh 15.79:34)

War is thus presented as a maintenance of the mandate of Heaven, just as the initial conquest was presented as a fulfillment of the mandate.

Throughout these inscriptions and poems, then, we see a recurring theme: Heaven (or Di) is the director, and the Zhou follow his divine plan. Each successive king is posed as adhering to the model of his predecessors, and each act of conquest, consolidation, and domestication is presented as simply a continuation of the ancestors' work. Moreover, the king's aides are presented as simply serving the royal house in its work, a service accomplished by modeling themselves on their forebears. The living, in such rhetoric, do nothing but respect the model of the ancestors. Unlike the potentially antagonistic relationship of man and divinity in the Shang, then, the Western Zhou writings seem to pose Heaven as acting with the king.

But does the Western Zhou represent a fundamental break from the Shang in terms of the perceived relations between humans and spirits? I think not. The problem here is that we must be careful to contextualize statements and understand why they were written. Above all, we must avoid the temptation to take statements at face value and read them as common beliefs or assumptions of the time. In what follows I will argue that perhaps Eno, Bilsky, and Pankenier are jumping too quickly from statements made in a particular context to claims about an overall belief system of the time. More specifically, the view that there existed a belief in the early Western Zhou of the identity of the king and Heaven seems to me suspect.

---

69. Guo Moruo (*Liang-Zhou jinwenci daxi tulu kaoshi*, p. 20b) reads this *cai* 才 as the exclamatory *zai* 哉. Tempting though such a reading may be, I am not sure it is justifiable. I have instead read it as *zai* 在, as is common in Western Zhou bronze inscriptions.

70. Following Guo Moruo (ibid.) in reading 杢 as *mei* 昧.

Pacifying the Spirits: Western Zhou Sacrificial Practice

The notion of a mandate is linked with the idea of proper sacrifices. In the "Duofang" chapter of the *Shangshu*, the Duke of Zhou is reported to have said: "It was your last king of Shang who took pleasure in his ease, scorned his governance, and did not keep the sacrifices pure. Heaven thus sent down timely disasters." Heaven then turned to the Zhou: "It was our Zhou king who efficaciously upheld the people, was able to utilize his power (*de*), and direct the spirits and Heaven. Heaven then instructed us to utilize his favor. He examined and gave us the mandate of Yin to administer your numerous regions."[71] Of note here is the fact that one of the fundamental distinctions drawn between the two rulers is an ability to utilize sacrifices properly. The last Shang king failed to do so, and Heaven thus sent down disasters. In contrast, the Zhou king was able to direct the spirits and Heaven properly, and he thus won the mandate. But what does it mean to use sacrifices properly?

The Tianwang *gui*,[72] which dates to the reign of King Wu, is inscribed:

The greatly illustrious deceased father King Wen
serves and pleases[73] the Di on high. (Sh 1.1:1)

The late King Wen, Wu's father, is presented as serving and pleasing Di. Here again, the ancestors are expected to do what they can to keep the highest power, Di, working on behalf of the living.

Although the ritual involved here is different from those discussed above, the concerns are quite similar. The inscription in the bronze vessel was presumably intended for the ancestors—in this case King Wen—who would thus read the inscription after descending to consume the sacrifices offered in the vessel.[74] The inscription, therefore, is not so much a statement of fact as an exhortation to Wen to serve Di: "May the greatly illustrious deceased father King Wen serve and please the Di on high!"

---

71. "Duofang," *Shangshu*, 17.5b, 6a. My translation has been aided by Karlgren, "The Book of Documents," pp. 64–65.

72. Also known as the Da Feng *gui*.

73. Guo Moruo reads this as 禴, a type of sacrifice that is being offered to Di (*Liang-Zhou jinwenci daxi tulu kaoshi*, p. 1b.) But since there is no *yu* 于 following the word, it seems difficult to read Di as the indirect object of a sacrifice verb. I thus read the word in its usual meaning.

74. For an extremely helpful analysis of meanings of bronze inscriptions, see Falkenhausen, "Issues in Western Zhou Studies." See also idem, *Suspended Music*.

This concern with coaxing or even controlling the ancestors appears frequently in bronze inscriptions. For example, in the Bo Dong *gui*, a vessel from the middle Western Zhou:

[I,] Bo Dong, for the first time will make
a treasure for the western palace. It is to be used to pacify (*sui* 妥: 綏) the spirits,
and to embrace and call out to the earlier, cultured men, who grasp
virtue and uphold generosity. It is to pray for ten thousand
years to have sons' sons and grandsons' grandsons eternally treasure it. (Sh 17.91:207)

The explicit statement that the vessel was made for use in pacifying the spirits through sacrifices, like the oracular material discussed in the preceding sections, implies a belief that the ancestors were at least potentially not supportive.

But if, in the Tianwang *gui*, it is Wen who serves and pleases Di, what happened to the Shang ancestors? How, in the aftermath of the conquest, were the Shang ancestors replaced by the Zhou in serving the Di? Hints can be found in the "Shifu" chapter of the *Yizhoushu*, a chapter that may indeed date to the early Western Zhou.[75] We are told that after conquering the Shang, King Wu declared: "In declaration to the earth altar, [Wu] said: 'It is I, the young one, who pacifies [my] cultured, deceased father. May it reach to [me], the young one.'"[76] The descendant, King Wu, claims to pacify (*sui*) his deceased father, King Wen, and hopes that this will result in benefits for himself. The term *sui* is the same one used in the Bo Dong *gui* to describe the pacification of the spirits. The declaration reveals that Wu is not at all certain of his deceased father's support.

King Wu's actions in the aftermath of the conquest are telling: "On *wuchen* [day 5], the king then performed an exorcism, made an inspection, and gave a commemorative sacrifice to King Wen. On this day, the king established the government."[77] All these actions, taken immediately after the conquest and immediately before the establishment of the Zhou state, appear to be acts of consolidation, aimed at driving away malevolent forces and settling the new order. The exorcism, as discussed above, serves to drive spirits away from the human realm—presumably, in this case, the spirits are the Shang ancestors. Sacrifices are then given to Wen—presumably to per-

---

75. See Shaughnessy, "'New' Evidence on the Zhou Conquest," pp. 60–66.
76. "Shifu," *Yizhoushu*, 4.12a–b.
77. Ibid., 4.10a.

suade him to accept the new order. These are the actions of a king who sees himself in a position similar to that implied by the oracular inscriptions discussed above: he is acting in ways that he is not convinced will be supported by the divine powers and hence performs ritual acts aimed at coercing their acceptance.

Another of the actions taken by Wu after the conquest, the beheading of the Shang masters of cauldrons,[78] is particularly intriguing. Bronze vessels were used to offer sacrifices to the ancestors and thus to pacify them and maintain their support. Cauldrons in particular were associated with such notions.[79] The beheading of the Shang cauldron makers can be understood as symbolizing the end of the Shang means of determining the will of the divine powers.

And the sacrifice of the last Shang king makes the transfer complete. The chapter records another announcement by Wu:

[Wu] announced in the Zhou temple, saying: "Earlier, I have heard, [my] cultured, deceased father cultivated himself on the standards of the men of Shang. With the dismembered body of Zhou [the last Shang king], I announce [the change in rulership] to Heaven and to [Hou] Ji."[80]

The announcement is directed both to Heaven (the high god) and to Hou Ji (the ancestor of the Zhou people). King Wu acknowledges that the Shang formerly held the rulership and that King Wen modeled himself on the Shang. By sacrificing the Shang king and beheading the Shang masters of cauldrons, Wu ends the sacrificial system to the Shang ancestors. The claim is that now the Zhou, not the Shang, will be the ones to serve Heaven.

In the aftermath of the conquest, it is King Wen who is called on to serve and please Di and thereby bring order to the realm. We thus find in the *Shijing*, Mao #235:

King Wen is above,
How glorious he is in Heaven.

---

78. Ibid., 4.11b.

79. Relevant here is the transfer of the Yin kings' cauldrons to Wu, also recorded in the *Yizhoushu* (4.10a). Later texts present such transfers as a standard occurrence during a legitimate change of dynasties. See, e.g., the *Zuozhuan*, Huan, second year, in which the Shang are reported to have transferred nine cauldrons to the Zhou. The *Shiji*, "Qinshihuang benji," records the failure of the first emperor to get the cauldrons from the Zhou, a failure understood to signify the illegitimacy of the Qin dynasty.

80. "Shifu," *Yizhoushu*, 4.12a.

Although Zhou is an old state,
Its mandate is new.
Are the rulers of Zhou not illustrious,
Was the mandate of Di not timely?
King Wen ascends and descends,
Residing to the right and left of Di.

Much is said in these few lines. The Zhou is an old state, but only with King Wen did Di grant it the mandate to rule. Thus, it is Wen who resides with Di, descending to the human realm to receive sacrifices and ascending to the heavens to serve Di and maintain his support for the Zhou. Wen thus serves the same function as the Shang ancestors had earlier.

These ritual exhortations to ancestors continue throughout the dynasty. But what about the descendants? The inscription on the Tianwang *gui* concludes:

King Wen looks down from above. The greatly
illustrious king [Wu] makes the inspection, the greatly majestic king [Wu] becomes the successor. (Sh 1.1:1)

Here we see another side of the equation: the living, in this case King Wu, attempts to become a proper successor to the ancestor. The deceased Wen is presented as watching his descendant from above, and Wu claims legitimacy because of his ability to inspect Wen and serve as his successor. The relationship between them, therefore, is bi-directional: the living work to make the deceased into proper ancestors, who will work to maintain Di's favor for the living. But, as the deceased are made into proper ancestors, the living promise to make themselves into proper descendants.

These themes pervade the Western Zhou bronze inscriptional material. A further example is an extremely late vessel, the Hu *gui*, which was commissioned by King Li.[81] The vessel was cast in the twelfth, and possibly last, year of Li's reign before his forced exile:

[I], Hu [King Li], make this great sacrificial treasured *gui* tureen, with which to make tranquil and compliant my
august cultured and valorous grandfather and deceased father; may [they] go to the former cultured men,

---

81. Published in Luo Xizhang, "Shaanxi Fufeng faxian Xi-Zhou Liwang Hu gui." Although I disagree in a few specific points, my translation of the inscription generally follows that given in Shaughnessy, *Sources of Western Zhou History*, pp. 171–72.

may [they] frequently be in the court of the Di on High, ascending and descending,
continuously encompassing the august
[Di] on High's great and generous mandate, thereby commanding and protecting
our family, my
position, and Hu's person.

The presentation is similar to that seen in the earlier vessels, except that the
ancestral line is now older. King Li has ordered the vessel for sacrifices to his
deceased father and grandfather, whom he thereby hopes to "make tranquil
and compliant." The father and grandfather, rendered compliant through
sacrifices, are exhorted to approach the "former cultured men"—a reference
to the founders of the dynasty, presumably Kings Wen and Wu. The latter
in turn are called on to ascend and descend between the human realm and
the court of Di, preserving Di's mandate for the Zhou and thus protecting
the living king's position.

The inscription closes with the King's exhortation that he be able to continue his sacrifices and thus gain long life and a continuing mandate from Di:

May [I], Hu, for ten thousand years greatly bring to realization
my many sacrifices, thereby seeking long life and entreating an eternal mandate to
govern
in position and act as the stem below.

The text is a prayer to the king's ancestors to remain with Di in order to
protect the king's position.

The repeated claim throughout these poems and bronze inscriptions is
that the deceased must be made into proper ancestors who will then convince Di to maintain support for the Zhou royal line. The living represent
themselves as proper descendants to these proper ancestors. The living, in
other words, will follow the ancestors, but only after the deceased have in
fact been made into proper ancestors.

The bronze inscriptions and the poems from at least the "Zhousong" section of the Shijing may thus have been written from a perspective not unlike
that seen in the Shang oracle inscriptions, a perspective, namely, of living
humans attempting to coerce the divine powers to grant aid or, at least, not
to send down disasters. Statements in these works that the descendants are
simply following the example of the ancestors, who in turn were simply following the example of Heaven, should perhaps not be taken purely at face
value. Instead of reflecting an assumption that descendants should simply
follow their ancestors, such statements more likely arose as an attempt by

the descendants to coerce the ancestors, sometimes through rituals of control, sometimes through acts of rhetorical submission. The claim that in taking an action the speaker is simply continuing what the ancestors initiated should perhaps be read more as voicing an argument rather than an assumption: it may be the case that at least sometimes it is not that the descendants think they have followed the ancestors but that the descendants have acted on their own and then claimed that in so doing they were simply following the ancestors. Their goal would be to win the ancestors' support. Even the ancestor, then, must be urged to become linked with Heaven. And the descendants do follow the ancestors, but only when the ancestors have been made into proper ancestors. There was no more of an assumption concerning harmony in the Western Zhou than there was in the Shang.

A statement, quoted above, in the "Shao gao" chapter of the *Shangshu*, concerns the founding of Luoyang: "The king should come and continue the [work] of the Di on high, and himself serve in the center of the land."[82] The statement, attributed to the Grand Protector, clearly presents the founding of the city as the king continuing the work of the Di. But the He *zun*,[83] a vessel inscribed in the fifth year of King Cheng's reign, characterizes this act in a different way:

It was the time when the king [Cheng] first moved and settled at Chengzhou. He once again received

King Wu's abundant blessings from Heaven. It was the fourth month, *bingxu* [day 23].

The king made a statement to the young men of the lineage in the great hall, saying: "Earlier

your father, the duke of the clan, was able to accompany King Wen. And then King Wen

received this [great mandate].[84] It was when King Wu had conquered the great city Shang that he then, in court, announced to Heaven, saying: 'I will settle this central territory, and from it rule the people.'" (Sh 48.1:171)

King Cheng is presenting himself as fulfilling the plans of his father, King Wu, who is sending blessings from Heaven above.

---

82. "Shao gao," *Shangshu*, 15.5a.

83. For a fuller discussion of the He *zun*, see my *The Ambivalence of Creation*, pp. 33–34.

84. Two graphs are illegible here. Tang Lan ("He zun mingwen jieshi," p. 63n7) reads the graphs *da ming* 大命. For a discussion of his reading, see my *The Ambivalence of Creation*, p. 229n36.

But note King Cheng's statement. He quotes his father, after the conquest, as having announced to Heaven that he will settle the central territory to rule the people. This is an announcement along the lines of those seen in oracle-bone inscriptions: a statement of one's intentions to the divine powers, in this case Heaven, in order to request approval. This would hardly seem necessary if Wu was simply following Heaven's plan.

In these lines, the feeling is not dissimilar to that discussed above in relation to the late Shang: a potentially antagonistic relationship seems to hold between the king and the divine powers, and the king has to coax and influence those powers into accepting his work. Contrary to Wheatley's attempt to read such claims of centering as implying a correlative mode of thought, the notion here seems, rather, to involve an attempt by the king to stake out a political claim: he is announcing to Heaven his intention of establishing a center and is hoping thereby to gain Heaven's support. The assumption is not of correlativity but of potential antagonism.

Indeed, I think we can go even further. Note again that it is King Cheng who is making this announcement and that the inscription began with a reference to King Cheng's receiving abundant blessings from his father (King Wu) in Heaven. King Cheng's concern here is to maintain the support of his father, who is in Heaven and, Cheng hopes, maintaining Heaven's support. The point, then, is to emphasize to the ancestor Wu that it was in fact Wu's idea to establish Luo as the new political center. King Cheng thereby hopes to maintain the support of Wu, who in turn will work to maintain Heaven's support.

The concerns here are thus quite comparable to those found in the Shang. Heaven (or Di) is the powerful agent, but Heaven is relatively unresponsive to the rituals of the living. The living thus strive to receive the support of the ancestors, who are in turn called on to influence Heaven. The living may present themselves as following Heaven and the ancestors, but such a presentation is part of a larger goal of influencing first the ancestors and, through them, Heaven itself, to support the wishes of the living.

Overall, Western Zhou hymns and inscriptions were based on building a proper ancestral pantheon that would then work on behalf of the living to maintain Di's (or Heaven's) support. The ancestors were called on to descend to the human realm, receive sacrifices as well as ritual exhortations, and then ascend to the realm of Di to serve him and maintain divine support for the Zhou line. The cultic practices are directly comparable to those of the Shang, with the obvious difference that the Zhou, by sacrificing the last Shang king and beheading his cauldron makers, have replaced the Shang ancestral pantheon with the Zhou ancestral pantheon in the realm of Di.

The Art of Sacrifice: The "Sheng min" Poem of the Shijing and Hesiod's Theogony

Further evidence for this reading of cultic practices in the Bronze Age can be gleaned from the poem "Sheng min" (Mao #245).[85] Here I read the poem as a reflection on the themes of sacrifice—its origins and its significance.[86] More explicitly, I argue that the poem includes a rather complex presentation of the relationships between ancestors and descendants. After providing a close reading of the poem, I then turn to comparative material from Greece and reconsider the larger comparative claims made by the scholars discussed in the first part of this chapter.

The poem opens by describing the birth of Hou Ji, the ancestor of the Zhou people:

> The one who first gave birth to our people,
> This was Jiang Yuan.
> How did she give birth to the people?
> She was able to perform the *yin* sacrifice, and she was able to
>   perform the *si* sacrifice,
> so as to no longer be childless.
> She stepped on the big toe of Di's footprint,
> she was elated about that which enriched her and that which
>   blessed her.
> And so she became pregnant, and so it was soon,
> And so she gave birth and so she reared [him].
> This was Hou Ji.

Jiang Yuan was unable to have a child. But she had one great power: she was able to perform the *yin* and *si* sacrifices "so as to no longer be childless." The

---

85. My translation had been greatly aided by that of Bernhard Karlgren, *The Book of Odes* (Stockholm: Museum of Far Eastern Antiquities, 1950), pp. 199–202. Indeed, in some of the later sections of the poem below, I largely quote from Karlgren's translation.

86. My understanding of this poem has been greatly enhanced by the interpretations of David Knechtges, Stephen Owen, Willard Peterson, and Pauline Yu in *Ways With Words: Writing about Reading Texts from Early China*, edited by Pauline Yu, Peter Bol, Stephen Owen, and Willard Peterson (Berkeley: University of California Press, 2000).

poem does not explain precisely why this solves Jiang Yuan's problem, but the ensuing line implies an answer: Jiang Yuan, through her abilities to utilize the sacrifices, was able to make Di descend. She then stepped in his footprint and absorbed some of his potency.

Not only did this allow Jiang Yuan to become pregnant, but it also meant that her child, Hou Ji, was born with divine powers:

> And then she completed her months,
> The first giving birth was like sprouting,
> [There occurred] no bursting, no rending,
> without injury, without harm.
> Thereby manifesting his numinous nature (*ling*).

Hou Ji's gift is apparent at birth: his numinous nature allows him to emerge without harming his mother, and his birth is like the sprouting of a plant. He is thus immediately associated with the generative process.

Nonetheless, Di was angry.

> The high Di was not serene
> and not pleased with the *yin* and *si* sacrifices.
> [But] tranquilly she gave birth to the child.

The sense here would appear to be that Di did not approve of Jiang Yuan's actions. Jiang Yuan used the sacrifices to make Di descend, and without Di's approval, she stepped in his footprint and captured some of his divine power. Hou Ji, in other words, was born of a transgression, in which Di's potency was appropriated through a deceitful use of the sacrifices.

Presumably because of Di's displeasure, Jiang Yuan was forced to give up Hou Ji:

> And then she placed him in a narrow lane
> The oxen and sheep nurtured him between their legs
> And then she placed him in a forest on the plain.
> He was found by those who cut the forest on the plain.
> And then she placed him on cold ice
> Birds covered and assisted him.
> The birds then left.
> Hou Ji wailed
> Really spreading, really strong
> His voice then became loud.

Jiang Yuan keeps trying to abandon her child, but Hou Ji is repeatedly saved by animals and humans. Despite Di's displeasure, Hou Ji is still favored by those below on earth.

Hou Ji continued to grow and was soon able to feed himself by planting:

> And then he was actually crawling,
> able to stride, able to stand firmly
> so as to seek food for this mouth.
> He planted with large beans.
> The bare beans were waving like streamers,
> The grain that was cultivated was sprouting,
> The hemp and the wheat were thick,
> The gourds were ample,
> And then Hou Ji's husbandry
> had the way of helping.
> He cleared away the dense grass,
> He sowed it in the yellow earth.
> Really even, really dense.
> really growing, really becoming tall,
> really extending, really flowering,
> really strong, really good,
> really ripe ears, really solid kernels,
> He had his house in Tai.

Hou Ji's gift of being able to aid the generative process manifests itself again. The harvest is enormous, and Hou Ji, with ample food, is able to settle down.

Hou Ji then handed down the grains to the people and thus began agriculture. And thus, too, began the sacrifices:

> And then he sent down the fine grains.
> There was black millet, there was double-kernelled black millet,
> There was millet with red sprouts, there was millet with white sprouts.
> Planting them extensively, the black millet, the double-kernelled
>   black millet,
> Reaping them and taking them by the acre.
> Planting them extensively, the millet with red sprouts, the millet
>   with white sprouts,
> carrying them on his shoulder, carrying them on his back,
> So as to return and initiate the sacrifices.

At this point, the frame of the poem shifts from a narrative of Hou Ji's actions to the perspective of those chanting the poems. The sacrifices initiated by Hou Ji have been handed down, and the chanters describe their continued efficacy:

> And so, our sacrifices, what are they like?
> Some pound (the grain), some bale it.
> Some sift it, some tread it,
> Washing it until soaked,
> Steaming it until steamed.
> And so we plan and so we think it over.
> We take southernwood, we offer fat.
> We take a ram so as to sacrifice to the spirits of the road.
> Roasting and broiling,
> So as to start the following year.

The sacrifices, if accepted by the spirits, allow for the start of the next agricultural cycle. Indeed, these sacrifices are enjoyed even by Di himself:

> We fill in the *dou* vessels,
> in the *dou*, in the *deng* vessels,
> (when) the fragrance first ascends
> The high Di tranquilly enjoys it
> Oh how pungent it is.
> Hou Ji initiated the sacrifice
> May we not have any faults
> So they [the sacrifices handed down by Hou Ji] reach to the present.

The living are continuing the sacrifices initiated by the ancestor Hou Ji, and when performed correctly, they please Di.

Thus, a proper harmony of humans, spirits, and the natural world is maintained by humans continuing the agricultural and sacrificial practices initiated by Hou Ji. Indeed, the poem links agriculture and the proper use of sacrifices: the harmony of man and god is achieved through the successful appropriation of nature through agriculture and the proper utilization of that agricultural produce to feed the gods in sacrifice.

This may help explain what the poem means when it says that Hou Ji initiated sacrifices. He obviously was not the first to give sacrifices (since his mother had already done so). The sense instead is that Hou Ji was the first to institute correct sacrifices, in which the proper duties of humans and the god were delineated: humans aid in the growth of the natural world and then feed Di and the other spirits through sacrifices. The spirits in turn support the next year's cycle (presumably through the control of the rains). Humans and spirits thus have their designated duties and their designated spheres.

Thus, the contrast drawn here between the sacrifices of Jiang Yuan and those of Hou Ji is more than simply that the mother's were deceitful and the son's were not. The nature of the sacrifices has clearly changed as well. When Jiang Yuan performed sacrifices, Di was brought down to tread on the land. With Hou Ji's sacrifices, however, Di remains in the heavens, enjoying the ascending fragrance. Humans are in charge of the agricultural work of the earth, and Di remains in his proper place in the heavens, enjoying the sacrifices given to him.

But all this was possible only because Hou Ji possessed the numinous power gained from Di. That power enabled him to aid the natural generative process and thus to begin agriculture and sacrifice. And the only reason he possessed that power is because Jiang Yuan had used sacrifices to steal it from Di. And, even then, the only reason Hou Ji survived long enough to initiate agriculture and the proper use of sacrifices was because figures on earth protected him from Di's wrath. In other words, the successful creation of a proper hierarchy between humans and gods was accomplished when a human stole Di's potency and other humans and animals protected the resultant hero from Di's wrath. Because of Hou Ji, the product of these actions, the earth became productive and humans thrived. And this in turn allowed Hou Ji to begin the sacrificial practices that pleased Di and allowed a continued flourishing of humanity.

The poem does not, therefore, assume an inherent harmony between humans and Di. On the contrary, harmony is achieved only after Di's potency is stolen and Di's plans are thwarted. Harmony was established not by Di but by the human beneficiary of a theft, a theft that gave humans the power to create a hierarchy in which they could thrive. The sacrifices initiated by Hou Ji are presented as continuing to mollify Di and maintain his support. And the significance of this becomes clear when we realize that the poem itself is aimed at Hou Ji, not at Di. The living ("we") are calling on Hou Ji to ensure that the sacrifices continue to maintain Di's support. If he is a good ancestor, Hou Ji will play the crucial role of mediation and work to ensure the support of Di for the living.

The poem is thus playing on the very themes that have concerned us throughout this chapter—only here the themes are worked out in narrative form. Jiang Yuan makes a proper descendant by appropriating divine power through sacrifice, and that descendant then initiates proper sacrifices, which in time will transform him into a proper ancestor. The sacrifices result in a proper genealogical order of ancestors and descendants, each with its own proper sphere of activity. Humans use agricultural produce to keep Di in Heaven, served by the mediating ancestor Hou Ji, and Di's resulting blessings allow for the agricultural produce to continue. A perfect system of genealogical order is created.

These points, along with the analysis of Shang and Zhou rituals above, should lead us to rethink some of the larger comparative claims that have been made concerning Chinese Bronze Age views about the relations between humans and divinities. I quoted above Keightley's remark that "the Chinese knew neither a Prometheus nor a Zeus."[87] Let us turn to Hesiod to evaluate the statement.

In the *Theogony*, Hesiod accounted for sacrificial practice through the well-known narrative of the transgressions of the Titan Prometheus. According to Hesiod, Prometheus killed an ox and split it into two portions. The first portion consisted of the animal's meat, which the Titan wrapped in the stomach of the ox in order to make it look unappetizing, and the second was the bones, which were hidden in the fat. Prometheus allowed Zeus to pick the portion he wanted, and his ruse tricked the god into choosing the worst of the two. As a punishment for this ruse, Zeus denied man the fire with which to cook. Prometheus then stole fire and gave it to man, an act that again brought down the wrath of Zeus and prompted him to send down woman. This theft of fire, insofar as it gave humanity the ability to cook, thus won human beings autonomy from the gods, but at the cost of a tragic separation from divinity.

Sacrifice, in such a narrative, recapitulates the crime of Prometheus, serving both as a repetition of the ruse against the gods and as a reminder of the degree to which humanity is still beholden to them: whereas the gods, not dependent on meat, can be satisfied with bones, man, who must eat in order to survive, has to take the edible portion—knowing that the satisfaction of hunger is only temporary. The division of the offerings in the sacrifice thus reveals, under Hesiod's reading, the separation of man and divinity, a separa-

---

87. Keightley, "Clean Hands and Shining Helmets," p. 42.

tion resulting from the fact that man can gain autonomy from the gods only by transgressing their power and thereby resigning himself to an ultimately doomed life of labor and hardship. The sacrifice is thus an offering to the gods, but one that underscores, rather than alleviates, the radical disparity between humanity and divinity.

As Jean-Pierre Vernant has argued:

> In devouring what can be eaten, men simultaneously restore their failing strength and acknowledge the baseness of their human condition—confirming their absolute submission to those very Olympian gods whom the Titan Prometheus, when he established the pattern in the first sacrifice, once thought to trick with impunity. The alimentary ritual which establishes communication between man and divinity itself underscores the gulf which sunders them. That communication is founded upon a religious ritual which, by memorializing Prometheus's error, reaffirms on every occasion of its performance the existence of that uncrossable gulf. And it is the purpose of the myth, as told by Hesiod, precisely to lay bare the origins of the separation and to make plain its dire consequences.[88]

Thus, following the transgression of Prometheus, "contact can only be made with the gods through sacrifice, which at the same time consecrates the impassable barrier between mortals and immortals."[89]

The point is of interest, for according to Vernant and Marcel Detienne, much of early Greek sacrificial practice corresponded closely to Hesiod's reading. An example can be seen in the Athenian Skirophoria, the annual slaughter of an ox for Zeus in the last month of the year. After the animal was slain, its bones and fat were burned as an offering, and the meat was consumed by humans in a great feast.[90] This division of the sacrificial portions is identical to that seen in the narratives of Hesiod, a fact that Vernant interprets as meaning that Hesiod constructed his narratives in relation to contemporary religious beliefs and practices, and thus that the narrative of Prometheus may reveal some of the implicit meanings and significance of early Greek sacrificial practice.[91] And if, as I have argued, the "Sheng min" is

---

88. Jean-Pierre Vernant, "Sacrificial and Alimentary Codes in Hesiod's Myth of Prometheus," p. 61.

89. Vernant, "The Myth of Prometheus in Hesiod," p. 185.

90. Burkert, *Greek Religion*, pp. 55–59; and idem, *Homo Necans*, pp. 136–43. See also Jean-Louis Durand, *Sacrifice et labour en Grece ancienne*.

91. Vernant, "Sacrificial and Alimentary Codes in Hesiod's Myth of Prometheus," p. 62.

equally telling of some of the tensions that surrounded sacrifices in China at roughly the same time, a comparison of the two may yield helpful results.

I argued above that sacrifice is better conceptualized in terms of transformations than of a gift, and the comparatively interesting questions then become how particular sacrifices present different aspects of these transformations. For example, one such issue is the state to be achieved through the sacrifice. Is it posed, to list some possibilities, as simply a removal of some perceived lack, as a means of correcting the currently skewed positions of humanity and divinity, as a reconnection with the divine, or even as a partaking of the divine? Another issue is how this final state is achieved in the sacrifice. Is the sacrifice understood as submission to the divine or as another transgression, a further usurpation of divine power for the sake of humanity?

In the cases at hand, both poems deal with similar problems: both the "Sheng min" and this portion of the *Theogony* revolve around the themes of the introduction of sacrifice and the proper roles for humans and gods. But the transformations in the narratives move in opposite directions. Hesiod's narrative begins with humans and gods linked genealogically; Prometheus's transgression introduces discontinuity—winning autonomy for humanity but at the cost of a life of toil. In contrast, the "Sheng min" begins in discontinuity, and the goal is to achieve continuity. Jiang Yuan must use sacrifice to obtain divine potency, but Hou Ji later institutes sacrifices in which gods and humans are transformed into proper ancestors and descendants. The *Theogony* narrates the dissolution of a genealogical continuity; the "Sheng min" narrates its creation.

It is somewhat misleading, therefore, to say that China knew neither a transgressive figure like Prometheus nor a capricious god like Zeus. At the beginning of the "Sheng min," Di is quite capricious, and Jiang Yuan transgressively appropriates divine powers. What is striking in the comparison of the two narratives, in other words, is not that one involves human transgression and capricious gods and the other does not; both have this. What is striking is, rather, the presentation of the transforming sacrifices.

I mention these points of comparison between "Sheng min" and Hesiod not in order to proclaim these poems as "founding myths" of Chinese and Greek culture, respectively. As I have argued elsewhere, the entire notion of foundational myths needs to be rethought,[92] and, as I have argued in the In-

---

92. For my critique of the way the term "mythology" is used in early China studies, see chap. 3 of *The Ambivalence of Creation*. In brief, my critique is that the term is used to refer to a

troduction to this book, comparisons that define the cultures in question from the viewpoint of one particular practice are always misleading. The comparison of these two narratives points to a different way of approaching these issues. When scholars read this distinction in terms of differing assumptions in Greece and China—of tragic discontinuity and genealogical continuity, respectively—they are mistaking effect for cause and reading the normative product of sacrifice as a starting assumption. The point is of relevance, for, if I am right that these are normative claims for sacrificial action rather than pervasive assumptions, then a different form of cultural analysis is called for: instead of trying to read other aspects of these cultures in terms of such assumptions, we should situate these normative sacrificial claims within the larger cultural debate of which they were a part. If these are the normative claims of the sacrificial experts supported by the courts, then how were they received? As we shall see in the next chapter, both of these sacrificial models became the objects of significant critique, and one cannot understand those critiques without understanding the practices that were being criticized.

Conclusion

As discussed earlier in this chapter, both K. C. Chang and Julia Ching posited a primordial experience of shamanism underlying Chinese tradition, and both tried to connect this further to an even more primordial sacred experience of humanity in general. Indeed, both argued that insofar as such a primordial, shamanistic experience underlies all civilizations, China is thus closer to that sacred linking of Heaven and Earth than is the West. Even if Ching and Chang's arguments about China were correct, their attempts to characterize shamanism, as well as a belief in continuity between the human and divine realms, as primordial forms of human spirituality would still be highly suspect. Why is continuity somehow more primordial, and the discontinuity they see in the West what Chang calls an "aberration" in humanity's history?

---

primordial, unchanging system of beliefs rather than to ongoing, ever-changing narratives that are constantly being reworked and revised. Analysis should therefore focus on those activities of reworking and revising the stories rather than trying to reconstruct a single ur-myth behind the variety.

As Jonathan Z. Smith has argued:

It strikes me that historians of religion have been weakest in interpreting those myths which do not reveal a cosmos in which man finds a place to dwell and on which he found [sic] his existence, but rather which suggest the problematic nature of existence and fundamental tension in the cosmos. I have in mind such traditions as dualistic creation myths, Earth-diver traditions, Tricksters, or the complex narratives of Corn or Rice Mothers who create by "loathsome" processes (e.g., rubbing the dirt off their bodies, by defecation, secretion). Clearly these mythologies, many of which are extremely archaic, point to a different spiritual horizon than that described by Eliade as the fundamental "archaic ontology."[93]

I would go further than Smith here: I would question the very usefulness of terms such as "archaic" and "spiritual horizon." Nonetheless, the basic point Smith raises is an important one: there is no empirical evidence to support the notion that harmony with the "sacred" is somehow more primordial in human experience than are radical tensions and conflicts. Even for those scholars like Chang who wish to claim that such an assumption existed in early China, there is no basis for arguing that this assumption is closely linked to some archaic, primitive experience lost by other civilizations.

But, in the case at hand, the argument is not only methodologically flawed but also empirically inaccurate: I have followed Keightley in arguing against the hypothesis that shamanism was a guiding force in the state societies of Bronze Age China. Keightley's provocative argument about "making ancestors" presents the ritual systems of the Shang court as attempts to influence from the bottom up. The higher, non-ancestral gods were the most powerful beings, but they were also relatively impervious to human rituals. The spirits of deceased humans were more malleable, but, even here, a hierarchy held: the more distant in time the deceased human, the more powerful but less subject to influence it became. The concern of the ritual system was thus to transform these deceased humans into proper ancestors.

However, although my readings of the oracle-bone inscriptions have largely followed Keightley's, I reach different conclusions. In particular, I question Keightley's attempts to read the Bronze Age material as evidence of a proto-bureaucratic mentality as defined by Weber. The Bronze Age sacrificial systems supported by the Shang and Zhou courts do not, I have argued, reveal an assumption of harmony between humans and gods, nor do

---

93. Jonathan Z. Smith, "The Wobbling Pivot," p. 100.

they reveal a belief in a *do et des* vision of sacrifice. On the contrary. What we can reconstruct of Bronze Age religion reveals a highly agonistic world in which humans were constantly trying to force impulsive divine powers into roles defined by the living and to convince them to act accordingly. Keightley's argument about making ancestors, in other words, should lead us to see sacrifices as attempts to transform capricious divinities into figures who could be controlled by the living: humans, while in part submitting themselves to the ancestral powers, were also actively transforming and ordering them. In short, the concern in the ancestral sacrifices was not simply to submit to the ancestors; rather, it was to create proper ancestors to which the living could then become proper descendants. And these ancestors were then called on to pacify the higher, non-ancestral powers—including, most important, Di. The cosmos would thus, to the limited extent possible, become ordered by the living.

The Shang sacrificial system was an attempt to domesticate these highly agonistic forces and place them within a hierarchy manipulable for the sake of human interests. Far from revealing an assumption of harmony, a belief in the benevolent intentions of the divine powers, and a desire to adjust to the world as given, sacrificial practice in the Shang was aimed at a radical transformation of the divine world, a transformation undertaken precisely so that humanity could appropriate and domesticate nature for its purposes. Such an attempt to transform both the divine and the natural worlds does indeed involve an enormous investment in sacrificial action, but that investment emerged not from an assumption of harmonious collaboration between man and god but from a sense of radical discontinuity and lack of harmony.

I have argued that similar ideas are visible in the Western Zhou materials as well, and I therefore question the attempt to read the Western Zhou materials as evidence of a correlative mode of thinking. I suspect, in fact, that what we see in the Shang and Zhou are a shared set of practices common in the North China plain. The Zhou conquest simply meant a replacement of the Shang pantheon with the Zhou pantheon, but the general ritual principles were much the same. The basic notion was to try to use sacrifices to build support through the ancestral pantheon and ultimately win the support even of Di.

As I noted in the Introduction, most discussions of ancient China have been based on the claim that a belief in continuity and harmony between the divine and human realms pervaded the Bronze Age period. The comparative frameworks have then diverged in their reading of the later history of early China: Did such an assumption of harmony continue in early China, or was there a shift toward rationality and humanism with the rise of philosophy? But if, as I have argued in this chapter, no such assumption existed, then we will have to develop a rather different reading of Warring States and Han developments.

2 *Gaining the powers of spirits*
The Emergence of Self-Divinization Claims in the Fourth Century BC

Concentrate the *qi* as if a spirit, and all the myriad things will reside within. Can you concentrate? Can you unify? Can you not engage in crackmaking and milfoil divination and yet understand auspiciousness and inauspiciousness? Can you stop? Can you reach an end? Can you not seek from others and obtain it in yourself? Think about it, think about it, and think about it again. If you think about it but do not penetrate, the ghosts and spirits will penetrate it. This is not due to the power of the ghosts and spirits; it is due to the ultimate point of essential *qi*.[1]

The fourth-century BC authors of this passage from the "Neiye" chapter of the *Guanzi* are arguing for a *qi*-based cosmology in which spirits can understand the future not because they control it but because, as concentrated *qi*, everything resides within them. In a similar fashion, those humans who can concentrate their *qi* to the same degree as a spirit will also gain an understanding of auspiciousness without resorting to the arts of divination. As we will see, this statement is only one of a number of such claims voiced in this period about the abilities of humans to gain access to divine powers without the mediation of ritual specialists. The emergence of these views

---

1. *Guanzi*, "Neiye," 16.5a.

leads to one subject of this chapter: the question of why such claims arose at this time.[2]

As noted in the Introduction, much of the secondary scholarship on texts such as these is divided between two readings: one school of interpretation sees these texts as records of a shift from religion (based on an animistic worldview) to philosophy (based on a human-centered worldview); the other views them as an organic development of a set of deep assumptions concerning the continuity of humans and divinities. Both readings are based on the claim that philosophy in early China emerged from an earlier shamanism, but they disagree on the degree to which philosophy broke from this earlier tradition. As we saw in the preceding chapter, the shamanism hypothesis for the Chinese Bronze Age is questionable. In this chapter, I argue that the shamanism hypothesis, and hence our understanding of the development of Chinese thought, grows out of a misleading comparison of Greece and China and that the concerns evident in this quotation from the *Guanzi* were not outgrowths of an earlier shamanism. I offer an alternative explanation and argue for a different approach for comparing these developments with those found in ancient Greece.

Spirits Within Humans: The Issue of Shamanism in Early China and Early Greece

K. C. Chang was a strong advocate of the view that Chinese thought of the Warring States period evolved from earlier shamanistic practices:

What may be seen as the most striking feature of ancient Chinese civilization is that ideologically speaking it was created within a framework of cosmogonic holism. In the words of Frederick Mote, "the genuine Chinese cosmogony is that of organismic process, meaning that all of the parts of the entire cosmos belong to one organic whole and that they all interact as participants in one spontaneously self-generating life process." This organismic process, Tu Wei-ming amplifies, "exhibits three basic motifs: continuity, wholeness, and dynamism. All modalities of being, from a rock to heaven, are integral parts of a continuum. . . . Since nothing is outside of this continuum, the chain of being is never broken. A linkage will always be found between any given pair of things in the universe." This ancient Chinese world view, sometimes referred to as

---

2. Portions of this chapter are taken from my "Humans and Gods: The Theme of Self-Divinization in Early China and Early Greece."

"correlative cosmology," is surely not unique; in essence it represents the substratum
of the human view of the world found widely among primitive societies (see, e.g.,
Lévi-Strauss). What is uniquely significant about its presence in ancient China is
the fact that a veritable civilization was built on top of and within its confines.[3]

Julia Ching argues a very similar position,[4] and A. C. Graham develops a
comparable argument. Graham reads the "Neiye" as a meditation text based
on earlier shamanistic practice: "It is interesting also in providing clear evidence that the meditation practiced privately and recommended to rulers as
an arcanum of government descends directly from the trance of the profes-
sional shaman." But whereas shamanism dealt with actual spirits, the
"Neiye" deals with naturalistic, numinous forces: "By this period the gods
and ghosts, like Heaven itself, are in the direction of becoming depersonal-
ised though still vaguely numinous forces of nature. . . . Man himself can as-
pire, not indeed to omniscience (since Chinese thinking does not deal in ab-
solutes), but to that supremely lucid awareness which excites a shudder of
numinous awe." The meditation techniques of the "Neiye" thus involve a
shifting of emphasis from linking with the spirits to perfecting the self: "The
shamanic origin of the exercise is plain. The point of it however is not to become a medium for the gods or for deceased ancestors. This is a programme
for self-perfection, as usual addressed primarily to the rulers." As such, the
text "may well be the earliest Chinese interpretation of the experience of
mystical oneness."[5]

Although Graham does not go as far as Chang and Ching in directly
connecting shamanism to later notions of correlative cosmology, he does,
like Chang and Ching, see the notion of humans being fully linked to the
oneness of the cosmos as a philosophical re-reading of an earlier shamanistic
experience. Indeed, the main differences in the positions of these scholars
concern the relations between this earlier shamanism and later philosophy.
For Chang and Ching, shamanism marked the primordial experience out of
which later Chinese philosophy grew, whereas for Graham the philosophy
involved a significant reworking of the earlier shamanistic practice. Chang
and Ching are arguing for a fundamental assumption of monism in early

---

3. K. C. Chang, "Ancient China and Its Anthropological Significance," pp. 161–62.
4. Ching, *Mysticism and Kingship in China*, pp. 67–131.
5. Graham, *Disputers of the Tao*, pp. 101, 104.

China that can be traced to a shamanistic past, and Graham is utilizing a "religion to philosophy" framework in which part of the distinctiveness of Chinese philosophy emerged when thinkers turned from shamanism to self-cultivation.[6] In both approaches, however, shamanism lies behind Chinese philosophy.

These arguments by Chang and Graham are closely paralleled by a large body of scholarship on ancient Greece that argues that Greek philosophy emerged against a shamanistic background. The most influential thesis was that advanced by E. R. Dodds. Much as Graham claims for China, Dodds argues that a fundamental shift in notions of the self occurred in Greece in the fifth century BC:

The "soul" was no reluctant prisoner of the body [in pre–fifth century BC Greece]; it was the life or spirit of the body, and perfectly at home there. It was here that the new religious pattern made its fateful contribution: by crediting man with an occult self of divine origin, and thus setting soul and body at odds, it introduced into European culture a new interpretation of human existence, the interpretation we call puritanical.[7]

Dodds argues that this occult notion of the soul is traceable to Central Asian shamanistic practices:

Now a belief of this kind is an essential element of the shamanistic culture which still exists in Siberia. . . . A shaman may be described as a psychically unstable person who has received a call to the religious life. . . . His own soul is thought to leave its body and travel to distant parts, most often to the spirit world. . . . From these experiences, narrated by him in extempore song, he derives the skill in divination, religious poetry, and magical medicine which makes him socially important. He becomes the repository of a supernormal wisdom. (p. 140)

Dodds argues that this shamanistic culture entered Greece in the seventh century from Scythia and Thrace (pp. 140, 142)[8] and was picked up by fig-

---

6. Several other scholars have developed this same "religion to philosophy" argument in regard to the "Neiye," as well as the related "Xinshu" chapters. (I discuss the "Xinshu" texts in Chapter 4.) See, e.g., Shibata, "Kanshi shihen ni okeru shin to dō"; and Qiu Xigui, "Jixia Daojia jingqi shuo de yanjiu." Both Shibata and Qiu paint the same general narrative that Graham does—from a shamanistic practice based on external spirits entering the human body to a philosophical regimen based on the cultivation of an internal spirit.

7. Dodds, *The Greeks and the Irrational*, p. 139; hereinafter cited in the text.

8. Dodds is building here on Karl Meuli's work; see his "Scythia."

ures such as Pythagoras and Empedocles: "These men diffused the belief in a detachable soul or self, which by suitable techniques can be withdrawn from the body even during life, a self which is older than the body and will outlast it" (pp. 146–47). In short, the diffusion of shamanistic culture to Greece led to the emergence of a true dualism of body and soul—a dualism that had never existed before in early Greece.

> We have seen—or I hope we have seen—how contact with shamanistic beliefs and practices might suggest to a thoughtful people like the Greeks the rudiments of such a psychology: how the notion of psychic excursion in sleep or trance might sharpen the soul-body antithesis; how the shamanistic "retreat" might provide the model for a deliberate askēsis, a conscious training of the psychic powers through abstinence and spiritual exercises; how tales of vanishing and reappearing shamans might encourage the belief in an indestructible magical or daemonic self. (pp. 149–50)

Dodds goes on to detail how this notion of an occult self of divine origin was later appropriated by Plato (pp. 207–35).

These ideas have since been hotly debated. Jan Bremmer, for one, has strongly criticized Dodds's shamanism hypothesis. After a lengthy survey of the evidence, both in Greece and Scythia, Bremmer concludes: "No convincing evidence exists for shamanistic influence on Archaic Greece. . . . It has not yet even been shown that the Scythians who were supposed by Dodds to have influenced the Greeks knew a shamanistic journey of the soul!"[9] Peter Kingsley, however, has recently come out in defense of the hypothesis.[10] Carlo Ginzburg has referred favorably to it as a piece of what he sees as a widespread diffusion of shamanism across Eurasia in the early period.[11]

I will follow Bremmer in rejecting Dodds's hypothesis. Before doing so, however, I would like to stress the implications of Dodds's theory for the shamanism hypothesis made for China. Arguments that might at first glance appear similar to Dodds's diffusion hypothesis have been made for China. Victor Mair has argued, based on linguistic and archaeological evidence, that the *wu*, the Chinese term usually translated as "shaman" in reference to early

---

9. Bremmer, *The Early Greek Concept of the Soul*, pp. 34–53; quotation at p. 47.

10. Kingsley, *Ancient Philosophy, Mystery, and Magic*; see also idem, "Greeks, Shamans, and Magi."

11. Ginzburg, *Ecstasies*, pp. 218n4, 276n78.

China, might in fact have been Iranian *magi* who entered China during the Bronze Age.[12] And, of course, the Scythians, whom Dodds sees as having become so influential in Greece, were Iranians. This line of reasoning implies that both China and Greece received a similar diffusion of ideas and techniques from the same Iranian source. Moreover, H. S. Nyberg has famously argued that Zoroastrianism was influenced by Siberian shamanism.[13] Thus, were one to follow all these links, one could trace a shamanism arising in Siberia, influencing Iranian culture, and in turn influencing both Greece and China.

However, several problems arise for anyone who wished to trace such a historical development. First, Nyberg's arguments about links between Siberian shamanism and Zoroastrianism have been widely rejected by specialists.[14] Even Eliade himself, who argues explicitly that shamanism was diffused from Siberia to many cultures throughout the world, has questioned them. Eliade instead reads Zoroastrianism as revealing elements of a belief in a sacred link between heaven and earth—ideas, as discussed in the previous chapter, that Eliade reads as primordial elements of human experience. He thus opposes the attempt to see such elements as a result of a diffusion of shamanism from Siberia:

The ecstatic and mystical elements in the religion of Zarathustra that bear resemblances to the ideology and techniques of shamanism form part of a complex and hence do not imply any "shamanic" structure in Zarathustra's religious experience. The sacred space, the importance of song, mystical or symbolical communication between heaven and earth, the initiatory or funerary bridge—these various elements, although they form an integral part of Asian shamanism, precede and go beyond it.[15]

As I noted in the previous chapter, I reject Eliade's arguments concerning the primordiality of notions of sacred space in human experience. But it is relevant to the current discussion that even Eliade—the figure one would expect to be most sympathetic to Nyberg—has rejected his claims.

---

12. Mair, "Old Sinitic *Myag, Old Persian *Magus*, and English 'Magician.'"

13. Nyberg, *Die Religionen des Alten Iran*.

14. For an overview of the arguments, see Widengren, "Henrik Samuel Nyberg and Iranian Studies in the Light of Personal Reminiscences."

15. Eliade, *Shamanism*, p. 399.

Moreover, we have already seen that many classicists reject the claim of diffusion from Scythia to Greece. And, on other end of Eurasia, Mair has argued that the *wu*, who he claims were *magi* from Iran, were *not* shamans:

It has been customary for students of Chinese civilization to translate *myag* [i.e., *wu*] as "shaman," but this is wrong on several counts. In the first place, the shaman was the leading representative of a specific type of religious system practiced by Siberian and Ural-Altaic peoples. Perhaps the most characteristic feature of this tradition was the shaman's ecstatic trance-flight to heaven during initiation and other rituals. The shamans also served the community as a whole by retrieving the errant souls of sick people and escorting the spirits of the dead to the other world. This is in contrast to the *myag* who were closely associated with the courts of various rulers and who were primarily responsible for divination, astrology, prayer, and healing with medicines.[16]

Thus, the figure in Chinese studies who has most strongly argued for Iranian influence on China rejects the shamanism hypothesis. The apparent parallel with Dodds's view does not arise at all: although Mair argues for a significant diffusion of Iranian ideas and practices into China, just as Dodds argues for a significant diffusion from the same source into Greece, Mair does not see this diffusion as involving anything that might be called shamanism. Chang and Ching, of course, would disagree with Mair's opposition to the shamanism hypothesis. But since they argue that shamanism was an inheritance from China's primitive past, they, too, would strongly deny any claim that shamanism was diffused into China from Siberia via Iran.

The diffusion hypothesis thus faces severe problems on all fronts. But what interests me more at this point is the opposite ways that shamanism is employed as an explanatory principle by Dodds, on the one hand, and Chang and Ching, on the other. For Chang and Ching (and, to a lesser degree, Graham), shamanism is the causative factor behind the dominance of a monistic worldview in China. For Dodds, shamanism was behind the emergence of dualism in Greece. Once again, we see the same basic contrast of China and Greece, with China defined by monism and Greece by dualism.

When the same phenomenon (in this case, shamanism) is credited with such opposite ramifications in two traditions, the adequacy of the hypothe-

---

16. Mair, "Old Sinitic *Myag*," p. 35.

ses should at least be questioned. However, variation in itself does not refute the hypotheses; it is, after all, possible that the same phenomenon can have decidedly contrary ramifications in two cultures, particularly if, as so many scholars have tried to argue, the two cultures are based on different guiding assumptions. So, a full reconsideration of these issues requires that we look at the evidence in detail.

I first turn to a discussion of Empedocles—the figure who plays such an important role in Dodds's argument. I first critique Dodds's use of diffusion as an explanatory principle to understand Empedocles and will offer an alternative approach. I then analyze the relevant material from early China. I will argue that the shamanism hypothesis, as well as the larger contrastive framework for studying China and Greece, should be rethought. I will conclude by suggesting a different approach to this material, as well as to the larger issue of comparing China and Greece.

Humans and Gods in Early Greece

In the *Nicomachean Ethics*, Aristotle discusses what it means for one to practice the theoretical life:

Such a life would be superior to the human level. For someone will live it not insofar as he is a human being, but insofar as he has some divine element in him. . . . Hence if understanding is something divine in comparison with a human being, so also will the life that expresses understanding be divine in comparison with human life. We ought not follow the proverb-writers, and "think human, since you are human."[17]

A philosopher is one who has risen above the human and become, at least in part, divine.

This claim came out of traditions of self-divinization beginning at least a full century earlier and, as is clear by the polemic at the end of Aristotle's statement, was made in opposition to numerous other views at the time concerning the nature of divinities and humans and the proper demarcation between the two. As is well known, the importance of maintaining a strict separation between humans and gods is a recurrent theme in early Greek

---

17. Aristotle, *Nicomachean Ethics*, X.7,1177b26–34, in *Aristotle: Selections*, pp. 441–42.

writings, as is the injunction to avoid the hubris of trying to get too close to divinity.[18] In the *Iliad*, Apollo warns Diomedes:

> Take care, give back, son of Tydeus, and strive no longer
> to make yourself like the gods in mind, since never the same is
> the breed of gods, who are immortal, and men who walk groundling.[19]

Or, as Pindar wrote:

> It is a dispensation of the gods that gives men their might.
> And two things only tend life's sweetest moment:
> when in the flower of wealth, a man enjoys both triumph and good fame.
> Seek not to become Zeus.
> All is yours if the allotment of these two gifts has fallen to you.
> Mortal thoughts befit a mortal man.[20]

The theme also plays an important role in the Hesiodic cosmology and view of sacrifice discussed in the previous chapter.

Much of early Greek philosophy, however, involved attempts to break this demarcation, to criticize the ritual specialists of the day, and to emphasize the abilities of humans to gain direct access to divine powers. One of the earliest figures to make this argument was Empedocles,[21] as in, for example, this fragment on the golden age of man:

They did not have Ares as god or Kydoimos, nor king Zeus nor Kronos nor Poseidon but queen Kypris. Her they propitiated with holy images and painted animal figures, with perfumes of subtle fragrance and offerings of distilled myrrh and sweet-smelling frankincense, and pouring on the earth libations of golden honey. Their altar was not drenched by the slaughter of bulls, but this was the greatest defilement among men—to bereave of life and eat noble limbs.[22]

---

18. See the excellent discussion by Rosen, *Hermeneutics as Politics* (Oxford: Oxford University Press, 1987), pp. 58–59. I am indebted to Rosen for the quotations from Aristotle, Homer, and Pindar.

19. Homer, *The Iliad*, V.440–42, in *The Iliad of Homer*, p. 140.

20. Pindar, *Isthmians* 5, v.11–16, in *Pindar's Victory Songs*, p. 309.

21. My understanding of Empedocles has been greatly enhanced by Kahn, "Religion and Natural Philosophy in Empedocles' Doctrine of the Soul"; and Panagiotou, "Empedocles on His Own Divinity."

22. Diels fragment 128; in *Empedocles: The Extant Fragments*, #118, p. 282; hereinafter cited in the text in the form D128; #118, p. 282.

Empedocles is explicitly attacking the religious practices of his day—practices based on sacrificial offerings to a pantheon of anthropomorphic deities. Prior to this world, Empedocles argues, was a period ruled by Kypris, or Love.

This opposition to sacrificial practice is a recurring theme in Empedocles: "Will you not cease from the din of slaughter? Do you not see that you are devouring one another because of your careless way of thinking?" (D136; #122, p. 285). Below I consider why Empedocles attributed sacrifice to a "careless way of thinking." Here, I delineate why an opposition to the world of anthropomorphic deities and to sacrificial practice is so important to Empedocles. To do so, it is necessary to situate Empedocles within a series of contemporary claims being made in opposition to the sacrifices carried out in the name of the polis. As discussed in the previous chapter, Greek polis sacrifices involved claims of ritual separation between man and god. It was this ritual separation that figures like Pindar were supporting and that several movements in the sixth and fifth centuries BC were trying to break down. One example among many of these groups is the Orphics. As a series of startling paleographic finds has demonstrated, the Orphics were a presence in the fifth century BC.[23]

In explicating the Orphic critique of sacrifice, Vernant and Detienne turn to a narrative concerning humans, the Titans, and Dionysus.[24] The narrative recounts how the Titans dismembered and devoured Dionysus. But Dionysus was then reconstituted, and Zeus punished the Titans by killing them with a thunderbolt. Humans were then born from the Titans' ashes. As a consequence of this history, humans possess within themselves both the guilt of the Titans' crime and a divine spark from the devoured Dionysus. To erase this crime and cultivate the divinity within, man is called on to follow Orphic practices and renounce the sacrificial meat of the polis. Orphic

---

23. See Burkert, "Orphism and Bacchic Mysteries"; and Fritz Graf, "Dionysian and Orphic Eschatology."

24. Vernant and Detienne fairly uncritically accept the antiquity of this narrative. Although I accept their dating, there is an enormous body of secondary literature on the topic. Prior to the recent paleographic discoveries, the scholarly world was split on this question. See, e.g., Guthrie, Orpheus and Greek Religion; and Linforth, The Arts of Orpheus. For convenient summaries of the paleographic evidence for the antiquity of the narrative, see Kahn, "Was Euthyphro the Author of the Derveni Papyrus?" pp. 57–60; and Fritz Graf, "Dionysian and Orphic Eschatology," pp. 239–45.

practices, including vegetarianism, should thus be understood as an attempt to reject the sacrificial practices of the polis and its tragic separation of humans and gods and to instead strive to join with the gods once again. As Vernant argues:

> By consenting to sacrifice a living animal to the gods in the Promethean manner, as official worship requires, men only repeat the Titans' crime indefinitely. By refusing this sacrifice, by forbidding the bloodshed of any animal, by turning away from fleshy food to dedicate themselves to a totally "pure" ascetic life—a life also completely alien to the social and religious norms of the city—men would shed all the Titanic elements of their nature. In Dionysus they would be able to restore that part of themselves that is divine. By returning to the god in this way each would accomplish, on the human level and within the framework of human existence, this same movement of reunification that Dionysus himself knew as a god during the torment in which he was first dismembered and then reconstituted.[25]

The rejection of sacrifice by the Orphics was thus based on a larger rejection of the ritual separation of humans and gods maintained in the practices of the polis.[26] Indeed, one of the paleographic discoveries, a series of gold leaves from Thurii, includes the statement "Happy and blessed one, you will be god instead of mortal."[27] The Orphics were claiming the ability to transcend the discontinuity of gods and humans found in the sacrificial system and become divine themselves.

This gives us some context for understanding the quotation from Pindar given above. Pindar's call to humans to stop seeking to become gods was hardly a rhetorical flourish. The sacrificial practices of the day strongly asserted the radical separation of man from god, and movements that attempted to reject this separation and proclaim the potential of humans to divinize themselves had sprung up. Pindar was thus reacting to growing trends of his day.

---

25. Vernant, "At Man's Table," p. 51; see also Detienne, "Culinary Practices and the Spirit of Sacrifice," pp. 7–8.

26. A different interpretation has been given by M. L. West (*The Orphic Poems*, pp. 144–50), who reads the Orphic narrative of Dionysus as a shamanistic initiatory ritual. Like Meuli and Dodds, West reads shamanism as having entered Greece from Central Asia during the classical period, and he sees Orphism as a part of this diffusion. For the reasons provided below, I find the hypothesis of a diffusion of shamanism unconvincing.

27. Graf, "Dionysian and Orphic Eschatology," pp. 246, 254.

Empedocles, like the Orphics, strongly opposed this ritual separation humans and gods. In direct contrast to the tragic cosmology encoded in the sacrificial practice of the polis, Empedocles proposed a system in which humans and the gods are inherently linked. Empedocles began by redefining the deities as the roots underlying all that exists: "Hear first the four roots of all things: bright Zeus and life-bringing Hera and Aidoneus and Nestis, whose tears are the source of mortal streams" (D6; #7, p. 164). The gods are not anthropomorphic deities separate from the world yet in direct control of it; on the contrary, they are the elemental bases of the world. Empedocles elsewhere defines these roots as fire, water, earth, and air (D17, #8, p. 166) and explains the cosmos in terms of their interaction:

All these are equal and of like age, but each has a different prerogative, and its particular character, and they prevail in turn as the time comes round. . . . These are the only real things, but as they run through each other they become different objects at different times, yet they are throughout forever the same. (D17; #8, p. 167)

The cosmic process is then defined in terms of the interaction of these roots:

Under strife they have different forms and are all separate, but they come together in love and are desired by one another. From them comes all that was and is and will be hereafter—trees have sprung from them, and men and women, and animals and birds and water-nourished fish, and long-lived gods too, highest in honor. For these are the only real things, and as they run through each other they assume different shapes, for the mixing interchanges them. (D21; #14, p. 177)

In such a cosmology, everything—from gods to humans to objects—is composed of the same roots. Not only are humans and gods not separated, they are in fact inherently connected. Indeed, differentiated things exist at all only because of the strife that breaks apart the proper harmony of love.

Hence Empedocles' contempt for sacrifice: sacrifice incorrectly assumes a division between animals, humans, and gods—wherein animals are sacrificed by humans for the sake of the gods—when in fact all three of these are linked. In contrast to a theistic understanding of the universe, Empedocles calls for a "divine understanding": "Happy the man who has gained the wealth of divine understanding, wretched he who cherishes an unenlightened opinion about the gods" (D132; #95, p. 252).

Here we arrive at the crucial points. Having denied the Hesiodic claim of a division between humans and gods, Empedocles makes an argument as to the potential of thought or divine understanding. A hint of what Empedocles means by this can be found in another set of fragments: "For he is not equipped with a human head on a body, [two branches do not spring from his back,] he has no feet, no swift knees, no shaggy genitals, but he is mind alone, holy and inexpressible, darting through the whole cosmos with swift thoughts" (D133; #97, p. 253). This description of mind is quite close in language to another fragment that describes the sphere of Love: "There the swift limbs of the sun are not distinguished . . . in this way it is held fast in the close covering of harmony, a rounded sphere, rejoicing in encircling stillness" (D27, #21, p. 187). And to another that appears to describe either Love itself or the state achieved by a wise man: "For two branches do not spring from his back, he has no feet, no swift knees, no organs of reproduction, but he is equal to himself in every direction, without any beginning or end, a rounded sphere, rejoicing in encircling stillness" (D29/28; #22, p. 188). The implication of these fragments would appear to be that Love as well as thought is the state of perfect harmony for the four roots. Divinity, therefore, is located in harmony, not in anthropomorphic deities. Accordingly, divinity is fully achievable by humans through understanding, which is itself the divine harmony of Love.

Such ideas are expanded in Empedocles' discussion of daimons. As he argues in the *Katharmoi*, a daimon is one in whom the four roots are properly combined, and one, therefore, "to whom life long-lasting is apportioned" (D115: #107, p. 270). But, through error, the daimons, like everything else, fall into strife:

He wanders from the blessed ones for three times countless years, being born throughout the time as all kinds of mortal forms, exchanging one hard way of life for another. For the force of fire pursues him into sea, and sea spits him out onto earth's surface, earth casts him into the rays of blazing sun, and sun into the eddies of air; one takes him from another, and all abhor him. (D115; #107, p. 270)

Empedocles has discovered himself to be one such fallen daimon: "I too am now one of these, an exile from the gods and a wanderer, having put my trust in raving strife" (D115; #107, p. 270). For this reason, he is now a mortal man, just as before he has been various other mortal creatures: "For before now I have been at some time boy and girl, bush, bird, and a mute fish in the sea" (D111; #101, p. 261). Empedocles himself, then, is striving to reachieve the divine understanding of the daimon, just as all humans should do.

Humans, therefore, are simply a transitory form, but the thought of humans can be divine. And this understanding grants the practitioner the ability to control the strife of the roots:

You will learn remedies for ills and help against old age, since for you alone shall I accomplish all these things. You will check the force of tireless winds, which sweep over land and destroy fields with their blasts; and again, if you wish, you will restore compensating breezes. After black rain you will bring dry weather in season for men, and too after summer dryness you will bring tree-nourishing showers (which live in air), and you will lead from Hades the life-force of a dead man. (D115; #107, p. 270)

Overall, then, in direct opposition to the claims of a separation between humans and gods, Empedocles proposed a cosmology in which a basic substrate unites all things. Moreover, he defined thought as divine and as thus potentially capable of controlling natural processes themselves. As such, he denied the theistic conceptions on which the dominant sacrificial activities of his day were based. For Empedocles, sacrifice was wrong because it involved a destruction of what is inherently linked, and it was unnecessary anyway because humans, properly cultivated, can attain powers over natural phenomena on their own. Empedocles was thus substituting for the religious practices of the day a new regimen whose followers would no longer supplicate the gods but would, ultimately, become divine. This regimen, in short, was being proposed in full opposition to the civic culture of the day.

These attempts to propose methods of self-divinization became increasingly important during the fifth and fourth centuries BC. Plato, for one, appropriated and reworked such ideas in his formulation of the academy, an institution in which disciples would be trained in a rigorous process of self-cultivation. As he argues in the *Timaeus*, explicitly appealing to a vocabulary of the daimon:

As concerning the most sovereign form of soul in us we must conceive that heaven has given it to each man as a guiding daimon—that part which we say dwells in the summit of our body and lifts us from earth toward our celestial affinity, like a plant whose roots are not in earth, but in the heavens.[28]

Plato's ultimate call, of course, was for those who underwent such self-cultivation to lead the state.[29]

---

28. *Timaeus* 90a; in *Plato's Timaeus*, p. 114.
29. The argument is laid out most clearly in the *Republic*.

It is beyond the bounds of this chapter to trace the ways that such ideas were developed and reformulated in the later Greek tradition. Suffice it to say here that these claims of self-divinization became a crucial aspect of early Greek philosophy, which in part explains the uneasy relation that philosophers had with the polis culture of their day.

This historical explanation for the emergence of self-divinization movements in Greece is, I think, more convincing than the shamanism hypothesis offered by Dodds. As Bremmer has noted, there are significant problems with the hypothesis itself: there is no evidence of contact in Greece with shamanistic currents among the Scythians, and, indeed, there is no evidence that shamanistic ideas of this sort existed among the Scythians at all. Moreover, Dodds's attempt to interpret the philosophers in question according to a shamanistic vision leads to forced readings. For example, Empedocles does not discuss shamanic spirit journeys,[30] and, although Empedocles does posit a dualism of body and spirit, his ultimate position on the cosmos is monistic. Far more significant for my argument, however, is that Dodds is mistaken in trying to use diffusion as an explanatory principle. Even if evidence for diffusion existed, the basic questions that need to be asked are: What claims were figures like the Orphics, Empedocles, Plato, and Aristotle making, Why were they making them, and What were the implications of such claims? These questions can be answered only through a historical analysis of early Greek cultures, not through a purported diffusion from Scythia. I have therefore situated these figures in their historical context, have seen their claims of self-divinization in relation to an ongoing debate, and have shown how and why they were responding to the ritual specialists, as well as the entire polis organization, of the day.

Comparing China and Greece

In turning to China, one might at first think that we confront a culture that witnessed no comparable debate concerning gods and humans. If K. C. Chang is correct, one would not expect a debate about the relationship between humans and spirits in early China. On the contrary, one would expect that spirits, like humans, would be conceptualized as part of a larger

---

30. For spirit journeys, see Chapter 5 of this book.

monistic system. In other words, the type of cosmological system that Empedocles was presenting in opposition to the dominant views of the time in early Greece would be, if Chang is right, a starting assumption in early China.

Indeed, one could go a step further and argue that some of what we have seen in Empedocles might support Chang's views concerning shamanism. With a few revisions, it could even be portrayed as supporting Dodds's hypothesis as well. If Empedocles is a monistic, rather than a dualistic, thinker, then monistic notions of the cosmos might be linked with shamanism, and monism may have come to Greece only when shamanism entered through diffusion: because of its continuing shamanistic foundations, Chinese civilization adhered to a monistic cosmology as an assumption, whereas Greece developed this idea only when it became influenced from outside by shamanism. Thus, both Chang's thesis that shamanism should be associated with a monistic cosmos and Dodds's thesis that Empedocles was influenced by shamanistic currents from Central Asia would be confirmed.

As the analyses in this chapter and the preceding one have shown, both hypotheses are unconvincing. In this chapter I will question any linkage between monistic notions and shamanism and will argue that, in both China and Greece, monistic notions emerged at the same time as claims of self-divination—of the ability of humans to become like spirits—and that this occurred in opposition to the ritual specialists of the day. I will argue, in other words, that notions of monism and of the continuity of the human and divine realms were not foundational in early China but were, rather, as in Greece, consciously formulated ideas designed to critique beliefs and practices dominant at the time. The fact that some of these cosmological notions became dominant at the imperial court during the Han should not mislead us into thinking they were common assumptions in the pre-imperial periods. Instead, these cosmological notions grew out of a debate not unlike that which developed in early Greece. This is not to say, of course, that the positions taken within the two cultures were identical or that the course of the debates was similar. My argument is, rather, that the debates are comparable in terms of the motivating concerns and tensions. The interesting issue from a comparative perspective lies in discovering how and why the debates worked out as they did in the two cultures.

Humans and Gods in Early China

These new cosmological notions developed in reaction to the religious and political contexts of early China.[31] The first point to emphasize is the degree to which, just as in early Greece, a highly theistic vision of the world continued to pervade elite religious activities throughout the period discussed in this book. Although Mote admits that "it is true that in the vulgarized versions of this rather philosophical conception [of naturalism], spirits sometimes began to resemble 'gods,'"[32] I would argue that such notions were not vulgarizations of a more pervasive naturalistic orientation. On the contrary, many of the religious orientations seen in the Bronze Age continued through the Warring States period.

Crucial to this cosmology was the notion that natural phenomena were governed by distinct, active deities. One example among many can be found in the "Ji fa" chapter of the *Liji*:

The mountains, forests, rivers, valleys, and hills that can send out clouds, make wind and rain, and cause to appear strange phenomena are called spirits (*shen*). He who possesses all under heaven sacrifices to the hundred spirits.[33]

Natural phenomena, the text is claiming, are under the direct control of particular spirits, to whom the ruler must make continual sacrifices.

And since natural phenomena were directly controlled by spirits—and potentially fickle spirits at that—a great deal of religious activity during the Warring States accordingly was devoted to charting which spirits controlled which domain of power, understanding their intentions through divination, and influencing them with sacrifices. It is in this context, for example, that we should understand claims such as those found in the *Zuozhuan* that one of the civilizing acts of Yu consisted of casting cauldrons with images of the spirits, an act that allowed the people to "know the spirits."[34] Similarly, the "Wuzang shanjing" section of the *Shanhaijing* contains an exhaustive description of, among other things, the various spirits of each mountain and the particular powers that each possesses. A typical passage reads: "As for the

---

31. For an excellent discussion of early Chinese religious practices, see Poo, *In Search of Personal Welfare*.

32. Mote, *Intellectual Foundations of China*, p. 17.

33. *Liji zhengyi*, "Ji fa," 46.3a.

34. *Chunqiu Zuozhuan zhengyi*, Xuan, 3, 21.8b–9a.

appearance of their [i.e., these mountains'] spirits, they all have a human body and sheep horns. In sacrifices to them, use one sheep and, for grain offerings, use millet. These are the spirits. When they appear, the wind and rainwater make destruction."[35] The text then explains the types of sacrifices that dissuade these particular spirits from causing destructive winds and rains. Both of these texts make an argument for rulership through a control of local spirits: by gaining powers over enough divinities, the ruler can bring order to the world.[36]

Given the dominance of such notions, it is not surprising that several texts from this period present critical responses to the ritual specialists in charge of dealing with these spirits. I discuss four of these texts here: the *Lunyu*, early chapters from the Mohists, the "Chu yu, xia" chapter of the *Guoyu*, and the "Neiye" chapter of the *Guanzi*.

Heaven and Man in the *Lunyu*

One of the most often-quoted passages from the *Lunyu* is: "Fan Chi asked about knowledge. The master said, 'To work on behalf of what is proper for the people, to be reverent to the ghosts and spirits and yet keep them at a distance, this can be called knowledge'" (6/22). Although Confucius is often presented, at least in the "religion to philosophy" framework, as marking a shift away from "superstition" and toward "rationalism,"[37] Confucius was not claiming that spirits do not exist. Indeed, he explicitly called on people to be reverent toward them. His point is, rather, to keep them at a distance and to focus on the human realm.[38]

It is within this context that we should understand Confucius' statements about spirits. As his disciples claimed: "He sacrificed as if present. He sacrificed to the spirits as if the spirits were present. The master said, 'If I do not participate in the sacrifice, it is as if I did not sacrifice'" (3/12). The passage is

---

35. *Shanhaijing jianshu*, "Dongshan jing," SBBY, 4.7b.

36. For a discussion of these texts, see Harper, "A Chinese Demonography," p. 479; and Needham, *Science and Civilisation in China*, 3: 503.

37. See, e.g., Fung, *A History of Chinese Philosophy*, 1: 58.

38. "Confucius" here refers not to some historical Confucius but to a composite figure constructed from the *Lunyu* whose views are representative of a certain strand of late Chunqiu–early Warring States opposition to the dominant forms of religious practice. For an attempt to periodize the chapters of the *Lunyu* themselves, see Brooks and Brooks, *The Original Analects*.

a critique of contemporary sacrificial practice, in which one engaged a ritual specialist to perform sacrifices properly. The goal of such sacrifices was to transform the spirits so that they would act on behalf of humanity. Confucius' argument is that one should focus instead on the human realm: the point of sacrifice is not to persuade the spirits but to transform the human performing the ritual. Accordingly, one must perform the act oneself, and one must do so even though the spirits may not be present during the ritual. This position does not deny that spirits act in the world. Rather, it argues against the view that humans should attempt to control the spirits with sacrifices: the goal should be self-transformation.

Spirits, therefore, should not be the object of our concern: "The master did not speak of abnormalities (guai 怪), force, disorder, or spirits" (7/21). Here again, there is no claim that the items on this list do not exist. Nor is there any claim that they are insignificant. Clearly, disorder and force are subjects of obvious concern. The power of the passage, therefore, lies precisely in the implication that for most people these topics would usually be objects of great concern, yet Confucius did not speak of them at all. The sense running throughout these passages is that spirits do have great potency, but humans should not speak of them, should avoid worrying about them, and should perform ritual actions not to influence them but to cultivate themselves. And yet one must still revere them. Indeed, the highest way to revere them is precisely not to try to influence them.

In many ways this position heightens the tensions noted in Chapter 1. In the Western Zhou, a proper pattern for human life was emphasized. Heaven and the other spirits sometimes supported this pattern; at other times they did not. But ritual specialists could, to a limited extent, keep the divine powers within this pattern. But Confucius, by decrying the instrumental use of sacrifices by ritual specialists, denied the powers that were used in the Bronze Age to mollify divine forces and to make them work for the living. Instead, he urged that we simply cultivate ourselves and accept whatever the divine powers do.

This stance explains both the reverence that Confucius expressed toward Heaven, the greatest of the divine powers, as well as his view that we must not attempt to influence Heaven but accept whatever Heaven sends at us. Thus, for example, Confucius strongly embraced the idea that humans must follow the mandate of Heaven. Indeed, esteeming the mandate of Heaven was one point of difference between a gentleman and a lesser man:

Confucius said, "As for the gentleman, there are three things he esteems. He esteems the mandate of Heaven, he esteems great men, and he esteems the words of sages. A petty man, not understanding the mandate of Heaven, does not esteem it; he is disrespectful to great men, and he ridicules the words of sages." (16/8)

And Confucius famously defined understanding the mandate of Heaven as one of the achievements of his life:

The master said, "At age fifteen, I set my intent on studying; at thirty I established myself; at forty I was no longer deluded; at fifty I understood the mandate of Heaven; at sixty my ear accorded; at seventy I followed what my heart desired without transgression." (2/4)

For Confucius, however, the mandate of Heaven was not a simple granting of moral norms, nor did it involve rewarding the worthy or punishing the unworthy. Although Sima Qian would later, in his biography of Bo Yi and Shu Qi,[39] critique Confucius for believing that the good are rewarded and the bad punished, Confucius in fact held no such position. Indeed, for Confucius, the mandate of Heaven appeared to involve no ethical calculus whatsoever, and this presumably is a part of why it took Confucius until age fifty to understand it. For example, when his favorite disciple, Yan Hui, died young, Confucius exclaimed, "Alas. Heaven is destroying me! Heaven is destroying me!" There is no sense here that Yan Hui had done anything to deserve dying young. On the contrary, Confucius' response was to rail at Heaven, since it is Heaven that controls the mandate.

Ji Kangzi asked, "Of your disciples, who loved learning?" Confucius responded, "There was Yan Hui who loved learning. Unfortunately he had a shortened mandate, and he died. Now there is no one." (11/7)[40]

What is mandated is under the control of Heaven, and there is no ethical calculus involved.

Indeed, Confucius often emphasized the degree to which events are out of the control of humans. When a certain Gongbo Liao defamed someone, and Zifu Jingbo asked Confucius if he should have Gongbo Liao killed, Confucius responded: "If the Way is going to be put into practice, it is mandated (*ming*). If it is going to be discarded, that too is mandated. What does Gongbo Liao have to do with what is mandated?" (14/36). Even the question

---

39. *Shiji*, 120.2124–25.
40. A similar statement appears in 6/3.

of whether the Way will prevail is out of human hands: humans can put the way into practice only if Heaven wishes them to. As with Confucius' statements about his best disciple dying young, the attitude here is simply that one must accept what Heaven has ordained.

Nonetheless, Confucius held strongly to the view that no one should resent Heaven:

The master said, "No one understands me." Zigong asked, "What does it mean to say no one understands you?" The master replied, "I do not resent Heaven nor bear a grudge against man. I study here and reach to what is above. Only Heaven understands me." (14/35)

Indeed, Confucius believed that human culture itself derives in part from Heaven and argued that cultural patterns emerged when the initial sages modeled themselves on Heaven and then transmitted those patterns to humanity:

The master said: "Great indeed was the rulership of Yao. So majestic—only Heaven is great, and only Yao modeled himself upon it. So boundless, the people were not able to find a name for it. Majestic were his achievements. Illustrious are his patterned forms (wen zhang)." (8/19)

Heaven is also seen as being responsible for the continuation of these cultural patterns:

When the master was in danger in Kuang, he said: "King Wen has died, but are his cultural patterns (wen) not here? If Heaven had wanted to destroy these cultural patterns, then those who died later would not have been able to participate in the cultural patterns. Since Heaven has not destroyed these cultural patterns, what can the people of Kuang do to me?" (9/5)

Heaven is thus granted a normative role. The patterns of human culture (wen) emerged from Heaven, and it is Heaven that allows those patterns to continue.

Thus, the patterns that should guide human behavior can be traced to Heaven—they are patterns observed by the sages and brought from Heaven to humanity. However, the commands of Heaven do not necessarily involve support for those who follow these patterns. And yet man must not resent Heaven for this and indeed must strive to understand and even esteem these commands.

Such a position is a variant of the tensions present in the Western Zhou. Heaven is revered, and both living up to and accepting what Heaven ordains are man's highest goals. But since, in Confucius' view, man cannot influence Heaven through sacrifices (or, to be more explicit, through sacrificing to the spirits who then petition Heaven on behalf of the living), man must simply cultivate himself and accept whatever Heaven does.[41]

The Moral Cosmos of the Mohists

If Confucius responded to the tensions between humans and Heaven by embracing them and denying the ability of humans to transform Heaven, the Mohists took the opposite approach and denied the tensions altogether. For them, Heaven was a moral deity who acted according to a clear moral calculus: "Heaven desires propriety and detests impropriety."[42] Accordingly, humans must model themselves on Heaven in order to act properly: "The gentlemen who desire to act with propriety must accord with the intent of Heaven" ("Tianzhi, xia," 7.11a). Moreover, Heaven actively intervenes in human affairs to reward the good and punish the bad. If, for example, someone kills an innocent man, Heaven sends down a calamity ("Tianzhi, xia," 7.11a–b), as do the ghosts and spirits arrayed below Heaven ("Minggui, xia," 7.2b). Absent here is any sense that either Heaven or the spirits are capricious. All of them always act according to a clear moral calculus.

The Mohist advice to the rulers of the day was thus to simply follow Heaven, just as, the Mohists claim, the sage-kings of the past did:

Therefore, in ancient times the sage-kings made manifest and understood what Heaven and the ghosts bless and avoided what Heaven and the ghosts detest so as to increase the benefits of all under Heaven and eradicate the problems of all under Heaven. ("Tianzhi, zhong," 7.6a)

Like Confucius, the Mohists believed that humans must follow the commands of Heaven, but, unlike Confucius, the Mohists saw those commands as ethical.

---

41. For a somewhat different reading of these issues, see Ning Chen, "Confucius' View of Fate (*Ming*)."

42. *Mozi*, "Tianzhi, xia," 7.10a; hereinafter citations from the *Mozi* are given in the text.

Indeed, not only should humans follow the commands of Heaven, but it was Heaven itself who

made kings, dukes, and lords and charged them with, first, rewarding the worthy and punishing the wicked and, second, plundering the metals, wood, birds, and beasts and working the five grains, hemp, and silk so as to make the materials for people's clothing and food. ("Tianzhi, zhong," 7.7a)

Heaven instituted the political hierarchy and taught rulers how to rule and how to appropriate natural resources for the benefit of humanity. The hierarchy of the human world thus replicates the hierarchy of the cosmos, with the rulers rewarding the worthy and punishing the unworthy just as Heaven above does.

There is no sense here that humans, through their sacrifices, are transforming Heaven and the spirit world in order to persuade them to act on behalf of humanity, nor is there any sense that humans are utilizing sacrifices in order to make material resources available for human consumption. On the contrary, the hierarchy of Heaven and the spirits is a given, and that hierarchy is already predisposed to aid humanity. Indeed, it is Heaven that created the kings, and Heaven that directs humanity to appropriate the natural world. It is as if the goal of late Shang sacrifices became the foundation for Mohist thought.

Moreover, for the Mohists sacrifices are not transformative. Instead, they are simply a case of humans giving the spirits what the spirits need, just as the spirits give humans what humans need. It is with the Mohists, in other words, that one finds the bureaucratic vision of sacrifices that Keightley sees in the Shang. The Mohist narrative of the origins of sacrifices makes the point well. The narrative appears in a Mohist argument about the importance of identifying with one's superior. This is true at each level of the hierarchy, all the way up to Heaven. Thus, the argument goes, if one identifies with the ruler but fails to identify with Heaven, then Heaven will send down punishments. To prevent this, sacrifices were instituted:

Therefore, if it were like this, then Heaven would send down cold and heat without moderation, snow, frost, rain, and dew at the improper time, the five grains would not grow, and the six animals would not prosper. . . . Therefore, in ancient times, the sage-kings clarified what Heaven and the ghosts desire and avoided what Heaven and the ghosts detest. They thereby sought to increase the benefits of all under Heaven and push away the problems of all under Heaven. They thereby led the myriad peoples under Heaven to purify themselves, bathe, and make libations and offerings to sacrifice to Heaven and the ghosts. ("Shangtong, zhong," 3.5a–b)

Heaven and the ghosts desire sacrifices, and the sage-kings of the past therefore instituted them. Thenceforth, "favors from Heaven and the ghosts could be obtained" ("Shangtong, zhong," 3.5b). If humans sacrifice properly, then the divine powers will send down blessings. In short, the Mohist view of sacrifices is precisely *do ut des*—precisely the view that Keightley and Poo Mu-chou, incorrectly in my opinion, tried to read into Shang sacrifices. Indeed, stories abound in the *Mozi* about the importance of gauging the correct amount of sacrifices to give in order to receive the proper amount of divine blessings in return. As one example among many:

The sacrificer of Lu sacrificed one pig and sought one hundred favors from the ghosts and spirits. Master Mozi said to him, "This is unacceptable. If you give to others sparingly and yet expect them [in response] to give generously, then they will be afraid of your giving things to them. Now, if you sacrifice one pig and expect one hundred favors from the ghosts and spirits, then they will be afraid of getting sacrifices of oxen and sheep." ("Luwen," 13.6b)

Like Confucius, the Mohists opposed the use of sacrifice to coerce or transform the spirit world. But, unlike Confucius, the Mohists asserted that sacrifices should be used to gain benefits from the spirit world. Not only is it a moral cosmos, but it is also one that operates according to a hierarchical *do ut des* framework. For this reason, the Mohists argued strongly against the notion of fate.[43] Since the highest power, Heaven, is moral, the only issue is whether the ruler models himself on Heaven and acts properly to those below. If he does, there will be order; if he does not, Heaven will send down punishments.

When men of propriety are above, all under Heaven will be ordered. The High God, as well as the ghosts and spirits of the mountains and streams, will have their master of sacrifices, and the myriad peoples will receive great benefits. ("Feiming, shang," 9.3a)

Sacrifice, in short, is simply a part of the proper hierarchical functioning of the cosmos. It is not that sacrifices transform the spirits; rather, humans give

---

43. See the "Feiming" chapters, all of which, as their title implies, contain lengthy critiques of the notion of fate.

their superiors what they need. Indeed, when the Mohists argue that Heaven loves universally, they even give as one of their examples the fact that Heaven accepts sacrifices from all—and, if he accepts sacrifices from all, he will send down blessings to all ("Tianzhi, xia," 7.11a).

Like Confucius, the Mohists deny that sacrifices can transform Heaven and the spirits. But, for Confucius this meant that one simply had to accept the capriciousness of those powers. For the Mohists, on the contrary, it is unnecessary to transform Heaven or in any way act to coerce it; Heaven is explicitly the source of propriety, and, indeed, of all things that the Mohists deem good. And humans are simply called on to follow Heaven's commands and thus achieve the order that Heaven has made possible. For the Mohists, the cosmos is moral and is controlled by a moral deity and a moral pantheon of spirits, and humans should simply submit themselves to that deity in order to achieve a proper order. The tensions between humanity and divine powers are denied by arguing that Heaven and the spirits are not capricious and already act on behalf of humanity, and that the cosmos is already hierarchically structured and therefore not in need of human sacrifices to so order it. All humans need to do is follow the commands of Heaven, and those commands will always lead them properly.

Separating Humans and Spirits and Dividing Heaven and Earth: The "Chu yu, xia" Chapter of the *Guoyu*

Confucius and the Mohists, albeit for different reasons, rejected the use of sacrifices to coerce and transform the divine realm, but others attempted to define more carefully the relations that ritual specialists should maintain with the spirits. A clear example of this can be found in the "Chu yu, xia" chapter of the *Guoyu*, which critiques its own age by looking back to an earlier period when ritual specialists behaved properly.

This section includes a passage widely cited in the sinological literature on shamanism. Indeed, K. C. Chang's argument for shamanism in early China is based to a significant degree on his reading of this passage. Chang followed Derk Bodde's paraphrase:

Anciently, men and spirits did not intermingle. At that time there were certain persons who were so perspicacious, single-minded, and reverential that their understanding enabled them to make meaningful collation of what lies above and below, and their insight to illumine what is distant and profound. Therefore the spirits would descend into them. The possessors of such powers were, if men, called *xi* (shamans), and, if women, *wu* (shamanesses). It is they who supervised the positions of the spirits at the ceremonies, sacrificed to them, and otherwise handled religious matters. As a consequence, the spheres of the divine and the profane were kept distinct. The spirits sent down blessings on the people, and accepted from them their offerings. There were no natural calamities.[44]

Chang calls this "the most important textual reference to shamanism in ancient China."[45]

Fung Yu-lan understood this passage in a similar way. However, Fung, reading the passage according to his general "religion to philosophy" argument, denigrated the link between humans and gods that Chang celebrated:

What is said here shows in a general way the forms of superstition of the early Chinese. From the fact that sorcerers and witches were considered necessary to regulate the dwelling places, positions at the sacrifices, and order of precedence of the spirits, we may see how numerous these spirits were. The fact that the spirits were supposed to be able to bestow happiness, receive sacrifices, and to enter into human beings, shows that they were regarded as anthropomorphic beings. And the statements that "people and spirits were confusedly mingled," "people and spirits held the same position," and "the spirits followed the customs of the people," show us that the actions of the spirits were looked upon as being quite indistinguishable from those of human beings. The Chinese of that time were superstitious and ignorant; they had religious ideas but no philosophy; so that the religious ideas and spirits which they believed in were exactly like those of the Greeks.[46]

I will follow David Keightley in arguing that the passage in fact has little to do with shamanism.[47] Indeed, far from referring to a mixing of humans and spirits, the text is explicitly oriented toward defining humans and spirits as, normatively, separate. Like Pindar, the writers of this text were arguing against any attempt to weaken the boundary between humans and spirits.

The text revolves around King Zhao of Chu (r. 515–489 BC) and his minister Guan Yifu:

---

44. K. C. Chang, *Art, Myth, and Ritual*, p. 44. For Bodde's paraphrase, see his "Myths of Ancient China," p. 390.
45. K. C. Chang, *Art, Myth, and Ritual*, p. 45.
46. Fung, *A History of Chinese Philosophy*, 1: 23–24.
47. Keightley, "Shamanism, Death, and the Ancestors," pp. 821–24. The particular passage in question here is discussed in detail in Keightley's unpublished "Shamanism in *Guoyu*? A Tale of the *xi* and *wu*."

King Zhao asked Guan Yifu: "What does the *Zhoushu* mean when it refers to Chong and Li causing Heaven and Earth to have no communication? If this had not happened, would the people be able to ascend to Heaven?"[48]

The precise reference here is unclear. However, the "Lü xing" chapter of the *Shangshu* mentions the activities of Chong and Li in its description of the creation of punishments by the San Miao.[49] Di, heeding the cries of the people, decided to intervene:

Those who were oppressed and terrified and facing execution announced their innocence to the powers above. The high Di surveyed the people, but there was no fragrant virtue, and the punishments sent out a smell that was rank. The august Di pitied and felt compassion for those among the multitudes who, though innocent, were facing execution. He requited the oppressors with terror and put an end to the Miao people so that they had no descendants. He thereupon ordered Chong and Li to break the communication between Heaven and Earth so that there would be no more descending and reaching up.[50]

The passage clearly represents the interruption of communication between Heaven and Earth as a good thing: Di did so in order to establish a proper hierarchy. The sense would appear to be that the San Miao, in creating punishments, had usurped privileges that belonged to the god alone. The San Miao, in short, had transgressed the limits of what is permitted for humans.

In the "Chu yu" chapter, however, King Zhao asks if the passage perhaps had the opposite meaning: that the breaking of communication between Heaven and Earth was now preventing humans from ascending to the heavens. Guan Yifu immediately opposes such a reading: "This is not what it means. In ancient times, the people and the spirits did not mix" (18.1a). People and spirits were separated in antiquity, and, as Guan Yifu explains, a proper ritual separation was maintained between them. More specifically, ritual specialists were responsible for maintaining the proper sacrifices:

Those among the people whose essence was bright and never divided and who were able to be proper, reverential, correct, and rectified, their wisdom was capable of comparing the propriety of what was above and what was below; their sagacity was

---

48. *Guoyu*, "Chu yu, xia," 18.1a; hereinafter cited in the text.
49. For a detailed discussion of the "Lü xing" chapter, see my *Ambivalence of Creation*, chap. 3.
50. *Shangshu zhengyi*, "Lü xing," 19.10b–11b.

able to glorify what was distant and display what was bright; their clear-sightedness was able to glorify and illuminate it; their keen hearing was able to listen and discern it. As such, the illuminated spirits descended to them.[51] As regards males, they were called *xi* [male ritual specialists]; as regards women, they were called *wu* [female ritual specialists]. They were employed in order to regulate the placement, positions, precedence, and ranks of the spirits and to prepare the sacrificial victims, vessels, and seasonal garments. (18.1a)

The ritual specialists were rectified and proper, and the spirits thus descended to accept their sacrifices. The duties of these ritual specialists involved granting spirits their proper rank and precedence. Guan Yifu's argument parallels the views ascribed to ritual specialists in the Shang and early Zhou texts (see Chapter 1): the duty of such specialists was to order the spirits and grant them their proper position.

Because the ritual specialists performed their duties correctly, the tasks of humans and spirits were defined properly:

The people and spirits had different tasks. These were respected and not transgressed. Thus, the spirits sent them good harvests, and the people used the produce to sacrifice. Disasters did not come, and there were no deficiencies in what they sought for use. (18.1b–2a)

The ritual specialists regulated the positions of the spirits correctly, and the spirits in turn granted good harvests. The people then used the products of the harvest to sacrifice to the spirits. In short, because the ritual specialists observed their appropriate tasks, the worlds of humans and spirits were correctly demarcated and no disasters occurred.

Clearly, this is far removed from shamanism. The text is not describing the descent of spirits into humans, and its only reference to humans ascending is a negative one: it argues against any such attempt. Contrary to Chang's interpretation, the text is claiming that spirits and humans should be separated and placed within a proper hierarchy of functions. *Wu* here thus seems best translated as "ritual specialists"; I would agree with Mair's argument (see pp. 84–86) that the *wu* are not shamans at all.

---

51. This is the passage that Bodde read as "the spirits would descend into them" and that Chang used to build his argument for shamanism. In fact, however, the wording *jiang zhi* simply means "to descend and arrive"—which is exactly what spirits are supposed to do when effective ritual specialists entice them with the proper blandishments.

Guan Yifu continues:

> When it came to the declining period of Shao Hao, the Jiu Li brought disorder to the power (*de*). The people and spirits were mixed up. Things could not be assigned to their proper categories. People made their own offerings, and each family had a ritual specialist (*wu*) and a scribe. There was no demand for substance. The people exhausted themselves in sacrifices and yet knew no good fortune. They made offerings without proper moderation. The people and the spirits occupied the same position. The people profaned the proper covenants. There was neither respect nor reverence. The spirits had improper intimacy with the people; they did not purify their behavior. Bountiful harvests were not sent down, and there was no produce for use in making offerings. Misfortunes and disasters repeatedly came. No one used up their *qi*. (18.2a)

The ritual differentiation that had characterized the earlier period broke down, and humans and spirits became mixed. Each family employed its own ritual specialist, and the order and precedence of the offerings collapsed. Even though sacrifices increased, good harvests ended and disasters arose.

When Zhuan Xu took power, the situation was finally rectified:

> Zhuan Xu succeeded him [Shao Hao]. He thereupon ordered Chong, the rectifier of the south, to supervise Heaven and thereby assemble the spirits. He ordered Li, the rectifier of fire, to supervise Earth and thereby assemble the people. He made them revive the old rules. There were no more mutual usurpations and encroachments. This is what was meant by breaking the communication between Heaven and Earth. (18.2a)

When Chong and Li were assigned the tasks of supervising Heaven and Earth, respectively, each was demarcated properly, and this, Guan Yifu argues, was the meaning of breaking the communication between Heaven and Earth. Unlike King Zhao, Guan Yifu clearly sees this rupture as a good thing.

A similar problem arose when the San Miao appeared, but Yao was able to rectify things by supporting the descendants of Chong and Li:

> After this, the San Miao restored the power of the Jiu Li. Yao turned again to nurturing the descendants of Chong and Li. Those who had not forgotten the old were made to revive their regulating. From that point, down to the Xia and Shang, the Chong and Li families accordingly placed Heaven and Earth in order and distinguished their proper spheres of management. (18.2a–b)

This situation continued into the Zhou dynasty:

With the Zhou, Bo Xiufu of Cheng was their descendant. In the time of King Xuan, he lost his office and became part of the Sima clan. Esteeming his ancestors as spirits so as to hold the awe of the people, he said: "Chong truly raised heaven, and Li truly lowered Earth." (18.2b)

But, with the decline of the Zhou, the proper demarcation of Heaven and Earth was lost again:

But when they met the disorders of this age, none was able to withstand it. If such had not been the case, then Heaven and Earth would be complete and not altering. How can they be joined together? (18.2b)

The implication is that the problem confronting Guan Yifu and his contemporaries was the loss of the proper distinction between Heaven and Earth.

Far from being a shamanistic text, the "Chu yu, xia" is a call for a ritual separation of humans and spirits and a critique of any intermingling of the two. The goal is harmony through ritual separation. The text is defending a position much closer to that of Pindar.

Becoming Like a Spirit: The "Neiye" Chapter of the *Guanzi*

If the *Lunyu* reveals a concern with keeping spirits at a distance, if the Mohists asserted an absolute, pregiven hierarchy of humans and spirits, and if the "Chu yu, xia" chapter represents an attempt to maintain a ritual separation of humans and spirits, the "Neiye" chapter of the *Guanzi* is representative of attempts to break down the barriers between humans and spirits altogether.

The "Neiye," chapter 49 of the *Guanzi*,[52] builds its argument around three interrelated terms: *qi*, essence (*jing* 精), and spirit (*shen*). *Qi*, which I here leave untranslated, is the energy and substance of all things. In its most refined form, *qi* becomes essence: "Essence is the essence of *qi*."[53] Spirit is then defined as a refined *qi* as well; as we shall see, it becomes another name in this text for essential *qi*.

------

52. For an excellent translation and analysis of the "Neiye," see Roth, *Original Tao*. See also the invaluable discussions by Roth, "Psychology and Self-Cultivation in Early Taoistic Thought"; and Graham, *Disputers of the Tao*, pp. 100–105. Also extremely helpful is Qiu Xigui, "Jixia Daojia jingqi shuo de yanjiu." For a discussion of the dating of the "Neiye," see Roth, *Original Tao*, pp. 23–30; idem, "Redaction Criticism and the Early History of Taoism," pp. 14–17; and Rickett, *Guanzi*, 2: 32–39.

53. *Guanzi*, "Neiye," 16.2b; hereinafter cited in the text.

The text opens up with one of its more provocative renderings of this argument:

As for the essence (*jing*) of all things (*wu*), it is this that is life. Below it generates the five grains; above it becomes the arrayed stars. When it floats between Heaven and Earth, we call it ghosts and spirits; when it is stored within a person's chest, we call that person a sage. (16.1a)

As the life force, essence generates all things on earth and in the heavens. Spirits are simply the essence floating between Heaven and Earth, and sages are those who have such essence within. Human sages, in other words, contain within themselves the same essence found in spirits.

Indeed, the only significant difference between humans and spirits is that spirits are pure essence (and thus float between Heaven and Earth), whereas humans are a mix of essence and form:

As for the birth of humans: Heaven brings forth the essence, and Earth brings forth the form. They combine these to make humans. When they harmonize, there is life; when they do not, there is not life. If we examine the way of harmony, its essence cannot be seen, its signs cannot be classified. When there are arrangement and regulation in the mind, this thereby gives long life. If hatred and anger lose their measure, one should make a plan for them. Moderate the five desires, and expel the two evils. If one is not joyous and not angry, balance and correctness fills the chest. (16.5b)

Humans thus occupy a unique place in the cosmos because they combined the essence received from Heaven and form received from Earth. By harmonizing these, humans can attain longevity.

Harmonizing the essence and form requires one to live properly with Heaven and Earth:

Heaven values correctness; Earth values levelness; man values calmness and stillness. Spring, autumn, winter, and summer are the seasons of Heaven. Mountains, hills, streams, and valleys are the branches of Earth. Happiness, anger, taking, and giving are the schemes of man. For this reason, the sage alters with the seasons but is not transformed, follows things but is not changed. (16.2b)

The sage must recognize the proper values of Heaven, Earth, and man— correctness, levelness, and stillness, respectively. The sage must be still and not be transformed or changed by the alterations of Heavenly seasons, the shifts in the earthly landscape, and the schemes of other humans.

Doing so will allow him to have a settled heart and ultimately become a resting place for essence:

Only he who is capable of being correct and still is capable of being settled. If he has a settled mind within, ears and eyes that are keen of hearing and sight, and four limbs that are durable and strong, then he can be the resting place of the essence. Essence is the essence of *qi*. When the *qi* follows the Way, there is life. When there is life, there is thought. When there is thought, there is knowledge. When there is knowledge, one stops. In all cases, the forms of the mind are such that transgressive knowledge leads to a loss of life. (16.2b)

By becoming settled, the sage is able to develop a form that can bring essence to rest within himself. This grants him life and knowledge. The concern of the authors thus becomes clear. The problem is that our essence tends to dissipate from our form because of the changes, alterations, and schemes of Heaven, Earth, and man. Our goal, therefore, should be to keep our essence within our form and thus maintain the proper balance of Heaven and Earth within us.

Essence is the most refined state of *qi*. Moreover, *qi* that follows the Way allows for life—the very thing said about essence. The implication is that one refines one's *qi* by following the proper Way. If this is done, one's form becomes correct, one obtains longevity, and one's actions meet with success:

The Way is that about which the mouth cannot speak, the eye cannot see, the ear cannot hear. It is that with which one cultivates the mind and corrects the form. If men lose it, they die; if they obtain it, they live. If, in performing tasks, [the Way] is lost, one will fail; if it is obtained, the tasks will be completed. (16.2a–b)

To do this, however, the Way itself must be brought to rest, since it, too, has no fixed place. Thus, one must render one's mind still and bring one's *qi* into accord with the normative pattern (*li*): "Now, the Way is without a fixed place, but a good mind will bring it to rest and care for it. If the mind is still and the *qi* patterned (*li*), the Way can thereupon be brought to a stop" (16.2a). One's goal is to bring the Way to rest within one's form. Here again, change and movement are dangers, and longevity rests with stillness.

However, insofar as the Way fills all under Heaven, he who can bring it to rest within himself gains access to the entire cosmos:

The Way fills all under Heaven. It is everywhere that people reside, but people are unable to understand. With the liberation (*jie* 解) of the one word, one explores (*cha*) Heaven above, reaches to Earth below, and encircles and fills the nine regions. (16.3b.)

The Way pervades everything. Accordingly, he who can grasp it with the one word (i.e., the "Way") can be liberated and is able to explore Heaven and Earth and fill the world. The claim here is not that the adept actually explores the cosmos in person; the point is rather that the adept can gain these powers by grasping the one word that pervades the cosmos. As the text explicates:

What does it mean to be liberated by it? It resides in the stability of the mind. If one's mind is regulated, one's senses are thereby regulated. If one's mind is stabilized, one's senses are thereby stabilized. What regulates them is the mind, and what stabilizes them is the mind. The mind therefore stores the mind; within the mind there is also a mind. In this mind of the mind, tones precede words. Only after there are tones are there forms; only after there are forms is there the word; only after the word is there control; only after there is control is there regulation. If there is no regulation, there will inevitably be disorder. If there is disorder, there will be death. (16.3b–4a)

The process occurs entirely within the adept himself. The adept must stabilize his mind and thereby regulate his senses. The mind within his mind responds and hence experiences the inherent resonance that exists in musical tones. Only through this resonance can one grasp the one word—that which pervades everything. And by grasping that which pervades everything, one is thereby liberated.

Similarly, by obtaining the one word that pervades everything, all under Heaven will submit:

If a regulated mind resides within, regulated words will issue from one's mouth and regulated tasks will be applied to men. As such, all under Heaven will be ordered. When the one word is obtained, all under Heaven will submit. When the one word is determined, all under Heaven will obey. (16.3a)

The one word is the fulcrum of the cosmos. By obtaining the one word, the adept is able to make himself the fulcrum of the cosmos as well, and all under Heaven will submit itself to him.

The author make these same points about *qi* itself. A proper utilization of *qi* allows humans to possess within themselves the same qualities found in the rest of the cosmos: "Therefore, the *qi* of the people is bright as if ascending to Heaven and dark as if entering into an abyss; vast as if residing in the ocean and constricted as if residing in the self" (16.1a). The claim again is not that humans actually ascend to Heaven and encompass distant regions (claims, as we will see, that were indeed made later within comparable frameworks). The argument is rather that *qi* is what enables humans to have access, through something within themselves, to the rest of the cosmos.

And, since *qi* thus pervades the cosmos, an understanding of it allows the adept to make all under Heaven submit: "Rewards are not sufficient to encourage goodness, and punishments are not sufficient to correct the transgressive. When awareness of the *qi* is obtained, all under Heaven will submit. When awareness of the mind is settled, all under Heaven will obey" (16.4b). Indeed, if one can hold fast to the *qi* and not let it escape, one gains power over things:

Therefore, this *qi* cannot be stopped with force, but it can be made to rest through power (*de*); it cannot be called through sound, but it can be welcomed through musical pitch. Reverently hold fast to it and do not lose it. This we call "completing the power." When the power is complete and knowledge emerges, then the myriad things (*wu*) can be fully obtained. (16.1a–b)

By holding fast to that *qi* and not letting it escape, one can obtain the myriad things. Since *qi* pervades the cosmos and exists in the forms of all things, the ability to make the *qi* rest within oneself gives the adept an ability to control those things.

In short, the monistic cosmos posited by the authors allows them to make great claims for the potential powers of those who follow the teachings of the text. Not only is the adept able to transform with the changes of the world without altering his own *qi*, but he is in fact able to gain control of things:

To unify things and be able to transform them is called spirit (*shen*). To unify affairs and be able to alter them is called craft. Transforming but not altering the *qi*, altering but not changing one's craft: only the superior man holding fast to the One is able to do this. By holding fast to the One and not losing it, he is able to rule over the myriad things. The superior man controls things (*shi wu*); he is not controlled by them. He obtains the pattern (*li*) of the One. (16.3a)

Since the cosmos is monistic, it follows that there is an inherent pattern (*li*) to the oneness of the world. If the adept brings his *qi* into accord with this pattern and holds fast to it, then he can achieve mastery over the things (*wu*) that populate the world.

Indeed, he who can fully gain such powers and fill himself with essence, the most refined state of *qi*, is able to avoid all disasters and harm:

When the essence exists, it gives life of itself. On the outside, all will be settled and flourishing. Internally, one can store it so that it acts as the source of a fountain. Floodlike, harmonious, and tranquil, it acts as the depths of the *qi*. If the depths do not dry up, the nine apertures will thereupon open. They are thereby able to exhaust Heaven and Earth and cover the four seas. If within one has no delusions, then outside there will be no disasters. If the mind is complete within, the form will be complete on the outside. One will not encounter Heavenly disasters nor meet with injuries from others. This person we call the sage. (16.4a)

Since the essence pervades everything, access to it grants the adept full powers to penetrate everything, exhaust Heaven and Earth, and avoid disasters.

At times, the text refers to this essence as "spirit" (*shen*):

There is a spirit that of itself resides within the body, at times leaving, at times entering. No one is able to contemplate it. If you lose it, there will be disorder; if you obtain it, there will be order. Carefully clean its resting place, and the essence will of its own enter. Refine your thoughts and contemplate it; make tranquil your memories and bring it to order. Be reverent, generous, dignified, and respectful, and the essence will come and settle. Obtain it and do not dispense with it. Your ears and eyes will never go astray, and your heart will have no other designs. When a correct mind resides within, the myriad things will obtain their standard. (16.3a–b)

Each person, therefore, has a spirit—refined *qi*—within his own body. The goal of self-cultivation is then to keep this spirit within oneself.

By doing so, the adept is able to gain an understanding of the things of the world:

The extremity of divine illumination (*shen ming*)—so brilliant, it knows the myriad things. Hold it fast within, and do not be excessive.[54] Do not allow things to disorder the senses, and do not allow the senses to disorder the mind. This is called obtaining it within. (16.3a)

The adept is able to understand all things because he does not allow his senses to be disordered by things and holds fast to the divine illumination within.

---

54. Following Wang Niansun in dropping the *yi* as excrescent.

Indeed, the text argues, self-cultivation allows the sage to gain the powers of the spirits—without resorting to the arts of the religious specialists of the day:

Concentrate the *qi* as if a spirit (*ru shen* 如神), and the myriad things will all reside within. Can you concentrate? Can you unify? Can you not engage in crackmaking and milfoil divination and yet understand auspiciousness and inauspiciousness? Can you stop? Can you reach an end? Can you not seek from others and obtain it in yourself? Think about it, think about it, and think about it again. If you think about it but do not penetrate, the ghosts and spirits will penetrate it. This is not due to the power of the ghosts and spirits; it is due to the ultimate point of essential *qi*. (16.5a)

The argument here rests on the claim that the universe is composed of *qi*, and that change is a product of the alterations and transformations of this *qi*. *Shen*, the most highly refined form of *qi*, is able to understand the proper movements of the universe, and, since humans have this form of *qi* within themselves as well, they ultimately can attain the same comprehension through their own efforts.

The claim, in other words, is that there exist substances within oneself that, properly cultivated, can gain one the powers of a spirit. Thus, self-cultivation allows one to understand auspiciousness and inauspiciousness without resorting to divination. This understanding is attained not because the ghosts and spirits have given one information, and not because self-cultivation allows one to ascertain the intentions of particular spirits, but because one has attained sufficient refinement on one's own to understand the workings of the universe.

Thus, since all things consist of *qi*, that which possesses the most refined *qi* (as do the spirits) possesses both knowledge about and power over that which possesses less refined *qi*. By accumulating essence within himself, man becomes like a spirit: able to understand the changes of forms, avoid being harmed by them, and even gain control over them. In other words, the cosmology of the "Neiye" is one of hierarchical monism, and one's goal is to gain ever more potency over the world of forms by becoming ever more refined.

Man's powers and limitations are defined by the resulting hierarchy of Heaven and Earth. At his weakest, he is a thing like other things; at his strongest, he is capable of gaining the potency of the essence possessed by Heavenly powers like the spirits. The authors of the "Neiye" are thus teaching humans how to usurp powers that otherwise belong to spirits and to usurp abilities that ritual specialists claim as their own. Indeed, the text is a denial of the very distinctions argued for so strongly in the *Guoyu.*

Far from internalizing a shamanistic practice, the "Neiye" is rather an attempt to bypass the work of ritual specialists. Power and knowledge, the authors argue, can be gained by cultivating oneself and becoming like a spirit: this allows one to know the patterns of the cosmos and to be able to control things. I therefore disagree strongly with the reading of the "Neiye" offered by A. C. Graham. As mentioned above, A. C. Graham compares the text with the *Guoyu* passage quoted above. But Graham accepts a shamanistic reading of the *Guoyu* passage and then reads the "Neiye" as an attempt to shift shamanic practices toward self-cultivation. I have argued here for a different reading of both texts.

The point of the *Guoyu* passage was not to discuss the shamanistic linking of man and spirit but to emphasize the importance of maintaining a distinction between the two: properly trained ritual specialists, the text argues, will keep the worlds of man and spirit separate. This separation was presented as a prerequisite for an orderly world. The "Neiye," in direct contrast, is claiming that humans potentially possess the same essential *qi* as spirits and that humans can thus, through cultivation, achieve the powers of spirits. If the point of the *Guoyu* passage was to maintain a proper ritual separation between humans and spirits, the point of the "Neiye" is to argue that humans can overcome the distinction. And the *Guoyu* passage claims that disasters can be avoided only through such a separation; the "Neiye" that disasters can be avoided by the sage who crosses such boundaries.

Like Empedocles, the authors of the "Neiye" presented a cosmological model that redefines both humanity and spirits in a way that divine powers are obtainable by humans. By claiming to be in possession of techniques that allow the practitioner to obtain the powers of spirits without resorting to the arts of divination patronized at the courts, the authors were making an argument for their own authority: instead of trying to divine the intentions of the spirits and to control them through sacrifices, they claim the ability to divinize themselves.

These ideas were promulgated by figures outside the major courts, in an attempt to displace the ritual specialists by denying the theistic underpinnings of their practices. Far from being an assumption emerging from a

shamanistic substratum, monistic cosmology in China—just as in Greece—
was a language of opposition.

Conclusion

I have sketched the emergence, in early Greece and China, of claims of self-
divinization. In both cultures, these claims emerged within religious and
political contexts dominated by theistic beliefs and practices. Indeed, an
analysis of the two traditions reveals beliefs that spirits control natural
phenomena, that spirits are potentially capricious, and that humans and
spirits therefore have a potentially agonistic relationship. The major courts
in both regions maintained ritual specialists to influence, mollify, and gain
information from the spirits through divinatory and sacrificial arts. And, I
have argued, one of the main reasons that notions of a monistic cosmology,
of continuity between human and divine realms, and of the ability of
humans to gain the powers of divinities arose in both cultures was precisely
that such practices were seen by those outside the ritual system as an
effective response to the practices dominant at the courts of the day.

In neither case should shamanism be seen as the wellspring of fifth- and
fourth-century BC thought—whether as a fifth-century diffusion (in the case
of Greece) or as a deep-seated cultural practice (in the case of China). The
fact that the shamanism hypotheses of Dodds and Chang point in different
directions should be enough in itself to give cause for thought. For Dodds,
shamanism explained the emergence of dualism in Greek thought, and for
Chang the dominance of monism in China. In any case, the hypothesis is
unconvincing for either culture.

In Greece, the emergence of claims that humans could become gods was a
response to the practices of the ritual specialists. Although Greek thought is
often—in the sinological literature, at any rate—presented as having been
based on a tragic cosmology and as assuming an inseparable barrier between
humans and gods, the notion of humans becoming divine is in fact a crucial
motif in early Greek thought, and it developed precisely in opposition to a
tragic cosmology. In Greece, every bit as much as in China, there were competing cosmologies.

For China, there were at least four different responses to ritual specialists.
The *Lunyu* supports ritual specialists but opposes an instrumental reading of

ritual actions. Sacrifices should be performed for the purposes of cultivation, not in order to influence the spirits. Heaven, the highest divinity, is granted normative status, but in a specific sense: sages, those humans who cultivate themselves properly, understand the proper aspects of Heaven and model themselves on it. The latter-born should then follow the sages' model in cultivating themselves. However, with no ability to influence Heaven or the spirits, man simply has to accept whatever Heaven sends.

The early Mohists argued that the realm of Heaven and the spirits has its own innate hierarchy, and that hierarchy is not created through human rituals. Humans should simply follow the dictates of Heaven, who created the human political order, provided natural resources for human appropriation, and, along with the spirits, actively intervenes in human affairs to reward the good and punish the bad. The Mohists denied the ordering power of human ritual vis-à-vis the divine realm. The divine realm was already properly ordered; indeed, the divine realm was ordering the human realm. Sacrifice was thus defined within a hierarchical, *do ut des* framework.

The "Chu yu, xia" chapter of the *Guoyu* supported ritual specialists as a means of maintaining a proper hierarchy between humans and spirits and thereby obtaining a harmonious world for humans. The text was written in opposition to the attempt to overturn the proper distinction that, according to the authors, should prevail between humanity and the divinities. The authors thus took a position comparable to that found in the "Sheng min" poem discussed in the previous chapter; in the "Chu yu, xia," however, this position is clearly being asserted against those who might transgress the boundaries between humans and spirits. The "Chu yu, xia" is thus comparable to Pindar's attempt to maintain a distinction between humans and spirits against contemporary critiques.

Finally, the "Neiye" claims that humans have within themselves the ability to gain powers like those held by the spirits. Although the "Neiye" accepts the hierarchy of Heaven, Earth, and man, it holds that humans can gain the ability to control things and understand fortune and misfortune without resorting to ritual arts to divine the intentions of spirits. In short, the "Neiye" is asserting precisely the sort of position that texts like the *Guoyu* are rejecting.

Thus, not only were the claims of continuity between human and divine powers not an assumption in early China, but such claims were made in explicit opposition to ritual specialists of the day. Moreover, such claims were only one of a field of responses to such specialists that developed during the fifth and fourth centuries BC.

Monistic cosmology, far from being an assumption of the times, was initially a form of critique, based on an attempt to bypass the dominant modes of orientation toward the world of spirits. The advocates of these practices began articulating new definitions of the nature of spirits, the nature of humanity, and the relationship between the two. More precisely, these articulations involved attempts to reduce the distinction between humans and spirits, and to argue that, through proper practices, one can attain divine powers.

In other words, in China just as in Greece, monism was a later development, and in both cultures monistic cosmologies were formulated in opposition to the dominant practices supported by the state. The attempt to contrast these two cultures in terms of the claim that one assumed a tragic disjunction between humans and gods that the other, due to its shamanistic substratum, never possessed is unconvincing. Such a contrast requires taking particular texts out of context and reading them as assumptions of an entire culture. Some of the texts that are often cited in such contrastive frameworks were written within debates that were in fact quite similar in Greece and China. Certainly the "Neiye" offers a cosmology completely different from, say, that found in the *Theogony*, but it is far less different from that in Empedocles. And both Empedocles and the "Neiye" contain attempts to formulate a cosmological model with self-divinization claims in order to question the modes of authority dominant at the time.

There are, of course, significant differences in the monistic cosmologies proposed in these two cultures. In terms of the examples discussed in this chapter, Empedocles was dealing with numerous ideas—such as reincarnation—not found in the early Chinese material. But the more significant difference lies in the social claims of the figures in question. In the case of Empedocles, the emphasis of self-divinization was part of an attempt to form an alternative way of life and ultimately an alternative community—a claim that certainly holds true for Plato as well. Claims of self-divinization in early Greece, in other words, tended to be made by those groups in opposition to the polis.

In early China, such appeals were similarly made by figures who opposed the political and religious structures of the time, but they were rarely used in the attempt to build alternative communities. On the contrary, many such appeals were made in the form of advice to kings—calling on rulers to follow their practices and advice as opposed to those of the divinatory and sacrificial specialists dominant at court. Indeed, it was not until the Eastern Han that such self-divinization practices (in a very different form) were appropriated and utilized by religious Daoist communities to formulate the basis of an alternative political order.

The interesting comparison between Greece and China lies in the different ways that such claims were debated, the different groups that appealed to self-divinization practices, and the historical consequences of the ways in which such debates played out. The comparative approach that I advocate, therefore, is one in which the analyst attempts first to locate similar tensions and concerns in the cultures in question and then traces the varying responses to those tensions and concerns.

Such an approach has two advantages. First of all, it allows us to avoid the tendency in comparative frameworks to deny the individual as well as the differences that exist within cultures. If we focus on discovering common tensions rather than on contrasting different assumptions, then it is possible, once one has isolated the political and cultural tensions, to study the ways in which particular individuals, in particular contexts, try to deal with the perceived problems. The comparison then revolves around the attempts of individuals in other cultures to deal with similar political and cultural concerns. Second, by making explicit the tensions with which figures were grappling, it becomes possible to analyze particular statements as reflective of an attempt at solving a given problem and not as necessarily indicative of assumptions of the larger culture as a whole. It thereby helps the analyst avoid the tendency, for example, to read a given statement concerning the correlation of humans and spirits made in a single text as necessarily reflective of the beliefs of the time.

In this chapter, for example, I suggest that at least one of the ideas often promoted in comparative studies—the contrast between the "tragic" cosmology of early Greece and the "continuous" cosmology of early China—is based on a misreading of specific claims that were made within larger political and cultural conflicts. Rather than focus on a claimed difference between Greece and China, we should instead attempt to read these claims in a contextual and historical manner—as claims being made in particular contexts—and to ask why such claims were being made and against whom they were being made. Many of the interesting comparative issues then lie in discovering the different ways that these conflicts and debates unfolded historically.

In the next three chapters, I continue to explore claims about relations between humans and divinities made in the Warring States period. I trace what happens when the claims concerning the potentially divine powers of humans become more and more common over the course of the fourth and third centuries BC, as well as the historical implications of how such claims were received.

3 Accepting the order of heaven
Humanity and Divinity in Zhuangzi and Mencius

In the previous chapter, I explored the emergence in the fourth century BC of claims that humans could gain divine powers or, more explicitly, of claims that humans had more direct access to divine powers than was accepted in contemporary ritual practices. It is within this context, I will argue, that we must understand the thought of Zhuangzi and Mencius. I begin with Zhuangzi, focusing on his critique of the ritual specialists of the day and tracing his elaboration of the potentially divine aspects of humans—notions whose vocabulary is directly reminiscent of that of the "Neiye"—and his explanation of the relationship between these divine aspects and Heaven. I then turn to Mencius and his discussions of similar concerns. Mencius, I will argue, also sees humans as capable of gaining divine powers—a position that for Mencius gives rise to the possibility of tension between humans and Heaven. Ultimately, both Zhuangzi and Mencius argue that man must accept the order of Heaven. But, for both, acceptance is a far more problematic act than has often been portrayed.

"Nothing Can Overcome Heaven": The Notion of Spirit in the *Zhuangzi*

One of Zhuangzi's anecdotes opens with a description of a ritual specialist named Ji Xian:

In Zheng there was a specialist on spirits named Ji Xian. He could tell whether a man would live or die, survive or be destroyed, have good fortune or bad, live long or die young, and he could predict the year, month, week, and day as though he were a spirit.[1]

Ji Xian's powers, indeed, were such that the apprentice Liezi felt him to be superior to Liezi's own master. The remainder of the anecdote shows that the powers of the spirit specialist are, counterintuitively, quite limited and that Liezi's master is indeed far more impressive.[2]

I trace the details of the argument below. Here, it is sufficient to note that this critique of the ritual specialists of the day is a recurrent theme in the "Inner Chapters." In another anecdote, Zhuangzi, in a discussion of how trees useful to man are inevitably cut down, concludes:

Therefore, before they have lived out their years given by Heaven, they are cut down by axes in mid-journey. This is the danger of being something that can be used. Thus, in the Jie sacrifice, oxen with white foreheads, pigs with upturned snouts, or a man with piles cannot be offered to the river. This is something that all ritual specialists and invocators know, since they are considered inauspicious. But this is why the spirit-man considers them greatly auspicious. (12/4/80–83)

Here the contrast is drawn between, on the one hand, the ritual specialist and invocator (巫 祝) and, on the other, a spirit-man (*shen ren* 神 人), a term that appears frequently in the "Inner Chapters" of the *Zhuangzi*. Unlike the ritual specialists, Zhuangzi informs us, the spirit-man does not distinguish objects in terms of what is usable or unusable for sacrifices. Why this is significant is, again, something I will put off for the moment. Here, I simply wish to point out Zhuangzi's object of criticism.

As we saw in the previous chapter, this critique of ritual specialists was a common theme in the fourth century BC. The "Neiye," for example, argued against the concept of the relationships between humans and spirits held by the ritual specialists of the day and claimed that humans had more direct access to divine powers than was accepted in contemporary ritual practices. As we shall see, Zhuangzi, while borrowing a great deal of vocabulary from these texts, also opposed many assertions of human access to divine power.

---

1. *Zhuangzi*, Harvard-Yenching Sinological Index Series, 20/7/15–16; hereinafter cited in the text. My translations of the *Zhuangzi* have been aided greatly by those of Burton Watson and A. C. Graham.

2. Portions of this section on Zhuangzi are taken from my "'Nothing Can Overcome Heaven': The Notion of Spirit in the *Zhuangzi*."

In fact, much of the power of Zhuangzi's arguments comes from the degree to which he both builds on and questions contemporary views of the implications of gaining such powers. In this section, I look in detail at Zhuangzi's vision of divinity—how he defines it, why he defines it in this way, and how it compares with other definitions at the time.[3] This entails an analysis of many of the anecdotes in which Zhuangzi discusses the notion of spirit (*shen*), as well as an examination of Zhuangzi's cosmology.

Zhuangzi reserves the term "spirit-man" for some of the figures he most admires. Liezi, a figure, as we saw above, characterized in the *Zhuangzi* as an apprentice in self-cultivation, fails to measure up:

Liezi rode the wind with great skill. He only returned after fifteen days. He brought good fortune, but not in great amounts. And although he avoided walking, he still had that on which he depended. As for he who ascends the correctness of Heaven and Earth and rides the give-and-take of the six *qi* in order to wander without limit—what does he depend on? Thus I say: the perfect man has no self, the spirit-man (*shen ren*) has no merit, the sagely man has no fame. (2/1/19–22)

Liezi's failure lies in his dependence. The perfect man, the sage, the spirit-man, in contrast, do not rely on things, do not depend on things, and wander without limit.

Zhuangzi elaborates the argument in a dialogue between Lian Shu and Jian Wu. A disbelieving Jian Wu begins by quoting the words of a certain Jie Yu:

He said, "On the distant Gushe Mountain there lives a spirit-man (*shen ren*). His flesh is like ice and snow, and he is modest as a virgin. He does not eat the five grains but sucks in the wind and drinks the dew, ascends the vaporous *qi*, rides the flying dragons, and wanders beyond the four seas. When his spirit is concentrated, he makes things free from flaws and makes the harvests ripen." (2/1/28–30)

In addition to being free and unbounded, the spirit-man can, by concentrating his spirit, influence the natural world as well. This potency, however, does not consist of an ability to prognosticate—the power possessed by the spirit specialist from Zheng. Instead, the spirit-man can cause things (*wu*) to be perfect and plentiful. By concentrating his spirit, the spirit-man can make things flourish as they naturally ought, free from harm.

Lian Shu supports Jie Yu's words and builds on his claims:

---

3. My understanding of these issues has been greatly enhanced by Yearley, "Zhuangzi's Understanding of Skillfulness and the Ultimate Spiritual State."

As for this man, nothing can harm him. Great floods can reach Heaven, but he will not drown; great droughts can melt metal and stone and scorch the earth and mountains, but he will not burn. . . . Why would he worry about things? (2/1/32–34)

Spirit-men are not dependent since they are not controlled by, nor do they bother themselves with, things (*wu*). As Zhuangzi elsewhere states: one should be "able to overcome things and not be injured by them" (能 勝 物 而 不 傷; 21/7/33).

Another anecdote makes the point even more forcefully:

Wang Ni said: "The perfect man is divine (*shen*)! If the great swamps catch fire, he cannot be burned. If the Yellow and Han Rivers freeze, he cannot be made cold. If swift lightning strikes mountains and the gale winds shake the sea, he cannot be frightened. A man such as this rides the vaporous *qi*, mounts the sun and moon, and wanders beyond the four seas. Death and life do not alter him—how much less the principles of benefit and harm!" (6/2/71–73)

Natural phenomena—things—have no effect on the perfect man. Moreover, he is not contained by any boundaries: neither the four seas nor even death itself constrain him. Whereas the spirit specialist Ji Xian possessed knowledge of life and death, Zhuangzi claims that he who is divine is unaffected by life and death. The divine do not possess special knowledge of, nor power over, things; instead, they are simply unaffected by things. The distinction will prove to be crucial.

The point comes out clearly in a quotation attributed to Confucius:

Do not listen with your ears but listen with your heart; do not listen with your heart but listen with *qi*. . . . To refrain from leaving tracks is easy; to not walk on the ground is difficult. When acting for the sake of man, it is easy to deceive; when acting for the sake of Heaven, it is difficult to deceive. You have heard of using wings to fly; you have never heard of flying without using wings. You have heard of using knowing to know; you have not heard of using not knowing to know. . . . Allow your ears and eyes to penetrate on the inside, and place the understanding of the mind on the outside. Ghosts and spirits will come to dwell, not to mention the human. This is the transformation of the myriad things. (9/4/27–33)

The general perspective of this passage is the same as those quoted above: the sage can walk without depending on the ground; he can fly without depending on wings. By cultivating *qi*, the text argues, one can reach a point at which ghosts and spirits dwell within one.

This terminology of spirits coming to dwell (*she* 舍) within the adept calls to mind the "Neiye" chapter of the *Guanzi*. Indeed, one passage in the "Neiye" is quite similar to this passage from the Zhuangzi: "There is a spirit that of itself resides within the body, at times leaving, at times entering. No one is able to contemplate it. If you lose it, there will be disorder; if you obtain it there will be order. Carefully clean its resting place, and the essence will of its own enter."[4] Through self-cultivation, one can bring spirits (*shen*) and essence (*jing*) to dwell (*she*) within oneself.[5]

Although the *Zhuangzi* and "Neiye" use similar terminology, the goals of the two texts are radically different. In the "Neiye," the goal of the superior man is to unify and control things (*shi wu* 使 物) and, indeed, to gain power over them. The adept uses self-cultivation through *qi* to make all under Heaven submit, make the myriad things reside within, and gain an understanding of auspiciousness and inauspiciousness without resorting to divination. In the *Zhuangzi*, the spirit-man allows things to be as they naturally ought.

The argument of the "Neiye," then, is that by relying on *qi*, one can attain the powers to control phenomena and foretell the future that spirit specialists can achieve only through magical arts. Whereas a spirit specialist has to resort to divination to understand auspiciousness and inauspiciousness, the adept in the "Neiye" can do so through *qi*. But the end result is the same: both the spirit specialist and the practitioner described in the "Neiye" are seeking knowledge about things (*wu*) and hence power over them. This point is underlined by the fact that the terms used in the "Neiye" to describe the adept are similar to those used by Zhuangzi to describe the spirit specialist from Zheng: both the spirit specialist from Zheng and the adept in the "Neiye" can become "like a spirit" (*ru shen* 如 神) and can understand auspiciousness and inauspiciousness.

Thus, although the *Zhuangzi* uses terminology similar to that found in the self-cultivation literature, it is in fact offering a gnosis different both from that claimed by the spirit specialists and from that described in the self-cultivation literature. Indeed, the passage quoted above concerning spirits coming to dwell closed not with a discussion of the spirit-man's control

---

4. *Guanzi*, "Neiye," 16.3a–b.

5. See also the *Guanzi*, "Xinshu, shang," 13.1b: "If one empties one's desires, the spirit will enter and dwell (虛 其 神 將 欲 入 舍). If in clearing one does not cleanse fully, the spirit will leave."

over the myriad things but with a reference to the transformation of the myriad things. But what precisely does this mean? And if the gnosis offered by Zhuangzi is superior to that in which one gains the powers of prognostication held by spirits, then what precisely does it involve?

To answer these questions, let us turn to an anecdote that explicitly discusses the proper relationship of humans to the differentiated world of things (*wu*). The anecdote concerns two figures, Zi Si and Zi You. The latter is being refashioned by the Fashioner of Things (*zaowuzhe* 造物者) and is queried by Zi Si as to his feelings about this:

"The Fashioner of Things is making me all rolled up like this." Zi Si said: "Do you detest this?" Zi You replied: "No—how could I detest it? . . . One obtains life at the proper time; one loses it when it is fitting. If you are content with the time, and if you dwell in what is fitting, then anger and joy will be unable to enter you. This is what of old was called 'untying the bonds.' If you are unable to untie them yourself, then you will be bound by things. But things cannot ultimately overcome Heaven. What is there for me to detest?" (17/6/49–53)

The concern here for those who are bound by things is in some ways similar to that seen in the "Neiye" for those who are controlled by things. But the thrust of the argument is in many ways the opposite. The goal of cultivation is not to learn to control things but to liberate oneself (literally: "untie oneself" *zi jie* 自解) by no longer focusing on things. Things, Zi You assures us, can never overcome Heaven (*sheng tian*): all things are inevitably transformed into other things. To bind oneself to any one thing (including one's human form) is to commit oneself to cycles of joy and sorrow; only by complying with this ceaseless transformative process can one avoid resentment.

Unlike the "Neiye," which is concerned with making all under Heaven submit, the *Zhuangzi* calls on one to side with ceaseless transformation itself and to accept the flux of the world. And whereas the "Neiye" teaches one to understand good and bad fortune, the *Zhuangzi* teaches one to accept these as fate:

Life and death are fated (*ming*). That they have the regularity of day and night is a matter of Heaven. As for that with which man cannot interfere, they all belong to the essential qualities of things. They only take Heaven as their father, and yet we still love them. How much more that which surpasses them! (16/6/20–22)

Heaven governs the ceaseless transformation of things, including human life, and accordingly, we should acquiesce in Heaven's decrees.

The argument continues. If one hides one's possessions (for example, a boat), they may still be stolen. But if one hides all under Heaven in all under Heaven, then nothing will ever be lost (16/6/25–26). In other words, if one's view includes everything, then nothing can disappear. The same point holds for the human form: he who embraces the transformations of everything will not mourn the loss of his form at death (16/6/26–27). Accordingly, the author concludes,

Therefore the sage will roam where things cannot be hidden and where all exist. He takes pleasure in dying young, he takes pleasure in old age. He takes pleasure in beginnings, he takes pleasure in ends. If men take him as a model, how much more that to which the myriad things are tied and that to which each single transformation depends. (16/6/27–29)[6]

In the cosmology of the *Zhuangzi*, all things (*wu*) are tied to Heaven, and all things ceaselessly transform. The goal of the adept is not to control things—an act that would be portrayed within this cosmology as an attempt to overcome Heaven. One must, rather, take pleasure in the ceaseless transformations of the universe—among them, one's own life and death. Instead of attempting to overcome Heaven, one should glory in the transformations of Heaven. The goal, as Zhuangzi puts it elsewhere, is to "use to the utmost what one receives from Heaven" (盡其所受乎天; 21/7/32).

And, within this cosmology, spirit, too, is associated not with control but rather with properly following that which one is given from Heaven:

When Gongwen Xuan saw the Commander of the Right, he was alarmed and said: "What sort of man is this? Why is he so small? Is this due to Heaven or man?" The Commander replied, "It is due to Heaven, not man. When Heaven generates something, it makes it unique. Man's appearance is something given to him. This is how I know it is from Heaven, not man. A swamp pheasant walks ten paces for one peck and a hundred paces for one drink. But it does not seek to be nourished in a cage. Its spirit, even if treated as a king, would not be happy." (8/3/12–14)

The moral of the anecdote is that we must accept what Heaven has given. The spirit of the pheasant cannot be content unless it does what the bird is supposed to do—even if what it is supposed to do seems absurd, and even if the caged pet would receive royal treatment. The contentment of the spirit, then, depends on an acceptance of the order of Heaven.

---

6. Cf. Watson, *Chuang Tzu*, p. 77; and Graham, *Chuang Tzu*, p. 86.

At first glance, this stance might appear to be at odds with many of the statements quoted earlier that stressed a lack of dependency and liberation: the spirit-men roam freely, no longer depend on things, are no longer bound by things—they are, in fact, untied. In these passages, however, the stress is on acceptance: just as the spirit of the pheasant can be content only if it does what it is supposed to do, so must we learn to accept what Heaven has ordained for us.

For Zhuangzi, however, these two seemingly contradictory stances are in fact flip sides of the same coin: the liberation that arises from no longer being dependent on things arises from accepting the order of Heaven. This is what is behind the statement quoted above that nothing can overcome Heaven (*sheng tian*). To be dependent on the world of things is, for Zhuangzi, to attempt to overcome the order of Heaven. This is as true of someone who hoards things as it is of those who try to control things through gaining supernatural powers—whether such powers are gained through the mastery of magic or through the cultivation of qi. Zhuangzi is indeed calling on the spirit to become untied, but for Zhuangzi the untied spirit follows the order of the world. He wants the pheasant to be uncaged, but, Zhuangzi would emphasize, only so that it may walk ten paces for one peck and a hundred paces for one drink. The spirit untied will naturally do what it naturally ought.

This liberated spirit's relationship to the order of Heaven is seen perhaps most forcefully in the famous Cook Ding anecdote. A certain Lord Wenhui comments on the tremendous skills of Cook Ding in butchering, and Ding responds:

I am fond of the Way, which advances beyond skill. When I first started carving oxen, I could only see the ox. After three years, I never saw the whole ox. Nowadays, I follow along using my spirit, and I don't use my eyes to look at all. My senses and knowledge have stopped, but my divine desires move along. I accord with the Heavenly patterns. (7/3/5-6)

Cook Ding's greatness lies in the fact that he uses his spirit, not his eyes. By allowing the divine desires (*shen yu*) to go where they wish, Cook Ding accords with the Heavenly patterns (*tian li* 天 理).[7] Following the Way, according with the Heavenly patterns, means, in the case of a butcher, an abil-

---

7. For an excellent discussion of this passage, see Cook, "Zhuang Zi and His Carving of the Confucian Ox."

ity to move flawlessly through the natural divisions in the carcass. It does not, in other words, involve any form of transcendence, nor does it involve control over things. Following the desires of the spirit means following the patterns of Heaven.

We are now in a position to understand Zhuangzi's criticisms of ritual specialists. In both the anecdotes quoted at the beginning of this section, ritual specialists are singled out for failing to support the proper order of Heaven. In the second anecdote, they prevent things from living out their years given by Heaven (未 終 其 天 年), in contrast to the spirit-man, who wishes them to live out their allotted span. The criterion for valuation is, in other words, one's acceptance of the order of Heaven.

A similar argument underlies the anecdote about Liezi and the spirit specialist from Zheng. In the next part of the anecdote, Liezi tells his master, Huzi, about the great spirit specialist Ji Xian. Huzi has Liezi invite the spirit specialist over to use his skills in physiognomy to predict Huzi's fate. On four separate occasions, Huzi presents a different face to him; each is meant to signify an ever deeper stage of self-cultivation. The first time, Huzi shows him the patterns of earth (地 文), which Ji Xian misinterprets as meaning that Huzi will soon die. Next Huzi shows him "Heavenly, fertilized ground" (天 壤), which Ji Xian misunderstands as signifying that Huzi is revivifying. Then Huzi presents him with the "great void that none can overcome" (太 沖 莫 勝), which Huzi achieves by "balancing the impulses of the qi" (衡 氣 機). The spirit specialist cannot interpret this at all. Finally, Huzi presents himself as "not yet having emerged from one's ancestor" (未 始 出 吾 宗), and Ji Xian flees (20/7/25–29).

The spirit specialist, whose art is concerned only with attaining knowledge over life and death, fails before Huzi. Not only is Ji Xian unable to foretell the life and death of Huzi, but Huzi, through cultivation of his qi, is able to reach a state in which he is not bound by things, in which the very concerns of life and death become irrelevant. In this state, Huzi can reach back to the point before things were differentiated—symbolized here as the void that cannot be overcome and the state prior to the generation of things. The term for "overcome" is again *sheng*—the same word used in the dictum that things cannot overcome Heaven. Once again, for Zhuangzi the cultivated figure is one who gains access to the state that nothing can overcome.

This same point may explain the differences between Zhuangzi and the authors of a text like the "Neiye." Just as Zhuangzi opposes any attempt to become mired in things, so would he oppose any attempt to transcend the human form, become like a spirit, and gain control over things: he wants man neither to lose sight of Heaven nor to transcend himself and become like Heaven. If one is a human, then one should remain a human until the time ordained by Heaven occurs and one is transformed into something else.[8] In other words, for Zhuangzi the sage does not attempt to transcend humanity: "When neither Heaven nor man overcomes the other—this is called the True Man" (HY 16/6/20). Here the call on man not to attempt to overcome Heaven (*sheng tian*) is linked with the concurrent concern that man should also not be overcome by Heaven—which is to say, man should not strive to reject his humanity and simply become Heaven.

This framework also explains the famous anecdote at the end of chapter 5.[9] Zhuangzi calls on man to do without his dispositions (*qing* 情)[10] and thus to prevent "right and wrong" (*shi fei* 是 非) from entering. The person who can do this will be able to perfect his Heaven (*cheng qi tian* 成 其 天). Zhuangzi then has Huizi question the meaning of this stance: "How can a man who does without his dispositions still be called a man?" (人 而 無 情 何 以 謂 之 人; 14/5/54–56). Zhuangzi responds in full:

Distinguishing "right" and "wrong" is what I mean by the dispositions. What I mean by being without dispositions is that man should not allow likes and dislikes to enter and thus harm himself. He should always accord with the spontaneous and not add to life. (15/5/57–58)

Huizi then asks him what adding to life means, and Zhuangzi responds:

The Way gave us appearance, and Heaven gave us form. Do not use likes and dislikes to enter and harm the self. Now, you are putting your spirit on the outside, and wearing out your essence. (15/5/58–59)

The call here is for man to accept that which is given to him and not to add to life by categorizing things according to humanly constructed distinctions of right and wrong. Those who do so harm the self and thus prevent themselves from living out their allotted lifespan. Instead, one must accord

8. For a careful discussion of the relations between Heaven and man in the Zhuangzi, see Graham's "Introduction" to idem, *Chuang-tzu*, pp. 15–19.

9. For an excellent discussion of this passage, see Graham, "The Background of the Mencian Theory of Human Nature," pp. 61–63.

10. For the reasons behind my translation of *qing* as "dispositions," see my "Ethics of Responding Properly: The Notion of *Qing* in Early Chinese Thought."

with the spontaneous, keep one's spirit internalized, and not wear out one's essence. Here again, then, the notion of spirit is connected with the proper use of that which was given by Heaven and with the spontaneous way. Gnosis is not a matter of transcending the human but of continuing and perfecting the Heaven within man—a continuation that requires us to stop imposing distinctions on things and to cultivate that with which we were endowed.

By now it should be clear that we are to read the term "spirit-man" literally. Zhuangzi is not calling on humans to become spirits; he is calling on humans to cease being dependent on artificial attempts either to reify things or to categorize them according to artificial standards. A spirit-man is not a man who becomes a spirit but a man who fully cultivates his spirit and thus wanders free from things while allowing things (including his own human form) to fulfill their natural endowment.

For Zhuangzi, then, the ultimate goals are not to be dependent on things, not to control things, not to transcend the human form. He thus opposes the attempts either to impose artificial distinctions on things or to become a spirit and gain control over things. For Zhuangzi, *both* of these would be a failure to maintain the proper relationship with Heaven. It is wrong to be bound to things, and it is wrong to attempt to transcend the human—for Zhuangzi, becoming bound and overreaching are related. Just as Zhuangzi portrays unloosening and accepting the order of things as the same things, so he sees possessiveness and hubris as linked as well.

We often associate Zhuangzi with liberation, with a denial of boundaries, with a call for humanity to become uncaged. And, indeed, all these images do appear regularly in the text. Zhuangzi is clearly concerned that most humans spend their lives dependent on things, foolishly clinging to life and possessions. But, as we have seen, this concern with not being dependent on or bound by things, with becoming untied, with wandering beyond any boundary, is intimately and directly tied to a cosmological claim: the liberated spirit accords with Heavenly patterns, helps things be as they naturally ought to be, and allows things to fulfill their Heaven-given allotment. As Zhuangzi repeatedly argues, we cannot overcome Heaven, we must accept fate, and we must accord with the order of Heaven.

Through this argument, Zhuangzi is able both to call on man to cultivate himself and to strive to perfect his spirit and the Heaven within him and to undercut many of the claims being made at the time concerning the ability of man to gain the powers of spirits—whether through magic or cultivation of the qi. Zhuangzi is arguing against any attempt to gain knowledge or control over the universe; instead he calls on the spirit-man to take pleasure in the patterns of Heaven.

Contrary to the general perception, then, Zhuangzi is strongly committed to the notion that there are proper patterns in the natural world that a cultivated person inherently follows. This is a point, I think, that has been missed by those who portray Zhuangzi as a relativist. For example, Robert Eno has argued that Zhuangzi is calling on man to engage in skill-based activities that lead to a state of spiritual spontaneity. And, according to this reading, any skill-based activity would work: "Dao-practices can be adapted to any end: the dao of butchering people might provide much the same spiritual spontaneity as the dao of butchering oxen—as many a samurai might testify."[11] I would argue, on the contrary, that Zhuangzi is asserting that the cultivated human spirit acts in certain ways rather than others. He does so not by asserting that particular activities are ethically better than others but by making a cosmological claim: the truly human person will inherently behave in certain ways rather than in other ways. Just as the pheasant, if it is allowed to do as Heaven means it to do, will walk ten paces for one peck and a hundred paces for one drink, so will a human, if he uses his endowment properly, act in conformity with the Heavenly patterns as well. In this sense, Zhuangzi is not a relativist; he is, on the contrary, a cosmologist with a strong commitment to a certain view of the proper place of humanity in the universe.[12]

Zhuangzi's calls for liberation can thus be read as involving a careful redefinition of notions current at the time—spirit, Heaven, and man—to argue for a particular type of gnosis—a gnosis involving a breaking of boundaries and yet, at the same time, an acceptance of the patterns of Heaven. For Zhuangzi, liberation involves a proper and spontaneous acceptance of the order of the world. Anything else is an attempt to overcome Heaven—a project doomed to failure.

---

11. Eno, "Cook Ding's Dao and the Limits of Philosophy," p. 142. For another argument that Zhuangzi is a relativist, see Hansen, "A Tao of Tao in Chuang-tzu."

12. My conclusions are thus largely in line with those of Philip J. Ivanhoe, even though our respective conclusions were achieved through different routes; see his "Was Zhuangzi a Relativist?"

The Resignation of the Sage to the Order of Heaven: The Cosmology of the *Mencius*

Like Zhuangzi, Mencius calls on humans to accept the order of Heaven.[13] Indeed, as he bluntly states: "He who accords with Heaven is preserved; he who opposes Heaven is destroyed" (4A/7). Submission to the order of Heaven is for Mencius a crucial element along the path to sagehood. Indeed, Mencius at times argues that cultivating oneself is precisely the means by which one fulfills one's duty to Heaven. Preserving and nourishing the mind and nature endowed on us by Heaven are how one serves Heaven, and knowing one's nature is how one knows Heaven. And, as with Zhuangzi, a crucial part of this acceptance of the order of Heaven is that one accepts whatever Heaven ordains, without concern for living long or dying young:

Mencius said: "He who has fully used his mind knows his nature. If he knows his nature, he knows Heaven. Preserving his mind and nourishing his nature are the ways that he serves Heaven. Dying young and living long are not two distinct things. He cultivates himself so as to await what is to come. This is the means by which he establishes his destiny (*ming*)." (7A/1)

One establishes one's destiny by cultivating oneself and accepting whatever Heaven mandates.

Like Zhuangzi, Mencius accepts much of the vocabulary of the day for the potentially divine powers of humans. Indeed, several passages from the Mencius are reminiscent of the "Neiye." In describing his flood-like *qi*, for example, Mencius states: "If one cultivates it with straightness and does not harm it, it will fill the space between Heaven and Earth" (2a/2). Elsewhere, he argues that such a cultivation allows one to encompass all things: "The myriad things are complete in me" (7A/4). Because of these great powers, he who cultivates himself can transform the people and unite Heaven and Earth:

Mencius said, "If there is a hegemon, the people are happy. If there is a king, the people are contented. They do not become resentful if people are put to death, nor do they become lazy[14] if they gain profits. The people are daily moved toward the good, but they do not know what makes it so. Now, where a gentleman passes, he

---

13. Portions of this section are taken from my "Following the Commands of Heaven: The Notion of Ming in Early China."

14. Reading 慵 for 庸.

transforms; where he resides, he is divine (*shen*). Above and below, Heaven and Earth flow together. How can it be said that he is but a small addition?" (7A/13)

Indeed, Mencius even goes so far as to define reaching a state of divinity (*shen*) as being above sagehood itself:

Haosheng Buhai asked, "What kind of a person is Yuezhengzi?" Mencius said, "A good man, a trustworthy man." "What do you mean by 'good' and 'trustworthy'?" Mencius responded, "If one can desire it, one can be called 'good.' If one has it within oneself, one can be called 'trustworthy.' If one is filled with it and embodies it, one can be called 'beautiful.' If one is filled with it, embodies it and also has radiant brilliance, one can be called 'great.' If one is great and can transform it, one can be called 'sage.' If one is a sage but cannot be understood, one can be called 'spirit.' Yuezhengzi is in the first two of these, but is less than the last four." (7B/25)

Despite the similarities with texts like the "Neiye," the ultimate goals are quite different. The "Neiye" taught how to gain the powers of spirits—powers to understand fortune and misfortune and powers to control things—but Mencius is concerned with a different set of issues. Like Zhuangzi, he wants to define sagehood as meaning an acceptance of the order of Heaven.

Like Zhuangzi, then, Mencius is tying together two seemingly disparate bodies of thought: an emphasis on accepting the order of Heaven and support for the divine powers of humans. With Zhuangzi, these two are joined by claiming that the ultimate spirit will simply and spontaneously enact what Heaven ordained: the spirit spontaneously follows—and aids—the movement of Heaven. Thus, cultivating one's spirit and accepting the order of Heaven are for Zhuangzi one and the same thing. For Mencius, however, there is a potential tension here. In this respect, Mencius is building on Confucius.

Like Confucius, Mencius holds that Heaven is the source of the moral patterns that humans should follow. Because of his interest in placing divine powers within humans, however, Mencius argues that these patterns are obtainable not because the ancient sages modeled themselves on Heaven but because Heaven has rooted them in man himself. Heaven has granted humans a nature that, if cultivated properly, allows them to become fully moral: "The nature of the superior man is humaneness, propriety, ritual, and knowledge. They are rooted in his mind" (7A/21). Heaven has given all humans the potential for sagehood. But such a commitment means that the tension implicit in the *Lunyu* (discussed in the previous chapter) becomes all the more significant. If all humans have within themselves the potential to become a sage and if Heaven, not man, decides whether order will prevail, then the potential conflict between Heaven and man deepens.

Humans have within themselves both the potential to become fully moral and the potential to become spirits and bring order to the world. But, as with Confucius, the question of whether order will in fact prevail is decided by Heaven, not man. And man must accept what Heaven ordains. To quote the full passage in which the statement that opens this section appears:

Mencius said, "If all under Heaven has the way, those of small virtue serve those of great virtue, and the less worthy serve the greatly worthy. If all under Heaven lacks the Way, the small serve the big, and the weak serve the strong. These two are due to Heaven. He who accords with Heaven is preserved; he who opposes Heaven is destroyed." (4A/7)

Unlike Zhuangzi, Mencius does make moral judgments on historical periods, and he makes it quite clear that according with Heaven means, at times, accepting a state of affairs that runs counter to the normative way—a way that Heaven itself has given man the potential to bring about.

But what happens in such an event? Must humans simply resign themselves to a lack of order if such are the wishes of Heaven? This is a difficult question for Mencius to answer. The ultimate answer, of course, is that one must indeed accept the order that Heaven ordains. But for Mencius this must not imply simple resignation. As he argues:

Mencius said, "Everything is mandated (ming). One accords with what is correct. Therefore, one who understands what is mandated does not stand beneath a falling wall. One who dies after fulfilling his way has corrected his destiny (ming). Dying in fetters is not a correct destiny." (7A/2)

Everything is mandated, but this should not lead to shirking: the concern should, rather, be to correct one's destiny by trying to fulfill one's way.

But this stance opens several questions. Zhuangzi teaches that liberation involves an acceptance of the order of Heaven. Mencius also argues that one must accept the order of Heaven, but for him this is not a matter of liberation. Although sages must submit to what Heaven ordains, the path to sagehood does not rest on submission. Indeed, Mencius' formulations seem to imply that whatever is to come is not necessarily right—but one must accept it.

This potential conflict—unthinkable from the point of view of Zhuangzi—plays out forcefully in numerous places in Mencius' work. One obvious problem, given Mencius' political theology, is the issue of hereditary monarchy. If everyone has the potential to become a sage, then why is it not the case that, at any given time, the most cultivated person in the realm is the king? Indeed, for Mencius, most of the greatest sages since the introduction of hereditary monarchy have *not* been kings: Yi Yin, the Duke of Zhou, Confucius, and, perhaps, Mencius himself. Is hereditary monarchy therefore in opposition to the order of Heaven?

On the contrary. Mencius is committed to claiming that Heaven itself established the custom:

Wan Zhang asked: "Some people say that, when it came to the time of Yu, power (*de*) declined. He did not give power to the worthy but instead gave it to his son. Is this correct?" Mencius said, "No. It is not so. If Heaven had given it to a worthy, then it would have been given to a worthy. Since Heaven gave it to the son, it was given to the son." (5A/6)

Mencius recounts the history of the succession of Yao, Shun, and Yu and points out that, in each case, the worthy man worked with the ruler for several years, and the people grew to trust him. But this was not true of Yu's minister Yi, whom the people did not know well. Moreover, Qi, the son of Yu, was worthy, whereas the sons of Yao and Shun were not. All of this, according to Mencius, was mandated from Heaven and thus was not due to Yu:

All this was due to Heaven. It is not something that man could have done. If no one does it and yet it is done, then it is Heaven. If no one brings something about (*zhi* 致) and yet it is brought about, it is mandated (*ming*). (5A/6)

According to Mencius, thereafter hereditary monarchy became the norm: the kingship was always handed down to the son. Only if a ruler were truly horrible—as with Jie and Zhou—was the transmission from father to son interrupted. Otherwise, Heaven would not stop the succession. For Mencius, this explains why Yi, Yi Yin, and the Duke of Zhou could never be kings: their rulers were acceptable—even if not as sagely as Yi, Yi Yin, and the Duke of Zhou themselves.

But Mencius' argument begs the question. This may explain why Yu should not be criticized, but it hardly answers the larger point implied in

Wan Zhang's query: even if Qi was a better prospective ruler than Yi, it hardly follows that hereditary monarchy is in general a good thing. And, since Heaven chose the rulers, Heaven is responsible for the institution. Why, if Yi, Yi Yin, and the Duke of Zhou were more worthy, did they not become rulers? Or, to put the question more forcefully, why did Heaven ordain hereditary monarchy to be the norm? No answer to this is given. Of note here is that Mencius makes no attempt to claim that hereditary monarchy is a moral institution or even that Heaven had good practical reasons to maintain it. For Mencius, all we can say is simply that Heaven has mandated it, and we must therefore accept it.

But what happens when the mandates of Heaven clearly conflict with the ethical stance of the sage? The most forceful and poignant example of this occurs near the end of Mencius' career. Mencius spent several years traveling from state to state, trying to convince one of the rulers to listen to his advice. He received a position at the court of Qi, and, if the current text is to be believed, had audiences with the king of Qi on several occasions. As several commentators have noted, Mencius clearly perceived himself to be the Yi Yin of his era: just as Yi Yin had counseled Tang on how to bring order to the world and establish the Shang dynasty, so would Mencius advise the ruler of Qi how to bring order to the world and start a new dynasty.[15] However, the king did not follow Mencius' advice. Mencius did not become the next Yi Yin, and the world was not ordered. His life project in failure, Mencius left the state of Qi:

When Mencius left Qi, Chong Yu asked him on the way, "Master, you seem to look displeased. A few days ago I heard you say that 'a gentleman does not resent Heaven nor bear a grudge against men.'" Mencius responded, "That was one time; this is another time. Every five hundred years, it must be the case that a king will arise. In the interval there must arise one from which an age takes its name. From the Zhou until now, it has been more than seven hundred years. The mark has passed, and the time, if one examines it, is proper. Yet Heaven does not yet wish to bring order to all under Heaven. If Heaven wished to bring order to all under Heaven, who in the present generation is there other than me? How could I be displeased?" (2B/13)[16]

---

15. See, e.g., Robert Eno's discussion in *The Confucian Creation of Heaven*, p. 261n60. The relevant passages on Yi Yin are *Mengzi* 5A/7 and 5B/1.

16. My translation of this passage is heavily indebted to that of D. C. Lau, *Mencius*, p. 94. My understanding of the meaning of the passage has been aided tremendously by the analysis

The statement to which Chong Yu refers was uttered by Confucius. Indeed, the entire conversation between Chong Yu and Mencius is comparable to, and probably constructed with reference to, the passage from the *Lunyu* in which this quotation occurs:

The master said, "No one understands me."
Zigong asked, "What does it mean to say no one understands you?"
The master replied, "I do not resent Heaven nor bear a grudge against man. I study here and reach to what is above. Only Heaven understands me." (14/35)

In general terms, the passage from the *Mencius* reveals a similar view, but Mencius is clearly less accepting of the situation.[17]

Mencius argues strongly for a cyclical order, in which a king arises every five hundred years and in the interval there is a sage. This is a normative pattern in human history, and the moment for a sage to emerge has arrived. Mencius clearly feels that he is that sage. So why has Mencius' project ended in failure? The only possible reason is that Heaven does not wish for there to be order. There is no moral or practical reason: in preventing order from arising, Heaven is acting contrary to the normative pattern of human history and is blocking the path of a true sage. This is a much stronger claim than anything in the *Lunyu*. Confucius believed that Heaven was responsible for the state of the way and that Heaven was destroying him by making Yan Hui die young. But Confucius never implied that such acts stood in opposition to a normative order. In contrast, Mencius distinguishes between what is right and what Heaven actually does. Although the two should always accord, there are times, and Mencius clearly feels himself to be living in such a time, when they do not.

For Mencius, unlike Zhuangzi, there is a potential tension between the claims of Heaven and those of the sage. And yet, what can one do? For Mencius the conclusion is clear: if there is a disjunction between the normative patterns and the decisions of Heaven, one must side with Heaven. In Mencius' political theology, one must accept what Heaven ordains and try to do so without resentment.

---

in Lee Yearley's "Toward a Typology of Religious Thought." I discuss Yearley's overall argument concerning Mencius below.

17. I am reading the passage as revealing a level of anger on the part of Mencius. For somewhat different views of the passage, see Bloom, "Practicality and Spirituality in the Mencius"; and Ivanhoe, "A Question of Faith."

The commands of Heaven, therefore, do not necessarily agree with the normative order that Heaven itself has given man the potential to realize. Sages have the potential to bring order to the world, but Heaven can, for no apparent reason, thwart such plans—even though it was Heaven that gave humans this potential in the first place. This is not to say that Heaven is un-ethical, but according to both Confucius and Mencius, ethical action on the part of humans is not enough. It is not the case that the most ethical person will necessarily become a king or even the sage become a minister. The man-dates of Heaven are simply beyond our understanding.

Although Confucianism is often portrayed as fundamentally optimistic, Mencius' argument is based on a very different cosmology. Calling it "tragic" may be going too far, but Mencius clearly conceives a potential for tension between Heaven and man and advises us to side with Heaven. Indeed, we must side with Heaven and do so without resentment, even if what Heaven has decreed clearly contradicts the proper patterns.[18]

I therefore strongly agree with Lee Yearley, who focuses attention on what he calls "irresolvable but revelatory and productive tensions." With Mencius, Yearley finds "at one pole the notion of a human potential whose realization depends on each individual's effort; at the other, the notion of a sovereign power beyond man that creates the potential but also seems, in some way, to control and even frustrate its completion in most or all men."[19] Indeed, we can probably take Yearley's insight a step further. For Mencius, it is not just that Heaven frustrates the fulfillment of the potential that Heaven itself gives; at times, Heaven seems to work actively to prevent it.

The "Naturalism" of Zhuangzi and Mencius

In terms of the links between Heaven and humanity, Zhuangzi is often por-trayed as a purely naturalistic thinker, and Mencius is usually associated with the view that the linkage between them is moral. In both cases, however, there are strongly felt tensions between the divine aspects of humans and the order of Heaven. This tension clearly contradicts the standard reading of these two thinkers. Mencius and Zhuangzi are commonly cited as the prototypical "naturalistic" thinkers of early China. Indeed, Mencius and

---

18. For different readings of these passages on *ming*, see Slingerland, "The Conception of *Ming* in Early Confucian Thought"; and Ning, "The Concept of Fate in Mencius."

19. Lee H. Yearley, "Toward a Typology of Religious Thought," p. 433.

Zhuangzi are often presented as twin sides of naturalism: Mencius of the view that nature is moral and Zhuangzi of the view that it is amoral. For those scholars like Frederick Mote who wish to argue that early Chinese thinkers assumed a monistic cosmos, Mencius and Zhuangzi represent proof of that cosmology.[20]

Those who wish, to the contrary, to emphasize a transcendental break-through argue that Zhuangzi's and Mencius' emphasis on nature provides them a basis to critique their world. For example, Benjamin Schwartz focuses on Zhuangzi's "affirmation of nature" and his use of that to critique the "analytical discriminating consciousness of man." Such a critique marks Zhuangzi (along with Laozi) as "the most radical expression of transcendence in China."[21] Mencius, according to Schwartz, also roots values in Heaven, but with the opposite implication: "If we contrast Mencius with his contemporary, Zhuangzi, we find here almost a defiant Confucian reply to Zhuangzi's view that the distinctly human consciousness . . . is precisely what alienates him from the *dao*." Instead, Schwartz argues, Mencius asserts that "moral consciousness" is the "transcendental instrument of human salvation that unites man to Heaven." If humans properly use the "transcendental 'heart within the heart'" that Heaven has given them, they "are able to understand the world in which they live, to feel at one with it and at one with Heaven."[22] For Schwartz, then, both Zhuangzi and Mencius take naturalistic positions that emphasize the unity of man and Heaven, and in both cases this emphasis allows for a transcendental position. The only difference between them, for Schwartz, lies in the fact that Zhuangzi sees human moral consciousness as injuring man's harmony with Heaven and Mencius sees human moral consciousness as the basis for building that harmony.

Heiner Roetz, typically, takes this transcendental position one step further and sees Mencius and Zhuangzi as marking a new point in the progressive development of Chinese philosophy—a development consisting of a break from an earlier magical worldview and the positing of norms separate

---

20. Mote, for example, sees Mencius and Zhuangzi as representing opposite poles of the man-nature continuum: Zhuangzi criticizes man and valorizes nature, and Mencius valorizes man and reads nature in terms of man. Thus, Mote characterizes Zhuangzi as projecting the "ideals of living simply in harmony with nature" and Mencius as seeing the "well-being of human society as the measure of Nature's proper functioning" (*Intellectual Foundations of China*, pp. 74, 51).

21. Schwartz, "Transcendence in Ancient China," p. 66.

22. Schwartz, *The World of Thought in Ancient China*, p. 277.

from conventions. Thus, he sees Zhuangzi's "naturalism" as providing a "critique of the given order." But, Roetz claims, since Zhuangzi rejects convention altogether, his naturalism is ultimately "a postconventional recourse to the preconventional past. . . . In the final analysis, it constitutes a regressive evasion of development."[23] Roetz's reading of Zhuangzi is essentially the same as Mote's and Schwartz's; the difference lies in the explicitly evolutionary framework Roetz employs to interpret Zhuangzi's naturalism.

With Mencius, however, Roetz provides an argument that deserves closer scrutiny. Most previous scholars, with the exception of Lee Yearley, have read Mencius as assuming a linkage between humanity and nature. Roetz, consistent with his attempt to find in early China what Weber claimed existed only in the West, sees Mencius' appeals to Heaven as an attempt to define norms separate from the world of convention:

> What is the role, then, within this ethics of conspicuously nonreligious self-cultivation, of the no less striking appeals to Heaven? That Mengzi clings to Heaven is no 'archaism,' as Hsiao Kung-chuan has called it. The reason is because in doing so he can bring his ethics into a marked contrast with the realities of his time and especially with politics. Heaven becomes an embodiment of moral norms, on which it confers its distance from the world.[24]

In short, Roetz finds in Mencius the very tension with the world that Weber thought was lacking in Confucianism:

> Through the concept of Heaven, Mengzi can draw an ontological separation between the realm of the moral norms, among which humaneness, as the 'most honored of the ranks of Heaven,' holds the highest position, and the realm of the mundane authorities. What he formulates is no less than a counterpart of the occidental teaching of the 'two kingdoms.' It was this teaching which essentially contributed to the very 'tension with the world' that Weber contrasted with the alleged Confucian readiness for adaptation.[25]

If for Mote Mencius represents an attempt to read humanity into nature, and if Schwartz reads Mencius as positing a transcendental consciousness that allows for a unity of man, society, and nature, Roetz reads Mencius as conceiving, for the first time in Chinese history, a tension with the world.

---

23. Roetz, *Confucian Ethics of the Axial Age*, pp. 249, 251, 257.
24. Ibid., p. 196.
25. Ibid.

But Roetz is again too dependent on the Weberian paradigm. There is indeed a strong tension in Mencius, but its object is very different from the one Roetz wants to read into the tradition. Roetz, in a sense, has it backwards: the tension in Mencius is not with the world but with Heaven. Or, more particularly, it is between Heaven and the divine potentials of humans. Mencius is not arguing for a Weberian type of transcendence in which Heaven is the source of ideals that conflict with the mundane happenings of this world. The tension runs the other way: it is Heaven that is potentially in conflict with the proper order of man (even if Heaven is the ultimate source of that potential for order within man).

Although I disagree with Roetz's Weberian framework in general and his reading of Mencius in particular, his stress on tension rather than harmony in his reading of Mencius is of interest. I would suggest that perhaps one reason "transcendence" has become so influential a term in early China studies (beyond the attempt to argue that early Chinese thought meets one of Weber's standards of rationality) is precisely because it allows scholars, while working within a generally Weberian framework, to discuss tensions that clearly are there in the texts. For those like Schwartz who wish to argue that early Chinese thinkers did assume a harmonious cosmos, the notion of transcendence is a way of dealing with the tensions they find in early Chinese thought—tensions that a purely Weberian emphasis on harmony would tend to deny. In other words, the notion of transcendence allows scholars to avoid the dangers of reductionism that would result from reading early Chinese thinkers as assuming a harmonious cosmos. I suspect, for example, that Schwartz's somewhat ungainly notion of transcendence within immanence (discussed in the Introduction) was intended to do precisely this. And, for those scholars like Roetz who wish to reject the notion of an immanentist cosmology (at least for certain Warring States thinkers), the notion of transcendence allows them to argue, in essence, that the "tension with the world" found by Weber in Protestantism existed in early China as well.

But, if we turn away from the Weberian framework and its emphasis on harmony, we can see these tensions in a different and, I think, more powerful way. I have argued in this chapter that both Zhuangzi and Mencius should be read in the context of the developing claims concerning the potentially divine capacities of humans and the potential conflicts between such claims and notions of Heaven.

Mencius, like many thinkers of the fourth century BC, made strong claims that divine powers resided in humans, and for Mencius this meant that humans have the potential to bring order to the world. Heaven, in contrast, while being the source of those divine powers in humans, can potentially prevent the order that it has given humans the power to create. The central tension for Mencius, then, is that although Heaven is the ultimate source of moral patterns, it can and does arbitrarily act in opposition to those patterns. And yet we must accept what Heaven commands.

Zhuangzi also felt this tension, but he resolved it in a very different way: Zhuangzi denied that Heaven is the source of moral norms and thus denied that Heaven had to follow such norms. For Zhuangzi, moral norms are human inventions, with no basis whatsoever in Heaven. If Mencius saw such moral judgments as deriving from Heaven, Zhuangzi saw them as entirely due to man. Accordingly, for Mencius, the agon of Heaven and man arises because man makes moral judgments on the world. For Zhuangzi, man should accept whatever Heaven decrees; once men stop using moral norms to criticize Heaven, there will be no agon.

Although both Mencius and Zhuangzi could be characterized as "naturalistic," insofar as they both root values in Heaven, such a characterization misses several crucial points. Both Mencius and Zhuangzi were interested primarily in the divine potentials of humans, and part of what is so interesting about their differences lies in the ways they attempted to link such potentially divine powers of humans with a support for Heaven. In neither was there an assumption of continuity. On the contrary, both asserted at least partial continuity between the human and the divine realms, and for both this creates a potential problem with Heaven. Although both responded to this problem by supporting Heaven, the effort the argument required was tremendous.

4 *Descendants of the one*
Correlative Cosmology in the Late Warring States

Let us return to the origin of the cosmos:

Heaven and Earth had a beginning. Heaven was subtle so as to complete, and Earth blocked so as to give form. Heaven and Earth combining and harmonizing is the great alignment (*jing*) of generation (*sheng*).[1]

In the cosmogony sketched in the "Jingshen" chapter of the *Huainanzi*—the passage with which I opened this book—spirits aligned (*jing*) the cosmos.[2] This passage from the "Youshi" chapter of the *Lüshi chunqiu*, a text that dates to around 240 BC, posits neither spirits nor Heaven as active agents in the formation of the cosmos. Instead, Heaven and Earth simply emerge spontaneously, and their mating, which gives birth to the myriad things, is the alignment of generation itself.

Cosmological arguments like these began appearing at about the same time as the self-divinization movements described in Chapter 2. They ranged from five-phase speculation to monthly ordinances to attempts to place culture within cosmogonic schemata. Like the self-divinization claims, such cosmological frameworks were used to argue that a sage can, through variously defined processes of self-cultivation, achieve the power to understand the workings of the cosmos and thereby act correctly and gain control over them.

---

1. *Lüshi chunqiu*, "Youshi," 13.1a.
2. See Chapter 7, pp. 270–84, for a detailed discussion of this text.

The nature of early Chinese correlative thought has been a topic of lengthy discussion in both anthropological and sinological studies. Marcel Mauss and Emile Durkheim first proposed the famous thesis that early Chinese correlative thinking was based on "primitive classification" systems.[3] According to them, such systems in China were "a highly typical case in which collective thought has worked in a reflective and learned way on themes that are clearly primitive."[4] This thesis clearly fits the recurrent arguments of sinologists that China's significance lies in the degree to which it maintained (for better or worse, depending on the criteria of the scholar in question) links to a primitive, primordial period of human history.

Although Marcel Granet did not develop Mauss's and Durkheim's comparative claims, their sociological approach exercised an important influence on Granet's analysis in *La pensée chinoise*,[5] itself the single most influential work ever published on early Chinese cosmology. Largely because of Granet's work, Chinese correlative thought has come to play an important role in the anthropological study of cosmology. Claude Lévi-Strauss's *The Savage Mind*, a landmark study of primitive classification systems that superseded Mauss's and Durkheim's earlier work on the subject, for example, relies heavily on Granet.

In this chapter, I attempt to re-examine the origins and nature of correlative thinking in early China. I begin by surveying the secondary literature on the topic, in particular anthropological studies of sacrifice and cosmology and the ways that sinologists have both contributed to and worked from this literature. I then trace the rise of correlative thought in the late Warring States period and argue for a somewhat different approach to using the insights of anthropological studies of correlative systems.

The One and the Many: Secondary Scholarship on Early Chinese Cosmology

The discussion of early Chinese cosmology has both influenced and been influenced by anthropological analyses. Indeed, much of the scholarship on this issue has developed as scholars positioned themselves in different ways in relation to the work of Granet or Lévi-Strauss. I, too, will argue that an

---

3. Durkheim and Mauss, *Primitive Classification*, pp. 67–80.
4. Ibid., p. 73.
5. Granet acknowledges the debt in *La pensée chinoise*, pp. 484–85n22.

alternative reading of Granet and Lévi-Strauss might lead to a more successful approach to the problem of Chinese correlative thought.

As discussed in the Introduction, A. C. Graham criticizes Granet for reading Warring States and Han correlative models as characteristic of Chinese thought in general and argues instead that correlative thought is universal and exists in all forms of thinking save one: "What Granet saw as the difference between Chinese and Western thought may nowadays be seen as a transcultural difference between proto-science and modern science."[6] In making this argument, Graham presents himself as rejecting Granet and favoring Lévi-Strauss: "In exploring proto-scientific thinking it has been usual to start from what we find peculiar in pre-modern views of nature; here we have followed the example of Lévi-Strauss (although not the detail of his methods) in starting from the opposite direction, from structures common to pre-modern and modern thinking."[7] For Graham, late Warring States and Han cosmological systems should be understood as a particular, highly formalistic, example of an essentially human way of thinking.

David Hall and Roger Ames position themselves on the opposite side of each of these claims. They strongly defend Granet's argument that correlative thinking was a defining feature of Chinese thought in general, and they reject Graham's claim that Granet's arguments apply only to texts from the late Warring States and after. Hall and Ames trace Graham's "error" to Lévi-Strauss: Lévi-Strauss, they claim, misread Marcel Granet's arguments about correlative thinking, and Graham unfortunately based his reading on Lévi-Strauss.

[Graham] appeals explicitly to the theory of correlativity developed by Claude Lévi-Strauss. Lévi-Strauss had formalized the sense of correlativity contained in Marcel Granet's *La pensée chinoise* by recourse to the work of Roman Jakobson. . . . Lévi-Strauss applies Jakobson's notions of similarity and contiguity relations to Marcel Granet's speculations concerning the "Chinese mind," surmising that what Granet had called correlative thinking could be formalized by recourse to the metaphor/metonym distinction. . . . With this insight, so Lévi-Strauss believed, the notion of correlativity gained clarity and rigor. Applying this insight to the Chinese employment of analogical thinking, it would be possible, for example, to understand

6. Graham, *Disputers of the Tao*, p. 320.
7. Graham, *Yin-Yang and the Nature of Correlative Thinking*, p. 39.

the vast systems of classification associated with *yin-yang* cosmologies or the *Book of Changes* by appeal to these tropic devices.[8]

But Lévi-Strauss's attempt to analyze correlative thought more rigorously made it less applicable to China:

We are inclined to believe that the attempt to formalize the analogical mode of thinking by appeal to Jakobson's speculations has in fact overly rationalized analogical, first problematic thinking and made it, while more precise and rigorous as a method, less applicable to the Chinese context. The burden of the following discussion will be to reinstitute the former, more naive understanding of analogical thought.[9]

Indeed, the very distinction of metaphoric and metonymic relations is for Hall and Ames an example of the "rational intellect" and is based on "rational, causal assumptions."[10]

The problem with Graham, Hall and Ames argue, is that, by following the more formalistic reading of Lévi-Strauss, he was led to believe that correlative thought arose late in Chinese history. A return to Granet will correct this error.

Graham's judgment that correlative thought is to be consigned to periods beyond the classical is based upon his acceptance of the metaphoric/metonymic distinction as an essential formalizing element in all correlative operations. We believe that this acceptance of Lévi-Strauss's Jakobsonian interpretation of Granet's initial insight leads him astray, finally causing him to fail to appreciate the extent to which first problematic assumptions shape the entire sweep of the Chinese cultural sensibility.[11]

For Hall and Ames, correlative thought defines all of early China:

We only insist that the more formal, rationalized interpretation not be treated as exhausting the meaning of this activity. . . . Our argument will be that we shall be able to employ the term "correlative thinking" as a synonym for the analogical procedures associated with first problematic thought without losing any of the relevant meanings that have come to be associated with the term when applied to the interpretation of Chinese culture.[12]

---

8. Hall and Ames, *Anticipating China*, pp. 126–27.
9. Ibid., pp. 127–28.
10. Ibid., p. 296*n*44.
11. Ibid., p. 133.
12. Ibid.

Lévi-Strauss's attempt to generalize correlative thinking ended up limiting the meaning of the concept—and led Graham to restrict its applicability to only late Warring States and Han texts.

As should be clear from my discussion in Chapters 1 and 2, I side with Graham on this particular point: correlative cosmology is a late development in Chinese history. The problem is then to explain how and why it emerged. One recent attempt to do so is that of John Henderson. Henderson's *Development and Decline of Chinese Cosmology* is a brilliant narrative of the history of correlative thought in China. Although the question of the emergence of such thinking occupies only a small portion of this narrative, Henderson's comments are nonetheless provocative: "My own view on this question is that correlative systems in China were devised in a fully historical epoch, particularly the third and second centuries B.C., for largely historical reasons." Among the possible scenarios adduced by Henderson for the rise of correlative cosmologies is that particular philosophers created an "epistemological space (as Michel Foucault might say) in which correlative thought could develop." An example would be Laozi's calling on man to "pattern himself after heaven and earth." As a consequence, "later and lesser minds could interpret the classical Taoist calls for the harmonization of man and nature in a literalist fashion, devising anatomical, numerological, and psychological correspondences."[13] In this view, correlative cosmology is a literal reading by lesser minds of a metaphor. The problem with this explanation is that it unnecessarily denigrates correlativity and fails to explain why greater minds of a later period found correlativity convincing.

Another explanation offered by Henderson is institutional. In the Qin and early Han, "imperial ideologists" invoked correlative thought as a means of justifying imperial governance:

Through the invocation of the "mutual conquest" sequence of the five phases, by which earth (Han) conquers water (Qin), the Han was able to justify its overthrow of Qin rule and its assumption of power. Once the dynasty was established, imperial ideologists also found it useful to invoke the hierarchical relation of yang to yin and heaven to earth as a way of legitimating various authoritarian political and social relations.[14]

---

13. Henderson, *The Development and Decline of Chinese Cosmology*, pp. 30, 35.
14. Ibid., p. 36.

Critics of imperial rule then appropriated correlative thought "as checks on Han imperial despotism."[15] But this explanation also has problems. If correlativity arose as a means of imperial legitimation, why did the intended audience find it convincing? As with any argument in terms of legitimation, one needs to explain why the ideology was effective.

Yet another reason given by Henderson was that correlative thinking was utilized by Han thinkers to "weav[e] diverse strands of the classical literary legacy into a consistent whole."[16] But correlativity emerged before the Han and not in texts that could plausibly be seen as attempts to unify the literary tradition. Although I have questioned Henderson's explanations (and I emphasize again that these suggestions occupy only a small portion of an exceptionally cogent narrative), his search for historical explanations of why cosmology arose is a model for my own work.

Benjamin Schwartz approaches correlativity in a different way. He sees it as linked to the "absence [in early China] of clearly drawn boundaries between the divine and human," and he tries to connect this with ancestor worship:

I am tempted to speculate that this absence of boundary affects not only the realm of religion narrowly defined, but the entire realm of ontological thinking. Does the fact that in later Chinese high-cultural accounts of the origins of mankind or of the cosmos, the dominant metaphor is that of procreation or "giving birth," rather than that of fashioning or creating, have anything to do with the centrality of ancestor worship with its dominance of the biological metaphor? Does this in turn have something to do with the predominance of what some have called "monistic" and "organismic" orientations of later high-cultural thought?[17]

As we will see, some correlative systems in the Warring States and Han are indeed based on generative models, and many do quite explicitly play on ancestor sacrifices in their discussions. Schwartz sees this as a continuation of a mind-set datable to the Shang. But this explanation in fact explains little. The fact that the Shang worshipped ancestors does not *explain* why later authors built generative correlative systems. The question remains: Why did the authors in question choose to appropriate sacrificial language in developing their cosmological systems?

---

15. Ibid., p. 37.
16. Ibid., p. 41.
17. Schwartz, *The World of Thought in Ancient China*, p. 26.

Schwartz's response is to say that the family metaphor was highly important in China.[18] I have already questioned Schwartz's attempt to read familial holism and a continuity between the human and divine as guiding orientations in early China, and I will continue that questioning in this chapter.
But the complexities of Schwartz's arguments warrant careful attention.
Schwartz argues that earlier sacrificial practice in China should not be read
in correlative terms. Sacrifice and cosmology may have shared the same general vision of continuity, but they should not be equated. As discussed in the
Introduction, Schwartz is firmly committed to a general "religion to philosophy" model of rationalization. Thus, although he claims that certain
metaphors of the family and bureaucracy dominated early China, he
wants to see correlative thought as a late, philosophical development—a
movement away from religion and toward a rationalized worldview. Like
Graham, then, Schwartz reads correlativity as a late development in early
China, but unlike Graham, he bases this claim not on the notion that correlativity is a universal mode of thought but rather on the Weberian model of
rationalization.

In making this argument, Schwartz also appeals to Lévi-Strauss. But he
cites Lévi-Strauss not in order to emphasize the universality of correlative
thinking but to distinguish late Warring States correlative cosmology from
the sacrificial model that predominated in the Shang:

The fact is that neither the oracle bones, the bronze vessels, nor any of the earliest
texts we have seem to provide strong evidence of correlative cosmology, even though
some discern evidence of totemism in the iconography of the Shang ritual bronze
vessels. Much of the information furnished in these inscriptions sheds light not on
correlative cosmology, but on what Lévi-Strauss would himself define as the realm
of religion. Correlative cosmology in his view is a "science of the concrete" because it
relates concrete phenomena actually perceived in our ordinary experience to each
other "horizontally." Its materials are all drawn from the "real" world. Animals,
plants, the four cardinal directions, kinship organizations, human traits, and celestial bodies are all "real." A religious ritual—specifically the ritual of sacrifice—which
relates humans "vertically" to gods and spirits represents in this view an effort to establish "a desired connection between two initially separate domains," of which
one—the divine—is non-existent.[19]

---

18. Ibid., pp. 416–17.
19. Ibid., pp. 351–52.

Schwartz thus rejects Granet's argument that correlative thinking should be read as pervading early Chinese thought. Even if we adopt Lévi-Strauss's own terminology—the very terminology developed to argue the pervasiveness of correlative thinking—we are forced, Schwartz argues, to see that Chinese correlative thinking is a late development.

Ironically, this reading of Lévi-Strauss is comparable to that of Hall and Ames. Hall and Ames hope to demonstrate that correlative thinking defines all of Chinese thought, and Schwartz is arguing for a general movement from religion to philosophy, but all three believe that Lévi-Strauss's position, despite its overt claims for the universality of correlative thinking, leads to a rejection of Granet and to the position that correlative systems are late developments in China. Hall and Ames therefore reject Lévi-Strauss's position, whereas Schwartz agrees with it.

Although, like Schwartz, I argue that correlative cosmology is a late development in China, I nonetheless disagree with his (and Hall and Ames's) reading of Lévi-Strauss. Schwartz is misreading Lévi-Strauss, and his misreading is worth following in detail, for a closer reading of Lévi-Strauss, as well as of Granet, will lead to a somewhat different, and perhaps more promising, approach to the problem.

Totemism and Sacrifice: From Granet to Lévi-Strauss and Back Again

In the passage quoted by Schwartz, Lévi-Strauss refers to the distinction between "so-called" totemism and sacrifice.[20] In so-called totemism, two discontinuous series (human clans and natural species) are presented as analogies. In contrast, sacrifice "seeks to establish a desired connection between two initially separate domains." "Sacrifice therefore belongs to the realms of continuity."[21] According to Schwartz, this distinction, when applied to

---

20. The reason Lévi-Strauss uses "so-called" in referring to totemism is that he argues strongly against the category of "totemism" to describe the phenomenon of social groups connecting themselves with animals. Lévi-Strauss's basic move here is to subsume the category under a larger theory of structural classification: "So-called totemism is in fact only a particular case of the general problem of classification and one of many examples of the part which specific terms often play in the working out of a social classification" (*The Savage Mind*, p. 62). For his full critique of the term, see Lévi-Strauss, *Totemism*. Some of Lévi-Strauss's motivations for providing this argument are discussed below.

21. Lévi-Strauss, *The Savage Mind*, pp. 224–25; hereinafter cited in the text.

China, reveals a shift from sacrifice to totemism, from the Shang ancestral cult to correlative cosmology. But, in fact, Lévi-Strauss would argue something quite different.

The distinction Lévi-Strauss makes between totemism and sacrifice is based on the different ways that each conceptualizes continuity and discontinuity. Totemism, Lévi-Strauss argues, is a polygenetic system, in which discontinuity is assumed:

The homology they [the so-called totemists] evoke is not between social groups and natural species but between the differences which manifest themselves on the level of groups on the one hand and on that of species on the other. They are thus based on the postulate of a homology between two systems of differences, one of which occurs in nature and the other in culture. (p. 115)

Lévi-Strauss contrasts this with monogenetic systems, using Polynesia as an example:

Instead of a once-for-all homology between two series each finite and discontinuous in its own right, a continuous evolution is postulated within a single series that accepts an unlimited number of terms. Some Polynesian mythologies are at the critical point where diachrony irrevocably prevails over synchrony, making it impossible to interpret the human order as a fixed projection of the natural order by which it is engendered; it is a prolongation, rather than a reflection, of the natural order. (p. 233)

In short, polygenetic systems assume discontinuity, and monogenetic systems assume continuity.

To return to China, all the texts discussed in this chapter posit a cosmos generated naturally by a single ancestor—often referred to as the Great One (*Taiyi*). In Lévi-Strauss's terminology, these texts reflect monogenetic cosmologies, not the totemic systems of polygenesis. Moreover, Lévi-Strauss would certainly not cite the Shang ancestral cult as an example of totemism. Thus, Schwartz's attempt to use Lévi-Strauss's terminology to characterize the shift from Shang ancestral sacrifice to correlative systems as a shift from sacrifice to totemism is incorrect. For Lévi-Strauss, both the Shang ancestral sacrifices and the late Warring States correlative systems would be prototypically monogenetic. None of the systems we have looked at would be classified by Lévi-Strauss as a totemic system.

Indeed, Lévi-Strauss argues that no Eurasian civilization is totemic, nor are Eurasian civilizations based on totemic foundations. For Lévi-Strauss, totemism and sacrifice are two distinct systems: one does not lead to the other. He emphatically rejects the tendency in earlier anthropology to present totemism and sacrifice along evolutionary lines: "That it should have been possible to regard totemism as the origin of sacrifice in the history of religion remains, after so long, a matter of astonishment" (p. 223). Lévi-Strauss's move here is to defend the complexity of classificatory schemes in primitive cultures by denying that totemism represents an earlier, superseded period in the development of civilizations. Instead, he argues, the classificatory systems of the great civilizations are not based on totemism (see, e.g., p. 42). On the contrary. The great civilizations of Eurasia are monogenetic: "This perhaps explains what one is tempted to call the 'totemic void,' for in the bounds of the great civilizations of Europe and Asia there is a remarkable absence of anything which might have reference to totemism, even in the form of remains" (p. 232). And not only is totemism not a superseded level of culture, but it is in fact scientifically superior to sacrifice:

Totemic classifications have a doubly objective basis. There really are natural species, and they do indeed form a discontinuous series; and social segments for their part also exist. . . . The system of sacrifice, on the other hand, makes a pre-existent term, divinity, intervene; and it adopts a conception of the natural series which is false from the objective point of view, for, as we have seen, it represents it as continuous. . . . The system of sacrifice . . . represents a private discourse wanting in good sense for all that it may frequently be pronounced. (pp. 227–28)

Totemic systems are objectively valid, since they recognize discontinuity from the beginning. In contrast, sacrifice is "wanting in good sense," since sacrificial systems believe in continuity—and this is, from an "objective point of view," wrong.

Lévi-Strauss's polemic is not a passing rhetorical flourish. One of the recurrent arguments in *The Savage Mind* is that totemism is just as logical as modern science. It is simply a different form of logic (p. 269), a form that he calls "a science of the concrete" (pp. 1–35). And the crucial point about this science of the concrete is that it builds classifications based on an objectively accurate understanding of natural structures (pp. 1–35, 135–61). Note, for example, how Lévi-Strauss describes the idea of species in totemism: "We should understand how this idea can furnish a mode of sensory apprehension of a combination objectively given in nature, and that the activity of the mind, and social life itself, do no more than borrow it to apply it to the creation of new taxonomies" (p. 137).

In other words, for Lévi-Strauss there are two legitimate forms of science: the science of the concrete (found in totemism) and modern science:

Certainly the properties to which the savage mind has access are not the same as those which have commanded the attention of scientists. The physical world is approached from opposite ends in the two cases: one is supremely concrete, the other supremely abstract; one proceeds from the angle of sensible qualities and the other from that of formal properties. But the idea that, theoretically at least and on condition no abrupt changes in perspective occurred, these two courses were destined to meet, explains why both, independently of each other in time and space, should have led to two distinct though equally positive sciences. (p. 269)

So where does modern science come from? If it is not based on totemism, is it based upon sacrifice? Lévi-Strauss does not make an explicit statement on this point, but I suspect that he would say that modern science arose with the *transcending* of the sacrificial model. Totemism is a science (a science of the concrete), but the model of sacrifice is objectively wrong, and it needed to be overcome before a different, abstract science could arise. Lévi-Strauss is cagey on why this happened, but it is clear that he sees the crucial step as the introduction of abstraction in early Greece: "A dramatic change took place along the frontiers of Greek thought, when mythology gave way to philosophy and the latter emerged as the necessary pre-condition of scientific thought."[22] In other words, he is working with a version of the "religion to philosophy" argument. Moreover, he appears to view modern science as a unique creation of the West, the one Eurasian civilization that transcended the sacrificial model.

Given this framework, what would Lévi-Strauss say about China? Lévi-Strauss says almost nothing about China in his voluminous writings, but I think it is safe to say that Lévi-Strauss would not be sympathetic to Chinese correlative thought. And for *precisely* the same reasons that figures from Weber to Roetz have disparaged Chinese correlative thought: Chinese correlative thought fails to recognize the objective existence of discontinuities—the discontinuities that, the implicit argument goes, proved crucial for the emergence of modern science. The only difference is that Lévi-Strauss would not see Chinese correlative thought as primitive: unlike so many scholars—from Mauss and Durkheim to K. C. Chang—who see

---

22. Lévi-Strauss, *From Honey to Ashes*, p. 473.

the uniqueness of China as lying in its intimate connection to a primitive
past, Lévi-Strauss would *not* see primitive thought in China at all. Similarly,
Lévi-Strauss would not agree with Graham's presentation of Chinese correlative systems as simply another example (along with "primitive thought")
of "proto-science." One suspects that for Lévi-Strauss, Chinese correlativity would have involved an objectively incorrect claim of continuity. Primitive thought, in contrast, is to be found in totemism—a system that, like
modern science, but in a different way, accurately recognizes the truth of
discontinuity.

But where does this leave the study of early China? As the vast majority
of scholars who have studied early Chinese correlative thought have noted,
Lévi-Strauss's analyses are invaluable for the exploration of classification systems. But if we choose not to follow Lévi-Strauss's polemic, can we at least
use his terminology more effectively? First, is China monogenetic? I will argue no. Even if Schwartz is slightly misrepresenting Lévi-Strauss's argument,
Schwartz's intuition that China cannot be successfully defined according to
one pole of Lévi-Strauss's terminology is nonetheless correct. I will go even
further and question Lévi-Strauss's attempt to distinguish polygenesis and
monogenesis in the form that he does: categorizing entire cultures on the basis of such a dualistic framework is precisely what we should avoid in comparative studies.

Marshall Sahlins has suggested a way of utilizing Lévi-Strauss's distinctions in a more nuanced way. As noted above, Lévi-Strauss cites Polynesia as
an example of a monogenetic system—a system that defined everything as
based on a single continuous line of descent. Sahlins, an expert on Polynesia,
has modified this by pointing out that this description, while accurate, refers
only to one set of claims; other groups, in the same culture, emphasize polygenesis:

It appears in Fiji as the interchangeable contrast between unitary lineage organization of the social totality, an encompassment of the whole in the ancestry of a divine
king (*yavusa* system), and the scheme of society as a synthesis of indigenous and
immigrant peoples, joined by the marriage of a daughter of the land with a stranger-
king from the sea, and then ordered as a diarchic kingdom under a ritual paramount
from the foreigners and a warrior-king from the originals (land-sea or *vasu* system).[23]

---

23. Sahlins, "Foreword," p. x.

Certain groups define society and the cosmos monogenetically; others define it polygenetically. Historical analysis involves, among other things, the study of the interplay between these competing visions.[24]

Gregory Schrempp, one of Sahlins's students, has developed these arguments for the Maori through his notion of a "dual formulation," which he defines as "the co-existence of two different conceptions of the essential character and identity of a given concrete social unit."[25] These two conceptions correspond closely to Lévi-Strauss's distinction between monogenesis and polygenesis. Schrempp argues that Maori cosmogonic narratives can be grouped into two distinctive positions—positions that, Schrempp points out, can be mapped successfully with Kant's antinomies.[26] Kant's argument is that, in the history of Western metaphysics, one can find two distinctive, and mutually contradictory, positions. Take, for example, Kant's second antinomy in the *Prolegomena to Any Future Metaphysics*:

Thesis: Everything in the world consists of [elements that are] simple.
Antithesis: There is nothing simple, but everything is composite.[27]

According to Schrempp, Maori thought, just like Western metaphysics, can be categorized into one of these two positions.[28] And, what is more significant, the two constantly play off each other. To revert to Lévi-Strauss's terminology, neither monogenesis nor polygenesis is a founding assumption: rather, the two co-exist, and their antithesis endlessly gives rise to further developments in cosmological thought.

This way of using Lévi-Strauss's terminology points toward a means of explicating the complexities of competing cosmological formulations in a given culture. How do various cosmologies posit continuity and discontinuity, and what are the implications of this positing? And how do these competing cosmologies play off against one another? As we will see, in the case of early China, this is a crucial question for working through the correlative cosmologies posited in the late Warring States and early Han.

---

24. For related arguments by Sahlins's students for other areas of Polynesia, see Valeri, "Constitutive History"; Schrempp, *Magical Arrows*; and Michael Scott, "Auhenua."

25. Schrempp, *Magical Arrows*, p. 68.

26. Ibid., pp. 137–68.

27. Kant, *Prolegomena to Any Future Metaphysics*, p. 87. A fuller discussion can be found in Kant, *Critique of Pure Reason*, pp. 402–9.

28. For Schrempp's discussion of parallels between the second antinomy and aspects of Maori thought, see *Magical Arrows*, pp. 149–55.

Thus, although I have questioned Schwartz's presentation of Lévi-Strauss, I follow Schwartz in arguing that Lévi-Strauss's terminology may be extremely helpful in sorting out Chinese correlative thought but that it should be utilized in a new way. It will also be helpful to return to Granet, but in a way very different from that of Hall and Ames. I agree with Hall and Ames that we should attach much significance to the way Lévi-Strauss built his ideas on the foundation of Granet, but I will argue that the implications point in the opposite direction.

Although Lévi-Strauss is repeatedly read in the sinological literature as having claimed that all "primitive" thinking is based on the principles Granet discovered, the actual development of this thinking was far more complex. Although Lévi-Strauss built much of his structural analyses on Granet, he consistently charged Granet with failing to develop his ideas rigorously. For example, Lévi-Strauss faults the analysis of Chinese kinship structures in Granet's *Catégories matrimoniales et relations de proximité dans la Chine ancienne*:

In this work, a sinologist provides a decisive contribution to the general theory of kinship systems, but he presents his discoveries in the guise of Chinese material, and as interpretations of this material. However, when considered from this particular angle, these interpretations seem confused and contradictory, and sinologists have received them suspiciously, even when their own analyses were not contrary to them. Here, then, is a specialist who perhaps exceeds his proper role, but he succeeds in arriving at theoretical truths of a greater and more general significance.[29]

And I suspect that Lévi-Strauss would reach a similar conclusion about Granet's analysis of correlative thinking: invaluable for theory but confused for China. More specifically, I suspect that Lévi-Strauss thought that Granet treated China too much like a totemic system, when it in fact was, by Lévi-Strauss's reckoning, a monogenetic system.

More important, though, Lévi-Strauss would have rejected Granet's overall analytical framework. As mentioned above, Lévi-Strauss strongly opposed an evolutionary reading of totemism and sacrifice. Such a framework has a long pedigree and was most famously argued by William Robertson Smith. But it is a pedigree that includes Granet. Indeed, the shift from totemism to sacrifice is one of the underlying themes of Granet's evolutionary reading of early China.[30] Granet argues that early Chinese society was to-

---

29. Lévi-Strauss, *The Elementary Structures of Kinship*, p. 311.
30. See Granet, *Danses et légendes de la Chine ancienne*.

temic and that kingship arose when particular figures—the ancient sages—
sacrificed the totemic animals and captured their power. For example, according to Granet, the owl was the totemic "emblem" of Huangdi, but
Huangdi captured and devoured an owl. Similarly, Yao had to conquer the
sun before he could become a king: "Yao, the sovereign, . . . had to aim arrows at the sun before he could become a Son of Heaven. Thus he succeeded in overcoming his celestial double. As soon as he had conquered the
emblem of the sun, he was worthy to reign."[31]

Granet's reconstruction is not convincing in terms of the sinological materials; nor, I would agree with Lévi-Strauss, is it convincing theoretically.
Lévi-Strauss would certainly be correct in saying that Granet's decision to
analyze early China in terms of a shift from totemism to sacrifice was unfortunate. But if we accept Lévi-Strauss's critique of Granet's evolutionism, we
should also accept Sahlins's critique of Lévi-Strauss's form of cultural classification. All of this leaves us in a very interesting place when reading Granet.
Most of Granet's sources were late Warring States or Han texts, and the issues Granet was discussing as an evolution from totemism to sacrifice could,
à la Lévi-Strauss and Sahlins, be worked out in terms of the ways that various texts posit continuity and discontinuity.

With this in mind, let us return to Granet. Granet's point in emphasizing
that the early cultural heroes conquered emblems was that the origins of
Chinese correlative thought do not lie in an attempt to make the social
world correspond to the natural world. Rather,

the first necessity of the ruler is to furnish humans with the emblems that allow
them to domesticate nature. The emblems signal, for each being, its nature as well as
its place and position in the world. In the first days of Chinese civilization, Huangdi
acquired the glory of a heroic founder, for he saw the need to give all things a correct
name. . . . "To render the names correct" is, in effect, the first of governmental obli-
gations.[32]

This is why Granet emphasized that emblems were initially totems conquered by man: man did not so much recognize correlations between the social and the natural worlds as create correlations by appropriating, domesti-
cating, and placing natural objects within a framework that allows for
human consumption and control.

---

31. Granet, *Chinese Civilization*, pp. 197–98.
32. Granet, *La pensée chinoise*, p. 47.

Removed from its evolutionary framework of a shift from totemism to sacrifice, Granet's argument yields something close to what Sahlins was pointing toward: a correlative claim of continuity between humanity and nature was designed, and continues to function, only in opposition to an opposing claim of discontinuity. Or, in Lévi-Strauss's terminology, there is both polygenesis and monogenesis here, and neither can be understood without the other.

The Great Unity of the Cosmos: The *Taiyi sheng shui*

The *Taiyi sheng shui*, a text discovered in the Guodian tomb and probably dating to the late fourth century BC,[33] describes a cosmogony focused on Taiyi 太一, the Great One. In this text, Taiyi is the force that gives birth to the cosmos.[34]

The Great One gives birth to water. Water goes back and supplements [i.e., joins with] the Great One. They thereby complete Heaven. Heaven goes back and supplements the Great One. They thereby complete Earth. Heaven and Earth [return and supplement each other].[35]

In this opening portion of the cosmogony, the Great One is the primary power. It initially generates, on its own, water. Water and the Great One then join to give birth to Heaven. Then Heaven and the Great One combine to make the Earth. The Great One not only begins the process with a direct birth (without another partner), but it continues to be the force with which each successive substance copulates to complete the next substance. This process reaches its conclusion once both Heaven and Earth have been completed. Contrary to most early Chinese cosmologies, Heaven is not the highest power. Not only is Heaven subordinated to the Great

---

33. For a discussion of the Guodian find, see "Jingmen Guodian yi hao Chu mu." For analyses of the Guodian texts, see, in particular, Allan and Williams, *The Guodian Laozi*; and Guo Yi, *Guodian zhujian yu xian-Qin xueshu sixiang*.

34. Relatively little is known about Taiyi. He was evidently a god in at least the southern regions during the pre-Han period. He appears, for example, in the Baoshan divination texts from the state of Chu in the fourth century BC. For an excellent analysis of the paleographic references to Taiyi, see Li Ling, "An Archaeological Study of Taiyi (Grand One) Worship."

35. *Taiyi sheng shui*, strip 1; hereinafter strip numbers are given in the text; the entire text is reproduced in *Guodian chumu zhujian*, p. 125.

One, but it is placed within a generative process that it does not control. Heaven is not a potentially capricious power here; it is a part of a larger processual movement.

Following the completion of Heaven and Earth, the substances begin copulating among themselves, without the Great One: Heaven and Earth join together and complete two more substances, which in turn copulate and complete two more:

They thereby complete the spirits and the illuminated (*shen ming*). The spirits and the illuminated return and supplement each other. They thereby complete the yin and yang. Yin and yang return and supplement each other. They thereby complete the four seasons. The four seasons return and supplement each other. They thereby complete the cold and hot. Cold and hot return and supplement each other. They thereby complete the wet and dry. The wet and dry return and supplement each other. They thereby complete the year and then stop. (Strips 2–4)

Of interest here is that all these figures, from the Great One through Heaven, Earth, the spirits, and the illuminated (*shen ming*), were gods and spirits who received cult at the time. The authors of this text are thus building their cosmology from actual gods and reading them simply as substances in a balanced cosmos.

The next substances mentioned in the cosmology are the cold and hot and the wet and dry. The combination of the second pair results in the formation of the year, and this brings the process to its end. The cosmos is thus formed when the wet and the dry result in the natural generation of the year.

The text then recapitulates the process and underlines that it all began with the Great One:

Therefore, the year was generated by wet and dry. Wet and dry were generated by cold and hot. Cold and hot were generated by the four seasons. The four seasons were generated by yin and yang. Yin and yang were generated by the spirits and the illuminated. The spirits and the illuminated were generated by Heaven and Earth. Heaven and Earth were generated by the Great One. (Strips 4–6)

However, the text draws a further conclusion as well: the Great One pervades all that was generated from it and is in fact active in the seasons themselves:

Therefore the Great One is stored in water and moves in the seasons. Circulating and again [four graphs missing, probably: starting, it takes itself as] the mother of the myriad things. At times diminishing, at times flourishing, it takes itself as the alignment (*jing*) of the myriad things. (Strips 6–7)

The Great One pervades everything and is both the mother and the aligner of the myriad things. Spirits do not control natural phenomena, nor, as we will see later in the *Huainanzi*, do they align the cosmos. Instead, the One gives birth to the myriad things and aligns them.

It is therefore the one thing that cannot be controlled by Heaven, Earth, yin, and yang: "This is what Heaven is unable to kill, what Earth is unable to regulate, and what yin and yang are unable to complete. The gentleman who understands this is called . . . [characters missing]" (strips 7–8). He who understands that the Great One pervades and aligns everything understands the movement of the universe.

The authors then explain the alignment of the universe: "The way of Heaven is to value weakness. It reduces its completion so as to add to life. By cutting back on strength, making clear . . ." (strip 9). Part of the text is unfortunately lost, and it is impossible to reconstruct the full argument. But it is clearly intended to explicate the alignment that can be understood by the person who knows the Great One. The text continues: "Below is the ground; it is called Earth. Above is *qi*; it is called Heaven" (strip 10). The interaction of Heaven and Earth takes place through the Great One, also known as the Way: "The Way is also its style-name (*zi*). I beg to know its name (*ming*)" (strip 10). It can be given the style-name of "the Way," but the real name is unknowable. This is presumably a reference to contemporary religious practice. As we saw in Chapter 2, Yu's placing the images of spirits on cauldrons allowed for a degree of control over those spirits: naming domesticates deities by putting them within a system controlled by humans. Here, however, the name is unknowable: one cannot place the ancestor into a humanly defined system, and one cannot gain control over it. One must simply entrust oneself to its name:

He who follows affairs by means of the Way must entrust himself to its name. Thus, tasks are completed, and the body grows. As for the sage's following of tasks, he also entrusts himself to its name. Therefore, his achievements are completed, and his body suffers no harm. (Strips 10–12)

The sage accomplishes his tasks and suffers no harm. The reason for this is not that he can transform the spirits who control natural phenomena but rather that, by knowing the ultimate ancestor, the sage understands the ways that natural forces operate:

Heaven and Earth, the style-name and name, were established together. Therefore, if one transgresses the other's boundaries, each fits[36] with the other without thinking. [When Heaven was insufficient in][37] the northwest, that which was below raised itself through strength. When the Earth was insufficient in the southeast, that which was above [seven graphs missing; the last four are probably: If there is insufficiency above], there is excess below; if there is insufficiency below, there is excess above. (Strips 12–14)

The sage understands the degree to which forces of the natural world spontaneously respond to one another. As such, he is able to live and act effectively in the world. In this cosmology, neither humans nor spirits affect the environment: the cosmos is simply a set of natural forces that respond to one another. Sages are simply those who understand these processes properly by understanding the Great One—whose style-name is "the Way."

In this cosmology, natural phenomena are not controlled by individuated spirits. Rather, the authors of this text appropriated divinities and spirits and made them into cosmological forces. Like the texts discussed in Chapter 2, this text presents a gnosis different from that offered by the ritual specialists of the day: any attempt to manipulate the spirits of the world through divination and sacrifices would be useless within such a cosmology. However, the argument here departs significantly from the claims seen in Chapter 2. Instead of trying to establish forms of power within the adept, the authors of this text based power on the spontaneous nature of the cosmos—which operates independently of the actor. There is an inherent alignment in the cosmos, generated and maintained by the Great One, that provides the basis for human action. Power and knowledge are thus to be gained not by appropriating the powers of spirits but by understanding and subordinating oneself to the patterns of the cosmos. The cosmos is thus seen as following a normative pattern discernible by those who know how to understand it.

The consequence of this is that the tensions between humanity and Heaven found in Mencius are here completely erased. Heaven is here an offspring of a yet earlier ancestor—the Great One. And Heaven becomes simply a partner with another offspring, Earth, with whom it mates to generate the remainder of the cosmos. Heaven, Earth, and the remainder of the cos-

---

36. Following Qiu Xigui in reading the missing graph as *dang* 當; see *Guodian chumu zhujian*, p. 126n17.

37. Following Qiu Xigui in reading the three remaining missing graphs as 天 不 足; see ibid.

mos are generated and aligned by the One, and any movement by one force spontaneously brings about a movement by its pair. Neither Heaven nor any of the deities can be capricious in this schema.

This point allows us to reflect further on some claims made concerning Chinese cosmology. In particular, Joseph Needham's descriptions of early Chinese cosmology, discussed in the Introduction, deserve a closer look. Schwartz criticizes Needham's biological metaphors (particularly the description of the cosmology as "organismic"), arguing, among other things, that Needham's terminology is somewhat contradictory. As Schwartz correctly points out, Needham's notion of a harmony of wills implies distinctive wills that are then harmonized—exactly the opposite of what Needham is trying to imply: "There is much talk [in Needham] of 'cooperation' of parts or 'harmony of wills,' while avoiding the fact that the image of 'cooperation' inevitably suggests the notion of initially separate entities which come together to 'cooperate.'"[38] Although Schwartz's intent is to illustrate Needham's poor choice of words, I would argue that the poor choice is, unintentionally, quite felicitous: what is going on in Chinese correlative thought is precisely an attempt to pull together elements perceived to be distinct—an attempt to claim a form of continuity prevailing against disparate entities. Continuity is not assumed; it is created. In the case at hand, disparate deities are defined as descendants of the Great One, and that ancestor is presented as continuing to align and participate in the actions of the descendants. Accordingly, the actions of each of these powers are seen as a spontaneous response to the actions of the others. All, in other words, are imbued with the One.

This first instance of correlative thinking appears in a cosmological system in which the One is posited as the ancestor of the cosmos. As we shall see, the basing of correlative thinking in a claim of genealogical descent from a single ancestor will continue throughout much of the Warring States. The debate will turn then to issues such as What is the relationship of humans to this One? Do they simply conform to the patterns of the One, or can they achieve power by means of the One as well? And, if they can, under what circumstances is it acceptable to exercise such power? And does one use the traditional arts of sacrifice and divination to do this or some other means?

---

38. Schwartz, *The World of Thought in Ancient China*, p. 416.

Becoming an Ancestor to the People: The *Laozi*

In the Guodian cache, the *Taiyi sheng shui* text is linked with, and may have been attached to, the third of the texts containing chapters of the *Laozi*.[39] The *Laozi* does, indeed, compare in many ways with *Taiyi sheng shui*.[40] To begin with, it posits a comparable cosmogony:

> The Way gives birth to the One,
> the One gives birth to the two,
> the two give birth to the three,
> the three give birth to the myriad things.
> The myriad things carry the yin and embrace the yang,
> and blend the vapors so as to become harmonized. (Chap. 42)

Although worked out differently, the cosmogony of the *Laozi*, like that of the *Taiyi sheng shui*, is based on generation from an original ancestor, the Way.

Also like the *Taiyi sheng shui*, the *Laozi* discusses the Way in terms of its name (*ming*) and style-name (*zi*):

> There is a thing chaotically completed,
> born before Heaven and earth.
> Still and quiet,
> standing alone yet unchanging,
> going around yet never becoming weary,
> and capable thereby of being the mother of all under Heaven.
> I do not know its name (*ming*),
> Its style-name (*zi*) is "the Way."
> If forced to give it a name, it would be called "Great" (*da*). (Chap. 25)

The ancestor of all that exists can be given a style-name of "the Way," but its real name is unknowable. Here again, one cannot domesticate or control the divine power by learning its name.

Unlike the *Taiyi sheng shui*, however, the *Laozi* calls on the adept to return to this ancestor:

---

39. On the nature of the Guodian *Laozi* chapters, see Roth, "Some Methodological Issues in the Study of the Guodian *Laozi* Parallels."

40. My understanding of the *Laozi* has been aided greatly by the essays in *Religious and Philosophical Aspects of the Laozi*, edited by Mark Csikszentmihalyi and Philip J. Ivanhoe.

All under Heaven had a beginning.
It can be taken as the mother of all under Heaven.
Once you have obtained the mother,
you can thereby know the sons.
Once you have known the sons,
you can return and hold fast to the mother. Until the end there will
    be no harm. (Chap. 52)

The crucial point here is that the sage does *not* strive simply to understand, follow, and accord with the generative process of the Way. On the contrary, the sage reverses that generative process and returns to the source of power: the ancestor.

By doing so, the adept gains the same powers and generates the same harmony as the Way itself:

The Way is nameless.
Although the uncarved block is small,
no one is able to subordinate it.
If princes and kings were able to hold fast to it,
The myriad things will submit on their own,
and Heaven and Earth will harmonize with each other
and send down sweet dew.
The people will adjust themselves,
    yet no one will order them. (Chap. 32)

By holding fast to the Way, the adept is able to make all things submit to him, to control the populace without resorting to overt commands, and even to bring Heaven and Earth into harmony. He becomes, in a sense, like the ancestor: he is able to generate order and cause everything to submit to him.

The ruler is thus able to accomplish everything, but it will seem to the people as though everything is simply occurring naturally, without any directing will:

When his achievements are completed and tasks finished,
The commoners say that "We are like this naturally (*zi ran*)." (Chap. 17)

Since the people think the order brought about by the ruler is a spontaneous product of the Way, they readily accept it. In contrast to the sage of the *Taiyi sheng shui*, the sage of the *Laozi* is not according with a pre-existing natural order, nor is he simply following the order of the ancestor—the One.

Instead, the adept is according with the ancestor in order to gain its powers and create an order of his own choosing.

Although the *Laozi* is often characterized as an expression of a form of naturalism, I would argue that the epithet is even less appropriate for the *Laozi* than it is for Zhuangzi and Mencius. In the *Laozi* the sage does not model himself on nature: he models himself on the Way, which is the ancestor of the natural and human worlds. He thus gains power over both: the natural world, like the human world, submits to him, not the other way around. Moreover, the sage does not act naturally at all. To begin with, he reverses the natural generative process to return to the Way. He thereafter fools people into thinking the subsequent phenomena they witness are natural, when in fact they are simply his wishes.

In short, this is not a naturalism at all; it is yet another form of self-divinization—a claim that humans can, through self-cultivation, gain divine powers. But, in contrast to the "Neiye," the claim here is not made through a posited cosmology of *qi*, essence, and spirit, and the argument is not that humans have the ability to become like spirits. It is, rather, a genealogical claim in which the adept is able to appropriate and thus gain the powers of the ultimate ancestor of the cosmos.

Whether such a cosmology should be termed correlative depends on one's definition of the term. But I will argue that ideas such as those seen in the *Laozi* and *Taiyi sheng shui* were crucial for the development of late Warring States correlative cosmologies.

Using the One to Explore Heaven: The *Shiliujing*

The "Chengfa" chapter of the *Shiliujing*, one of the texts discovered at Mawangdui, reveals a concern with the One similar to that seen in the *Taiyi sheng shui*.[41] The chapter consists of a dialogue between Huangdi and his minister Li Hei. Huangdi is concerned about the growth of dissension in his realm:

Huangdi asked Li Hei: "It is only I, the One Man, who has united and taken possession of all under Heaven. But cunning people are continuing to grow, and clever debaters are using craftiness. They cannot be opposed with laws. I fear that some will employ them and thereby bring chaos to all under Heaven. I wish to ask if all under Heaven has complete laws that can be used to rectify the people?"[42]

---

41. My translation has been aided by Yates, *Five Lost Classics*, pp. 135–37.
42. *Shiliujing*, in *Mawangdui Hanmu boshu*, 1: 72; hereinafter cited in the text.

Li Hei responds by first discussing the ancient period:

Li Hei responded: "Yes. In ancient times, when Heaven and Earth had been completed, rectified were the names and in harmony were the forms. [graph missing] thereby held fast to the one name. They connected it to Heaven above and extended it to the four seas. I have heard of the complete laws under Heaven. Therefore it is said: Instead of the many, speak of the One and then stop. Accord with the name and return to the One, and the people will not bring disorder to the regulations." (1: 72)

In the implicit cosmogony here, names emerged with Heaven and Earth. Moreover, the one name is portrayed as fully graspable by humans. By according with it, the ruler can return to the ultimate ancestor and regulate all the descendants.

Huangdi then inquires whether the One can still be possessed, and Li Hei assures him that it has been accessible throughout history:

Huangdi said: "I wish to ask if all under Heaven can still possess the One." Li Hei responded: "In ancient times, august Heaven made the phoenix descend to say one word and then stop. The five thearchs employed it, using it to clear Heaven and Earth, calculate the four seas, cherish the people below, and rectify the officers of the first generation. For this reason, all the slanderous people retreated, and the worthy men arose. The five evils were expunged, and the clever debaters stopped. They accorded with the name and returned to the One, and the people did not bring disorder to the regulations." (1: 72)

By according with the name, the thearchs were able to right Heaven and Earth and order the world.

Huangdi next asks about the One itself:

Huangdi asked, "As for the One: is it the One and that's all? Does it also grow?" Li Hei said: "The One is the root of the Way. How could it be so and yet not grow? [two graphs missing] is lost, it is because no one is holding fast to the One. The liberation (*jie*) of the One allows an exploration (*cha*) of Heaven and Earth. The pattern (*li* 理) of the One extends to the four seas." (1: 72)

The pattern of the One extends throughout the world. Consequently, by holding fast to the ancestor, the adept is liberated and thus able to exceed normal human limitations and to explore Heaven and Earth. Moreover, the pattern of the One extends throughout the world. The statement is almost precisely the same as the one discussed in Chapter 2 from the "Neiye":

The Way fills all under Heaven. It is everywhere that people reside, but people are unable to understand. With the liberation (*jie*) of the one word, one explores (*cha*) Heaven above, reaches to Earth below, and encircles and fills the nine regions. What does it mean to be liberated by it? It resides in the stability of the mind.[43]

As noted above, however, the "Neiye" presents this liberation as occurring entirely within the mind of the adept. Here, the One is presented as the ancestor and the unifying link of the cosmos, and the adept is called upon to link himself to it.

Li Hei continues:

How can one understand the endpoint of complying and the comprehension of far and near? Only the One is not lost. The One thereby impels transformations. The few can be used to know the many. Now, for gazing throughout the four seas, reaching the farthest points above and below, with the four directions embracing each other: each follows its own way. Now, a hundred words have a basis, a thousand words have essentials, and a myriad words have totality. As for the numerousness of the myriad things: all pass through one hole. (1: 72)

The One thus becomes the ground for control:

Now, if not a rectified person, who would be able to regulate this? He must be a rectified person, thereby able to manage rectification so as to rectify the strange, grasp the One so as to understand the many, expel what is harmful to the people, and support what is appropriate for the people. He manages all by holding fast to the One, and he shares the same endpoints as Heaven and Earth. He can thereby know the good fortune and misfortune of Heaven and Earth. (1: 72)

By holding fast to the One, one is able to understand and regulate all. Again, as in the "Neiye," one is able to understand good fortune and misfortune. But, if the adept in the "Neiye" is liberated through inner cultivation, the sage of the *Shiliujing* frees himself by holding fast to that which generated and continues to pervade everything.

All three of the texts discussed thus far—the *Taiyi sheng shui*, the *Laozi*, and the "Chengfa" chapter of the *Shiliujing*—have a similar monogenetic cosmology: everything that exists, we are told, was generated from a single ancestor—usually termed the One. Accordingly, great powers over the descendants of that ancestor—including Heaven and Earth themselves—can be obtained if one can return to that ancestor. The exact method for

---

43. *Guanzi*, "Neiye," 16.3b.

returning varies by text, as do the powers that can be obtained. But what is of interest here is how this cosmology reverses that seen in the sacrificial models. The sacrificial models assume a radical disjunction between the human realm and the world of spirits. The goal was thus to try, within the limits of what was possible, to anthropomorphize the spirit world, beginning with the local and most immediate spirits and working one's way up the pantheon to, one hoped, Heaven itself. In these cosmological models, however, the claim is not that there exists an inherent disjunction between the human, natural, and spirit realms but rather that all things—humans, nature, and the entire pantheon of gods (including Heaven)—are descendants of a single ancestor, and all things are thus directly related by descent. Thus, by understanding or (in other texts) holding fast to this ancestor, one can gain knowledge or even direct power over all things. These cosmological texts are, in short, an attempt to reject a sacrificial model of the cosmos by asserting absolute monogenesis and by claiming a consequent ability to return directly to the ultimate ancestor instead of having to work up (and transform) the pantheon with sacrifices beginning at the local level.

Becoming a Spirit: The "Xinshu" Chapters of the *Guanzi*

Read in this way, the cosmological texts under consideration in this chapter are similar to those discussed in Chapter 2. And, indeed, the authors of the "Xinshu, shang" and "Xinshu, xia," chapters 36 and 37 respectively of the *Guanzi*,[44] modeled their arguments directly on the "Neiye." Not only is the overall cosmology quite similar to that seen in the "Neiye," but significant portions of these chapters are based on passages from the "Neiye." However, the arguments concerning self-divinization go much farther than those found in the "Neiye."

The authors of the "Xinshu, xia" begin by focusing on the rectification of the form and the resting of the essence within: "If the form is not rectified, the power (*de*) will not arrive. If the essence is not within, the mind will not be regulated. Rectify the form and illuminate the power, and all the myriad things will arrive on their own."[45] The passage is almost identical to one

---

44. For an excellent discussion of the relationship between the "Neiye" and the "Xinshu" chapters, see Roth, "Redaction Criticism and the Early History of Taoism"; and idem, *Original Tao*, pp. 23–30. See also Rickett, *Guanzi*, pp. 56–58, 65–70.

45. *Guanzi*, "Xinshu, xia," 13.5b–6a; hereinafter cited in the text.

from the "Neiye": "If the form is not rectified, the power (*de*) will not arrive. If you are not still within, the mind will not be regulated. Rectify the form and assist the power."[46] Building on the arguments of the "Neiye," the authors of the "Xinshu, xia" posit a cosmology based on form and essence. Maintaining these properly allows one to obtain power, regulate the mind, and thereby bring the myriad things to oneself.

As in the "Neiye," the cosmos is monistic. He who grasps the One is thus able to explore everything: "Therefore, as for the sage, the one word liberates him. He explores Heaven above and explores Earth below" (13.8a). Although the sage never leaves his form, he is able to explore the cosmos simply by grasping the one word. And, again as in the "Neiye," this allows him to rule all the myriad things:

He who grasps the One and does not lose it is able to become the ruler of the myriad things. He shares the same brightness of the sun and moon and shares the same pattern as Heaven and Earth. The sage regulates things; things do not control him. (13.6b)

The claim here exceeds anything seen in the "Neiye." Grasping the One not only gives the sage access to the cosmos, it in fact allows him to gain the same pattern as Heaven and Earth and achieve the same brightness as the sun and moon. He has the same powers of control as Heaven itself.

This emphasis on the divine powers of humans is particularly clear in the way the authors play off the discussion in the "Neiye" concerning *shen*. The text defines spirit as that which is so refined as to be immeasurable by ordinary human experience and yet understands everything: "As for the spirit, no one knows its ultimate point. It brilliantly knows all under Heaven and penetrates the four ultimate points" (13.5b–6a). The text then quotes the "Neiye" passage on divination. Intriguingly, however, it omits the admonition to concentrate "as if a spirit" (*ru shen*; see p. 115):

Can you concentrate? Can you unify? Can you not engage in crackmaking or milfoil divination and yet understand auspiciousness and inauspiciousness? Can you stop? Can you reach an end? Can you not ask others and obtain it in yourself? Therefore it is said: "If you think about it and think about it but do not obtain it, the ghosts and spirits will teach it. This is not due to the power of ghosts and spirits; it is due to the ultimate point of the essential *qi*." (13.6a–b)

---

46. *Guanzi*, "Neiye," 16.3a.

The passage concludes by defining the sage in precisely the same terms used to describe the spirit: "He brilliantly knows all under Heaven and penetrates the four ultimate points" (13.7b). The claims are essentially those of the "Neiye," but the authors take the additional step of implying that one can in fact become a spirit and gain full knowledge of all under Heaven.

Another chapter of the *Guanzi*, the "Xinshu, shang," makes the point explicit. The text at one point makes a claim clearly reminiscent of the "Neiye": "If one empties one's desires, the spirit will enter and dwell. If in clearing one does not cleanse fully, the spirit will leave." It then provides a commentary to this statement:

That which regulates man is essence. If you discard desires, then you will be all-embracing. If you are all-embracing, then you will be still. If you are still, you will be of essence. If you are of essence, you will establish yourself alone. If you are alone, you will be illuminated. If you are illuminated, you will be a spirit. The spirit is the most valued. Thus, if a hallway is not opened and cleared, then a valued person would not reside in it. Therefore it is said: "If you do not cleanse, the spirit will not remain."[47]

Utilizing the same cosmology and same terminology as the "Neiye," the authors of the "Xinshu, shang" make the full claim that humans can in fact become spirits.

Like the "Chengfa" chapter of the *Shiliujing*, the authors of these two chapters posit a monistic cosmology in which the adept should attempt to grasp the One. But, whereas the "Chengfa" is built on an argument for the necessity of understanding and controlling the many by means of the One, the authors of these chapters are arguing that the sage can in fact become a spirit—ruling over the myriad things, possessing the same pattern as Heaven and Earth, and penetrating to the four points of the cosmos. Despite their differences, however, both follow a similar move: both present a monogenetic cosmos, and both claim that the ruler can gain great powers by returning directly to the One.

Becoming Like Heaven: The *Lüshi chunqiu*

Many of these cosmological arguments were further elaborated in the *Lüshi chunqiu*, a text put together by Lü Buwei at the court of Qin around 239 BC. The text is, among other things, an argument for universal rulership. Com-

---

47. *Guanzi*, "Xinshu, shang," 13.1b, 3a–b.

piled at a time when the Qin unification of the states became a real possibility, the text appears to be part of a court debate over what the ideology of the state of Qin should be.

The received tradition holds that Lü Buwei commissioned a number of scholars to write chapters for a work that would encompass all knowledge of the time. Why such a tradition would develop is clear: the overall claim made by the text is one of inclusivity. Although the specific arguments vary from chapter to chapter, each chapter attempts to pull together distinct positions into larger, totalizing systems. Moreover, and more important for the concerns of this chapter, the attempt is usually made within cosmological frameworks. The text thus reveals an array of cosmological positions taking shape in the mid-third century BC: since the place of humans varies from chapter to chapter, the text serves as an excellent series of examples of some of the disparate late Warring States attempts to envision rulership within a cosmological framework.

The text also provides a snapshot of a debate at the Qin court on the eve of the imperial unification. In the short run, as we shall see, the positions associated with the *Lüshi chunqiu* failed to win out at court: soon after the work was completed, Lü Buwei fell from power, and the Qin court thereafter provided little support for such ideas—nor did it do so after the formation of the Qin empire. We thus gain a glimpse as well of the precarious position of correlative cosmology at the courts of the day.

The text continues the critique of ritual specialists, as well as the critique of rulers of the day for employing them. For example, the "Jie shu" chapter sees attempts to manipulate the world of spirits as causing the problems they are supposed to prevent: "In the current generation, the rulers use crackmaking and milfoil divination, praying, and sacrificing. Therefore, sickness and disease come all the more."[48] The same chapter has similar critiques of the "spirit specialists and physicians"—figures whom the "the ancients held in contempt."[49] Such criticisms show the degree to which, even as late as 240 BC, cosmologists still perceived themselves to be a minority voice at the court and thought it necessary to argue that the rulers of their day should not resort to such ritual arts as divination and sacrifice. The point is worth emphasizing, since many twentieth-century analyses take the cosmological

---

48. *Lüshi chunqiu*, "Jieshu," 3.5a.
49. Ibid.

claims in texts like the *Lüshi chunqiu* as evidence of fundamental structures of Chinese thought and overlook the origins of these texts as polemics against the dominant practices at the courts of the day. And they were arguments that would continue to be, for much of the next two centuries, quite unsuccessful.

"Dayue"

The "Dayue" chapter, an essay on music, opens with a cosmogony designed to place both the origins of music and the sages' utilization of music within a broad generative framework—a framework reminiscent of the *Taiyi sheng shui*:

> The origins of tones and music are distant. They were generated of measures and rooted in the Great One (Taiyi). The Great One produced the two forms, the two forms produced the yin and the yang, the yin and the yang changed and transformed, one above and one below, joining and completing, confused and chaotic, separating and then again joining, joining and then again separating. This is called the constancy of Heaven. Heaven and Earth were the wheel of a chariot, ending and then again beginning, reaching the extreme and then again returning.[50]

As in the *Taiyi sheng shui*, the cosmogony here centers around the Great One. But unlike that earlier text, the role of the Great One was to give birth to two forms, which then gave birth to the yin and yang.

The interaction of these two created the seasons, and out of this the myriad things were born:

> The four seasons repeatedly arose, now hot, now cold; now short, now long; now soft, now hard. The myriad things were what emerged, initiated (*zao*) by the Great One, transformed by the yin and yang, germinating, sprouting, developing, growing, growing cold, and freezing—all so as to be formed. (5.3b)

The proper and harmonious functioning of the cosmos allows for the continued growth of things. The sounds produced from the ensuing harmony became the basis for the sages' formation of music: "The form and substance have a place; everything has a sound. Sound is produced from harmony, harmony is produced from being fitting. When it was harmonious and fitting, the former kings determined (*ding*) the music. (Music) was generated from

---

50. *Lüshi chunqiu*, "Dayue," 5.3a; hereinafter cited in the text.

this" (5.3b). Harmonious sound is thus a product of the growth of the cosmos itself, and the sages created music by determining those natural harmonies. Music thus exemplifies this natural harmony: "All music is the harmonizing of Heaven and Earth and the blending of yin and yang" (5.4a). Hence, the sages use music to maintain Heaven and Earth in proper harmony.

The Great One is the source of this harmony. As the authors argue in a passage almost identical to statements in both the *Taiyi sheng shui* and the *Laozi*: "The Way is the utmost essence. It cannot be formed; it cannot be named. If you are forced to do so, call it the Great One. Therefore, the One regulates and commands, and the two follow and obey" (5.4a–b). Consequently, humans who can use the One are able to bring harmony to nature:

He who can use the One to bring order to his body will escape from disaster, live a long life to the end, and keep intact his Heaven (Tian). He who is able to use the One to govern his state will cast out depravity and licentiousness, attract the worthy, and complete the great transformation. He who is able to use the One to regulate all under Heaven will cause cold and heat to be moderated and the wind and rain to be timely, and will become a sage. (5.4b)

By utilizing the One, an adept can bring the natural world to its proper fruition: the individual will live out his allotted lifespan, the ruler of a state will bring order to his realm, and the supreme ruler of all under Heaven will properly modulate the forces of nature.

Humans thus play a crucial role in moderating not only human nature but the entire natural world. Music occupies a middle position here—it is based on the generative processes of nature, and yet it is one means humans use to regulate nature. Humanity is thus, even in the formation of music, the fulfiller of natural processes. The way to control the wind and rain, therefore, is not by trying to manipulate the spirits who control such forces but by connecting oneself to the Great One and thereby helping to maintain the harmony of the cosmic forces. As in the "Chengfa," the argument here is that the adept should conform to an external One.

"Bensheng"

In contrast to the "Dayue" chapter and the "Chengfa," the authors of several other chapters in the *Lüshi chunqiu* built their cosmological arguments on claims concerning *shen*. The "Bensheng" chapter, one of the most interesting of these essays, makes cosmological claims for the potentially divine powers

of humans through a complex argument concerning ancestors and humans.[51]
The opening statement plays on the title of the ruler, the "son of Heaven"
(*tianzi*): "That which first gives birth (*sheng*) is Heaven; the one that nour-
ishes and completes is man. The one who is able to nourish what Heaven
generates without perverting it is called the Son of Heaven."[52] Heaven is a
generative power, and humans nurture what Heaven has generated. However, such activities risk a perversion of the inheritance, a perversion that can
be avoided only by the Son of Heaven—that is, he who is a proper son,
properly following what the parent, Heaven, has generated.

The text continues:

> The actions of the Son of Heaven take the completing of Heaven as their cause. It is
> for this reason that officials are established. The establishment of officials is done in
> order to complete life. The deluded rulers of the present age set up many officials
> but contrarily use them to harm life. They thus lose the purpose for establishing
> them. (1.4a)

The sole goal of the state should be to complete Heaven. And the same
point holds at the level of human nature. Again, the emphasis is on the necessity of nurturing human nature and on the dangers of perverting it:

> It is the nature of man to be long-lived. But things (*wu*) disorder it; therefore, it does
> not obtain long life. Things are used to nurture the nature; they are not what uses
> the nature to be nurtured. (1.4a)

The concern, therefore, is not to use oneself to help things but the exact
opposite:

> Of those who are deluded in the present age, many use the nature to nurture things.
> They do not understand [the distinctions of] lightness and heaviness. He who does
> not know lightness and heaviness takes heavy as light and light as heavy. As such,
> every action fails. (1.4a–b)

The ability to nurture correctly thus resides in a correct understanding of
distinctions. Accordingly, the sage consumes only those things that are
beneficial:

---

51. My understanding of this chapter has been helped by the insightful comments in Graham, "The Background of the Mencian Theory of Human Nature," pp. 13–15. I, however,
question Graham's attempt to read the chapter as "Yangist."

52. *Lüshi chunqiu*, "Bensheng," 1.3b–4a; hereinafter cited in the text.

Therefore, as regards a sage's relation to sounds, colors, flavors, and tastes: if they are beneficial to his nature, he takes them. If they are harmful to his nature, he rejects them. This is the way of completing his nature. (1.4b).

And completing his nature is tantamount to completing his Heaven:

Therefore, the sage regulates the myriad things so as to complete his Heaven. If his Heaven is complete, then his spirit will be harmonized, his eyes will be clear-seeing, his ears keen of hearing, his nose good at smelling, his mouth quick, the 360 joints all connected and sharp. (1.51)

By thus regulating the myriad things, the sage is able to perfect his heavenly endowment. His powers and faculties then connect properly with the rest of the cosmos: as his spirit becomes harmonized with the cosmos, his senses are able to perceive without error. As a consequence, the sage himself becomes like Heaven and Earth:

His essence will penetrate Heaven and Earth, and his spirit will cover the universe. As regards things: there are none he does not receive and none he does not internalize. He is like Heaven and Earth. (1.5a).

The cycle is complete. Heaven gives birth to man, and man thus has a part of Heaven within him. The goal of man is to utilize the things of the world to complete that which Heaven has given. The true sage—the person who is able to complete this process—ultimately internalizes all things within himself, and his essence and spirit penetrate the universe. The Son becomes comparable to that which gave birth to him: he becomes like Heaven and Earth themselves.

The sage's achievement of a spirit that encompasses the cosmos is thus the teleological completion of what Heaven initially generated. In such a cosmology, man does not exist in a potential agon with Heaven, nor does man follow Heaven; instead man—if he fully achieves his potential— completes Heaven's generative process and thereby regulates the myriad things of the universe. Things are therefore to be used to aid in man's completion of this generative process. In short, Heaven established the cosmos for man: if the Son of Heaven accepts what benefits his own nature and rejects all that does not, he will rule over the world properly.

The argument is in some ways a radicalization of the claims of Mencius. Mencius believed that sages, by cultivating that which Heaven gave them, could encompass the myriad things and harmonize Heaven and Earth. But he also felt that Heaven, for reasons that were mysterious, at times blocked the sage's proper ordering of the world. In this chapter of the *Lüshi chunqiu*, however, the sage's ordering of the cosmos is defined as the normative movement of the generative process begun by Heaven. The potential agon found from the Western Zhou through Mencius, which figures like Zhuangzi rejected by defining the spirit as spontaneously following Heaven, is here denied entirely: in achieving the ability to encompass the universe and regulate the myriad things, the sage brings to completion what Heaven has generated.

A closer look, however, reveals that the argument of the "Bensheng" parallels the ritual behavior toward the ancestors discussed in Chapter 1: it is the living who must both fulfill the processes begun by the ancestors and place those ancestors in the proper location. Only here the process moves in the opposite direction: instead of trying to order his ancestors and ultimately influence Heaven, the ruler becomes like Heaven and personally brings order to the entire cosmos. The method advocated is therefore self-cultivation, not sacrifice and divination. As in the "Neiye" and "Xinshu" chapters, powers usually conceived to be obtainable only by ritual specialists in their dealings with spirits are here presented as obtainable by certain humans through self-cultivation. The conflict between humans and spirits is denied by representing the sage as capable of divinizing himself and thereby internalizing all of the cosmos within himself.

"Lunren"

The "Lunren" chapter plays with these notions in a slightly different way. The chapter opens by explaining that the most important thing for a ruler to do is to revert to his true nature:

What is meant by turning back to oneself? Making one's ears and eyes appropriate, modulating one's lusts and desires, forsaking cleverness and plotting, expelling craftiness and precedent, letting one's intentions roam (*you*) in the inexhaustible realm, and exercising one's mind on the path of spontaneity.[53]

Neither precedent—following the past—nor craftiness—shifting with the times—is of use. The goals are to return to one's true self, wander throughout the cosmos, and embrace spontaneity. On the face of it, this sounds very much like Zhuangzi.

---

53. *Lüshi chunqiu*, "Lunren," 3.7b; hereinafter cited in the text.

As in the "Bensheng" chapter, by following this program, the ruler protects the Heaven within him:

As such, there will be nothing that will harm his Heaven. If there is nothing that will harm his Heaven, then he will know his essence. If he knows his essence, then he will know his spirit. Knowing his spirit is known as obtaining the One. Now, the myriad forms are completed after obtaining the One. Therefore, he who knows the One can respond to the alterations and transformations of things. (3.7b)

Here too, the possibility of conflict with Heaven is denied; on the contrary, one's highest goal as a human is to protect that piece of Heaven within oneself. But the "Lunren" adds to this argument a cosmology based on essence, spirit, and the One. These are arrayed in a hierarchy: not harming his Heaven allows the adept to know his essence, which in turn allows him to know first his spirit and then the One. Since all things, it is implied, are subordinate to the One, his knowledge of the One allows the adept to respond to things flawlessly.

As in the "Bensheng" chapter, this ultimately allows one to be like Heaven and Earth:

Therefore, if his knowledge consists in knowing the One, then he will be like Heaven and Earth. As such, then what affair cannot be overcome? What thing (wu) will he not respond to? (3.8a)

The ruler thus, in a sense, transcends being a thing (wu). He instead knows the One and is like Heaven and Earth: he witnesses the alterations and transformation of things and responds properly. In some ways, this argument is reminiscent of that in the "Neiye": by cultivating himself, the adept is able to obtain the One and rule effectively. But here the implication is not that one, as in the "Neiye," controls things; the sense is, rather, that one is able to respond effectively to things. This is, in a way, a political reading of the cosmology of texts like the Zhuangzi. But instead of simply accepting the order of Heaven and thereby spontaneously according with the proper way, the ruler here becomes like Heaven and Earth and thus maintains the same spontaneous direction over things that Heaven and Earth themselves exercise. The Zhuangzi repeatedly advises us to stop trying to overcome Heaven; the concern here is precisely to allow the adept to overcome things. The path to political power, therefore, lies not in becoming like a spirit but in attaining the same spontaneous guidance of the cosmos exercised by Heaven.

"Wugong"

Yet another variant of the cosmological argument is to be found in the "Wugong" chapter. As in the "Lunren," the argument of the "Wugong" chapter is based on a linkage of spirit and the Great One. The sage-king, the authors argue,

> nourishes his spirit, cultivates his power (*de*) and transforms. . . . Bright, like the illumination of the sun, he alters and transforms the myriad things, and nothing is not put in motion. His spirit is harmonized with the Great One.[54]

By nourishing his spirit, the sage-king harmonizes his spirit with the Great One and gains power over things:

> His essence penetrates to the ghosts and spirits. Deep, minute, dark, mysterious; no one sees his form. If today he faced south, the hundred heterodoxies would correct themselves and all under Heaven would return to their dispositions. The people would fully take pleasure in their intentions and peacefully cultivate their natures, and none would act without completing. (17.9b)

These powers would ultimately allow him to become like the ghosts and spirits, and he would rectify the world.

The claim here is in some ways comparable to a statement from the *Lunyu* (15/5):

> The master said: "Not doing anything and yet putting things in order, this was Shun. What did he do? He made himself reverent, was rectified, and faced south; that is all."

Shun was able to put all in order by assuming the proper ritual position. The passage from the "Wugong" chapter makes a similar point but at a cosmological level: by making his spirit harmonize with the Great One, the sage-king penetrates to the ghosts and spirits and brings order to the world.

Several interrelated claims are being made here. The most important is that humans can, through self-cultivation, gain the same powers as ghosts and spirits. Precisely what powers ghosts and spirits have is not clear: they certainly do not seem to be the ghosts and spirits of contemporary religious practice—beings who act willfully and (from the point of view of humans) sometimes arbitrarily, and who therefore need to be manipulated by means

---

54. *Lüshi chunqiu*, "Wugong," 17.9a–b; hereinafter cited in the text.

of arts such as divination or sacrifice. The implication is that the spirits are without form yet can nonetheless order things—powers that a human can attain as well.

However, nothing in the text implies that ghosts and spirits face south and thereby make all under Heaven follow their wishes. Humans can penetrate to the ghosts and spirits, but humans are also granted a particular and crucial role in ordering the cosmos. As with Confucius, that role is based on ritual positioning, but here it is discussed in terms of a cosmological potency. As a consequence, the sage-king is able to bring all within his realm into the form that he desires:

In general, the ruler resides in evenness and stillness and employs virtue and transformation so as to follow his needs. In this way, he gives form to nature (*xing*). (17.10b)

The sage-king does precisely what the Great One does: he gives form to things by guiding their nature—their innate potentiality.

The sage's realm is thus a microcosm of the larger cosmos. By nourishing his spirit, the ruler can attain the power to transform things and give them form. This is yet another variant of the attempt to claim continuity in the cosmos and to position the human ruler, by linking with the ultimate ancestor, as the ordering force of the cosmos.

Each of these chapters from the *Lüshi chunqiu* involves attempts to develop a cosmological argument based on a claim of genealogical descent. If everything is descended from a common ancestor, then how does man gain power vis-à-vis this ancestor? As I have noted, the answers to this question are complex cosmological reworkings of the issues discussed in Chapter 1 concerning ancestral sacrifices. Correlative cosmology in China may be an attempt to supersede sacrificial models, but the authors of cosmological systems often appeal to the model of ancestral sacrifice in making their arguments. As Granet (according to my reading of him) has argued, cosmology in early China often recapitulates sacrificial claims.

The Pattern of Heaven and Earth: The *Xunzi*

All the texts discussed thus far in this chapter advocate a cosmology based on a common descent of everything (including man) from a single ancestor, and all reject practices such as divination and sacrifice. I turn now to Xunzi, one of the pre-eminent thinkers of the third century BC.[55] Many scholars would argue that although Xunzi rejects divination and sacrifice, he does not accept the cosmological arguments developing around him. Indeed, Heiner Roetz portrays Xunzi as a full rationalist[56] and argues that although Xunzi at times appears to make cosmological arguments, he does not intend them as such. In Xunzi, "the cosmological diction is rhetoric."[57]

I will dispute each of these points: Xunzi was indeed extremely interested in cosmological notions, and unlike so many of his contemporaries, he *supported* sacrifice and divination. Although he agreed that sacrifice and divination could not coerce spirits, he argued that they were nonetheless traditional practices and should be accepted as such. Thus, in contrast to those calling for a rejection of sacrifice and divination on the grounds that the sage can achieve the same ends through *shen*-like intuition, Xunzi argues that such practices are culture (*wen* 文). As he states in the "Tianlun" chapter:[58]

If we sacrifice and it rains, what does this mean? I say: it does not mean anything. It is the same as not sacrificing and having it rain. When the sun is eaten by the moon [i.e., when there is an eclipse], we save it; when Heaven has a drought, we sacrifice; we engage in crackmaking and milfoil divination and only then decide a great event. But we do not thereby obtain what we seek; we are placing culture (*wen*) upon it. Therefore, a gentleman takes this as culture, but the hundred families take it as divine (*shen*). To take it as culture is auspicious; to take it as divine (*shen*) is inauspicious.[59]

But what precisely does Xunzi mean in distinguishing *wen* and *shen*? Tellingly, Xunzi defines *wen* in relation to sacrificial action. His full argument is worth following in depth.

At the *xiang* sacrifice, we are told, water, raw fish, and unflavored soup are offered: "At the great *xiang* sacrifice, one offers a goblet of water, places

---

55. My overall understanding of Xunzi has been helped greatly by the analyses in Goldin, *Rituals of the Way*; and the essays in Kline and Ivanhoe, *Virtue, Nature, and Moral Agency in the Xunzi*. Of particular help for the specific issues of interest in this section has been Campany, "Xunzi and Durkheim as Theorists of Ritual Practice."

56. See, e.g., Roetz, *Confucian Ethics of the Axial Age*, pp. 213–26.

57. Ibid., p. 230.

58. My understanding of the "Tianlun" chapter has been aided tremendously by Ivanhoe, "A Happy Symmetry"; Machle, *Nature and Heaven in the Xunzi*; and Eno, *The Confucian Creation of Heaven*, pp. 154–67.

59. *Xunzi* (hereinafter cited in the text), "Tianlun," 11.13a.

raw fish on the offering table, and serves first the unflavored soup. This is to honor the foundations (*ben* 本) of food and drink" ("Lilun," 13.3b). But one then goes on to offer prepared foods:

At the *xiang* sacrifice, one offers the goblet of water but then utilizes wine and sweet wine; one first has glutinous and panicled millet but then eats rice and spiked millet; at the sacrifices, one takes the unflavored soup but then gets filled with various delicacies. One is thus honoring the foundations yet embracing how they are used (*yong* 用). ("Lilun," 13.3b)

The sacrifices allow us to honor both the raw and the cooked.

Xunzi then associates these two poles with *wen* and *li* 理, respectively: "Honoring the foundations is what we call cultural forms (*wen*). Embracing how they are used is what we call pattern (*li*)" ("Lilun," 13.3b). Offering a goblet of water, placing raw fish on the offering table, and serving unflavored soup is an example of cultural form—of actions that direct the participants' attention to the foundations observable in nature. And the second part of the sacrifices allows us to embrace human preparation of food and drink for consumption. "When these two are combined with completed cultural forms, they thereby return to the Great One. All of this is what we call the Great Flourishing" ("Lilun," 13.3b). The "completed cultural forms" thus return us to the Great One—the original foundation—just as lesser cultural forms return us to such basics as raw food.

Xunzi has thus posited an extremely complex set of interlocking definitions. We have foundations, cultural forms that help us honor those foundations, patterns that allow us to embrace how humans put those foundations to use, and completed cultural forms that, combining cultural forms and patterns, return us to the Great One—the primary foundation. Sacrifices for Xunzi thus involve a focus on the nature of human action in relation to the world. Indeed, they encapsulate the entire process of humans' taking elements of nature, preparing them, and then consuming them.

At one level, this may seem like a very "rational" understanding of sacrifice. Indeed, it closely corresponds with some of Lévi-Strauss's analyses of ritual. But Xunzi's final claim that humans are thus honoring the Great One reveals a greater cosmological interest than Roetz is willing to admit. To make sense of this, let us take a closer look at Xunzi's conception of "foundations," cultural forms, and patterns. For Xunzi, cultural forms and patterns are human artifice, whereas the foundations are part of nature.

Therefore I say that the nature (*xing*) is the foundation, the beginning, the material, and the substance; artifice is the cultural form (*wen*), pattern (*li*), abundance, and flourishing. If there were no nature, there would be nothing for artifice to add to. If there were no artifice, the nature would be unable to beautify itself. Only when the nature and artifice combine are the names of the sages unified and the accomplishments of all under Heaven completed. ("Lilun," 13.10a)

And artifice *must* be combined with nature in order for the myriad things to be brought to order:

Therefore, I say that when Heaven and the Earth combine, the myriad things are born; when yin and yang join, changes and transformations arise; when the nature and artifice combine, all under Heaven is put in order. Heaven can give birth to things but cannot distinguish things; the Earth can bear man but cannot put men in order. Within the universe, the myriad things generate those who belong to the human race; they await the sage and only then are they differentiated. ("Lilun," 13.10a)

It is the combining of cultural forms and patterns with the foundations that brings order to the world. As I have argued elsewhere, there is an implicit teleology in Xunzi: humans fulfill their proper duty through artifice and thereby bring order to that which Heaven generated.[60]

Elsewhere, Xunzi speaks of patterns (*li*) as something the sages properly brought to the world of nature:

Therefore, Heaven and Earth gave birth to the gentleman. The gentleman gives patterns to Heaven and Earth. The gentleman forms a triad with Heaven and Earth, is the summation of the myriad things, and is the father and mother of the people. Without the gentleman, Heaven and Earth have no pattern, ritual and righteousness have no unity; above there is no ruler or leader, below there is no father or son. This is called the utmost chaos. Ruler and minister, father and son, older and younger brother, husband and wife, begin and then end, end and then begin. They share with Heaven and Earth the same pattern and last for ten thousand generations. This is called the Great Foundation (*ben*). ("Wangzhi," 5.7a–b)

The gentleman forms a triad with Heaven and Earth, and he in turn becomes the father and mother of the people. And this entire hierarchy is defined as the Great Foundation.

The order of sages is thus the teleological completion of the generation of Heaven. As in the "Bensheng" chapter of the *Lüshi chunqiu*, the sage is the son of Heaven in a literal sense of carrying out the inheritance of Heaven.

---

60. See chap. 2 of my *The Ambivalence of Creation*.

But the sage does not, through cultivation, become like Heaven. On the contrary, Heaven and man have distinct duties in the proper ordering of the cosmos. They are genetically related, but in this cosmology the son does not become like the ancestor.

So what about *shen*? If in this cosmology the sage completes the work of Heaven, then does the sage become a spirit?

The arrayed stars follow in circles, the sun and moon shine in alternation, the four seasons take charge in succession, yin and yang greatly transform, the wind and the rain disseminate broadly. As for the myriad things, each obtains what harmonizes with it in order to be born, and each obtains its nurturance in order to become complete. We cannot see the activity, but we can see the accomplishments. This is what we call "divine" (*shen*). All understand that by which it has been completed but no one understands its formlessness. This is what we call "Heaven." Only the sage acts without seeking to understand Heaven. ("Tianlun," 11.9b–10a)

The cosmos operates according to specified patterns in order to allow things (*wu*) to live and receive nourishment. The fact that the cosmos so operates is *shen*. Xunzi uses the term not to describe spirits with control over natural phenomena: the word does not imply particular spirits as the causal agents of each event. He is, rather, using it to describe the divine qualities of the patterned cosmos, the fact that it so operates to allow things to flourish. And "Heaven" refers to the origin of this cosmos. But, we are told, the sage seeks not to understand any of this.

Xunzi then turns to man. Like the rest of the cosmos, man is born from Heaven: "When the work of Heaven has been established and the accomplishments of Heaven have been completed, the form is prepared and the spirit (*shen*) is born" ("Tianlun," 11.10a). As in texts like the "Neiye" and "Xinshu," humans have spirit within themselves. Man's inheritance is then described as coming from Heaven:

Likes, dislikes, happiness, anger, sorrow, and joy are stored within him: these are called the Heavenly disposition. The ears, eyes, nose, mouth, and body—each has that with which it connects, but they cannot substitute for one another: these are called the Heavenly faculties. The mind resides within the central emptiness so as to rule the five faculties: this is called the Heavenly ruler. It makes into produce what is not of its species in order to nurture its species: this is called the Heavenly nurturance. Those who accord with their species are called fortunate, and those who oppose their species are called unfortunate; this is called the Heavenly governance. ("Tianlun," 11.10a)

And the sage is the figure who most successfully utilizes his inheritance from Heaven:

> The sage clears his Heavenly ruler, rectifies his Heavenly faculties, prepares his Heavenly nurturance, accords with his Heavenly governance, nourishes his Heavenly disposition, and thereby brings completion to the Heavenly accomplishments. If he does so, then he knows what he is to do and not to do. Heaven and Earth then perform their functions, and the myriad things serve him. His movements are fully ordered, his nurturance fully appropriate, and his life is without injury. This is called knowing Heaven. ("Tianlun," 11.10b)

If man utilizes properly what Heaven has given him, then the myriad things serve him. Man's duty in the cosmos, therefore, is to bring order to things. And, for Xunzi, *this* represents knowing Heaven. In other words, to attempt to study the workings of the cosmos directly (as many correlative texts of the time were advocating) is mistaken; rather, the goal should be to cultivate oneself, utilize the Heavenly inheritance properly, and thereby take a dominant role in ordering things.

The order that results is a further example of *shen*. For example, in one passage, after discussing how all natural objects and creatures are utilized by man for man's benefit, Xunzi concludes:

> Thus, as for what Heaven nourishes and Earth carries, all that is beautiful is utilized, and all that is useful is brought forth. Above, it is used to adorn the worthy and good, and below it is used to nourish the hundred families and give them pleasure. This is called the "Great Divinity" (*da shen*). ("Wangzhi," 5.6b)

The appropriation by humanity for its own use of all that has been nourished and carried by Heaven and Earth is the proper, divine order of the cosmos.

And the sage who is able to maintain order in the cosmos is himself divine (*shen*):

> What is called the One? I say: holding fast to the divine (*shen*) and being resolute. What is called divine (*shen*)? I say: the utmost goodness and full ordering is called divine. If none of the myriad things (*wu*) are able to overturn him, then he is called resolute. He who is divine and resolute is called a sage. ("Ru xiao," 4.7a)

By definition, the sage is resolute and divine. Resoluteness is the ability not to be overturned by things: the sage should rule things, not vice versa. Divinity (*shen*) is specified as "utmost goodness and full ordering (*zhi*)." This is consistent with Xunzi's other uses of the term *shen*: *shen* is what brings things to their proper order. Thus, the functioning of the cosmos itself is divine (*shen*), the sage who properly uses the endowment given to him by Heaven to rule over the myriad things is divine (*shen*), and the resulting order is greatly divine (*da shen*).

The passage continues: "The sage is the manager of the Way. The Way of all under Heaven is managed by him; the Way of the hundred kings is unified by him. Therefore, the *Poetry, Documents, Rituals*, and *Music* return us to him" ("Ru xiao," 4.7a). The traditions of the sages, recorded in what we now call the Classics, allow later generations to know the teachings of the sages. But since Heaven has endowed everyone with the ability to become a sage, anyone who studies these ancient records can achieve the same powers:

If you make a man in the street submit to techniques and engage in study, concentrating his mind and unifying his will, thinking, inquiring, examining, adding each day for a long time, accumulating goodness without ceasing, then he will penetrate to the divine clarity (*shenming*) and form a triad with Heaven and Earth. ("Xing'e," 17.6b)

But these powers grant the student neither control over phenomena nor a flawless understanding of the cosmos but, rather, an ability to bring proper order to himself and the world. Xunzi thus utilizes much of the increasingly common cosmological vocabulary of the time but alters it so as to emphasize the crucial importance of following the earlier sages, of continuing the ritual and textual traditions of the past.

We are now in a position to understand Xunzi's reading of sacrifice and divination. In the passage quoted at the beginning of this section, Xunzi defends these practices as *wen*, but not as *shen*. The "Neiye" and "Xinshu" claim divination to be unnecessary because such powers of prognostication are obtainable through human cultivation; Xunzi encourages these practices. But he opposes any attempt to understand the spirits or Heaven, and he opposes any attempt at prognostication: he rejects the claim that one can truly understand a future event (either through divination or intuition). Nonetheless, the practice still has value, for it is a tradition handed down by the sages.

But what does Xunzi mean when he says that sacrifice and divination are not *shen*? For practices to be *shen*, in Xunzi's terminology, they have to bring about a proper order, even though the ultimate causal mechanism is outside ordinary human perception. So, if sacrifice resulted in order, it would be *shen*; if divination succeeded in showing what activities are auspicious, it would be *shen*. But sacrifice and divination cannot do these things, and the belief that they can represents for Xunzi a foolish attempt to control and understand the cosmos—things that are outside the powers of humans and their arts. Humans can bring about order only by cultivating themselves to utilize their faculties properly and thereby make the myriad things serve them, but they do not have the power to control the wind and rain.

But sacrifice and divination are still *wen*: if understood properly, these practices help humans to understand their proper role in the cosmos. Thus, Xunzi's argument is based not on a claim of rationalism but on the nature of humanity and the nature of the cosmos. Xunzi opposes attempts by humans to use sacrifice and divination to influence spirits, and he equally opposes claims that humans can themselves become spirits and directly exercise control over the cosmos. His response is to argue that humans have a crucial role to play in the cosmos. the human artifices of culture and pattern bring order to the cosmos not by allowing humans to control the wind and rain but by allowing them to cultivate themselves properly, create a correct society, and appropriate natural objects for their own benefit. The cosmos is structured such that humans can emerge and, in this specific sense, give it order. Xunzi thus fully accepts the arguments concerning divinization and the crucial role humans play in the ordering of the cosmos, but he shifts the meaning of each of these terms dramatically. Humans do not become like Heaven; rather, they play a Heaven-given role in bringing order to the world.

And, through this argument, Xunzi provides himself a basis for supporting cultural traditions handed down from the past. Unlike the other texts discussed in this chapter, Xunzi supports sacrifice and divination and opposes the claim that humans can control or understand natural processes.

Submitting to the Trigrams: The *Xici zhuan*

The *Xici zhuan*, a commentary to the *Yi*, or *Book of Changes*, is one of the most oft-cited texts in discussions of correlative cosmology in China. At first glance, it appears to be yet another late Warring States text, like the chapters of the *Lüshi chunqiu* and *Guanzi*, arguing that a human can through cultivation come to understand the workings of the cosmos and thereby be effective in the world or, in short, become a sage. Without question, the terminology of the text, with its emphasis on a spontaneous, self-generating cosmos which the sages should strive to understand and pattern themselves on, resembles that found in the roughly contemporary texts mentioned above. Nonetheless, appearances aside, the *Xici zhuan* is quite critical of many of these texts. Contrary to the usual interpretation, its argument is in some ways comparable to that found in portions of the *Xunzi*.

In particular, unlike almost all the texts discussed thus far, the *Xici zhuan* was written in *support* of the art of divination. Unlike the critiques in texts such as the "Neiye" and "Xinshu," the authors of the *Xici zhuan* argue strongly for the efficacy of divination. And unlike Xunzi, the authors of the *Xici zhuan* support divination not because it is *wen* but because it is *shen*.

The authors of the *Xici zhuan* argue that the cosmos operates through changes put in motion by the alternation of yin and yang. Since change is based on a definable series of processes, the alternation can be formulated numerically.

The numbers of Heaven are twenty-five, the numbers of Earth are thirty. In all, the numbers of Heaven and Earth are fifty-five. It is by means of these that the alternations and transformations are completed and the ghosts and spirits are put into motion.[61]

Hence, to understand change itself is to understand the spirits:

The master said: "He who knows the way of alternations and transformations understands what it is that the spirits (*shen*) do." (A/9)

Spirits, in this definition, are not willful agents who direct phenomena on their own. Instead, they operate through understandable processes of change.

The key, therefore, is to understand these processes. And the way to do it, according to the *Xici zhuan*, is to understand "the Pivot." The Pivot is the point of the alternation of yin and yang, the basis on which all change occurs. Thus, he who understands this mechanism is able to understand change and hence what actions will be auspicious. And because this knowledge gives him the ability to act properly, it means that he, too, can be called divine (*shen*):[62]

The master said: "The one who understands the Pivot, is he not divine? . . . The Pivot is the minutest beginning of movement, the first manifestations of auspiciousness. The superior man sees the Pivot and acts, without waiting until the end of the day." (B/5)

---

61. *Xici zhuan*, A/9; hereinafter cited in the text. My numbering of each passage follows the Zhu Xi arrangement.

62. Willard J. Peterson ("Making Connections," pp. 103–10) provides an excellent discussion of the notion of *shen* in the *Xici zhuan*. In what follows, I attempt to supplement his study by noting the historical significance of the claims made in the text.

However, the text claims that the *Yi*, or *Changes*, is also divine:

The *Yi* is without thought and without action. Still and not moving, responding and then penetrating the causes of everything under Heaven. If it were not the most divine (*shen*) of all under Heaven, how would it be able to participate in this? (A/10)

Moreover, the passage continues, it was only by means of the *Yi* that the sages were (the past tense, as I will argue later, is necessary here) able to understand phenomena:

The *Yi* is that by which sages went to the limit of the deep and investigated the Pivot. Only because it is deep were they therefore able to penetrate the will of all under Heaven; only because it is a Pivot were they therefore able to complete the work of all under Heaven. Only because it is divine (*shen*) were they therefore not hurried and yet fast, not moving and yet arriving. (A/10)

But note that it is not just that the *Yi* gives one access to the Pivot; in the second sentence, the authors describe the *Yi* itself as a Pivot.

Several questions immediately arise. How can the *Yi* be called divine? How can the *Yi* itself be described as a Pivot? and If it is the text that guided the sages, then where did it come from? I will deal with each of these in turn.

As Willard Peterson has convincingly argued, the basic claim of the *Xici zhuan* is that the *Yi* is itself in accord with the processes of nature:[63]

The *Yi* is adjusted to Heaven and Earth. Therefore it is able to complete and classify the way of Heaven and Earth. Looking up, it observes the patterns of Heaven; looking down, it examines the principles of the Earth. (A/4)

The reason the *Yi* possesses the ability to replicate the changes of the world is that it possesses the Pivot of change itself:

It is for this reason that the *Yi* possesses the Great Pivot (*Taiji*). This generated the two insignia. The two insignia generated the four images. The four images generated the eight trigrams. The eight trigrams determine auspiciousness and inauspiciousness. Auspiciousness and inauspiciousness generate the great undertakings. (A/10)

This passage can be read either as a cosmogony of the universe or as a statement of the generation of the *Yi*. And that is precisely the point: it is both. In other words, the changes in the hexagram lines of the *Yi* mirror the

---

63. Peterson, "Making Connections."

changes that occur in the natural world, and the work is thus a microcosm of
the processual changes of the universe itself:

The hard and the soft push each other and generate changes and transformations.
(A/2)

As a consequence, the Yi corresponds to the movement of Heaven and
Earth itself:

The broad and the great[64] match Heaven and Earth; the alternations penetrate and
match the four seasons; the propriety of yin and yang matches the sun and moon.
The goodness of ease and simplicity[65] matches the utmost potency. (A/6)

But what makes the Yi invaluable for humans is that not only does it correspond to the movements of Heaven and Earth, but it actually penetrates
these processes and is thus able to understand what changes are to come:

One yin and one yang is called the Way. That which continues it is called good; that
which completes it is called nature. . . . Generating and generating is called change.
Completing the images is called Qian; imitating the models is called Kun. Going to
the limit of numbers to understand what is to come is called prognostication; penetrating alternations is called serving. What yin and yang cannot measure is called
shen. (A/5)

The movement of the universe is defined by the interplay of yin and yang;
the interplay of yin and yang lines in the Yi therefore replicates the interplay
of yin and yang forces in the cosmos at large. And that which defines this interplay is divine and therefore not explicable in terms of yin and yang. The
Yi is divine precisely because it penetrates to the workings of change itself.

And the process of divination grants humans—those with forms—an
understanding of these changes.

It is for this reason that the power of the milfoil stalks is round and divine (shen), the
power of the trigrams is square so as to understand, and the propriety of the six lines
is changeable so as to provide. (A/10)

---

64. The "broad" and the "great" refer to Qian and Kun, respectively; these terms are used
to define Qian and Kun in the lines immediately preceding those given here.

65. "Ease" and "simplicity" are further references to Qian and Kun, respectively. An earlier
line in the work reads: "Qian knows by means of ease; Kun is capable by means of simplicity"
(A/1).

The first part of divination involves the use of milfoil stalks, which are divine and hence attuned to the changes themselves. They are thus round—like Heaven. The milfoil stalks point the user to the trigrams—which are square and thus within human comprehension.[66] The lines then explain what is to come.

Only the sages of antiquity, those who were able to perceive properly, were able to understand how to use the text:

Divine (*shen*) so as to understand what is to come, understanding so as to store what had come, who would be able to participate in this? It is those of antiquity who were sharp of hearing and clear of vision, perceptive and understanding, divinely (*shen*) martial without putting people to death. This is the means by which they illuminated the way of Heaven and explored the practices of the people. (A/10)

The sages of antiquity understood the way of Heaven and the practices of the people because of the *Yi*.

And where did the *Yi* come from?

The sages set forth the trigrams and observed the images. They attached words to them and clarified auspiciousness and inauspiciousness. (A/2)

Here we seem to encounter a paradox: the sages created the *Yi*, and yet they became sages only by following the *Yi*. This paradox is not, however, the result of confused thinking on the part of the authors. On the contrary, it is precisely the point. The lengthy, and frequently quoted, passage that describes the creation in detail will help explicate this point:

In ancient times Baoxi [i.e., Fuxi] was the king of all under Heaven. Looking up he observed the images in Heaven, and looking down he observed the models on Earth. He observed the patterns of the birds and beasts and the suitability of the earth. Near at hand he took them from his body, and at a distance he took them from things. (B/2)

Baoxi is here posed as purely an observer of patterns in the natural world. He generated the eight trigrams in order to understand and categorize these patterns:

He thereupon first created the eight trigrams in order to penetrate the potency of the divine clarity (*shenming*) and in order to categorize the dispositions (*qing*) of the myriad things. (B/2)

---

66. As the authors explain elsewhere, "spirits (*shen*) are not square" (*Xici zhuan*, A/11).

By taking the patterns in the natural world and refining them into the tri-grams, Baoxi was able to understand the cosmos.[67]

The text then illustrates the divine potency of the trigrams by narrating how the trigrams inspired the sages to create cultural implements. As Willard Peterson correctly points out: "In contending that the great innova-tions were inspired by trigrams and hexagrams, the 'Commentary' [*Xici zhuan*] effectively subordinates to the *Yi* the sages who were venerated by the society as culture heroes."[68]

Why does the *Xici zhuan* give such extraordinary prominence to the *Yi*, even to the point of subordinating the sages themselves? I suggest that the text is a critique of the claims being made for sagehood that were becoming increasingly common in the late Warring States period. To oppose the as-sertions that one can attain the powers of, even become, a spirit, the text subordinates sagehood to textual authority. The implications of this move were crucial for late Warring States culture.

Although translations of the *Xici zhuan* commonly utilize the present tense to refer to the actions of the sages, I argue, on the contrary, that the past tense is almost always more appropriate. The *Xici zhuan*'s account of the creation of the *Yi* by the sages is a historical narrative, one not unmarked by problems:

As for the arising of the *Yi*, was it not in middle antiquity? Did those who made the *Yi* not have anxiety and troubles? (B/7)

The hexagrams are datable to the earliest sages, but the text of the *Yi* came later, in middle antiquity. And the fact that such explications were necessary is a further sign of decay from the early sages:

The master said: "The Qian and Kun are the gates of the *Yi*. Qian is a yang thing, and Kun is a yin thing. Yang and yin unite potency, and the hard and soft have em-bodiment. They thereby embody the arrangements of Heaven and Earth and pene-trate the potency of the divine clarity (*shenming*). Their appellations and names are mixed but do not transgress. In examining their categorization, they are the ideas of an age of decline." (B/6)

---

67. For a fuller discussion of the creation of the trigrams, see chap. 2 of my *Ambivalence of Creation*.

68. Peterson, "Making Connections," p. 112.

The Qian and Kun hexagrams may exhibit the potency of divine clarity, but the text itself reflects an age of decline, more specifically, the era of King Wen, at the end of the Shang dynasty:

As for the arising of the *Yi*, was it not fitting to be during the end of the Yin and the flourishing potency of the Zhou? [Was it] not fitting to be at the events between King Wen and Zhou? (B/11)

That the text had to be composed at all was a sign of degeneracy, of a period that desperately needed reform.

The vision of history set forth in the *Xici zhuan* is one of gradual loss, with each stage in the process of degeneration being marked by the need for more elaboration of the *Yi*. The final text of the *Yi* was put together in middle antiquity, at the end of the Shang dynasty, and, the text is arguing, it is this textual record that must now guide us in this period of even greater degeneration. Our only means of attaining an understanding of the universe is through the *Yi*, the text authored by the sages of antiquity so that we may act properly in this world. And, the *Xici zhuan* is at pains to point out, the *Yi* does indeed give us access to the proper understanding held by the sages of antiquity:

The master said: "Writing does not fully express words, and words do not fully express ideas. As such, as for the ideas of the sages, can they not be seen?" The master said: "The sages established the images in order to express ideas fully, set up the hexagrams in order to express the essential and the artificial fully, appended statements to them in order to express their words fully, alternated and penetrated them in order to express the beneficial fully, and drummed them and danced them in order to express their divinity (*shen*) fully." (A/12)

Consequently, a properly trained gentleman will turn to the *Yi* before he undertakes any actions:

Therefore, when a gentleman is about to take an action, or is to begin moving, he makes a vocal inquiry to it. (A/10)

As I read it, this argument is directed against those who were arguing that, through self-cultivation, one can attain sagehood and achieve divine powers. The authors of the *Xici zhuan*, on the contrary, placed the text of the *Yi* between their contemporaries and divinity: we can only attain a proper understanding of fortune and misfortune through the *Yi*. The *Xici zhuan* does not, of course, argue that it would be impossible for a new sage to arise, but the text does imply that even a new sage would need to be guided by the *Yi* (although not by the line statements), just as the great sages of antiquity were. Moreover, since the *Yi* is already divine, this cosmology does not appear even to entertain the possibility that the *Yi* could be superseded.

In short, the *Xici zhuan* is arguing for textual authority, for a commitment to past teachings, for a recognition that at best the outcome of self-cultivation would be a replication of the sages of antiquity. Hence the recurrent quotations attributed to Confucius and the recurrent quotations from the *Shijing*.

When read this way, one can see a surprising, and somewhat counterintuitive, parallel with the *Xunzi*'s concerns: both texts share an interest in supporting divination as a traditional practice, and both argue that we should follow the teachings of the past sages. But they build these arguments in very different ways. The *Xici zhuan* argues that divination does indeed lead to an understanding of the cosmos—an argument Xunzi would have rejected as a misguided and improper attempt to know Heaven. Xunzi opposed this type of cosmological speculation because it might pull man away from a proper cultivation in the traditions of the past sages; the *Xici zhuan* is claiming that, to the contrary, cosmology and textual authority are inherently linked. In other words, the *Xici zhuan* argues that cosmological knowledge depends on a mastery of the traditions of the ancient sages.

In saying this, I am not claiming that the authors of the *Xici zhuan* were "Confucian," or that they would have perceived themselves as offering a Confucian response to Xunzi.[69] But I am claiming that the *Xici zhuan* is making an argument for the authority of past sages and that it was presenting the *Yi* as the proper textual authority for cosmological speculation.

---

69. The discovery of the Mawangdui version of the text has sparked a debate whether the *Xici zhuan* was "Confucian" or "Daoist." See, in particular, Wang Baoxuan, "Boshu *Xici* yu Zhanguo Qin Han Daojia *Yi* xue"; and Liao Mingchun, "Lun Boshu *Xici* yu jinben *Xici* de guanxi." For an excellent overview of the debate, see Shaughnessy, "A First Reading of the Mawangdui *Yijing* Manuscript." As I have explained in the Introduction, I oppose the attempt to categorize Warring States texts in terms of schools.

As for the question of the relationship between the Mawangdui and the received versions of the *Xici zhuan*, for the specific issues discussed in this chapter, the variants between the Mawangdiu *Xici zhuan* and the received text are minor. Although the Mawangdui *Xici zhuan* does not contain the passages concerning the text in middle antiquity, it does include the vast majority of the other statements quoted. Overall, I think the reading given here applies to the Mawangdiu *Xici zhuan* as well.

As noted in Chapter 3, the *Mencius* argues that the sage must follow the proper patterns derived from Heaven—even if the actions of Heaven itself are not always in accord with these patterns. In the *Xici zhuan*, however, the patterns that the sages found in nature themselves guide the natural world; in other words, the natural world operates by those patterns, and the sages must emulate them and bring them to other humans. In the *Xici zhuan*, the natural world is more than the repository of normative patterns that can be discovered by a discerning sage; it itself is normative.

But, like the *Lunyu* and unlike the *Mencius*, the *Xici zhuan* relegates the period of the sages—the period when humans were able to model themselves on the cosmos—to the distant past. Textual authority is thus defended through a claim of gradual degeneration: the sages of antiquity discerned the patterns properly, and those born later must use divination and the reading of hexagram line statements to gain access to the patterns. As long as one submits to the divination practices of the *Xici zhuan*, fortune and misfortune are fully knowable. Whereas the authors of the "Neiye" and "Xinshu" had claimed fortune and misfortune to be knowable by those who practiced self-cultivation to gain the powers of spirits, the authors of the *Xici zhuan* argue that they are knowable only by following the traditions handed down from the ancient sages.

Instead of claiming that divination has been superseded by self-cultivation techniques and instead of supporting divination as *wen*, the authors of the *Xici zhuan* present divination as a crucial art—not because it determines the actions of the spirits but rather because it forms a microcosm to the patterns of the cosmos. The authors of the *Xici zhuan* thus used correlativity to call for a subordination to the traditions of the past sages.

Conclusion

As mentioned earlier in this chapter, Marshall Sahlins, in his re-reading of Lévi-Strauss, argues that Polynesian cultures can be read as both mono-genetic and polygenetic—or more precisely, they can be read as either, depending on the perspective of the cultural actors in question and the practice in play. The interesting issue then becomes how these principles are articulated in any given situation. Which is the marked term: continuity or discontinuity? For example, Sahlins argues that in Fiji sacrificial action assumes continuity, and the goal of the sacrifices is thus to introduce and maintain discontinuity.

Recall that in Polynesian thought, as distinguished from the so-called totemism, all men are related to all things by common descent. The corollary would be that, rather than the ancestral or kindred species being tabu, Polynesian social life is a universal project of *cannibalisme généralisé*, or even of endocannibalism, since the people are genealogically related to their own "natural" means of subsistence. . . . All useful plants and animals are immanent forms of the divine ancestors—so many *kino lau* or "myriad bodies" of the gods. Moreover, to make root crops accessible to man by cooking is precisely to destroy what is divine in them: their autonomous power, in the raw state, to reproduce. . . . Yet the aggressive transformation of divine life into human substance describes the mode of production as well as consumption. . . . Fishing, cultivating, constructing a canoe, or, for that matter, fathering a child are so many ways that men actively appropriate "a life from the god."[70]

The concern, in other words, is to introduce discontinuity, to separate the divine from the human, to mark off a human realm distinct from the divine:

Men thus approach the divine with a curious combination of submission and hubris whose final object is to transfer to themselves the life that the gods originally possess, continue to embody, and alone can impart. It is a complex relation of supplication and expropriation, successively bringing the sacred to, and banishing it from, the human domain. Man, then, lives by a kind of periodic deicide. Or, the god is separated from the objects of human existence by acts of piety that in social life would be tantamount to theft and violence—not to speak of cannibalism.[71]

In this sense, Fijian sacrifice operates according to principles very similar to those found in early Greece (see Chapter 1).

If we were to accept the recurrent arguments of sinologists, we would certainly conclude that China, too, is monogenetic and assumes continuity between the human and the divine realms. And, at first glance, much of the evidence appears to support such a reading. In looking at the sacrificial material discussed in Chapter 1, one could conclude that the predominant concern was similar to that Sahlins describes for Polynesia: an attempt to create discontinuity between the human and the divine realms, to distinguish humans and spirits, to appropriate for human use phenomena controlled by spirits (for example, divinations for the purposes of opening a field for agriculture or setting the boundaries of the capital in part reveal a desire to appropriate land controlled by divine powers and mark it off for human use). One could similarly argue that the correlative cosmologies of the fourth and

---

70. Sahlins, *Islands of History*, pp. 112–13.
71. Ibid., p. 113.

third centuries BC reveal a recurrent belief in the absolute consubstantiality of all things within a single ancestral line: everything is born from the One, and thus literally everything in the cosmos is related by birth. In such a reading, China, from the Bronze Age through the correlative cosmologies of the late Warring States period, is prototypically monogenetic.

But I have argued for a different reading of this material. In the sacrificial and ritual actions of Bronze Age China, the concern for demarcating a human realm apart from the divine was only a part (and a lesser part at that) of the whole story. The main concern was to transform the spirit world into a pantheon of ancestors that acted on behalf of the living king. Humans were not just claiming land from the spirits; they were transforming the spirits into (deceased) humans. The concern, in short, was to transform a capricious and potentially antagonistic spirit world into a hierarchical pantheon of ordered genealogical descent interested in its living descendants' welfare. The goal was not to introduce discontinuity but to anthropomorphize the divine and thus create genealogical continuity. Both divine and human powers were to be transformed into ancestors and descendants. And the paradigmatic relationship was that of the king and Heaven—through the sacrifices, Heaven would become the father to the king: hence the royal title "Son of Heaven."

Several of the correlative cosmological texts played with these models of ancestral sacrifice because their authors wished to make comparable arguments—with a crucial twist. Whereas divination and sacrifice assumed a world populated by spirits who had control over natural phenomena— spirits who were to be transformed into ancestors—the correlative texts posit a cosmos descended from a single ancestor. More pointedly, if the sacrificial practices assumed an agonistic world, the texts discussed in this chapter argue for a single, continuous cosmos within which all gods, spirits, humans, and nature are linked by chains of genealogical descent.

The debates then turned on the relationship between the sage and that ancestor. Should he strive to be the proper descendant of the One and follow the natural patterns laid down by the ancestor? This is the position taken by the *Taiyi sheng shui* and the "Chengfa" chapter of the *Shiliujing*. Or should the sage go against the natural genealogy and return to the ancestor? This is the position of the *Laozi*, which argues that the sage should return to the One, gain its powers, and thereby give birth to a world of his own. By linking himself to the ancestor of the cosmos, the sage generates his own ordered political realm. Or does the cosmos work in such a way that the proper descendant comes to be like his ancestor? This is the position of the "Bensheng" chapter of the *Lüshi chunqiu*: the Son of Heaven, if he cultivates himself properly, ultimately becomes like Heaven and exercises the same powers over the cosmos that Heaven had earlier done.

Throughout these texts, the concern is not to demarcate the human from the divine but the exact opposite—to link man with the ancestor of the cosmos, either through the return of the sage to the ancestor, or through the growth of the sage into the power that the ancestor was, or through the divinization of the sage himself, or through a subordination of oneself to the movements of a series of images handed down by the sages of the past. In other words, the concern, as with so many Warring States texts, is with the divinization of man rather than the de-divinization of nature. And the recurrent concern of all these texts was to deny the agonistic world of the sacrificial specialists who were dominant at the courts.

The authors are thus playing with the model of ancestral sacrifice, but they do not assume monogenesis: in all these practices, monogenesis is the goal, not an assumption. Instead, the authors use ancestral sacrifice because it provides a perfect vocabulary for their claims: just as in ancestral sacrifice, correlative cosmology involves taking spirits and making them into ancestors who can then be understood or even controlled. And the resulting interplay that we have noted in this chapter is therefore similar to that discussed in Chapter 1: the living could be presented as simply following the wishes of the ancestors, or they could be presented as creating the ancestors and pacifying them. The concern in both the sacrificial systems and the correlative texts is to anthropomorphize the divine, either by making the divine into the image of man through sacrifices or by divinizing man and thus literally making the divine human. But, the agonistic world assumed in sacrifice is denied in correlative cosmology, and correlative cosmology grants the sage much more power over this world than does any sacrificial system.

And it was precisely in opposition to positions such as these that Xunzi and the authors of the *Xici zhuan* reasserted the importance of divination and (in the case of Xunzi) sacrifice in order to assert a form of discontinuity, with humans and Heaven fully separated. In the *Xici zhuan*, for example, humans act properly by following a set of refined images that crystallize, in a series of full and broken lines, the movements of the cosmos. The images are continuous with the pivot of the universe, but humans, because they are separate from the pivot, can act properly only by subordinating themselves to those images. The *Yi*, therefore, was placed between humanity and the rest of the cosmos. Divination was thus reinstated, although without the agonistic cosmology that defined earlier divination practices.

All of this brings us back to Granet. As noted earlier in this chapter, Granet argued that Chinese kingship arose from the sacrifice of totemic creatures: the rulers conquered the gods their people had earlier worshipped. Lévi-Strauss—correctly—would have questioned Granet's discussion of such themes in terms of an actual evolution from totemism to sacrifice—or in terms of an evolution at all, since Granet was discussing texts dating almost exclusively from the third and second centuries BC. I have therefore followed Lévi-Strauss in discussing the texts in terms of the ways they posit continuity and discontinuity. But Granet's point is crucial: even the statements about continuity reveal an attempt to gain for the sage tremendous power over the cosmos. Reading Granet through Lévi-Strauss thus gives us a powerful means of correcting the many sinologists who argue that the early Chinese assumed a continuous universe—a position, ironically, that many of them developed by reading Granet.

Correlative cosmology should not be interpreted as a general "Chinese" way of thinking, nor should it be understood as part of a shift from "religion" to "philosophy." It was, rather, an attempt to transcend the conflict between humans and spirits by overcoming the world of spirits altogether: spirits and the natural phenomena they control, as well as humankind, are placed in a descent line emanating from a single ancestor, with whom the sage, if he follows certain techniques, can gain a special relationship. Correlative cosmology was not an assumption in the Warring States period; it was a rhetoric of critique.

5 The ascension of the spirit

Liberation, Spirit Journeys, and Celestial Wanderings

The *Shiwen* (Ten questions), one of the texts discovered at Mawangdui, discusses how one becomes a spirit, becomes liberated from one's form, and ascends to the heavens:

Long life is generated through storing and accumulating. As for the increasing of this life, above one explores the Heavens, and below one distributes to the Earth. He who is capable will invariably become a spirit. He will therefore be able to be liberated from his form. He who clarifies the great way travels and traverses the clouds.[1]

Although this text was discovered fairly recently, the themes of liberation and ascension appear in a number of received works from the late Warring States and early Han periods as well, such as the *Chuci* and *Zhuangzi*. Modern analyses of these narratives of spirit journeys and ascensions often refer either to earlier shamanistic traditions or to later religious Daoism. I will briefly review these claims and then argue for a different approach.[2]

---

1. *Shiwen*, in *Mawangdui Hanmu boshu*, 4: 146; hereinafter cited in the text. My translation of this passage, as well as all other passages from the *Shiwen*, is heavily indebted to the excellent translation and study by Donald Harper in *Early Chinese Medical Literature*, pp. 384–411. Moreover, my understanding of the content itself is indebted as well to the superb analyses in ibid., pp. 112–25.

2. Portions of this chapter are taken from my "The Ascension of the Spirit."

How to Read the Ascension Literature

Many scholars explain the ascension literature as a survival of earlier shamanistic traditions dating to the Bronze Age. K. C. Chang, for example, reads the various mentions of spirit journeys in third- and second-century BC writings as remnants of an earlier shamanism that had dominated the cultures of Neolithic and Bronze Age China.[3] This shamanistic worldview was predicated on the belief that Heaven and Earth were interconnected, and shamans were perceived to be the figures who connected the two realms: "The shamans—religious personnel equipped with the power to fly across the different layers of the universe with the help of animals and a whole range of rituals and paraphernalia—were chiefly responsible for the Heaven-Earth communication."[4] Chang thus reads the ascension literature in texts such as the *Chuci* as "shamanistic poems" containing "descriptions of shamans and their ascent and descent."[5]

Similar arguments can be found in the work of Arthur Waley, Isabelle Robinet, and Jordan Paper, who refers to passages from the *Chuci* and *Zhuangzi* as examples of "shamanic ascent."[6] Perhaps not surprisingly, Mircea Eliade adopted this approach as well: "As for the Daoists, whose legends abound with ascensions and every other kind of miracle, it is probable that they elaborated and systematized the shamanic technique and ideology of protohistorical China." He refers explicitly to the "Yuan you" poem in the *Chuci* as shamanic: "A long poem by Qu Yuan mentions numerous ascents to the 'gates of heaven,' fantastic horseback journeys, ascent by the rainbow—all of them familiar motifs in shamanic folklore."[7]

There are, however, several problems with this theory. In addition to the questions about the shamanism hypothesis raised in Chapters 1 and 2, there are, in the extant corpus, no references to spirit journeys or ascensions in China until (at the earliest) the fourth century BC. We are dealing not with a tradition whose roots lie deep in the Neolithic (or Paleolithic) but with a

---

3. K. C. Chang, *Art, Myth, and Ritual*, pp. 44–55.
4. K. C. Chang, *The Archaeology of Ancient China*, p. 415.
5. K. C. Chang, "Ancient China and Its Anthropological Significance," pp. 163–64.
6. See Waley, *The Nine Songs*; Robinet, *Taoism*, pp. 35–36; and Paper, *The Spirits Are Drunk*, pp. 55–58.
7. Eliade, *Shamanism*, pp. 450–51.

phenomenon that arose at a specific and (relative to the chronology provided by these scholars) late period of time.

Moreover, the connection between the ascension literature and a belief in a shamanistic/monistic cosmos does not hold. Just as with the issues concerning self-divinization claims discussed in Chapter 2, there is again a clear parallel with Greece: references to spirit journeys and the ascension of the spirit appear widely in Greek texts at roughly the same time as they do in China.[8] Here again, Chang's attempt to distinguish China and its shamanistic/monistic cosmology from the West and its dualistic cosmology is unconvincing. Spirit journeys and ascensions cannot be linked to any one type of cosmology: claims of ascension can be made from either a dualistic or a monistic stance. Indeed, such claims were based on both monistic and dualistic cosmologies in Greece, and, I will argue, the same is true in early China: several early Chinese texts posit a monistic cosmology, but others are, I will try to demonstrate, at least partially dualistic. The China/West model, in other words, breaks down again, as does any attempt to connect ascension with monism.

How have ascension claims in Greece been interpreted? Until recently, the dominant explanation for the emergence of ascension literature in Greece was diffusion. Wilhelm Bousset, for example, saw that literature as a diffusion from Persia.[9] (This is slightly different from Dodds's argument that the Greeks were influenced by Siberian shamanism via the Scythians [see Chapter 2]. Bousset was attempting to account for a particular type of ascension practice, and, for example, he traced Plato's narrative about Er to Persia.)[10] This argument has since been widely rejected on the grounds that the Persian texts from which the Greek practices purportedly derived are demonstrably later than the Greek texts in question.[11] Another attempt to account for ascension narratives dispenses with diffusionist explanations entirely. Ioan Culianu argues that ascension is simply a product of the human mind.[12] The problem with this argument, however, is that it provides no ex-

---

8. A clear example would be the narrative of the soul in Plato's *Phaedrus*, which I discuss later in this chapter.

9. Bousset, *Der Himmelreise der Seele*.

10. Ibid., p. 66. Plato's narrative on Er is found in the *Republic*, book 10.

11. See Culianu, *Psychonadia I*, pp. 16–23.

12. Culianu, *Psychonadia I*.

planation why particular claims of ascension are made at particular times: cultural and historical specificity is again undervalued.

In discussing the emergence of ascension literature, we thus find ourselves in much the same position as we were in Chapter 2 in accounting for the emergence of self-divinization claims. The arguments for either survival or diffusion fail to convince. Not only is empirical evidence lacking for either explanation, but neither explanation in fact explains anything. To say that ascension literature appears in the third-century BC texts as a survival of an earlier shamanism or as a diffusion from another culture leaves aside the basic question of why authors began discussing ascension at this time. Even if the authors did get the notion from earlier sources or from another culture (and evidence is lacking for either argument), this does not explain why they appropriated it. And ascribing ascension to a universal way of thinking fails to explain the fact that claims for ascension are made only at certain times in certain contexts.

Instead of interpreting late Warring States and early Han ascension texts as remnants of an earlier shamanism or as products of either diffusion or a universal mind-set, I will analyze these texts from a historical perspective and ask why the themes of becoming a spirit, being released from one's form, and ascending to the Heavens became so important in the late Warring States and early Han. I will ask what claims were being made in each text, and why, in the context of the time, such claims were seen as significant.

As for the attempt to read these texts in terms of later Daoism, there is no question that religious Daoist movements utilized notions of divinization and ascension. In fact, as many scholars have pointed out, the reference in the passage quoted above to *xingjie* (being liberated from one's form) strongly resembles the later Daoist notion of *shijie* (being liberated from the corpse). However, labeling any of these third- or second-century BC ideas as "Daoist" is dangerous. Our first goal should be to understand the claims being made in these texts in terms of the contemporary context. Since there is no evidence that any of the figures making these claims considered themselves to be "Daoist," the term is not helpful in analyzing their arguments. The later appropriation of these ideas by religious Daoist movements is a separate issue.[13] I will hint at my own response at the end of the concluding chapter and will discuss the issue in depth in a forthcoming study.

---

13. Anna Seidel and Donald Harper have done pioneering work demonstrating the implications of Warring States and Han paleographic finds for our understanding of the religious

The Liberation of the Spirit: Question
Four of the *Shiwen*

The first question that arises with the *Shiwen* is What sort of a text is this? Donald Harper, one of the leading scholars of Warring States paleographic materials and author of a superb translation of this text, argues that we should see texts like the *Shiwen* as embodying a core set of elite practices during the Warring States period. Indeed, he argues, the texts represent a moment when practices that had earlier been the preserve of religious officiants and shamans were written down and became part of a more widely transmitted set of teachings:

> As documented in the Mawangdui medical manuscripts, incantations and magico-religious operations were collected together with other medical recipes. If such practices had once been the preserve of religious officiants and shamans, or formed part of oral folklore, they acquired a new kind of prestige as they were incorporated into the books of specialists in natural philosophy and occult knowledge. Magic became a technique to be taught and transmitted in books along with other techniques; it became a segment of occult thought.[14]

In Harper's view, the practices described in these texts should be understood as common among elites of the day: "I assume that the hygienic practices in Li fils' manuscripts were customary, rather than exceptional, among people of his class; and that the 'Way of Ancestor Peng' in Yinshu was a standard guide to healthful living."[15] And if texts such as the *Shiwen* are representative of elite practices, texts such as the "Neiye" and *Zhuangzi* should be read as philosophical and mystical programs—a product of philosophers, not of religious practitioners: "The Mawangdui and Zhangjiashan macrobiotic hygiene texts describe a kind of baseline macrobiotics hygiene for the elite that focuses on care of the body, not on the more philosophical and mystical programs of the 'Neiye,' *Zhuangzi*, or *Laozi*."[16]

Thus, for Harper, these texts are radically different in nature: the *Shiwen* is more popular, whereas the "Neiye" and *Zhuangzi* are more "philosophical" or "mystical." I disagree. The *Shiwen* was written as a response to other posi-

---

practices out of which Daoism later arose. See, e.g., Seidel, "Traces of Han Religion in Funeral Texts Found in Tombs"; and Harper, "Warring States, Ch'in and Han Periods."

14. Harper, *Early Chinese Medical Literature*, p. 43.

15. Ibid., p. 116.

16. Ibid., p. 114.

tions, and reading it as representative of a common set of practices and thus distinct from other, "philosophical" texts strikes me as potentially misleading. Moreover, the *Shiwen* is, as I show later in this chapter, generically identical to two narratives from the "Outer Chapters" of the *Zhuangzi*—a text that Harper would classify as "philosophical." Finally, I question, for the reasons elaborated at the beginning of this chapter, any attempt to read the *Shiwen* as an outgrowth of an earlier shamanistic folklore.

In short, I question the classifications of "popular" versus "philosophical." It is not clear that the *Shiwen* is more popular than the "Neiye" or the *Zhuangzi*. All three texts are polemics, and all in fact use a similar form of argumentation. I will read the *Shiwen* as part of the debates discussed in the preceding chapters and will argue that it is one in a series of claims made in the late Warring States and early Han concerning the potentials of humans to liberate themselves from the forms of the world and travel to other realms.

Before turning to the analysis, I should note that the precise placement within the *Shiwen* of a passage discussed below is a topic of debate. The editors of the Mawangdui texts initially placed this section within question number six. However, the passage makes no sense there. Question number six is concerned with the use of particular sexual practices for self-cultivation—topics that are not discussed at all in this narrative. Qiu Xigui has argued, convincingly in my opinion, that the passage belongs instead in question number four—a dialogue between Huangdi and a certain Rong Cheng concerning longevity.[17] By providing a close reading of the entire question, I hope to help demonstrate the strength of Qiu Xigui's suggestion.

The narrative opens with Huangdi asking Rong Cheng why people live and die:

Huangdi asked Rong Cheng, "When people first extend the pure that flows into their form, what is obtained so that they live? When this flowing into form becomes a body, what is lost so that they die? Why is it that, among people of the time, some are bad and others are good, some die young and others live long? I desire to hear why people's *qi* flourishes or yields, relaxes or strengthens." (4: 146)

"Flowing into the form" refers to the gestation of the embryo.[18] Another Mawangdui text, the *Taichan shu*, uses the same term to refer to the first

---

17. Qiu Xigui, "Mawangdui yishu shidu suoyi." Harper also follows Qiu's recommendation.

18. Harper, *Early Chinese Medical Literature*, p. 393n2.

month of the life of an embryo in a womb.[19] This notion that life begins with a flowing into the form sets the background for some of the crucial claims made later in the narrative.

The remainder of the narrative consists of Rong Cheng's response:

Rong Cheng answered, "If Your Majesty desires to be long-lived, then accord with and observe the disposition of Heaven and Earth. The *qi* of Heaven is exhausted monthly and then flourishes monthly. It can therefore live long. The *qi* of Earth is yearly cold and hot, and anger and ease take from each other. The Earth is therefore lasting and does not decay. Your Majesty must examine the disposition of Heaven and Earth and put it into practice in himself." (4: 146)

Both Heaven and Earth consist of *qi*, and both follow cycles. Heaven's *qi* flourishes and is exhausted monthly. (One manifestation of this, presumably, is the cycle of waxing and waning of the moon.) And the balancing of the *qi* of earth by cold and hot leads to the seasonal cycle. The key for self-cultivation lies in examining these qualities and putting them into practice within oneself.

However, only a man of the Way is able to fully do so:

There are signs that can be understood. At the present moment, even a sage is not capable of this; only one of the Way can understand them. The utmost essence (*jing*) of Heaven and Earth is born from the signless, grows in the formless, becomes complete in the bodiless. (4: 146)

One of the Way is superior to a sage, since only he can understand signs. And he can do so because only he understands that the utmost essence is born from the signless. Life may begin with a flowing into form, but one of the Way properly understands how to turn to the formless.

Rong Cheng continues:

He who obtains it will have longevity, he who loses it will die young. Therefore, he who is good at controlling the *qi* and concentrating the essence becomes accumulated with the signless. Essence and spirit (*shen*) will overflow like a fountain. Inhale the sweet dew so as to make it accumulate. Drink the jade fountain and numinous winepot so as to make them circulate. Get rid of the bad and enjoy the habitual, and the spirit will then flow into the form. (4: 146–47)

---

19. *Taichan shu*, in *Mawangdui Hanmu boshu*, 4: 136. See the translation in Harper, *Early Chinese Medical Literature*, p. 378.

The key to longevity lies in obtaining the utmost essence. The implication here is that spirit is born from a concentration of essence and an accumulation of the signless. And when spirit is abundant, it will flow into one's form.

The image of "flowing into the form" (*liu xing*) clearly refers back to Huangdi's initial question concerning the birth of humans. By means of this initial cultivation, Rong Cheng is arguing, the spirit will once again fill one's form as it did at the time of the initial birth.

In many ways, the argument thus far is based on a vocabulary and cosmology highly reminiscent of those found in much of the self-cultivation literature from the Warring States period. For example, as was discussed in Chapters 2 and 4, respectively, the "Neiye" and "Xinshu" chapters make a strikingly similar set of claims. The arguments of such texts are built around the interrelated terms *qi*, essence (*jing*), and spirit (*shen*). Both *jing* and *shen* are defined as highly refined *qi*—definitions that the *Shiwen* is utilizing as well. And, like the *Shiwen*, one of the goals of human cultivation is to concentrate more of this essence and spirit—this highly refined *qi*—within one's body.

Despite the apparent similarities between the "Neiye" and "Xinshu" chapters and this portion of the *Shiwen*, however, there are also several crucial differences. The arguments of the "Neiye" and "Xinshu" rest on the claim of a monistic cosmos: the entire universe is composed of *qi*, and spirit, the most highly refined *qi*, controls the less rarified *qi*. Accordingly, he who accumulates more of this refined *qi* within himself gains great power to understand and control phenomena, avoid injuries and disasters, and understand auspiciousness and inauspiciousness without resorting to divination. All these arguments rest on the claim of monism: since the universe is composed of *qi*, and since all change is a product of the alterations and transformations of this *qi*, then spirits, the most highly refined form of *qi*, are able to control phenomena and understand the proper movements of the universe. And, since humans have this spirit within themselves as well, they can, with proper cultivation, ultimately become (it is argued in the "Xinshu" chapters) spirits.

The *Shiwen* shares some of these concerns and much of this vocabulary, but the argument develops in a very different direction. Whereas the highest state that a human can reach in the "Xinshu" is that of a sage, the *Shiwen* explicitly states that its teachings are aimed at "one of the Way." The authors of the *Shiwen* are proclaiming themselves to be in possession of a higher teaching than that possessed by sages. And only one of the Way understands that "the utmost essence of Heaven and Earth is born from the signless, grows in the formless, becomes complete in the bodiless." Essence is born, grows, and becomes completely separate from the forms—and only the one of the Way fully grasps this.

Essence, in other words, is not simply a more refined type of what exists in the forms; the two are distinct. In contrast to the authors of the "Neiye" and "Xinshu" chapters, the authors of the *Shiwen* are not necessarily committing themselves to an explicitly monistic cosmology. There is no claim here that everything is composed of *qi*; rather, the argument is presented in terms of the relationship of *qi*, essence, and spirit on the one hand to forms on the other. I am certainly not trying to argue that the framework here is comparable to the fully dualistic claims of, for example, Gnosticism. It is possible that the authors of the *Shiwen* would have held that the form is in fact unrefined *qi*, and thus their position would still be, at a fundamental level, monistic. My point is, rather, that the argument itself is couched in a dualistic framework: instead of arguing, as other authors certainly did, that forms were simply unrefined *qi* and thus capable of being understood and controlled by more refined (more spiritlike) *qi*, the authors here make no claims concerning the substance of forms. Whatever their position on the monism (or lack thereof) of the cosmos, the argument itself rests on a dualism between form and spirit. The implications of this will become clear as we continue to follow the text.

Rong Cheng next explains how spirit should be drawn into the form:

As for the way of inhaling *qi*, one must direct it to the extremities. Essence will be born and not cut off. Above and below, all is essence. Cold and warmth are peacefully born. Breathing must be deep and long-lasting. The new *qi* is easy to hold fast to. Stale *qi* is old; new *qi* is long-lived. He who is good at controlling *qi* makes the stale *qi* dissipate nightly and the new *qi* collect in the morning so as to penetrate the nine apertures and fill the six cavities. (4: 147)

The method recapitulates Rong Cheng's earlier statement that the practitioner needs to put into practice the disposition of Heaven and Earth. Thus, just as the *qi* of Heaven becomes exhausted and then flourishes, so must the ruler do the same with his own *qi*. Moreover, this must be done in accord with the earthly seasons:

There are prohibitions for eating *qi*: in the spring avoid turbid *yang*, in the summer avoid the hot winds, in the autumn avoid the frigid mist, in the winter avoid icy *yin*. Discard the four defects, and then breathe deeply so as to achieve longevity. (4: 147)

This parallel between Heaven and the ruler continues:

As for the intent of breathing in the morning: when breathing out, strive to harmonize with Heaven; when breathing in, estimate the duality of the doors[20] as if gathering in a deep pool. Then the old *qi* will be daily exhausted, and the new *qi* will daily flourish. And then the form will glow deeply and be filled with essence. One can therefore live long. (4: 147)

The consequence of such a practice is, again, that the form becomes filled with essence, and one will thus, like Heaven and Earth, live long.

Rong Cheng then outlines the type of breathing that should occur in each of the four periods of the day:

As for the intent of breathing during the day: exhaling and inhaling must be subtle, the ears and eyes must be keen and perceptive, the yin and yang must move the *qi*. Within, there is nothing dense or rotten. Thus the body is without pains or injuries. As for the intent of breathing at dusk: deeply breathe, long and carefully, cause the ears to not hear, and thereby peacefully go to bed. The *hun* and *po* will be peaceful in the form. Therefore you can live long. As for breathing at midnight: when you awake, do not alter the form in which you were sleeping. Deeply and carefully expel your strength, with the six cavities all shining forth. You will take longevity to the extreme. (4: 147)

The goal of all these exercises is to gain the practitioner a form whose disposition is like that of Heaven and Earth; a constant replenishment of *qi* fills the form with essence and spirit and thus allows it to be long-lived.

At this point, the narration shifts to the longevity of the spirit:

If you wish to make the spirit long-lived, you must use the skin's patterns to breathe. When it comes to controlling the essence of *qi*, one exits death and enters life. Happy and joyous, one uses this to fill the form. This is called concentrating the essence. Controlling the *qi* has an alignment. The task lies in accumulating essence. When essence flourishes, it invariably leaks. The essence that exits must be supplemented. As for when to supplement what has leaked: do it during sleep. (4: 147)

---

20. Harper (*Early Chinese Medical Literature*, p. 395n4) suggests that the term *guiliang* 閨 誦 be read as "dual-entry doorway," referring to the nostrils.

This practice is a continuation of that already laid out. Rong Cheng is telling Huangdi to continue filling his form with concentrated essence.

Exit[21] and enter so as to cultivate the skin's pattern.[22] When the firm and white are completed within, what sickness can there be? As for this life having misfortune, it is invariably because the essence of the yin has leaked out and the hundred vessels have become infirm and decrepit. Happiness and anger will not be timely, one will not clarify the great way, and the *qi* of life will depart him. The common man lives recklessly and then depends on ritual specialists and doctors. When one has lived half one's years,[23] one's form will invariably be buried young. To kill oneself by laboring in affairs is truly lamentable and pitiful. (4: 148)

In the final stage, one can store up the essence to such a point that the *qi* does not leak out:

Wherever death and life reside, the discerning man regulates them. By solidifying what is below and storing up the essence, the *qi* does not leak out. If the mind controls death and life, who can be defeated by them? Carefully hold fast and do not lose it, and long life will continue across generations. For continuous generations there will be contentment, joy, and long life. Long life is generated through storing and accumulating. As for the increasing of this life, above one observes in the Heavens, and below one distributes to the Earth. He who is capable will invariably become a spirit. He will therefore be able to be liberated from his form. (4: 148)

The successful adept ultimately becomes a spirit and achieves liberation from his form.

Huangdi's initial questions revolved around the flowing into form that occurs at the beginning of existence: What is such a life and how can it be preserved? Rong Cheng began by explaining how the life span of this form could be extended. But the ultimate goal is to become liberated from one's form altogether. One begins the process by cultivating the form in order to keep the spirit within it. Next one cultivates the spirit within the form until it becomes long-lasting. Finally, one becomes the spirit, and the spirit is liberated from the form altogether. Human life, in other words, normally

---

21. The section that Qiu Xigui has argued should be moved from question six to question four (slips 52–59) begins here.

22. Harper (*Early Chinese Medical Literature*, p. 397n1) convincingly argues that the character transcribed here as *mei* 美 should be transcribed as *zou* 奏, and read as 腠.

23. Following Harper's (ibid., p. 397n3) suggested reading of the characters in question as *wei ban* 未半.

begins with the joining of form and spirit; but since forms deteriorate, each life must come to an end. However, if life can be concentrated only in the spirit, then immortality is possible.

Once this occurs, Rong Cheng argues, one becomes liberated from all boundaries that would normally limit the form:

He who clarifies the great way travels and traverses the clouds. From the Collected Jade above, as the water flows he can traverse far, as the dragon ascends he can reach high, fast and not wearied of strength. (4: 148–49)

Rong Cheng concludes with an anecdote about a certain Wucheng Zhao:

[Seven graphs missing.] Wucheng Zhao [two graphs missing] did not die. Wucheng Zhao used the four seasons as his support and Heaven and Earth as his alignment (*jing*). Wucheng Zhao was born together with the yin and yang. The yin and yang do not die; Wucheng Zhao can be seen with them. The master who possesses the Way is also like this. (4: 149)

The significance of Rong Cheng's earlier claim that "the utmost essence of Heaven and Earth is born from the signless, grows in the formless, becomes complete in the bodiless" now becomes clear. The utmost essence with which the practitioner fills himself allows him to leave the world of forms and join Heaven and Earth. Like them, he never dies.

Wucheng Zhao thus takes Heaven and Earth as his alignment. The word that I am translating as "alignment" here is *jing*. This is the same word (along with *ying*, "orient") that, as discussed in the Introduction, was used to describe the aligning of the cosmos by two spirits in the "Jingshen" chapter of the *Huainanzi*. It is also the same word, discussed in Chapter 4, used in both the *Taiyi shengshui* and the "Youshi" chapter of the *Lüshi chunqiu* to describe the alignment of the cosmos. As I will discuss in detail in Chapter 7, the authors of the "Jingshen" chapter of the *Huainanzi* were arguing that spirits arranged the alignment of Heaven and Earth. In this passage from the *Shiwen*, however, the implication appears to be that Heaven and Earth were born from the formless essence and naturally gained their alignment. The adept, by filling his form with essence, is ultimately able to leave his form and become aligned with Heaven and Earth.

A comparison with the "Xinshu" chapters is instructive. The cosmology of the "Xinshu" chapters is also based on *qi*, and the text teaches how a human can achieve the ultimate that a human is capable of achieving—namely, to become a sage and acquire understanding of the world of forms and power over it. By accumulating essence within himself, the adept becomes a spirit—able to understand changes, avoid being harmed by them, and even gain control over them. The cosmology of the "Xinshu" chapters is one of hierarchical monism, and one's goal is to gain more and more control over the world of forms by becoming ever more refined.

In contrast, question four of the *Shiwen* calls for the liberation of the spirit from the world of forms. When the adept becomes a spirit, he becomes one with Heaven and Earth, traverses the cosmos, and does not die. The basis for this argument lies precisely in the claim of a distinction between—and the potential separability of—the spirit and the form. The concern here is not understanding the less refined *qi* of the world of forms or gaining power over them or avoiding being harmed by them; the goal is to use the form to accumulate and store essence until one escapes the form altogether.

A closer scrutiny of the term *xingjie*—liberation from the form—will make this point clearer. We have seen the term *jie*, liberation, several times before. In an anecdote from the "Inner Chapters" of the *Zhuangzi* discussed in Chapter 3, Zi You taught the importance of *xianjie*, a liberation from bonds. For Zi You, this meant a full acceptance of the forms within which the Fashioner of Things has placed us: we are liberated when we stop trying to overcome the order of Heaven and accept the form in which we have been placed. Whereas the *Zhuangzi* calls on us to accept the processes of life and death, the *Shiwen* teaches a transcendence of death. Zhuangzi's sage achieves liberation by accepting his form; the adept of the *Shiwen* by leaving his form.

In other texts, however, the claim is that one can be freed from the usual limits of the human form. In the "Neiye," the claim is that grasping the one word allows one to survey the cosmos: "With the liberation of the one word, one explores (*cha*) Heaven above, reaches to Earth below, and encircles and fills the nine regions." We saw a similar argument in the "Chengfa" chapter of the *Shiliujing*: "The liberation of the One allows an exploration (*cha*) of Heaven and Earth." But in neither case does this involve a separation of the spirit from the body: the argument is that the human form is limited, but grasping the One allows the adept to understand the cosmos as if he were a spirit—as if, in other words, he were not limited by a human form.

The authors of the *Shiwen* passage have shifted the argument. Here, the successful adept does indeed become a spirit, transcend the limitations of the human body, and explore the heavens personally. Instead of teaching that one should accept one's form, or that grasping the One allows one to transcend the limitations of one's form, the authors here are arguing that one can fully divinize oneself and transcend the world of forms altogether.

Not only are self-divinization practices not based on an assumption of monism, but the *Shiwen* text under discussion here does not imply a monistic worldview at all. The goal is thus to assert not continuity but discontinuity and separate the divine from the human—with the crucial proviso that the adept stay on the divine side. In the self-divinization process, the adept nurtures that divine element in himself and then cuts off the human elements. Divinization is a product of discontinuity.

The fact that this argument is presented in the form of a dialogue with Huangdi is of interest as well. In the "Chengfa" chapter of the *Shiliujing*, Li Hei's admonition to grasp the One is directed at Huangdi, and it is part of a larger argument about bringing order to the world and names and forms into accord: Li Hei is teaching Huangdi to become a good ruler. In the *Shiwen* question, the argument is again presented in terms of a dialogue with Huangdi, only here the concern is to transcend the world of forms and align oneself with Heaven and Earth themselves. Huangdi does not become a better ruler; he transcends rulership altogether.

Liberation and Ascension in the Outer Chapters of the *Zhuangzi*

An examination of other works written at roughly the same time as the *Shiwen* will help us place its dualistic argument in context. One such work is a dialogue in chapter eleven of the *Zhuangzi* between Huangdi and Guang Chengzi, which contains striking parallels with the *Shiwen* dialogue between Huangdi and Rong Cheng.[24]

The narrative opens with Huangdi as the reigning Son of Heaven:

Huangdi had been established as the Son of Heaven for nineteen years. His commands had been spread throughout all under Heaven.[25]

He thereupon goes to meet Guang Chengzi:

---

24. My understanding of this text has been greatly aided by Roth, "The Yellow Emperor's Guru."

25. *Zhuangzi*, chap. 11, 4.18a; hereinafter cited in the text.

I have heard that you have reached the utmost Way. I dare to ask you about the essence of the utmost Way. I wish to grasp the essence of Heaven and Earth so as to aid the five grains and nurture the people. I also wish to manage the yin and yang so as to perfect all that lives. How should I do this? (4.18a)

Huangdi is attempting to understand, manage, and utilize the cosmos in order to aid all living things.

Guang Chengzi responds to Huangdi's question negatively:

What you wish to ask about is the substance of things, but what you wish to manage is the remnants of things. From the time that you have been ruling all under Heaven, the rain has come without even waiting for the *qi* of the clouds to gather, the leaves of grasses and trees have fallen without waiting to turn yellow, and the brightness of the sun and moon has increasingly fallen to waste. The heart of a flatterer may be clever, but undeserving of being told about the utmost Way. (4.18a)

Huangdi thereupon retreats, renounces all under Heaven, and lives in a shack for three months. He then returns to see Guang Chengzi, who is sleeping with his face turned south—the direction that the ruler should face. Huangdi bows and asks a different question:

I have heard that you have reached the utmost Way. I dare to ask you about correcting the body. How should I do this so that it will be long-lived? (4.18a)

This question Guang Chengzi accepts:

Good question. Come. I will tell you of the essence of the utmost Way. The essence of the utmost Way is obscure and dark. The extreme point of the utmost Way is abstruse and silent. Do not look, do not listen. Embrace the spirit so as to be still, and the form will correct itself. You must be still and pure. Do not labor your form, do not agitate your essence. Your eye will have nothing that it sees, the ear nothing that it hears, and the heart nothing that it knows. Your spirit will hold fast to your form, and your form will then live long. (4.18b)

The teaching clearly resembles that seen in texts like the "Neiye" and the first part of the *Shiwen*: by keeping the spirit within one's form, the form will live long.

Take care of your insides, and block what is outside you. To know too much is to be destroyed. For you I will proceed to the height of the great clarity, going there, going to the source of the yang. For you I will enter the gates of the obscure and dark, going there, going to the source of the yin. Heaven and Earth have managers, yin and yang have repositories. Carefully hold fast to your body, and things will become strong of themselves. I hold fast to their oneness so as to reside in their harmony. Therefore I have been cultivating my body for 1,200 years, and my form has not yet declined. (4.18b–19a)

Instead of trying to manage the yin and yang, one should accept that they manage themselves. One should hold fast to their source (and hence their oneness, their harmony), and thus prevent one's form from declining.

Huangdi then bows again and says, "Guang Chengzi is Heaven." Guang Chengzi continues:

Come. I will tell you. Its things are inexhaustible, yet men all believe they have an end. Its things are without limit, yet men all believe they have a limit. He who obtains my way will begin as august and end as a king; he who loses my way will begin by seeing light and end by becoming dirt. Now, everything springs from the earth and then returns to it. Therefore, I am going to leave you. I will enter the gates of the inexhaustible so as to wander in the fields of the limitless. I will form a third luminary with the sun and the moon, I will be constant with Heaven and Earth. Near me will be obscurity, far from me there will be darkness. Humans will all die, but I alone will exist! (4.19a–b)

The final movement of the dialogue presents a higher form of transcendence. Earlier, the concern had been to keep the spirit within the form and thereby achieve a long life. However, Guang Chengzi decides not to remain in the world of forms. The precise mechanism for this transcendence is not explained. But we are told that Guang Chengzi will leave the world in which things return to the earth in death and will instead journey through the limitless, form a triad with the sun and the moon, and achieve constancy with Heaven and Earth.

The text is clearly a critique of any attempt to manipulate the world of forms. Huangdi's attempt to do so would have resulted in the destruction of the natural world. Guang Chengzi advocates instead a regimen of personal cultivation—one that will ultimately enable the practitioner to transcend the cycles of decline and decay that characterize the inconstant world between Heaven and Earth.

The structure of the argument is remarkably similar to that in the *Shiwen*. Both are cast as dialogues between Huangdi and an adept, and in both the adept calls for a process of cultivation in which one first achieves long life by filling the form with spirit and then reaches a stage of transcendence in which the adept ascends, becomes immortal, and joins with Heaven and Earth.

The argument is paralleled in another dialogue from chapter eleven of the *Zhuangzi*, between Yun Jiang and Hong Meng. Yun Jiang argues that the *qi* of the cosmos is not blending properly and the seasons are hence improperly modulated; he hopes to bring order to the world to nourish all living things.[26] Hong Meng rejects him. A narrative much like that between Huangdi and Guang Chengzi ensues, and the story concludes with Hong Meng explaining what really matters:

Mind nurturing. If you follow your place and do not act, then things transform of themselves. Let fall your form and frame. Spit out your keenness of hearing and brightness of seeing, let your relationship with things be forgotten, and fully join with the boundless. Liberate your mind and set free your spirit. Be tranquil and without a soul. The myriad things will sprout, but each will return to its root.[27]

Things with forms sprout and die, but the adept is able to free his spirit from the form and not return. Hong Meng's teaching involves an explicit rejection of refining the form: unlike the "Neiye," which explicitly argued that cultivation allowed one to gain keenness of hearing and sight, Hong Meng argues that these should be rejected.

Transcending Heaven and Earth: The "Yuan you" of the *Chuci*

The growing popularity of this argument by the late Warring States and early Han is clear from its appearance in a poem dating from roughly the same period.[28] The poem in question is the famous "Yuan you" of the *Chuci*, a text that revolves explicitly around many of the issues discussed in this chapter.

The poem opens with the poet in distress:

My spirit darted forth suddenly and did not return;
My form withered and decayed, left behind, alone.

---

26. *Zhuangzi*, chap. 11, HY 27/11/46–47.

27. Ibid., 53–55.

28. Paul Kroll, among others, argues that the text is roughly contemporary with the *Huainanzi* and that the two works reflect a similar way of thinking: "A plausible speculation is that the author may have been one of the many *littérateurs* who gathered during the 130s BCE at the court of Liu An" ("Yuan you," p. 157). As I will argue in Chapter 7, however, the *Huainanzi* is more likely a somewhat later work, and the "Yuan You" should be dated to earlier than Kroll postulates.

> I looked inward with proper resolution,
> And sought the source of the proper *qi*.[29]

The concern expressed here is quite similar to that seen in such texts as the "Neiye" and the first part of the fourth question of the *Shiwen*: the fear is that the spirit is leaving the form. And, again as in these other texts, the solution is to turn inward and cultivate one's *qi*.

The first hint that the poet is moving in a direction different from that found in texts like the "Neiye," however, can be seen in the recurrent references to the dreariness of the cosmic cycles:

> I fear the recurring sequences of the Heavenly seasons,
> The bright numinousness glows and moves westward   (5.3a–b)

The fact of seasonal change on which such texts as the "Neiye" rest their arguments is presented here as simply a movement toward death, and the concern is to transcend it.

In searching for how to do so, the poet invokes Huangdi and Wang Qiao:

> I cannot aspire to take Xuan Yuan [i.e., Huangdi] as my precedent;
> I will follow Wang Qiao and play in amusement. (5.4a)

Huangdi is too exalted a figure for the poet to emulate. Instead, he turns to Wang Qiao, who, along with Chi Songzi, was commonly invoked during the early Han as a practitioner of techniques of liberation and immortality. For example, in the "Qisu," chapter eleven of the *Huainanzi*:

Wang Qiao and Chi Songzi blew, vented, exhaled, and inhaled. They purged the old and brought in the new. They left behind their forms and expelled knowledge. They embraced the simple and returned to the genuine so as to wander in the subtle minuteness. Above they penetrated to the cloudy heavens. Now we wish to study their Way. We do not obtain their nourishing of the *qi* and bringing the spirit to dwell, but we imitate their purging and then inhaling, at the right time crouching, at the right time straightening. That we will be unable to ride the clouds and ascend to greatness is clear indeed.[30]

The poet then begins undergoing self-cultivation—in a form quite similar to what we saw above:

---

29. *Chuci*, "Yuan you," 5.2a; hereinafter cited in the text. The following translations of the "Yuan you" have benefited from the excellent translations by David Hawkes (*The Songs of the South*, pp. 191–203) and Paul Kroll ("Yuan you").

30. *Huainanzi*, "Qisu," 11.9b.

> I preserved the clear purity of the divine illumination;
> Essential *qi* entered, and the foul was expelled. (5.4b)

Wang Qiao tells him to continue such practices in order to incorporate more refined *qi*:

> Unify the *qi*, deepen the spirit,
> And preserve it in the middle of the night. (5.5a)

These teachings are reminiscent of Rong Cheng's initial advice to Huangdi: cultivate one's *qi*, bring in more spirit, and maintain it during the night.

These practices lead to a refining of the spirit and ultimately allow it to be released:

> My essence (*jing*), unmixed and pure, began to strengthen,
> My substance (*zhi*) melted and fused so as to become soft
>   and straightened,
> My spirit (*shen*) vital and subtle so as to overflow, released. (5.5b)

The poet then ascends, travels upward on a floating cloud, and enters the palace of Di. He thereafter leaves the palace and assembles a procession that includes Yushi (the Lord of Rain) and Leigong (the Duke of Thunder). Using reins and a whip, he leads the procession throughout the cosmos (5b–8b).

In the Shang ritual, the ancestors were called on to ascend to the realm of Di and direct the nature spirits to act on behalf of the living. Here, in this metaphorical discussion of something quite similar, the adept performs the ritual on himself and achieves powers while he is still alive. The ascending adept becomes more powerful than the spirits in charge of rain and thunder, and he is in fact able to command and direct them.

Indeed, the adept directs these spirits over the entire cosmos:

> I surveyed (*jing ying*) the Four Wastes,
> and flew around the Six Boundless Regions. (5.11a)

As we will see in the next two chapters, the terms *jing* and *ying* came to be commonly used in the ascension literature to discuss the surveying of the cosmos by the ascending adept. As we saw in the Introduction of this book, the same terms were used in the opening cosmogony of the "Jingshen" chapter of the *Huainanzi* to describe the aligning and orienting of the cosmos by spirits. *Jing* also appears in the *Shiwen*, where it is used in reference to Wucheng Zhao's taking Heaven and Earth as his alignment (*jing*). These terms deserve a fuller discussion here.

As noted in the Introduction, when used to describe a survey undertaken before an act of construction, the terms have the sense of "align" and "orient." But when used to describe figures traveling over an established area, they carry a meaning of "surveying" or "inspecting." For example, two poems in the *Shi* refer to war expeditions as "*jing ying* the four quarters."[31] The expeditions involve an inspection of the land under the king's control to be sure all is in order. This dual meaning of *jing ying* is, happily, contained in the English "surveying" as well. In the "Yuan you," the terms are used in the sense of inspecting the area under one's control. Leading the lesser spirits who control natural phenomena, the adept surveys the cosmos. By guiding these spirits as he surveys the universe, the adept helps keep the cosmos in order.

However, the adept soon transcends even these powers and gradually becomes like those forces that first generated the cosmos. Indeed, the adept ultimately reaches back to the point before Heaven and Earth were distinguished:

> In the depths below there was no Earth,
> in the expanse above there was no Heaven.
> . . . .
> Surpassing *wuwei* for the utmost clarity,
> Becoming a neighbor with Taichu (the Great Beginning). (11a–b)

The narrator transcends even Heaven and Earth. If Wucheng Zhao took Heaven and Earth as his alignment, the adept here transcends them. Like the passages from the *Zhuangzi* and the *Shiwen*, the "Yuan you" is a call for ascension, of a liberation and release of the spirit, of a transcendence of this world.[32]

Conclusion

The three texts explored in this chapter play off similar themes. All three utilize vocabulary and refer to practices found in the self-cultivation literature like the "Neiye" and "Xinshu" chapters, and all represent shifts away

---

31. *Shi* #205 and 234.

32. For a different interpretation, see Holzman, "Immortality-Seeking in Early Chinese Poetry," pp. 105–7. Holzman contends that the "Yuan you" is "closer to philosophical Taoism than it is to the immortality seekers" (p. 106). Here, too, I would reject the distinction between practitioners and philosophers. Just as in early Greece, the figures who are now classified as "philosophers" were also practitioners.

from the concerns of those texts. These texts seek to transcend the hierarchy of Heaven, Earth, and man found in texts like the "Neiye." They call for some form of escape from the world of forms and exhibit either a lack of interest in or overt opposition to any attempt to control or manipulate the world. The practices they espouse are to be used not to gain understanding or control over this world but to transcend it. The one possible exception to this might be the "Yuan you" poem, which grants the adept power over the spirits of rain and thunder. Even here, however, the concern is not so much to impose the adept's will on the world. As implied by the use of *jing ying*, the adept surveys the cosmos and guides the spirits as they should be guided. In other words, the adept is not a human manipulating the spirits who control natural phenomena, nor is he a practitioner of self-cultivation techniques who directly gains control over natural phenomena. Instead, he surveys the cosmos and helps keep it in order—a state akin to Wucheng Zhao's taking Heaven and Earth as his alignment. Thereafter, the adept even transcends this state and returns to the states before Heaven and Earth came into being.

All these texts enjoin the adept to reverse the process of generation in an implicit cosmogony: Heaven and Earth were generated from an essence or great beginning, and Heaven and Earth then gave birth to the myriad formed things. Heaven and Earth do not die, but the formed things do. Each of these texts then teaches how humans can dispense with their form and, joining Heaven and Earth, traverse the cosmos and achieve immortality. With the "Yuan you," the adept is able to retreat yet further—to the stage before Heaven and Earth were even formed.

The cosmologies are thus in some ways comparable to many of those analyzed in Chapter 4, but the argument is taken a step further. In the "Bensheng" chapter of the *Lüshi chunqiu*, for example, the ruler is called on to become like his ancestor Heaven and to maintain that ancestor's order; here, an earlier ancestor is posited, and the goal is to transcend the world of forms altogether.

The key move in these texts is to build on earlier cosmological and self-cultivation texts, but to posit a potential dualism between the form and the spirit. If texts like the "Xinshu" chapters of the *Guanzi* were arguing for a monistic cosmology in which one could become a spirit while remaining fully within the limitations of the human form, the concern in these texts is to distinguish the two and to liberate the spirit from the body.

And, perhaps most significant, these texts are not written in the form of advice on rulership. Indeed, the "Yuan You" is not written to a king at all; the other two, while addressed to kings, advise the ruler to transcend the world of forms and to give up the attempt to gain power over that world. Thus, here we get one of our first glimpses at the use of divinization techniques to claim autonomy from the existing order. This is not unlike what we find in ancient Greece, where, as I mentioned in Chapter 2, divinization claims became increasingly associated with movements that rejected the polis. In Greece divinization practices were also extended into narratives of ascension. An example would be the narrative of the soul in Plato's *Phaedrus*,[33] which I read as a development of the same claims discussed in Chapter 2 regarding the divinity of man's soul. Plato compares the soul to a charioteer with a pair of winged horses. The horses and charioteers of the gods are purely good, but the charioteers of human souls have only one noble horse—the other is lowly.[34] As Plato describes the ascension:

The natural function of the wing is to soar upwards and carry that which is heavy up to the place where dwells the race of the gods. More than any other thing that pertains to the body it partakes of the nature of the divine. But the divine beauty, wisdom, goodness, and all such qualities; by these then the wings of the soul are nourished and grow, but by the opposite qualities, such as vileness and evil, they are wasted and destroyed. Now the great leader in heaven, Zeus, driving a winged chariot, goes first, arranging all things and caring for all things. He is followed by an army of gods and spirits, arrayed in eleven squadrons.[35]

In this ascension to the highest levels of the cosmos, Zeus, the highest god, leads the procession, followed by an array of other gods and spirits. And humans follow as well. The wings of human souls are the most divine, and they therefore tend to ascend with the gods. But the lesser parts of the human soul pull it back down. The higher the procession goes, the more difficulty those with less cultivated souls have:

They proceed steeply upward to the top of the vault of heaven, where the chariots of the gods, whose well matched horses obey the rein, advance easily, but the others

---

33. My understanding of the *Phaedrus* narrative has been greatly helped by the insightful analysis of Bruce Lincoln, in *Theorizing Myth*, pp. 151–59.

34. Plato, *Phaedrus*, 246a–b.

35. Ibid., 246d–47a; translation by Harold North Fowler from Plato, *Euthyphro, Apology, Crito, Phaedo, Phaedrus*, pp. 473–75; hereinafter cited as Fowler.

with difficulty; for the horse of evil nature weighs the chariot down, making it heavy and pulling toward the earth the charioteer whose horse is not well trained.[36]

Finally, the procession goes beyond the heavens and reaches the level of truth, absolute justice, and knowledge.[37] The gods are able to reach this highest level, as are the best of the human souls. The others, however, fail and fall back to earth—some having glimpsed the highest level, others having not seen it at all.[38] These souls fall back to earth and are reborn in a new body. The resulting humans are arranged in a hierarchy based on how much of the world of truth each soul saw during its ascension:

The soul that has seen the most shall enter into the birth of a man who is to be a philosopher or a lover of beauty . . . and the second soul into that of a lawful king or a warlike ruler, and the third into that of a politician or a man of business or a financier, the fourth into that of a hard-working gymnast or one who will be concerned with the cure of the body, and the fifth will lead the life of a prophet or someone who conducts mystic rites; to the sixth a poet or some other imitative artist will be united, to the seventh, a craftsman or a husbandman, to the eighth, a sophist or a demagogue, to the ninth, a tyrant.[39]

As one might expect from a follower of Empedocles, the philosopher is placed at the head of the hierarchy followed by rulers and religious specialists and then the rest of society.[40] Plato is thus claiming to have access to a divine status unattainable through the sacrificial system of the polis. As in the material from early China discussed in this chapter, ascension represents a radicalization of divinization claims.

Instead, therefore, of seeing these early Chinese texts as a survival of an earlier shamanism, I would argue that these claims for ascension arose only in the third and second centuries BC for specific historical reasons. They emerged only after divinization practices had developed. The ascension literature proliferated by appropriating and radicalizing these divinization practices in order to assert the ability of individuals to transcend their roles, the political order, and the world of forms itself. The same argument would hold as well for the emergence of ascension literature in Greece at roughly the same time. In both cases, this literature arose out of a radicalization of

---

36. Plato, *Phaedrus*, 247b–c; trans. from Fowler, p. 475.
37. Plato, *Phaedrus*, 247d–e.
38. Ibid., 248a–b.
39. Ibid., 248d–e; trans. from Fowler, p. 479.
40. See Lincoln, *Theorizing Myth*, pp. 153–56.

earlier self-divinization practices, which themselves arose as a reaction to the arts of the sacrificial and divination specialists of the day.

As we shall see in the next two chapters, such claims of ascension proliferated dramatically. I will trace how the debates concerning the relationship of the spirit to the form and the degrees of power that the adept can and should exercise over things developed in the early imperial period.

6 *A theocracy of spirits*
Theism, Theomorphism, and Alchemy in the Qin and Early Han Empires

In 218 BC, the First Emperor, in the twenty-ninth year of his reign, had an inscription carved on Mount Zhifu. It read in part:

The bright potency of the August Thearch (Di) aligns (*jing*) and arranges (*li*) all within the universe.[1]

The Qin ruler, having entitled himself *huangdi* (lit. "august god"), notes that he has aligned the universe and given it patterns to follow. As we saw in Chapter 4, the term *jing* was widely utilized to describe both the spontaneously generated alignment of the cosmos and, in the ascension literature, an adept's surveying of the cosmos. Here, the claim is that the ruler himself, now called a Di, has personally aligned the cosmos.

Although such statements would be characterized in the early Han as excessively boastful, the works of this period accepted, and frequently iterated, the notion that particular figures have power over the natural world. They disagreed, however, over the means of achieving such powers and the proper moments for using them. Among the questions debated were How do natural processes work? To what extent should humans manipulate these processes? And if manipulation is acceptable, how can it be accomplished, and under what circumstances is it legitimate? In this chapter, I sketch the

---

1. *Shiji*, "Qin Shihuang benji," 6.241.

development of this debate in the Qin and the early Han and analyze the issues of concern. I focus on the questions of what cults were supported by the
early imperial states, what claims were made concerning the powers of the
rulers over the natural and the human worlds, and why several figures at
court turned to correlative models during this period.

Intimately related to these questions, I will argue, was the issue of human
mortality. Both the First Emperor and Emperor Wu of the Han employed
specialists to help them overcome human limitations and achieve a bodily
ascension to the heavens. Many of the themes analyzed in the previous chapter reappear during this period, but in a very different form. I will try to dis-
entangle the competing cosmologies of the time and the various claims concerning human potency. In order to situate this argument, I begin by
discussing the anthropological literature on divine kingship and sacrifice—a
literature in which China, again because of the work of Marcel Granet, holds
an important place.

Kingship and Sacrifice: From Granet to Dumézil and Back Again Through Sahlins

As we saw in Chapter 4, Granet's analyses of China strongly influenced the
anthropological literature on cosmological thinking. The same is true of the
anthropological literature on divine kingship. Georges Dumézil, one of Granet's students and a leader in the study of kingship, devoted his life to the
study of Indo-European materials, but Dumézil explicitly built on Granet's
work in his analyses. Dumézil, however, turned away from the evolutionary
model Granet favored and toward a study of the generation of permutations
from a given structural paradigm. Moreover, his explicit goal was to provide
a framework for comparative analysis. His attempt is worth following, both
to follow the insights his approach has yielded as well as to note the losses.

In his classic study of kingship, *Mitra-Varuna: essai sur deux représentations
indo-européennes de la souveraineté*, Dumézil argued, within a comparative
framework, for the existence in Indo-European texts of a basic dualism in
concepts of sovereignty: a passive, sacerdotal form of kingship, and an active,
militaristic form.[2] It is in these terms, for example, that he analyzed two of

---

2. Dumézil dedicates the book jointly to Granet and Marcel Mauss, and in the preface to
the second edition, he emphasized his debt to Granet; see *Mitra-Varuna*, pp. 13–14. Dumézil
also discusses some of Granet's work in his conclusion, a point to which I will return below.

the first legendary rulers of Rome: Romulus, the exemplar of violent aggressiveness (*celeritas*), and Numa, the model of sacerdotal powers (*gravitas*).[3] Dumézil's comparative approach consisted of analyzing the appearances of this dualism in various texts in different Indo-European traditions. However, Dumézil's emphasis on studying these permutations synchronically led to an unfortunate tendency on his part to chart appearances of a given structure, in this case a diarchical system of kingship. Indeed, when he mentions the studies of Granet in the conclusion to his work, he discusses not the complex analyses of narratives of rulership in *Danses et légendes* but the analyses of yin and yang in *La pensée chinoise*.[4] For Dumézil, the dualistic structure of kingship in early Indo-European societies functioned as a complementary (or contrastive) pair in the same way that yin and yang did in early Chinese thought.

The comparison is unfortunate, for many of the ideas in Granet's studies of narratives in *Danses et légendes* would have been far more useful to a comparative discussion of kingship.[5] The problem with Dumézil's approach is that he tends to focus on the final structure of kingship rather than on the emergence of that structure, or, to put this another way, he tends to focus not on the tensions that led to a certain presentation of kingship in a particular narrative but on the final, synchronic structure itself. This approach derives in large part from his contention that this structure is traceable to the culture of the early Indo-Europeans. Dumézil argued that the early Indo-European community had an ideology based on a tripartite structure of sovereignty (itself divided into the dualism mentioned above), the warrior function, and the function of fecundity. His comparative method is thus focused on discovering this structure in various Indo-European narratives, discoveries that would then serve to validate his basic contention.

Whatever the truth of Dumézil's argument concerning the Indo-European community,[6] his method is not particularly helpful for comparative research. In the case of early China, for example, the approach would lead only to a comparison based on the negative claim that no such structure

---

3. Ibid., pp. 47–55.

4. Ibid., pp. 175–81.

5. For a discussion of Granet's discussion of mythical narratives in early China, see chap. 3 of my *The Ambivalence of Creation*.

6. For critiques of Dumézil, see Lincoln, *Death, War, and Sacrifice*, pp. 231–68; and idem, *Theorizing Myth*, pp. 121–37.

existed in early China. Since none of the narratives characterize the social order in terms of a diarchical kingship (or, for that matter, a more general tripartite structure), one could say only that the early Chinese narratives do not work in terms of the structure that Dumézil claimed to find in the Indo-European materials.

Among the recent critiques of Dumézil's arguments, Marshall Sahlins's attempt to shift the discussion away from a Dumézilian emphasis on synchronic structures and toward a generative approach provides a more promising comparative method. Of particular interest to the present study is Sahlins's discussion of the "stranger king."[7] Sahlins based this notion on narratives and rituals that present the state as having emerged from contact between a peaceful, indigenous populace and a transgressive outsider. The consequence of this contact is the emergence of a third term, sovereignty, which is itself dualistic and consists of peaceful and warlike elements. Instead, then, of focusing on a static system, this model emphasizes a diarchical structure of kingship as the result of an earlier conflict. The permutations found in different narratives from disparate cultures are then analyzed as the working out of various combinations of these dualistic forces, a process characterized by almost endless degrees of complexity.

Like Dumézil, Sahlins analyzes the legends concerning the creation of the Roman state. And as did Dumézil, Sahlins focuses on the accounts (primarily from Livy, Plutarch, and Dionysius of Helicarnassus) that portray the founding of Rome as a union between the followers of Romulus on the one hand and the Sabines on the other.[8] Dumézil, reading this material in terms of his tripartite structure, argued that we should see here the common Indo-European theme of a war between the functions, with sovereignty (Romulus) and the warrior function (his followers) paired against the function of fecundity (the Sabines).[9]

Sahlins, in contrast, reads the material in generative terms as a narration of the emergence of the state. The war then represents the combining of the powers of transgressive, military violence with the fecundity of the Sabines,

7. Sahlins, *Islands of History*, pp. 73–103.

8. See, e.g., Plutarch, *Lives*, "Romulus," 14–21.

9. Dumézil, *Gods of the Ancient Northmen*, p. 24. Dumézil discusses the account in comparison with the Norse myth of the war between the Æsir (who, he claims, represent the first two functions) and the Vanir (representing the third); see ibid., pp. 3–25.

and it is out of this combination that Roman kingship emerges.[10] Moreover, Sahlins argues, the reason that Roman kingship is divided into the dualism explored by Dumézil is precisely because it is posed as emerging from this combination of violence and fertility. Thus, the first instantiation of this dualism is seen in two early rulers of Rome, the same two figures analyzed by Dumézil as representing the dualism of Indo-European sovereignty: Romulus ("by nature a lover of war," as Plutarch put it) and Numa, himself a Sabine, who turns away from the militancy of Romulus' rule and establishes the religious order and organizes society and the calendar.[11] As Sahlins puts it:

Numa, Romulus's successor, weans Rome from war and founds the priesthood and cult, means of civic order. Numa's reforms represent the more general popular interest which he, as member of the indigenous people, is disposed to incarnate. Thereafter, the Latin kingship will alternate between *celeritas* and *gravitas*, magical war kings and religious peace kings.[12]

Such a reading opens up far more room for comparative research than does the synchronically based method of Dumézil. Instead of a focus on finding a given structure in various societies, the approach points toward the study of underlying tensions. The implication of this methodology is that, in comparing materials, we should first emphasize locating a common tension and then compare the diverse historical solutions to that tension and the different historical consequences of those solutions. In this model, for example, narratives that trace the origins of a kingship divided into militaristic and sacerdotal characteristics to a previous combination of violence and fecundity are seen as one method of dealing with this problem.

Indeed, following a passing reference from Dumézil, Sahlins draws a comparison with Polynesian materials, especially from Fiji and Hawaii.[13] Although the exact myths and rituals differ, the common concern in these cultures with posing society in terms of a combination of a peaceful populace and an intrusive transgressor provides the ground for comparison. In other words, the basis of the comparison is not a similar synchronic structure but a common generative approach to the emergence of the state.

---

10. Sahlins, *Islands of History*, pp. 84–91.

11. For the references to Romulus and Numa, see *Plutarch's Lives*, "Romulus," 24.1; and "Numa," 3.3, 8–14, 17–18.

12. Sahlins *Islands of History*, p. 91.

13. For Fiji, see ibid., pp. 84–89, 94–102; and for Hawaii, pp. 92–94.

The crucial point for the comparison is the role discontinuity plays in Polynesian cosmologies. As discussed in Chapter 4, Sahlins argues that Polynesian sacrificial systems emphasize the need to introduce discontinuity in order to achieve a life for humanity:

> Polynesians were ever and again engaged with the divine in a curious combination of submission and opposition whose object was to transfer to themselves the life that the gods originally possess, continue to detain, and alone can bestow. By successive rituals of supplication and expropriation, the god is invited into the human domain, to give it life, and then banished that mankind may take possession of the divine benefits.[14]

Sahlins argues that the "stranger king" is utilized in Polynesian narratives of the origin of the state to account for the introduction of discontinuity from outside. This also explains for Sahlins the existence of human sacrifice in Hawaii: the concern again is to introduce discontinuity, to separate the human from the divine. "Prerogative of the king, human sacrifice is what puts the god at a distance and allows mankind to inherit the earth. . . . So the temples consecrated in Hawaii by human sacrifice, separating the 'sacred' (heavenly) from the 'secular' (earthly) or tabu (*kapu*) from *noa*, would liberate the rest of the terrestrial plane for mankind."[15]

Sahlins quotes Beckwith's assertion that, in Polynesia, gods and men are "one family under different forms, the gods having superior control over certain phenomena, a control which they may impart to their offspring on earth." Thus, Sahlins argues, "The triumph of the warrior associated with human sacrifice over the peaceful and productive god represents the appropriation by man of the fructified earth."[16] The sacrifice of the peaceful god allows humans to take control of the land. As in the Roman materials, therefore, sovereignty is associated with the introduction of discontinuity—although here the issues are worked out in terms of a human sacrifice and appropriation of the power of a god. Granet argued along similar lines that in China kingship emerged through the conquest and sacrifice of previously divine figures: kingship was thus a form of divinization through the appropriation of divine powers.[17] Sahlins's reinterpretation of Dumézil, therefore, in a sense returns to Dumézil's teacher, Granet.

---

14. Sahlins, How "Natives" Think, p. 24.
15. Sahlins, Islands of History, p. 115.
16. Sahlins, How "Natives" Think, p. 25.
17. Granet, however, read Chinese narratives as evidence of an actual historical evolution rather than as later attempts to explain the nature of the contemporary state.

Can these discussions of divine kingship narratives help us understand the tensions surrounding the formation of the Chinese empire? I hope to show that they can. The narratives of the founding of the Roman state outlined above derive from Plutarch—a Greek living under Roman imperial rule. I suspect Plutarch intended to draw an unflattering parallel between the founding of the original Roman state and the founding of the Roman empire during the first century BC. Plutarch explicitly describes Caesar's assassination as a sacrifice.[18] Plutarch may be drawing a parallel here with Romulus, the mythological transgressor who created the original state. According to Plutarch, both Romulus and Caesar were sacrificed by senators who feared their growing usurpation of the Senate's power.[19] Just as the state was successfully consolidated only after the sacrifice of Romulus, so was empire consolidated by Augustus only after the death of Caesar: it took a transgressor like Caesar to begin the autocracy, but, by the same token, he was too transgressive to consolidate a new form of government. That job went instead to Augustus, the "second Caesar."[20] And, although Plutarch draws a comparison between Caesar and Romulus, he makes it clear that Augustus was not quite Numa:

[Janus] also has a temple at Rome with double doors, which they call the gates of war; for the temple always stands open in times of war, but is closed when peace has come. The latter was a difficult matter, and it rarely happened, since the realm was always engaged in some war, as its increasing size brought it into collision with the barbarous nations which encompassed it round about. But in the time of Augustus Caesar it was closed, after he had overthrown Antony. . . . During the reign of Numa, however, it was not seen open for a single day, but remained shut for the space of forty-three years together, so complete and universal was the cessation of war. For not only was the Roman people softened and charmed by the righteousness and mildness of their king, but also the cities round about, as if some cooling breeze or salubrious wind were wafted upon them from Rome, began to experience

---

18. Plutarch, *Lives*, "Caesar," 65.6.

19. Ibid., "Romulus," 27.5–6

20. Ibid., "Numa," 19.4. This may be the source of Hegel's famous argument that, in Rome, empire was instituted only after its initiator, Caesar, was sacrificed. Although Brutus, Cicero, and Cassius felt that the assassination would lead to the reinstatement of the Republic, history, according to Hegel, proved them wrong: "But it became immediately manifest that only a single will could guide the Roman State, and now the Romans were compelled to adopt that opinion; since in all periods of the world a political revolution is sanctioned in men's opinions, when it repeats itself" (Hegel, *Philosophy of History*, p. 313).

a change of temper, and all of them were filled with longing desire to have good government, to be at peace, to till the earth, to rear their children in quiet, and to worship the gods.[21]

Like Numa, Augustus brought peace. But it was not a peace comparable to that of the reign of Numa, who, through his "devotion to religion,"[22] brought the populace back to a proper worship of the gods.

But that which was the end and aim of Numa's government, namely, the continuance of peace and friendship between Rome and other nations, straightway vanished from the earth with him. After his death the double doors of the temple which he had kept continuously closed, as if he really had war caged and confined there, were thrown wide open, and Italy was filled with the blood of the slain. Thus not even for a little time did the beautiful edifice of justice which he had reared remain standing, because it lacked the cement of education. "What, then," some say, "was not Rome advanced and bettered by her wars?" That is a question which will need a long answer, if I am to satisfy men who hold that betterment consists in wealth, luxury, and empire, rather than in safety, gentleness, and that independence which is attended by righteousness.[23]

The moral is clear: Augustus may have succeeded in bringing peace, as had Numa, but Augustus' peace was a lesser peace—an autocratic and imperial one.

Plutarch clearly favored a return to what he envisioned as a traditional form of morality, religiosity, and statehood, in which humans engaged in peaceful agriculture and displayed proper reverence for the gods. In other words, he is overtly critical of aspects of the Roman empire and is calling for a ruler like Numa. Although Plutarch never wrote a biography of Augustus, one suspects that he strongly opposed the divinization of rulership that accompanied Augustus' consolidation of the emperorship.[24] In short, Plutarch's narrative of the origin of the state in Rome was written, I would argue, with the formation of the Roman empire in mind.

---

21. Plutarch, Lives, "Numa," 20.1–3; trans. Perrin, pp. 373–75.

22. Plutarch, Lives, "Numa," 22.7; trans. Perrin, p. 383.

23. Plutarch, Lives, "Lycurgus and Numa," 4.6–7; trans. Perrin, p. 399.

24. On the divinization of the Roman emperors, see Taylor, The Divinity of the Roman Emperor; and Pollini, "Man or God." Also helpful are Weinstock, Divus Julius; Yavetz, Julius Caesar and His Public Image; and Zanker, The Power of Images in the Age of Augustus.

And the more recent analyses of Plutarch's narrative discussed above were certainly written with such concerns in mind as well.[25] Sahlins develops his argument about the stranger-king not simply to draw a comparison between the Roman and the Polynesian narratives but also to discuss how these themes played out historically in Polynesia. Sahlins reads the great mid-nineteenth-century Fijian war in terms of an interplay between the claims of sacerdotal kingship and those of militant kingship.[26] Sahlins's move here is to work out the cultural tensions surrounding notions of kingship and then analyze the historical implications of the way these competing claims play out. Valerio Valeri, using a similar methodology, traces how such tensions played out in Hawaii when Kamehameha conquered other warring chiefdoms and went on to form a unitary state.[27]

All these analyses focus on the crucial historical tensions surrounding the emergence of empire—an approach far more powerful than an emphasis on permutations of a synchronic structure. In this form, the themes are even applicable to a discussion of the rise of empire in early Greece—a culture that Dumézil always had difficulty placing within his framework.

In early Greek historiography, empire (*arche*) is often presented in terms of a dialectic between human and divine powers. Indeed, empire and hubris were commonly linked by the Greek historians, who portrayed empire as a transgression of the proper order of the gods, the Greeks, or the traditions of the city-states.[28] Thucydides in his account of the Peloponnesian War, for example, presents empire as a human act of hubris against the city-states' traditional arrangements with the gods. In contrast to the Spartans, the Athenians are radical innovators, supporting rebellions and attempting to create an empire. Thucydides frequently quotes critiques of the hubris of the

---

25. Bruce Lincoln argues that Dumézil's analysis in *Mitra-Varuna*, the first edition of which was published in 1940, was in part written as a critique of the German empire and support for Mussolini's form of fascism. According to Lincoln, if Rome for Dumézil represents a proper ordering of Romulus and Numa, *celeritas* and *gravitas*, then German narratives tell of a dangerous turn to the military. Lincoln reads a link here with Mussolini's preservation of the Vatican and the monarchy on the one hand and Hitler's aggrandizement of power on the other: "Insofar as these patterns remain ideals, Germany—ancient and modern—appears as the problem, while Rome and its contemporary heir appear as the solution" (see Lincoln, *Theorizing Myth*, p. 136; for Lincoln's full discussion, see pp. 121–37).

26. See, e.g., Sahlins, "The Return of the Event."

27. Valeri, "The Transformation of a Transformation."

28. The most obvious example is Herodotus' earlier presentation of the Persian empire.

Athenians and argues that ultimately Athens will overreach its resources and be destroyed. Early in the work, for example, the Corinthians, while trying to convince Sparta to join the war against the Athenians, describe the Athenian empire in precisely these terms:

An Athenian is always an innovator, quick to form a resolution and quick at carrying it out. You [the Spartans], on the other hand, are good at keeping things as they are; you never originate an idea, and your action tends to stop short of its aim. Then again, Athenian daring will outrun its own resources; they will take risks against their better judgment, and still, in the midst of danger, remain confident.[29]

The very strength of the Athenians will ultimately lead to their defeat: as innovators and originators, they will inevitably transgress their limits and bring destruction on themselves.

This linkage of empire and transgressive innovation recurs throughout the narrative. For example, Pericles notes this in his famous funeral oration: "I shall begin by speaking of our ancestors. . . . They certainly deserve our praise. Even more so do our fathers deserve it. For to the inheritance that they had received they added all the empire we have now, and it was not without blood and toil that they handed it down to us of the present generation."[30] Empire was a recent creation, an addition to the inheritance from earlier generations of Athenians.

Later, when the war was going badly for the Athenians, Pericles offers a further reflection on this creation: "Your empire is now like a tyranny: it may have been wrong to take it; it is certainly wrong to let it go."[31] In Thucydides' account, Pericles admits that this addition of empire to the ancestral heritage introduced a dangerous element into the culture.

But it is right to endure with resignation what the gods send, and to face one's enemies with courage. . . . The reason why Athens has the greatest name in all the world is because she has never given in to adversity, but has spent more life and labour in warfare than any other state, thus winning the greatest power that has ever existed in history, such a power that will be remembered forever by posterity, even if now (since all things are born to decay) there should come a time when we were forced to yield.[32]

---

29. Thucydides, *Peloponnesian War*, 1.70; trans. Warner, pp. 75–76.
30. Thucydides, 2.36; trans. Warner, pp. 144–45.
31. Thucydides, 2.63; trans. Warner, p. 161.
32. Thucydides, 2.64; trans. Warner, p. 162.

Resigned to the inevitable destruction of the gods, the Athenians can nonetheless go down knowing they have created the greatest empire in history up to that point.

What is powerful in this speech and, indeed, powerful in Thucydides' narrative in general is that the Athenian empire is consistently presented as heroic but, as an effort that runs counter to the traditional arrangement of the city-states, doomed. Once Athens became an empire, Thucydides is implying, it was doomed. Thucydides associates empire with transgressive innovation and therefore with hubris. For Thucydides, the history of an empire can only be a tragedy.

This background may help to explain Alexander's progressive moves toward deification as he established his empire:[33] if empire contravenes the gods, then only a god can successfully establish an empire. Initially, Alexander's claims of divine attributes were based on the figure of Heracles, whom he claimed as an ancestor,[34] and who was one of the few mortals said to have joined the gods on Olympus. During the campaign in India, Alexander decided to scale the Rock of Aornas and capture it because, according to legend, Heracles had failed in a similar attempt. By capturing the Rock, Alexander was claiming to have surpassed even the great warrior Heracles.[35] Alexander similarly saw himself in competition with Dionysus and claimed that he had penetrated further into India than had the god.[36]

But the most significant act occurred in 324 BC, when the Greek states began debating whether to worship Alexander with divine honors.[37] By at least 323 BC, several Greek states were worshipping Alexander as a living

---

33. For recent discussions of the issue of Alexander's deification, see Bosworth, "The Divinity of Alexander," in idem, *Conquest and Empire*, pp. 278–90; and Fredricksmeyer, "Three Notes on Alexander's Deification."

34. Plutarch, *Lives*, "Alexander," 2.1.

35. Diodorus 17.85; and Arrian, *Anabasis*, 4.28, 30; 5.26.

36. Arrian, *Anabasis*, 5.2

37. Plutarch, *Moralia*, 219e. There is a large scholarly debate on whether Alexander requested that the Greek states give him divine honors or whether the states did so in order to court Alexander. See Hamilton, *Alexander the Great*, pp. 138–41; and Fredricksmeyer, "Three Notes on Alexander's Deification," pp. 3–5. Both see the evidence as indicating that Alexander did indeed request it. As Bosworth has argued, the evidence reveals at least that "the enactment of divine honours was well known to be something the king greatly desired" (*Conquest and Empire*, p. 288).

god.[38] Empire was successfully created, and it was created by a god: empire and deification developed together.

> [Alexander's] progress was complete. Beginning as a Heraclid and descendant of heroes, he had become son of Zeus and competitor with the heroes. Finally he had become a god manifest on earth, to be honoured with all the appurtenances of cult. The precedent for the worship of a living man was firmly established, and cults were offered to his Successors with greater frequency and magnificence.[39]

Similar themes of deification played out in the emergence of empire in early China as well, where we see the emergence, for the first time (as far as we know) in Chinese history, of claims by the ruler himself to be a god. The emergence of imperial rule in early China coincided with the rise of a new type of theomorphic claim. Building on the divinization and ascension literature, although accepting a largely theistic cosmos and a ritual order based on sacrifice, the Qin ritual system involved an appropriation of divine powers—the very issues that Granet discussed. As we have seen, comparable claims accompanied the rise of centralized states and empires in numerous areas. But the concern among those attempting to claim divine kingship in China was not, as Sahlins has discussed for Polynesia, to sacrifice the gods and appropriate the land; rather, the goal was to ascend to the heavens and be transformed into a god. The rest of this chapter attempts to answer the questions How and why were such claims articulated? Who opposed these claims? and What were the historical ramifications of the ways the ensuing conflicts developed? In short, what were the crucial tensions surrounding the formation of empire in early China?

Competing Cosmologies in the Qin and Early Han

Those who approach early Chinese thought historically tend to associate the emergence of correlative thinking in the late Warring States and early Han with the rise of centralized states concerned with building ideological systems different from the Heaven-based ideology of the Zhou. In Chapters 2 and 4, I argue that, to the contrary, monistic cosmologies were formulated by figures opposed to the ritual specialists employed at the dominant courts of the time, and that such cosmologies failed to gain significant backing for some time. An example is the *Lüshi chunqiu*. Once Lü Buwei fell from power,

---

38. Fredricksmeyer, "Three Notes on Alexander's Deification," p. 5.
39. Bosworth, *Conquest and Empire*, p. 290.

the Qin court ignored such ideas, as did the early Han emperors. Monistic cosmologies, far from being the imperial ideology, were used to oppose the cosmology dominant at the imperial court.

The views that dominated the Qin and early Han courts were indeed far removed from the Heaven-based system of the Zhou, but they were also little influenced by correlative systems of thought. Instead, early imperial ideology continued to be based on a theistic system, wherein natural phenomena were seen as governed by distinct, active deities. At the head of this celestial hierarchy was Di, and below him were arrayed various spirits, each with its own domain of power. Ritual specialists continued to be employed to use forms of divination or sacrifice to determine, influence, or even control the spirits of each domain.

Thus, for example, Sima Qian claims that Emperor Wen (r. 179–157 BC), after noting the growing prosperity of the empire, stated: "With my lack of virtue, how could I take credit for this? It is a gift of Shangdi and all the spirits."[40] He thereupon increased the sacrifices to the spirits. Whatever the veracity of this account, such statements are nonetheless telling of early Han political rhetoric: one could claim to be a humble ruler by crediting one's successes to the *di* and *shen* and by proclaiming one's indebtedness to them through copious sacrifices and ritual obeisance.

In stating that such a cosmology was predominant, however, I in no way mean to imply that all the early emperors expressed the type of humility toward the *shen* that Sima Qian ascribes to Emperor Wen. To the contrary, the predominance of this cosmology meant that many of the tensions surrounding the ideological claims of the early emperors revolved around the relationship between the emperors and the spirits. Although humility was one possible rhetorical posture, it was hardly the only one. In the remainder of this chapter, I attempt to reconstruct the sacrifices of the early emperors and the specialists they hired in order to trace these varying claims over the course of the early imperial era.

Emperors and Gods in the Early Imperial Courts

When Qin created the first imperial state in 221 BC, it attempted to forge an imperial ideology of unification. The most important sacrifices were offered at the Qin cult center of Yong to the four gods—the white, green, yellow,

---

40. *Shiji* (hereinafter cited in the text), "Fengshan shu," 28.1381.

and red *di* (*Shiji*, "Fengshan shu," 28.1376). The first of these sacrifices had been instituted in 771 BC, when the Zhou court recognized Duke Xiang of Qin as a feudal lord. Since the state of Qin was in the far west, Duke Xiang created an "altar of the west," at which sacrifices were made to the white *di*, the god of the west ("Fengshan shu," 28.1358). Over the next several centuries, Qin introduced sacrifices to the gods of the other three directions as well— presumably as a claim to prominence as Zhou power waned ("Fengshan shu," 28.1360, 1364).

Not only did Qin maintain these sacrifices, however, but it also attempted to co-opt the significant cults of each region in the empire. According to Sima Qian:

When Qin united all under heaven, [the first emperor] commanded that the offerings frequently performed by the officials of sacrifice to Heaven, Earth, the famous mountains, the great rivers, the ghosts, and the spirits be obtained and placed in order. ("Fengshan shu," 28.1371)

The First Emperor himself undertook several tours of his empire and personally performed many of the most significant of these sacrifices. The sacrifices to other important deities were placed under the control of a great invocator, who "offered the sacrifices according to the appropriate time of the year" ("Fengshan shu," 28.1377).

These attempts to gain control over cults to regional spirits involved a claim to rulership different from the one found in the Shang and Western Zhou material. The Zhou conquest had involved an attempt to replace the Shang pantheon of ancestors with the Zhou pantheon (see Chapter 1). The concern was to utilize one's ancestors to gain the support of Heaven. One thus performed sacrifices to build support from the lower, more accessible levels of the pantheon up to the higher, and the higher ancestors then worked to pacify Heaven itself. Since the goal of the sacrificial action was to build toward higher powers, there was no inherent tendency to expand sacrificial sites; all the ruler needed was one platform to reach his ancestors.

In contrast, the First Emperor's claims were based instead on a ritual system in which the ruler maintained personal control over all the land. The sacrifices were placed under centralized control, and the First Emperor traveled constantly throughout his realm and personally performed sacrifices in each area. He marked these occasions by erecting stelae announcing his achievements.

It is within this context that we see a flowering of interest at the imperial court in techniques to gain immortality,[41] as well as the rise to prominence of those specialists that Sima Qian called *fangshi*, or masters of formulas.[42] The *fangshi* claimed to possess formulas that enabled them to contact and summon spirits and to thereby secure divine support. One of the major commissions given these figures by the First Emperor was to seek out transcendents who had achieved long life and to find drugs that would make the emperor immortal (*Shiji*, "Qin Shihuang benji," 6.245, 252, 258, 263).

These searches became associated with the attempt to become a True Man (*zhen ren*). Sima Qian reconstructs a discussion between the *fangshi* Lu Sheng and the First Emperor:

> Lu Sheng told the First Emperor, "I and others have searched for *zhi* plants, strange medicines, and transcendents, but we have not found them. Strange creatures have prevented us. The formulas say that a human ruler must move secretly, at the appropriate time, in order to avoid the evil ghosts. If the evil ghosts are avoided, then the level of True Man can be attained. If the ministers know where the ruler resides, then harm will come to his divinity (*shen*). A True Man enters water without getting wet, enters fire without getting burned, crosses over cloudy *qi*, and lives as long as Heaven and Earth. Now, Your Majesty has put all under Heaven in order, but he has not yet been able to attain tranquility and peacefulness. When Your Majesty resides in the palace, do not allow people to know. This way, the drugs of immortality can perhaps be obtained." ("Qin Shihuang benji," 6.257)

Lu Sheng is calling on the ruler to become a True Man, and his description of the True Man is reminiscent of the descriptions of the adept discussed in the previous chapter: a True Man is unaffected by the elements, can ascend to the skies, and lives as long as Heaven and Earth. To Lu Sheng's suggestion, the First Emperor reportedly replied, "I hope to become a True Man. I will refer to myself as 'True Man,' rather than as 'I'" ("Qin Shihuang benji," 6.257). The First Emperor thereafter had the scholars (*bo shi*) compose poems on transcendents and true men, as well as on his travels (*you*) throughout the empire ("Qin Shihuang benji," 6.259). The form of rulership the

---

41. My understanding of the claims of immortality in this period have been greatly aided by Yü Ying-Shih, "Life and Immortality in the Mind of Han China"; idem, "'O Soul, Come Back!' A Study in the Changing Conceptions of the Soul and Afterlife in Pre-Buddhist China"; Needham, *Science and Civilisation in China*, 2: 93–113; and Poo, *In Search of Personal Welfare*, pp. 103–22.

42. On the masters of formulas, see Chen Pan, "Zhanguo Qin Han jian fangshi kao lun"; and Ngo, *Divination, magie et politique dans la China ancienne*.

First Emperor envisioned therefore became associated with the ascension literature discussed in the previous chapter: the ruler travels and attains immortality.

Such attempts to gain immortality were paralleled by the Qin ruler's own theomorphic claims. The title invented for the First Emperor, *huangdi* or "august god," had clear theomorphic pretensions (consider the inscription with which I open this chapter, p. 225). The First Emperor was claiming to possess the powers of a *di*, a god, as well as the power to impose his will on the natural phenomena of the world.

Moreover, as a *di*, his rule presumably extended over the lesser spirits as well. The First Emperor's assertion of direct control over regional cultic sites may imply such a claim. How far his claims went is impossible to say, given our limited sources. Certainly, however, numerous later stories portray him as having such pretensions. In a famous story from the *Shiji*, the First Emperor encounters troublesome winds and attributes them to the ill-will of a local spirit. The emperor is not without means of dealing with such miscreants:

Floating down the Yangzi River, he arrived at the shrine of Mount Xiang. He encountered a strong wind and was almost unable to cross. He asked the scholars, "Which spirit is the ruler of Xiang?" The scholars responded: "We have heard that she was the daughter of Yao and the wife of Shun, and that she is buried here." The First Emperor was thereupon very angry and sent three thousand convicts to cut down the trees on Mount Xiang. The mountain was left bare. ("Qin Shihuang benji," 6.248)

Although this may well be a later story intended to show the hubris of the First Emperor, it may nonetheless be revealing of the sorts of claims prevalent at the Qin court: if the ruler is a Di, then spirits should submit to him.

The early Qin imperium, therefore, was based on a theomorphic claim of rulership. The ruler himself claimed to be a Di with the power to order the world and employed ritual specialists to summon spirits. He presented himself along lines similar to the sages seen in the ascension literature discussed in the previous chapter, and he clearly entertained hopes of gaining immortality and ascending to the heavens. Such an ascension would have fully instantiated himself forever as a Di.

If Sima Qian is to be believed, however, the first few emperors of the Han dynasty were more modest in claiming power over the world of spirits.

Indeed, as we have already seen, Sima Qian presents Emperor Wen as extremely humble before the deities. Emperor Wen also abolished the position of "secret invocator"—the position instituted by the First Emperor to channel blame away from the ruler ("Fengshan shu," 28.1380). The move was clearly intended to portray the emperor as a ruler willing to accept responsibility before the spirits and gods.

With Emperor Wu (r. 140–87 BC), however, the relationship with the world of spirits changed once again. I discuss the sacrificial system under Emperor Wu in more detail in Chapter 8; here it is enough to mention that he restored many of the theomorphic claims made by the First Emperor. Like the First Emperor, Emperor Wu was deeply concerned with overcoming human limitations and achieving immortality; he undertook constant tours of his lands and personally performed the sacrifices; he also employed *fangshi* and was interested in the ascension literature.

The court poet Sima Xiangru immortalized the Emperor Wu's interest in ascension in his "Daren fu" (Prose-poem on the Great Man). The Great Man leads a retinue of spirits on a journey through the cosmos and is presumably a reference to the emperor. The work is clearly modeled on the "Yuan you" (see pp. 217–20) and in several places repeats the wording of the earlier poem, including the discussion of the surveying of the cosmos itself:

> . . . they observe the four wastes . . .

> they survey (*jing ying*) the Fiery Mountain and drift along the
>   Soft River. (*Shiji*, "Sima Xiangru liezhuan," 117.3060)

Similarly, the poem describes the Great Man as having direct power over spirits. Thus, for example, when the skies grow dark, the Great Man has Yushi (the Lord of Rain) and Fengbo (the Duke of Wind) punished ("Sima Xiangru liezhuan," 117.3060). The Great Man, therefore, has direct control over the wind and rain, for he controls the spirits who direct such phenomena.

The poem concludes with the Great Man leaving behind his procession and continuing alone:

> In the depths below there was no Earth,
> in the expanse above there was no Heaven.
> Looking about confusedly and with closing eyes, he sees nothing,

Listening indistinctly and uncertainly, he hears nothing.
Riding emptiness and nothingness, he ascends above
Transcending, without friends, he resides alone.
("Sima Xiangru Liezhuan," 117.3062)

The Great Man ultimately transcends the world of forms and Heaven and Earth themselves. The poem, in short, defines the Great Man as both totally dominating the world of forms and being completely free of dependence on anything within the world of forms—including other humans. If such views represented, in the "Yuan you," a claim of autonomy, here they represent, when utilized to describe the ruler, a claim of absolute power.

The Ascension of Huangdi: Divine Kingship in the Qin and Early Han

How can we account for the new sacrificial system of the Qin and early Han? And how should we interpret these claims of ascension and immortality? The ingestion of medicines and other substances as a means of attaining immortality is a clear difference from breathing exercises that concentrated the *qi* (see Chapter 5, pp. 209–11). But can we go further than this? It is important to avoid a simple dichotomy of "philosophical" discussions of ascension and immortality versus a more "superstitious" view on the part of the First Emperor and Emperor Wu. We need to develop a position from which we can understand the competing cosmologies of the time and the implications of those cosmologies. Unfortunately, our evidence is limited: we possess no writings from the *fangshi*, and our knowledge of court practices is limited to Sima Qian's statements and to the First Emperor's inscriptions.[43] However, we have enough to piece together at least part of what was going on.

Sima Qian portrays the *fangshi* as, among other things, liberating themselves from their forms (*xingjie*). As he describes the *fangshi* at the court of the First Emperor: "They practiced formulas and the way of the transcendents. Their forms were liberated, smelted, and transformed. They relied on the activities of ghosts and spirits" ("Fengshan shu," 28.1368–69). The term *xingjie* appeared in the *Shiwen* passage discussed in the preceding chapter. Here, however, the liberation is accomplished through means different from those described in the *Shiwen*: the *fangshi* rely on ghosts and spirits.

---

43. For an excellent analysis of the First Emperor's inscriptions, see Kern, *The Stele Inscriptions of Ch'in Shih-huang.*

Both the First Emperor and Emperor Wu supported the *fangshi* in the belief that these figures would help them gain access to the world of spirits and ultimately immortality. Indeed, the *fangshi* claimed that their control of the spirits enabled them to share in those spirits' power. According to Sima Qian, Li Shaojun, an important figure at the court of Emperor Wu, claimed to be able to "control phenomena" (*shi wu*). Since such powers were regularly ascribed to spirits, people at the time "took Li Shaojun to be a spirit" ("Fengshan shu," 28.1385).

These abilities to control phenomena are the same as those the authors of the "Neiye" attributed to their practitioners. However, the "Neiye" argues that the adept obtains these powers through particular forms of self-cultivation, and this claim, as we saw, is based on a monistic cosmology: insofar as everything consists of *qi*, then the more refined, the more spiritlike, one can become, the more power one has over less refined *qi*. In contrast, the *fangshi* claim these abilities through their utilization of formulas, formulas that allow them to gain control over both spirits and forms. Most of the references to the *fangshi* in the *Shiji* portray their attempts to summon (*zhi* 致) spirits. One example among many is Sima Qian's description of a certain Shaoweng. His knowledge of "formulas for ghosts and spirits" gains him an audience with the ruler. In response to Shaoweng's proposals, the emperor builds a palace at Ganquan to summon the spirits ("Fengshan shu," 28.1387–88).

It is clear from Sima Qian's accounts that Huangdi was a major figure for the *fangshi*. Indeed, many of the sacrificial reforms of the Qin and early Han empires were responses to the *fangshi*'s claims concerning Huangdi's ritual actions and eventual ascension to Heaven. For example, a certain Gongsun Qing presented a letter to Emperor Wu relating how "Huangdi had become a transcendent and ascended to Heaven." Gongsun Qing claimed the letter had been given him by Shen Gong, like Gongsun a native of Qi. Shen Gong wrote:

Of the seventy-two kings who have attempted the *feng* and *shan*, only Huangdi was able to ascend Mount Tai and give the *feng* sacrifice. The Han ruler who attempts it will also ascend and perform the *feng*. If he does ascend and give the *feng*, he will be able to become a transcendent and climb to Heaven. ("Fengshan shu," 28.1393)

Gongsun Qing also told the emperor:

These five mountains [Mounts Hua, Shou, Tai Shi, Tai, and Dong Lai] were where Huangdi often traveled and met with spirits. Huangdi at times fought wars and at times studied to become a transcendent. He was concerned that the hundred families opposed his way, so he thereupon had anyone who opposed ghosts and spirits beheaded. After more than a hundred years he was able to obtain communication with the spirits. ("Fengshan shu," 28.1393)

Gongsun Qing further recounted that a dragon came down from the sky to meet Huangdi. Huangdi and seventy court officials mounted the dragon and ascended to Heaven. Upon hearing this, the emperor expressed a wish to be like Huangdi ("Fengshan shu," 28.1394).

During the preparations for the *feng* and *shan* sacrifices, Sima Qian tells us, the emperor also invoked Huangdi:

The Son of Heaven had heard from Gongsun Qing and the *fangshi* that when Huangdi and those before him had performed the *feng* and *shan* sacrifices, they had summoned prodigious things and had communicated with the spirits. "I desire to imitate Huangdi and those before him by achieving contact with the spirits and transcendents on Penglai." ("Fengshan shu," 28.1397)

Behind these references is the *fangshi*'s claim that Huangdi had become a transcendent and ascended to Heaven by communicating with the spirits. The *fangshi* claimed to possess the formulas that would allow this to happen.

Clearly, there are similarities here with the ascension literature discussed in Chapter 5. For example, the authors of question four of the *Shiwen* also refer to an ascension, claim to possess teachings that allow one to become liberated from the form, and mention Huangdi. But the similarities end there. The arguments of the *fangshi* rest on a theistic cosmology populated by spirits, and their claims are based on their purported abilities to summon and control those spirits with their formulas. And, since ascension and immortality are obtainable by communicating with these spirits, those who possess the formulas to summon the spirits can help their patrons obtain immortality. In contrast, the arguments of the *Shiwen* rest on a *qi*-based cosmology. Since the spirits are highly refined *qi*, and since human life is the flowing of that spirit into a form, one attains immortality by refining oneself until one becomes a spirit—that is, until one reaches the stage of being life without a form.

The types of immortality to be achieved are accordingly distinct as well. In the story told by Gongsun Qing, Huangdi and his retinue ascend to the Heavens on the back of a dragon. There is no claim here of becoming a spirit or of achieving the separation of the spirit from the body. Indeed, Li Shaojun was described not as becoming a spirit but as being seen as a spirit (because of his ability to control phenomena). Even *xingjie* seems to mean something different from what it does in the *Shiwen*. The statement that the *fang-shi* have the ability to have their "forms liberated (*xingjie*), smelted, and transformed" does not appear to mean that the spirit is liberated from the form. The claim is instead linked to the statement that the *fangshi* can control phenomena: the *fangshi* can transform their forms just as they can transform and control other forms. Despite the similarity of vocabulary with the *Shiwen*, the claims are in fact quite different. In contrast to the ascension literature, there seems to have been no interest in liberating the spirit from the body. On the contrary, the evidence points toward a claim of bodily ascension.

Perhaps we are now in a position to understand the claims underlying the efforts of the First Emperor and Emperor Wu. The Qin-Han sacrificial system involved a radically new approach. The goal was for the ruler to contact personally as many divine powers as possible in order to obtain their power. And the *fangshi* were employed as specialists precisely for their ability to summon these divine powers. This overt concern for divinization and immortality may appear to be quite similar to the concerns of the ascension literature, but here the goal was neither to transcend the world of forms nor to grasp the One and thereby gain power over the world of forms. The goal was rather to become a Di and to exercise direct power over the world of forms. In short, ideologically the empires under the First Emperor and Emperor Wu functioned as a celestial imperium, with the rulers as the organizing thearchs.

The Order of Textual Authority: Lu Jia's *Xinyu*

The dominance of claims that the emperor and his ritual specialists exercised direct power over the natural world helps to explain why opponents of such aspects of the Qin and Han imperial order continue to utilize monistic cosmologies. As discussed in Chapters 2 and 4, monistic cosmologies developed during the Warring States period in opposition to the ritual specialists employed at the courts of the day. During the early Han, several figures began appropriating the vocabulary and claims of such texts to make similar critiques of the developing imperial order. The significance of this point becomes clear when we turn to those thinkers who were highly critical of just these theistic aspects of the Han imperial system. Much of their polemic was aimed at those who claim the ability to control or even in part to become a *shen*.

As early as the beginning of the Han dynasty, Lu Jia issued a strong critique of much of this theistic cosmology. Lu Jia was firmly committed to basing practice on the precedents laid out in the Five Classics. In his reading, the Five Classics had been established by sages during the decline that set in following the end of the three dynasties. Their goal was to allow later generations to correspond once again to Heaven. In Lu Jia's worldview, then, a proper subordination to textual authority was a necessity.[44]

Lu Jia's criticisms of forms of rule that transgress textual precedents can be seen in his discussion of King Ling, who ruled Chu from 541 to 529 BC. Ling had a well-established reputation in Warring States narratives as a transgressor. For example, the *Zuozhuan* presents him as follows:

Formerly, King Ling performed crackmaking and said, "May it be that I will possess all under Heaven." It was not auspicious. He flung down the tortoise shell and, cursing Heaven, yelled, "This is such a small thing, and yet you will not give it to me. I must take it for myself." The people were troubled about his never being satisfied. They thus flocked to the rebellion as if they were returning home.[45]

King Ling's attempt to usurp power on his own brings his downfall.

All of this makes Ling an ideal target for Lu Jia. However, Lu Jia does not stop at simply presenting King Ling as departing from proper ritual practices. Like the First Emperor, the king gains territory through esoteric arts rather than moral governance:

King Ling of Chu occupied a territory of a thousand *li* and enjoyed a state of a hundred cities. He did not place humaneness and propriety first, nor esteem the way and the power. He embraced strange arts [four graphs missing].[46]

By "strange arts," Lu Jia is presumably referring to the sorts of esoteric practices dominant at the court of the First Emperor. The possibility that this may be Lu Jia's object of criticism becomes all the more likely from Lu Jia's subsequent comments: King Ling "built a tower at Ganqi of a hundred *ren*. He hoped to ascend (*deng*) the floating clouds and look into the patterns of Heaven. As such, he died at Qiji" ("Huai lü," B.5a). The explicit critique here is the attempt to understand the patterns of Heaven through ascension

---

44. For discussions of Lu Jia and the *Xinyu*, see Luo Genze, "Lu Jia *Xinyu* kaozheng"; Xu Fuguan, *Liang Han sixiang shi*, 2: 85–108; and Ku, *A Chinese Mirror for Magistrates*, pp. 12–23.
45. *Zuozhuan*, Duke Zhao, 13.
46. Lu Jia, *Xinyu* (hereinafter cited in the text), "Huai lü," B.5a.

and the use of esoteric arts. And Lu Jia's belief in the uselessness of such an attempt is made clear by his pithy summation: King Ling died.[47]

Lu Jia's mini-narrative on King Ling anticipates many concerns expressed throughout the *Xinyu*. Lu Jia was deeply concerned with both the growing centralization of the empire and the predominance of esoteric arts. As we can see in his criticisms of King Ling, Lu Jia's point is that these two are interrelated: extreme imperial centralization exceeds the proper bounds of the human and attempts to appropriate the powers of the divine.

Accordingly, Lu Jia views the sages of the past as those who maintained the proper hierarchy of the political and religious spheres through the creation and maintenance of sacrifices. Lu Jia's exemplar here is the Duke of Zhou:

The Duke of Zhou regulated and created the rituals and music, gave suburban sacrifices to Heaven and Earth and the *wang* sacrifice to the mountains and streams. Armies were not instituted, and punishments, rules, and laws were suspended. And yet from all within the four seas tribute came. ("Wuwei," A.7a)

The antithesis of the proper rulership of the Duke of Zhou is the use of laws, punishments, and military expansion by the First Emperor ("Wuwei," A.7a). The contrast drawn is thus between the First Emperor, who crossed both temporal and spatial boundaries (breaking precedent, conquering foreign lands), and the Duke of Zhou, who maintained them properly.

Given this viewpoint, it is perhaps not surprising that Lu Jia was also alarmed at the rise of figures who devoted themselves to the search for spirits and immortality rather than to the texts transmitted by the sages:

This is like people who are not able to embrace humaneness and put in practice propriety. They differentiate the minute and subtle and gauge Heaven and Earth and thereupon exert their bodies and labor their forms to enter into deep mountains in search of spirits and transcendents, neglect their parents, injure their bones and flesh, cut off the five grains,[48] discard the *Poetry* and *Documents*, turn their backs on the valuables of Heaven and Earth, and seek the way of immortality. This is not the

---

47. Lu Jia's critique here is similar to Arrian's negative portrayal of Alexander's claims of deification: "Successive delegations from Greece also presented themselves, and the delegates, wearing ceremonial wreaths, solemnly approached Alexander and placed golden chaplets on his head, as if their coming were a ritual in honour of a god. But, for all that, his end was near" (Arrian, *Anabasis*, 7.23.2; trans. Aubrey de Sélincourt, in Arrian, *The Campaigns of Alexander*, p. 388).

48. Reading *gu* 谷 as *gu* 穀.

means to penetrate the age and guard against those who oppose it. ("Shen wei," A.11a)

Such critiques, indeed, are common throughout Lu Jia's writings. Elsewhere he states:

Now, people of the present day do not study the *Poetry* or the *Documents*, practice humaneness and propriety, [graph missing] the way of the sages, or search the depths of the classics and arts. They instead discuss unverified words, study absurd events, map out the physiognomy of Heaven and Earth, discuss the irregularities of disasters and alterations, [two graphs missing] the way of kings, and differ from the ideas of the sages. They delude the minds of the scholars and influence the intents of the commoners. . . . Those who hear them take them to be spirits (*shen*). ("Huai lü," B.5a–b)

The problem for Lu Jia is that those who try to attain such powers may claim for themselves, and influence others to claim, complete autonomy from the teachings of the past sages. Even if their practices are ineffective, even if they cannot really become spirits, such figures may delude the emperor into thinking he can claim complete independence from the moral and political order of the past sages. In short, for Lu Jia, one of the primary problems of his age was precisely that beliefs in divinization led rulers to seek inordinate power for themselves and to attempt to transcend the proper role of humans in the cosmos. These beliefs also promoted the emergence of groups of people claiming to be spirits. In both cases, the teachings and ritual forms of the past sages were being rejected.

Perhaps in part because of such concerns, Lu Jia attempted to formulate a radically different cosmology, one that redefined the normative standards of human activity within the world. Lu Jia argues that humans should be subordinate to Heaven and that humans accordingly should act to complete the process begun by Heaven: "Heaven gives birth to the myriad things and uses earth to nourish them. Sages bring them to completion" ("Dao ji," A.1a). Valuable objects

are generated by the breath of Heaven and controlled by the numinosity of the spirits. Subtle, elegant, clear, and pure, they float or sink with the spirit. One can work to make them useful, and exhaust their essence to make them into utensils. Therefore I say: Sages complete them. This is the means by which one regulates things, penetrates change, controls essence and nature, and makes manifest humaneness and righteousness. ("Dao ji," A.2b)

Although spirits control the natural world, the human appropriation of those things involves an attempt neither to control the spirits nor to become a spirit. On the contrary, human sages have their own proper activity within the natural world, and that is fundamentally different from, and yet fully accords with, the powers of the spirits. Moreover, these acts of human appropriation are explicitly seen as a process of bringing things to their proper completion.

In other words, the sage who has properly cultivated himself through a study of morality and past exemplars will understand and be able to complete the natural processes begun by Heaven and overseen by the spirits. Humanity, therefore, has a crucial and necessary role to play in the proper unfolding of the natural world. Although human potency is not, for Lu Jia, comparable in nature to that exercised by the spirits, the human action of appropriating natural materials for human consumption is a necessary moment in the proper unfolding of the process begun by Heaven. In short, the particular powers of humans are fully distinct from, even while forming a complement to, those of the spirits. As such, the actions of the sages are in accord with the harmony that guides the movement of Heaven and Earth, yang and yin: "Their actions harmonize with Heaven and Earth, and their power (de) matches yin and yang" ("Dao ji," A.3a).

Lu Jia develops this position by arguing for a monistic cosmology in which humans are inherently linked to the rest of nature through qi. Accordingly, he argues, incorrect actions on the part of humans generate negative qi, which in turn generates abnormalities in the natural world: "Bad governance generates bad qi; bad qi generates disasters and irregularities" ("Ming jie," B.7b). Disasters and irregularities, therefore, are signs that humans have acted improperly. And Lu Jia also draws the full conclusion of this argument. If bad governance creates irregularities in the natural world, then it follows that good governance results in an orderly natural universe. In other words, order in the natural world depends on proper human behavior. In his cosmology, humans are responsible for ordering the cosmos: nature requires proper human conduct in order to function as it should.

Lu Jia develops this argument in full in the "Shen wei" chapter. He asserts again that the sages acted in accord with the proper patterns of Heaven and the proper movement of yin and yang:

It is like the rulership of Tang and Wu, and the ministership of Yi Yin and Lü. They practiced punishments in accord with the seasons of Heaven, and they acted by following yin and yang. Above they studied the patterns of Heaven, and below they examined the hearts of the people. ("Shen wei," A.11a)

But, he goes on, the sages, precisely by following the patterns of Heaven, brought the world into proper accord: "They adjusted Heaven and Earth and summoned (zhi) the ghosts and spirits" ("Shen wei," A.11b). By following the patterns of Heaven, the sages provided the cosmos with its proper hierarchy. They also thereby summoned the spirits—following the patterns of Heaven thus conferred on the sages the powers claimed by the fangshi.

Once the cosmos was properly ordered by the sages and the spirits were summoned, the patterns of Heaven were further revealed through diagrams and writings: "The Yellow River produced the diagrams, and the Luo River produced the writings" ("Shen wei," A.11b). This revelation appears as well in the Xici zhuan:

Therefore Heaven and Earth generated the spiritual things; the sages patterned themselves on them. Heaven and Earth changed and transformed; the sages imitated them. Heaven hung down the images and revealed auspiciousness and inauspiciousness; the sages represented them. The Yellow River produced the diagrams, the Luo River produced the writings; the sages patterned themselves on them.[49]

In the Xici zhuan, the movement is entirely one way, and the sages simply imitate the patterns revealed by the cosmos. With Lu Jia, the process begins with the sages following the patterns of the cosmos, and the sages thereafter order the world in its proper hierarchy. And only then are the diagrams and the writings produced. In the Xici zhuan the sages are imitators; for Lu Jia they are responsible for the proper formation of the cosmos.

The sages thereby obtain the Way: "Therefore, as for the Way, they lodged it between Heaven and Earth. Is this not what in ancient times was called obtaining the Way?" ("Shen wei," A.11b). The role of the sages is again noteworthy: the sages placed the Way in its proper position and thereby allowed humans to practice it. If for Zhuangzi obtaining the Way means finding a source of power outside human custom, for Lu Jia it means following the way of the sages within the cosmos adjusted by the sages.

The full implication of this argument is that it was the patterning of the sages that brought the cosmos to its proper completion. As Lu Jia argues in the "Ming jie" chapter:

---

49. Xici zhuan, A/11.

With the patterning (*li*) of the sages, kindness reached to the insects and moisture reached to the grasses and trees. All that was generated by receiving the *qi* of Heaven and that moved by following cold and heat stretched [four graphs missing] and inclined their ears to listen and be transformed. The sages examined things without any loss. Above they reached the sun, moon, stars, and constellations, and below they extended to the birds, beasts, grasses, trees, and insects. ("Ming jie," B.8a)

It was the sages, therefore, who brought order to the cosmos, from the heavens above to the animals below.

They further gave laws and calculations to order the entire world—human and natural alike:

Even the birds, beasts, grasses, and trees hoped for each to attain its position. They guided them with laws and regulated them with calculations. How much more so humans! The sages received the brightness of Heaven, rectified the movements of the sun and moon, and recorded the measures of the stars and constellations. They accorded with the benefits of Heaven and Earth, defined the appropriateness of high and low, instituted the advantageousness of the mountains and rivers. They leveled the four seas and divided the nine regions. They brought likes and dislikes together and unified the customs. The *Yi* says, "Heaven arrayed the images and showed auspiciousness and inauspiciousness. The sages patterned themselves on them." Heaven sent out the good way, and the sages obtained it. They spoke of managing the changes of divination, charts, and constellations. If below there were declining customs, they would transform the deficiencies so as to correct their decline and make them flourish. They regulated things and settled the age. Afterward, there was no rectification that could not be put into practice, and no one who could not be regulated. Therefore it is said, "Pattern [yourself on] the brightness of Heaven and accord with the benefits of Earth. Observe the transformations of Heaven and extend them to the categories of the various myriad events." ("Ming jie," B.8a–b)

The quotation attributed to the *Yi* is in fact taken from the *Xici zhuan*.[50] But the argument goes far beyond anything found in that work. The sages are

---

50. Lu Jia's references to the *Xici zhuan* may provide clues as to why that text became so important for Han Confucians. Perhaps one of the reasons for the later importance of the *Xici zhuan* was that Han Confucians saw the work as an effective argument for appropriating cosmological thinking *and* for studying the classical texts handed down from antiquity. The *Xici zhuan* wedded cosmological thinking with an assertion of the importance of the past—a crucial issue for the Han figures who were trying to do just that. Although there is no evidence to suggest that the authors of the *Xici zhuan* would have seen the *Yi* as a text in any way comparable to the *Shi* or the *Shangshu*, it is nonetheless possible that one of the reasons that

not just patterning themselves on the cosmos but are in fact bringing the cosmos into accord with the proper patterns.

Lu Jia underlines this argument by contrasting the rulers of the past with those of the present day. He begins by discussing the ancients:

> The calculations of Heaven and Earth are the signs (*xiang*) of fate. The sun [missing eight graphs] eight constellations are all arrayed, each with its own ruler. The myriad sprouts take different paths, and the thousand models have different forms. The sages accorded with their propensities (*shi*) and adjusted them. They caused small and large to not mutually [one graph missing] and squares and circles to not conflict with each other. [The sages] divided them with standards and regulated (*ji*) them with measures. The stars could not be seen in the daylight, the sun did not shine at night, thunder did not appear in the winter, and frost did not descend in the summer. If the ministers did not attack the ruler, then yin would not encroach upon yang. If at the height of summer it was not hot, if in extreme winter there was no frost; if black *qi* bound the sun, comets scattered in brightness, rainbows appeared in winter, torpid insects hibernated in summer, Mars brought disorder to the constellations, and various stars lost their orbits—if this occurred, the sages accorded with these alterations of Heaven and rectified their losses, patterned (*li*) their extremities, and rectified their root. ("Si wu," B.9b–10a)

The sages followed the movements of Heaven and Earth to understand fate. They then grasped the propensities of things and adjusted them accordingly. Here again, the sages are granted tremendous power over the natural world, but only because they understand fate and recognize the proper propensities of things. They thus regulate things according to their correct tendencies. In other words, they exercised power over the cosmos not by altering it to fit their will but rather by according with fate and the natural propensities of things.

And Lu Jia explicitly contrasts such sages with the rulers of his own day: "Those who are rulers in the present time are not like this" ("Si wu," B.10a). The rulers of his own day reject the proper patterns of Heaven. Like King Ling trying to ascend to the skies and gaze on the patterns of Heaven, the rulers of the day are, according to Lu Jia, trying to appropriate divine powers

---

the *Yi* ultimately came to be considered one of the classics was because of the *Xici zhuan*: perhaps Han Confucians saw in the *Xici zhuan* a powerful argument as to how to combine cosmology with classical scholarship, leading them both to include the *Yi* among the classics and to designate the *Xici zhuan* as one of its commentaries.

to themselves rather than trying to bring the cosmos into accord with the proper patterns.

The decline at issue here is comparable to the one presented by both Mencius and the authors of the *Xici zhuan*. Because of this decline, Confucius, a latter-born sage, was forced to establish the classics in order to allow humanity to again bring itself into accord with the patterns of the cosmos: "The later ages declined and fell to waste. Thereupon, the later sage [i.e., Confucius] established the Five Classics and clarified the six arts to correspond to Heaven, govern Earth, and probe affairs" ("Dao ji," A.2b). Confucius was not a king and therefore could not order the world himself. Accordingly, he had no choice but to establish the classics. This at least opened for later kings the possibility of bringing order to the world again by following the teachings of the classics.

In the "Benxing" chapter of the *Xinyu*, Lu Jia discusses Confucius's compilation efforts: "He traced and put in order past events so as to rectify the generations to come; he examined and recorded the charts and diagrams so as to understand nature and fate (*ming*)" ("Benxing," B.6b). Using the diagrams and maps given to the earlier sages by the Yellow and Luo rivers, Confucius was able to understand nature and fate—the ability said to be possessed by the adept in texts like the "Neiye."

The classics edited by Confucius thus embody the way of Heaven: "The *Poetry*, *Documents*, *Rituals*, and *Music* have obtained their place. These were what were established by the way of Heaven and put into practice by the great propriety" ("Benxing," B.6b). Even though Confucius himself did not have the position that would allow him to bring order to the cosmos, he was able to fully harmonize with and follow Heaven in his compilation of the classics: "The sage [i.e., Confucius] upheld the authority of Heaven and harmonized with the *qi* of Heaven. They inherited the achievements of Heaven and imaged the appearances of Heaven" ("Benxing," B.6b). Confucius' establishment of the classics is thus portrayed as essentially equivalent to the actions taken by the earlier sages.

Accordingly, the scholar who studies the classics can gain full knowledge of the cosmos as well:

Now, if a scholar penetrates the alterations and transformations of the spirits and the numinous, understands the opening and closing of Heaven and Earth, [three graphs missing] relaxing and stretching, the shortness or length of nature and fate (*xing ming*), where fortune and honors reside and where destitution and poverty are no more—if he does all this, his hands and feet will not be wearied, his ears and eyes will not become disordered, his thoughts will not [one graph missing], his plans will be without error. Above, he will determine[51] right and wrong on the patterns of Heaven. ("Si wu," B.9a–b)

The abilities to penetrate the transformations of the spirits and to understand fate and fortune are those often ascribed either to ritual specialists or, in texts like the "Neiye," to the adepts of self-cultivation. In typical fashion, Lu Jia assigns these powers to those who study and grasp the patterns of Heaven. And, since the classics make manifest the patterns of Heaven, the scholar who follows them is able to gain the powers usually ascribed to those who practice self-cultivation.

And here we can return to Lu Jia's critique of the practitioners of esoteric arts. As mentioned earlier, he criticized such figures for, among other things, discussing "the irregularities of disasters and alterations." However, Lu Jia was concerned not with omenology per se (which, after all, he practiced himself) but with defining its proper methods and proper goals. Lu Jia's point is that such techniques must be based on a correct understanding of the place of humans within the cosmos, rather than in mistaken attempts to gain personal immortality or to bend the cosmos to the will of theomorphic powers.

In other words, Lu Jia's cosmological claims enable him to accept aspects of the practices of the day, but to argue that only those like himself—those who have read and understood the classics—are capable of accurately interpreting the signs of nature. Since the later sages organized the classics in part to explicate the proper way that humans should conduct themselves and correspond to Heaven, only those who have studied such works should provide guidance to rulers.

Accordingly, Lu Jia appropriates the language of the ascension literature but argues that these powers are obtainable only through those who understand how properly to use the past for the present:

Those who are good at speaking of the past harmonize it with the present. They are able to transmit the distant and examine it with the nearby. Therefore, when they discuss affairs, above they array the accomplishments of the five thearchs and contemplate these within themselves; below they rank the failures of Jie and Zhou and take these as precautions for themselves. If they do so, their power (de) can be made

---

51. Reading *jue* 決 for *jue* 訣.

to match the sun and moon, their actions can be made to harmonize with the spirits (*shen*) and the numinous (*ling*). They can ascend (*deng*) high, extend far, reach the darkness, and see through the obscure. They hear it even without sound and see it without form. ("Shu shi," A.4a)

The text posits a hierarchy, with humans fully distinguished from the heavens and the spirits. In this cosmology, humans cannot become spirits. However, Lu Jia borrows the language of ascension and divinization to describe the sage: his powers match those of the sun and moon, his actions harmonize with those of the spirits, his understanding ascends and extends to all, and he has keen sight and hearing.

Lu Jia's repeated move, then, is a double argument: there are normative patterns of humaneness and propriety given by Heaven, and humans, like the cosmos itself, must abide by these normative patterns. This is an argument he appropriates, quite explicitly, from the *Xici zhuan*. But he also wants to claim that sages bring order to the cosmos. Heaven may provide normative patterns, but the cosmos itself (including the actual movements of Heaven—the sun, stars, and constellations) does not always follow those patterns. Thus, the sages must organize the cosmos to accord with its proper patterns.

This argument is in some ways a radicalization of some of the points found in the *Mencius*: with Mencius, there was a hint (although certainly he never explored it explicitly) that the fullest manifestation of the proper order was to be found in the sages, not in the empirical actions of Heaven itself. Heaven is the source of the proper order, insofar as Heaven is the force that grants humans the nature that, properly cultivated, generates a true sage. But Mencius also implies that Heaven itself, for arbitrary and inexplicable reasons, sometimes acts in opposition to the proper order.

Lu Jia takes this a step further. Heaven is still the source of the normative patterns. But sages are the ones who organize the cosmos to fit such patterns. It is not just that the cosmos—including Heaven—sometimes fails to follow the proper patterns; it is that the cosmos needs the sages to organize it into the normative patterns. Indeed, Lu Jia emphasizes, even after the sages initially aligned the cosmos, the seasons occasionally appear at the wrong time, and stars occasionally wander from their orbits. Sages are still required to return things to their proper alignment. The sages do not follow the natural world; they organize it.

The crucial point, then, is that sages can find a normative pattern in the operations of Heaven, but Heaven itself does not always act in accordance with these proper patterns. The patterns that should guide humanity can be discovered in the natural world, but the natural world itself does not necessarily operate in terms of these patterns. In short, the proper normative development of nature is realizable *only* in humanity. Indeed, it is humanity who must bring this normative pattern to nature. Heaven itself only plants the seed for this development, but even Heaven does not always realize the perfection that should be attained. It is the sage, not Heaven, who fully realizes the normative pattern that should naturally exist. By building this into a teleological argument, Lu Jia is able to deny the tension that pervaded Mencius.

The obvious question then arises: why? Why did Lu Jia radicalize the Mencian position? And why do so with explicit reference to the *Xici zhuan*, a text that in part was written *in opposition* to attempts to grant sages such powers and in opposition to much of the self-cultivation literature whose vocabulary Lu Jia is borrowing? I suspect the answer lies in Lu Jia's political position. His opposition to the theomorphic claims of the First Emperor is clear throughout his writings, as is his opposition to attempts to become spirits. His recurrent evocations of the arguments in the *Xici zhuan* thus appear to be a call for rulers to recognize and subordinate themselves to moral patterns. Hence his critiques of figures like King Ling for trying ascend to the heavens and to the First Emperor himself for his transgressions of the proper hierarchy of the world.

Instead, however, of simply arguing for subordination to the normative patterns of the cosmos, Lu Jia's move is to claim that the sages of antiquity followed these patterns to give the cosmos its proper order. Sages are granted enormous power over the universe, but such powers are achievable only by those who follow the proper patterns. Sages ordered the cosmos, but only by following a normative hierarchy.

And then they died. The sages did not transgress or avoid fate; they understood it and acted accordingly. In this sense, Lu Jia is following Mencius: even if Mencius hinted that sages at times enacted the proper patterns better than Heaven itself, he still emphasized the importance of following fate, of accepting what Heaven ordained. And Lu Jia, while granting far more power to the sages than Mencius ever did, equally argues the importance of knowing and subordinating oneself to fate. Although he appropriates the language of the ascension literature to describe the True Man, he strongly opposes the notion that we can transcend the forms of this world. Accordingly, he is as committed to the notion of fate as was Mencius.

Conclusion

It is clear that claims to ascension and divinization had become a common idiom by the Qin and early Han periods. As I have argued, however, one has to pay careful attention to precisely what types of claims are made in each of these texts: what forms of divinization are called for, what types of practices are involved, and why such practices are invoked.

In this chapter and the preceding chapter, we have seen texts positing several different cosmologies. In the methods associated with the *fangshi*, the concern was to gain control over those spirits who control forms and thus to be able to appropriate their numinous powers. The ultimate result of this is the full divinization and ascension of the patron. In this model, Huangdi achieves bodily ascension because of his ability to summon spirits, communicate with them, and gain their powers. Such a model achieved prominence in Qin and early Han imperial ideology, which was forged around a claim of theomorphic dominance—the ruler as he who could control spirits and bring order to the world. In contrast to this, the authors of, for example, the "Xinshu" chapters of the *Guanzi* (discussed in Chapter 4) argued for a monistic cosmology in which one could gain powers over phenomena but only through techniques of self-cultivation, and in which one could become a spirit but only within the limitations of the human form.

Both these models involved claims on the part of the practitioners that they could control phenomena, but the methods employed and the cosmologies posited were radically different. In contrast to both of these, one finds cosmologies that offered not a method of controlling phenomena but a call for a transcendence of forms and liberation from them. In varying ways, this framework can be found in the "Yuan you," the dialogue between Huangdi and Guang Chengzi from the *Zhuangzi*, and question four of the *Shiwen*. In all three texts, Huangdi is presented as having achieved, or as having received teachings of how to achieve, a full ascension from the world. No claims were made for controlling natural phenomena, nor was it claimed that these methods would benefit humanity. On the contrary, the explicit concern was with transcending the realm of the human and ascending to a higher level.

Lu Jia appropriated much of the ascension vocabulary, but he did so to argue in favor of following textual precedents. In his system, humans maintain the cosmos, but they only do so to fulfill the process begun by Heaven. Humans and Heaven are ritually separated, and each has its distinct roles and duties. And humans must follow the textual guides transmitted to them. For Lu Jia, submission to textual precedents entails a rejection of claims of autonomy from the world of the past sages—claims he saw as rampant among divinization practitioners, from the emperor on down.

These texts allow us a glimpse of a fascinating moment in early Chinese history, a moment in which opposing forms of self-cultivation practice, visions of human power over the natural world, and notions of proper rulership were debated in terms of competing claims about ascension and divinization. These texts made claims for different cosmologies, different modes of self-cultivation, and different modes of rulership involving different methods of bringing order to the world. Still other texts called for yet another form of ascension that involved a full transcendence of the human and a rejection of attempts to gain such control over natural phenomena altogether.

Thus, if Granet was wrong in his evolutionary interpretations of China, he was right to see a highly agonistic world in Han texts based on the constant concerns of humans to appropriate the powers of gods. The specific articulation of this conflict, however, did not involve a sacrifice of the gods, as Sahlins describes in Polynesian cultures, nor an appropriation of the fecundity of the people, as in Plutarch's narrative. The concern in the early imperial courts of the First Emperor and Emperor Wu was rather to gain control over increasing numbers of cultic sites, to gain access to and thus obtain the power of ever more powerful gods, to become more and more divine, and, ultimately, to ascend to the higher realms directly.

In short, the empire in China emerged in conjunction with claims of divinization. And such claims were not based on an assumption of continuity between man and the divine. Rather, the power of such claims arose precisely from a sense of appropriation and transgression—of rulers' transgressing earlier ritual systems and appropriating divine powers to themselves. And so potent were such claims that, for this brief period, even the critics of aspects of these imperial practices made use of the vocabulary of divinization and ascension while trying to reassert a separation of the ritual powers of humans and the spirits.

7 Aligning and orienting the cosmos
Anthropomorphic Gods and
Theomorphic Humans in the *Huainanzi*

A passage that we looked at briefly in the Introduction from the "Dixing" chapter of the *Huainanzi* describes the process of self-cultivation in terms of a metaphor of climbing high mountain peaks:

If one climbs twice as high as Kunlun, [the peak] is called the Mountain of Liang-feng. If one ascends it, one will not die. If one climbs twice as high, it is called Xuanpu. If one ascends it, one will become numinous and be able to control the wind and the rain. Twice as high, it stretches up to Heaven. If one climbs it, one will become a spirit. This is called the Realm of the Great God (Di).[1]

The cosmology presented here is similar to that which dominated the Han court: Di presides over spirits,[2] who possess powers over natural phenomena. Humans try to gain these powers by approaching ever closer to Di, first by achieving immortality, then by gaining control over the winds and rain, and ultimately by becoming a spirit.

But the hierarchy of stages here implies that the goals of this process are quite different from those of the masters of formulas. Spirits are immortal and control natural phenomena, and humans can gain these powers. But immortality and control over nature are (literally) lower stages of cultivation.

---

1. *Huainanzi*, "Dixing," 4.3a. I have benefited from the excellent translation by John Major in his *Heaven and Earth in Early Han Thought*, pp. 158–61.

2. The hierarchy is discussed in more detail in *Huainanzi*, "Dixing," 4.9a.

The goal of becoming a spirit is higher than both of these goals. Moreover, theomorphic powers are obtained through techniques of self-cultivation, rather than formulas of control. One does not seek to control the spirits who control natural phenomena; rather, one practices self-cultivation in order to become a spirit oneself.

The passage reveals a series of arguments that appear throughout the *Huainanzi*. Several chapters of the text claim that there is no distinction between humans and spirits and that humans are fully capable of becoming spirits. The authors posit a cosmos populated by theomorphic humans and anthropomorphic gods, linked together within a monistic cosmos of natural patterns (*li*). As a consequence, many passages in the *Huainanzi* replay themes we have seen in preceding chapters, but with significant shifts.

For example, another *Huainanzi* chapter has a discussion of the tilt in the heavens from the northwest to the southeast described in the *Taiyi sheng shui*. The *Taiyi sheng shui* sees this as evidence of the way that the forces of the natural world spontaneously respond to one another (see Chapter 4). The *Huainanzi* authors, however, present it as the result of a battle between theomorphic beings of the past. To quote John Major's excellent translation:

> Anciently Gong Gong and Zhuan Xu fought, each seeking to
>   become the Thearch.
> Enraged, they crashed against Mt. Buzhou;
> Heaven's pillars broke, the cords of Earth snapped.
> Heaven tilted in the northwest, and thus
> The sun and moon, stars and planets shifted in that direction.
> Earth became unfull in the southeast, and thus
> The watery floods and mounding soils subsided in that direction.[3]

Again and again in the *Huainanzi*, themes we have seen in earlier works—particularly the notions of ascension, self-divinization, and the control of natural phenomena—are rewoven in a complex fashion. What is this text doing? Why does it posit a cosmos run by theomorphic beings, in which humans can become spirits and gain power over the world?[4]

---

3. *Huainanzi*, "Tianwen," 3.1a–1b; trans. John Major, *Heaven and Earth in Early Han Thought*, p. 62.

4. For an excellent study of the textual history of the *Huainanzi*, see Roth, *The Textual History of the Huai-nan Tzu*. My understanding of the text has been greatly aided by the analyses in Kanaya, *Rosō teki sekai*; Charles Le Blanc, *Huai-Nan Tzu*; Major, *Heaven and Earth in Early Han Thought*; and Vankeerbergen, "The *Huainanzi* and Liu An's Claim to Moral Authority."

Following the Way: The "Yuandao" Chapter

The first chapter of the work, the "Yuandao,"[5] opens with a description of the Way, which is more primordial than either Heaven or Earth: "The Way covers Heaven and carries Earth, extends the four corners, and opens up the eight points."[6] The text then introduces two ancient beings whose actions set the cosmos right: "The two earliest and most ancient august ones[7] obtained the handle of the way and positioned themselves in the center. Their spirits roamed (*you*) with the transformations so as to pacify the four quarters" (1.1b). Here, as repeatedly throughout the *Huainanzi*, the language of the ascension literature is borrowed and given a political implication. But, unlike Lu Jia, the authors of the *Huainanzi* accept the claims of the ascension literature. The move, in other words, is not to appropriate and reinterpret the language of ascension but to accept the claims and then read them politically.

The natural world flourishes under the two august ones:

Their power (*de*) made Heaven and Earth flourish and harmonized the *yin* and *yang*, modulated the four seasons, and instigated the five phases. By [their] giving breath to, guiding, sheltering, and nurturing, the myriad things were all born. . . . "Rainbows did not emerge, and meteors did not appear. This was all brought about (*zhi*) by their cherishing power." (1.2a).

The august ones have the power to bring about harmony simply by holding fast to the Way.

The texts then returns to a discussion of the Way: "Now, the uppermost way generates the myriad things and yet does not possess them; it completes and transforms the images and yet does not control them" (1.2a–b). The political argument here is that just as the Way gives rise to everything and ends in possession and control, so will the ruler who can hold fast to the Way.

---

5. My translations of this chapter have been greatly aided by those given in Lau and Ames, *Yuan Dao*.

6. *Huainanzi*, "Yuandao," 1.1a; hereinafter cited in the text.

7. The precise identity of these two figures is unclear: some commentators read them as Fu Xi and Nü Wa; others read them as Fu Xi and Shen Nong. Based on references elsewhere in the *Huainanzi* (such as the "Lanming" chapter discussed below), Fu Xi and Nü Wa may well be the figures intended here. However, their precise identity is irrelevant: the important point is that the authors are appealing to primordial figures who preceded Huangdi.

Since the august ones organized the cosmos through their *de*, those among the later-born who are able to ascend can unify themselves with the harmonized cosmos. As an example, the authors discuss the ancient charioteers Ping Yi and Da Bing:

As for the charioteering of Ping Yi and Da Bing in ancient times, they mounted the cloudy chariots and entered the clouds and rainbows. They roamed the subtle mists. . . . They surveyed (*jing ji*) the mountains and rivers, tread on Kunlun, and entered the gates of Heaven. Charioteers in an age of decline, even if they possessed light chariots, good horses, strong whips, and sharp goads, would be unable to compete with them. (1.2b–3a)

As we have seen, the term *jing* had become common in the ascension literature to describe an adept's surveying of the cosmos. The term is utilized with that same meaning here in order to discuss the ascension of Ping Yi and Da Bing.[8] The analogy between charioteering and rulership is clear: the ruler cannot succeed with strong controls.

The great man, therefore, is one who links with Heaven and Earth directly: "Therefore, a great man (*da zhang fu*) is calmly without forethought and tranquilly without anxiety. He takes Heaven as his shelter and Earth as his carriage; the four seasons as his horses, and yin and yang as his charioteer" (1.3a). The great man becomes one with Heaven and Earth. He ascends and joins in the movements of the cosmic transformations themselves: "He mounts the clouds and crosses through the mists. He is together with the maker of transformations (*zao hua*). He releases his intentions and relaxes his rhythms so as to race to the Great Dwelling" (1.3a). He follows the patterns laid out by the two august ones and thereby guides the spirits of wind and rain:

He orders (*ling*) the Master of Rains to clean his path and commands (*shi*) the Baron of Winds to sweep off the dust. Lightning he uses as his whip and thunder as his wheels. Above he roams (*you*) in the wilds of the mist and clouds, and below he emerges from the boundless gates. (1.3a–b)

Unlike Lu Jia, the authors present the wind and rain as being under the control of spirits. The adept can gain control over the elements by linking him-

---

8. A similar statement can be found in the "Shuzhen" chapter: "His [the True Man's] spirit surveys (*jing*) Lushan and Taihang without difficulty, enters the four seas and nine rivers without becoming wet" (*Huainanzi*, "Shuzhen," 2.12a).

self to the patterns of the cosmos. Here again, the vocabulary is drawn directly from the ascension literature: as in the "Yuan you" poem (see Chapter 5), he who ascends is presented as being able to command and control these spirits.

And, again as in the "Yuan you," the adept then achieves a higher level: after ascending and roaming throughout the cosmos, the adept returns to the Pivot—the point, as we saw with the two august ones, of power: "After inspecting and illuminating all, he goes back to hold fast within so as to make himself whole. He surveys (*jing ying*) the four corners and returns to the Pivot" (1.3b). He inspects everything and then turns to himself; he surveys everything and then returns to the Pivot. The parallels between these sentences imply that the adept's body becomes a microcosm of the cosmos.

Thus, although he surveys the entire universe, the adept never leaves his form. By grasping the Way, he roams the cosmos and yet stays in his body:

This is why he goes fast and yet does not get agitated, goes far and yet does not get tired. His four limbs are not moved, his keen hearing and sight are not damaged, yet he knows the boundaries and forms of the eight points and nine regions. How? By grasping the handle of the way and roaming (*you*) through the land without limit. (1.3b)

Since his body is one with the cosmos, he is able to control everything without manipulating anything:

Therefore, by taking Heaven as his shelter, there is nothing that is not covered; by taking Earth as his carriage, there is nothing that is not carried; by taking the four seasons as his horses, there is nothing that is not controlled (*shi*); by taking the yin and yang as his charioteer, there is nothing that is not completed. (1.3b)

As the authors argue later in the chapter:

Now, all under Heaven is something that I possess, and I am something that all under Heaven possesses. Between all under Heaven and myself, how can there be any distinction? As for possessing all under Heaven, why must one maintain measures, administer authority, and manage the handles of life and death so as to carry out one's requests and commands? What is called possessing Heaven does not mean this. All it means is obtaining oneself. If I obtain myself, then all under Heaven obtains me. If I and all under Heaven obtain each other, then we will always possess each other. How could anything come between us? What is called "obtaining oneself" is to make oneself whole. He who makes himself whole then becomes one with the Way. (1.14b–15a)

The analogy with rulership is clear, and the authors make the political implications of the cosmology explicit. They strongly oppose harsh laws and punishments (1.5a), aspects of statecraft closely associated in the early Han with the state of Qin. They further argue against a state based on the will of a single ruler—another probable reference to the Qin:

> Therefore, if we rely on the abilities of one man, it will be insufficient to regulate even a land of three *mou*. But if you cultivate the successions of the Way's patterns (*dao li*) and accord with the spontaneity of Heaven and Earth, then even the six harmonies will not require balancing. Therefore, Yu, in clearing and draining, took according with the water as his guide. (1.5b)

Proper rulership means according with the patterns of the Way and the spontaneous movements of Heaven and Earth. This is, in a sense, a political reading of the "Inner Chapters" of the *Zhuangzi*: the sage-king's goal is simply to be in harmony with the natural patterns.

The authors use this cosmology to argue for a non-agonistic vision of rulership. They thus describe the ruler in terms strongly reminiscent of the *Laozi*:

> He thereby positions himself above, yet the people do not regard him as heavy; he resides in front, yet the multitudes do not view him as injuring them. All under Heaven turn to him, while the licentious and depraved fear him. Since he does not struggle with the myriad things, no one struggles with him. (1.4a)

As in the *Laozi*, the sage is able to lead, but the people do not realize he is leading them. But there is a crucial difference here. The *Laozi* emphasizes an agonistic situation in which the adept-ruler was struggling with the Way, with his subjects, and with his rivals. For example, the authors of the *Laozi* underline the fact that the people would not recognize the sage standing before them because that is a wise strategy for controlling the people. In contrast, the authors of the *Huainanzi* chapter are denying any kind of conflict.

Moreover, the authors of the *Huainanzi* do argue that the ruler has a function in the cosmos: the ruler needs to do more than simply accord with a pre-existing order. The order was established by the two august ones by holding fast to the Way. And the goal of the later-born ruler is to help continue these processes:

> Thus, the affairs of all under Heaven cannot be managed (*wei*); one accords with their spontaneity and pushes them. The alterations of the myriad things cannot be examined; one grasps their essentials, returns to them, and hastens them. (1.3b)

Thus, as the authors describe Shun: "He grasped the mysterious power (*de*) in his mind, and the transformations were hastened as if he were a spirit (*ruo shen*)" (1.7b). By implication, the spirits in this cosmology have the power to hasten the transformations of the cosmos. The two august ones established the cosmos originally by holding fast to the Way, and spirits serve to keep these processes running. Humans have the potential to become like spirits as well and thus can help maintain this order.

This reference to becoming like a spirit is reminiscent of the argument of the "Neiye." And, indeed, in some ways the argument of the "Yuandao" is similar. For example, as did the authors of the self-cultivation chapters of the *Guanzi*, the *Huainanzi* authors develop their argument in terms of the interaction of form, *qi*, and spirit: "The form, spirit, *qi*, and intention, each resides where it is fitting so as to follow what Heaven and Earth do. The form is the dwelling of life, *qi* is the filling of life, and spirit is the regulator of life" (1.16a–b). In contrast to the *Shiwen* chapter discussed in Chapter 5 but very much as in the self-cultivation chapters of the *Guanzi*, the concern here is to keep these three properly linked:

> Now, man is able to see clearly and hear keenly. His form and frame are able to be raised, and his hundred joints can be bent and stretched. In analyzing he is able to distinguish black and white and see ugliness and beauty. In understanding he is able to differentiate identity and difference and clarify right and wrong. How? It is because his *qi* fills up for him and his spirit directs for him. (1/16b)

The key is to have the spirit control the form, instead of the opposite: "Thus, if one takes the spirit as the master, the form will follow and be benefited. If one takes the form as controlling, the spirit will follow and be harmed" (1.17a–b). Indeed, the main role for the form is to provide a proper resting place for the spirit: "His essence and spirit are thereby daily depleted and travel distantly. If for a long time it overflows and does not return, the form will close its openings and the spirit will have nowhere to enter" (1.17b).

Despite these similarities to the "Neiye," however, and despite the comparable claims that a human can, through self-cultivation, become "like a spirit," the overall argument of the "Yuandao" is quite different. For the authors of the "Neiye," by becoming like a spirit, the adept gains the ability to control things (*shi wu*) and can understand good and bad fortune without resorting to divination. Spirits, in other words, have direct control over natural phenomena, and humans who gain the spirits' power do the same. In the cosmology presented here, spirits also have control over natural phenomena, but these phenomena are part of a normative process. Their actions, in other words, are defined precisely as they are in the "Inner Chapters" of the *Zhuangzi*: spirits simply do what they are supposed to do within the order of Heaven. And, therefore, humans, when they become like spirits, do the same. As with Zhuangzi, the sense here is that any conflict between man and Heaven is entirely the fault of man. The way to overcome it is to follow one's spirit and accord with the order of Heaven.

This point is spelled out in the authors' discussion of self-cultivation. The concern here is to define a fully non-agonistic notion of self-cultivation: proper self-cultivation, the authors argue, involves not a usurpation of divine powers but a proper acceptance of them. The argument is made by building on elements of Zhuangzi:

When a human is born, he is still; this is the Heavenly nature. He moves only when he is affected. This is the goodness of nature. Things arrive, and the spirit responds. This is the movement of knowledge. Knowledge connects with things, and likes and dislikes are born therefrom. When likes and dislikes are completed into forms, knowledge is seduced from the outside. He is unable to return to himself, and the Heavenly patterns (*tian li*) are extinguished. Thus, one who reaches the Way does not use the human to change Heaven. He transforms with things on the outside but does not lose his disposition on the inside. (1.4a)

Humans have within themselves a Heavenly nature. If one moves only in response to external stimuli, one will not lose that nature. The authors define this as the spirit responding. The spirit is thus clearly linked to Heaven. However, if one allows one's responses to become hardened into preferences, then one loses that Heavenly nature and extinguishes the Heavenly patterns. The conclusion the authors draw is that the person in possession of the Way does not try to change Heaven.

As with Zhuangzi, therefore, the spirit should follow Heaven. Forms seduce one into the attempt to change (Zhuangzi would say overcome) Heaven. The key is to tailor one's response as closely as one can to the patterns of Heaven. However, the crucial difference between the argument in the "Yuandao" and that in the *Zhuangzi* is that the authors of the "Yuandao" want to claim that grasping the Way grants one powers of control. Even if these powers are nothing but the ability to direct and hasten the normative patterns, they are nonetheless powers that can, like the work of the two august ones, bring order to the cosmos.

But this raises an important point for the political arguments of the chapter. The authors are committed to claiming that by following their teachings, the adept will gain control; yet, because of the way they build on Zhuangzi, they are also committed to saying that this power is potentially available to *whoever* grasps the patterns of the Way. This does not mean that anyone can become a ruler; on the contrary, like Zhuangzi, they see such an issue of social position as outside the control of humans. But they do want to claim that the power to control can be gained by anyone, regardless of social position:

He who grasps the patterns of the Way (*dao li*) so as to pair himself with alterations, controls followers when leading and controls leaders when following. How is this so? If he does not lose that which enables him to control others, then others are unable to control him. (1.8b)

Like Mencius, these powers are available to anyone. But, unlike Mencius, these authors do not see the ruler as the only figure able to achieve such control.

The authors also quote a variation of the same passage about the liberation of the One that we have followed from the "Neiye" to the *Shiliujing* to the *Shiwen*: "As for the Way: when the One is established, the myriad things are generated. Therefore, the pattern (*li*) of the One extends to the four seas, and the liberation (*jie*) of the One reaches the border of Heaven and Earth" (1.11b). This passage is essentially identical to the version in the "Chengfa" chapter of the *Shiliujing*: "The liberation (*jie*) of the One allows an exploration (*cha*) of Heaven and Earth. The pattern (*li*) of the One extends to the four seas." But, in contrast to the "Chengfa" chapter, the *Huainanzi* is not arguing for the creation of a centralized state apparatus with unifying laws. On the contrary, the argument is that linking oneself to the One allows for the things to be generated properly. As in the *Laozi*, then, the adept is called on to link with the One and thereby become an ancestor to the myriad things. But, in contrast to the *Laozi*, this text accepts that there is a proper pattern to the cosmos that the adept, by establishing the One, will generate.

The authors of this chapter of the *Huainanzi* are thus building on both the ascension literature and texts such as the *Shiliujing* and the *Laozi*, but they are altering both. Indeed, despite these overt parallels, the argument is most indebted to Zhuangzi's notion of the spirit as spontaneously following the order of Heaven: "liberation" involves subsuming oneself to the order of Heaven. And the authors of the *Huainanzi* are working out the political implications of this.

The Ascensions of Huangdi and Fu Xi:
The "Lanming" Chapter

Similar concerns underlie the "Lanming," chapter six of the *Huainanzi*. The authors argue that, by practicing the proper techniques of self-cultivation, a process that includes, among other things, accumulating one's spirit (*shen*), one gains enormous power over the natural world.[9] One figure who practiced such techniques had phenomenal powers: "The Duke of Luyang was in battle with Han. As the battle became intense, the sun began to set. [The Duke] grasped his spear and waved it. The sun on his behalf went back three mansions" (6.1b). Of interest here, however, is the mechanism by which he achieved the power to move the sun from its orbit: the mastery of correlative influence through self-cultivation. "These are evidences of the mutual influence of the divine *qi* (*shen qi*)" (6.2b). The spirits control natural phenomena through correlativity: *shen* is the most refined form of *qi*, and hence the most resonant. The more refined, the more *shen*-like, one becomes through self-cultivation, the more resonant one becomes. Moreover, the processes by which such resonance occurs, the authors explicitly argue, are spontaneous, *ziran* (6.4a).

As in the "Yuandao" chapter, the authors develop this argument by citing exemplary charioteers. Instead of a whip, Qian Qie and Da Bing use essence and spirit to guide the horses: "Their desires and wants formed in their chests, and their essence and spirit (*jing* and *shen*) pass over to the six horses. This is the way that they drove them without driving" (6.6b). These arguments provide a cosmological underpinning for the larger political claims the authors want to make. The sage should indeed become theomorphic, should indeed possess tremendous power vis-à-vis the natural world, but such powers can be gained only through a process of self-cultivation that brings one more into alignment with the spontaneous processes of the universe and more in accord with the naturally given order. In short, the sage in such a system gains control over the natural world only by placing himself within a normative order of refinement.

To explicate the political implications of this argument, the authors relate a story about Huangdi's ordering of the world:

---

9. *Huainanzi*, "Lanming," 6.1a; hereinafter cited in the text. See the very helpful analysis in Le Blanc, *Huai-Nan Tzu*.

In ancient times, Huangdi put in order all under Heaven, and Li Mu and Taishan Ji assisted him. He thereby put in order the courses of the sun and the moon, put in order the *qi* of yin and yang, regulated the lengths of the seasons, corrected the numbers of the calendar, differentiated male and female humans, distinguished male and female animals, made clear the upper and lower, and ranked the noble and the common. . . . Laws and commands were clear and not obscure. (6.6b)

Because of Huangdi's actions, the cosmos functioned properly:

Thereupon, the sun and moon were rarified and bright, the stars and constellations did not lose their courses, the wind and the rain were timely and moderated, the five grains grew and ripened, the tigers and wolves did not recklessly bite, vultures did not recklessly seize, phoenixes flew over the courtyard, and the *jilin* roamed in the country. (6.7a)

Even so, the age did not equal that of Fu Xi, who, among other things,

directed the ghosts and spirits, ascended to the Nine Heavens, and attended the court of the Di at the Numinous Gate. . . . He held within himself the way of the True Man so as to follow the firmness of Heaven and Earth. How so? The way and power were penetrated above, and knowledge and precedent were extinguished. (6.7b–8a)

The authors then discuss the reign of the current Son of Heaven—Emperor Wu of the Han. They call on Emperor Wu to follow in the traces of Fu Xi and point out that, unlike Huangdi, Fu Xi did not use laws. An explicit contrast is drawn with the ideas of Shen Buhai, Han Feizi, and Shang Yang— figures whose ideas were highly influential on the development of imperial institutions (6.9b–10a).

The chapter is clearly intended as a critique of significant aspects of the Han imperial order, particularly the imperial vision of rulership in which the emperor imposes his will on the cosmos and orders the world through laws and commands. During this period, this aspect of Han ideology was clearly associated with Huangdi, and the authors of the *Huainanzi* argue the point by portraying Huangdi's methods of ordering the world as inadequate. Fu Xi is the exemplar of a superior way.[10]

---

10. Elsewhere I have argued against the attempt by many scholars to categorize the *Huainanzi* as a "Huang-Lao" text (see *The Ambivalence of Creation*, pp. 260–61n72). Here we see another reason to question such a categorization: Huangdi (the "Huang" of "Huang-Lao") is explicitly presented as a lesser ruler than Fu Xi.

The argument of the "Lanming" chapter is quite different from that found in the texts of spiritual liberation discussed in Chapter 5. For example, in contrast to the *Shiwen*, which utilizes a dualistic framework to argue for a liberation of the spirit from the form, the "Lanming" chapter uses a monistic framework to call on the ruler to bring order to the universe through resonance.

Nonetheless, there are striking parallels with these other texts. For example, the practices advocated here include "concentrating essence" and "accumulating spirit" (6.7b–8a). Fu Xi, moreover, is explicitly described as ascending to the heavens, and, just like the adept in the "Yuan you," he is explicitly described as attending the court of Di. Although this chapter does not refer to the liberation of the spirit from the form, it does have many of the same generic elements seen in the ascension texts discussed in Chapter 5.

Thus, the authors of the "Lanming" chapter of the *Huainanzi* are appropriating a monistic cosmology and self-cultivation techniques in order to critique aspects of the prevailing imperial ideology. The model posited here is a monistic one, based on a cosmology and set of practices traceable to texts such as the "Neiye." In the "Lanming" chapter, Huangdi is praised as a figure who was successful in bringing order to the cosmos, but he is clearly inferior to Fu Xi, the figure who ascended to the heavens and ruled through inaction. The arguments are similar to those of the *Shiwen* and the *Zhuangzi*, but here there is an explicit attempt to read the issues politically.

A Cosmos Aligned by Spirits: The "Jingshen" Chapter

We are now in a position to understand the chapter with which I opened this book: chapter seven of the *Huainanzi*, the "Jingshen"—one of the richest and most complicated texts on divinization and cosmology written in the early period. Having traced the claims concerning divinization and cosmology up to the mid-second century BC, we can now attempt a full reading of the chapter—to see what is behind its treatment of the subjects of spirits, divinization, and cosmology. I will argue that the "Jingshen" can be understood in its full richness only by placing it squarely within the context of the debates of the second century BC.

The chapter begins with a cosmogony:

Long ago, in the time before there existed Heaven and Earth, there was only figure (*xiang*) without form (*xing*). Obscure, dark, vast, and deep—no one knows its gate. There were two spirits born together; they aligned Heaven, they oriented Earth. So vast—no one knows its end or limit! So overflowing—no one knows where it stops! Thereupon, they divided and became yin and yang, separated and became the eight pillars. Hard and soft completed each other, and the myriad things were thereupon formed (*xing*). The turbid *qi* became insects, and the refined *qi* became humans.[11]

The cosmogony is in some particulars comparable to that given in texts such as the *Taiyi sheng shui* and the "Dayue" chapter of the *Lüshi chunqiu*. But the crucial difference is that in the "Jingshen" chapter spirits align and orient the cosmos. Although the cosmos is not actively constructed but emerges spontaneously, spirits organize and arrange it. The spirits are themselves generated spontaneously: the word used here is *sheng*, literally, "born." These spirits then actively plan and orient the cosmos.

To some extent, this cosmology is similar to that dominant at the Han court—spirits have the power to control natural phenomena. But the phrase used to characterize the way they control phenomena is *jing ying*. As we have seen, these terms have a long history of association with the surveying work of sages before an act of construction and became important in the ascension literature to describe the surveying of the already formed cosmos that an adept undertakes during a spirit journey. The authors play on both of these meanings in the chapter.

Through the opening cosmogony, the text has defined the cosmos as monistic, with Heaven and Earth being separate yet composed of the same substance. Within this monistic cosmology, humans are composed of refined *qi*. Moreover, the duality of Heaven and Earth inheres in humans: "This is the reason that the essence and the spirit are possessions of Heaven, whereas bones and limbs are possessions of Earth. When the essence and the spirit enter their gate, and when bones and limbs return to their root, how can 'I' exist?" (7.1a). This duality is clearly reminiscent of the dualistic systems analyzed in preceding chapters. And the question that closes the passage seems to imply a concern with preserving the individual from death: if at death the essence and spirit return to Heaven and the bones and limbs return to Earth, then the goal of cultivation, presumably, would be to keep the two together as long as possible.

That the authors are headed in a very different direction becomes clear in the next sentence: "Thus, the sage models himself on Heaven and follows his disposition (*qing*). He does not adhere to custom; he is not seduced by men"

---

11. *Huainanzi*, "Jingshen," 7.1a; hereinafter cited in the text.

(7.1a). The immediate move of the chapter, then, is not to present a program for achieving immortality but to claim an alternative to tradition or custom as the basis of authority: one's innate disposition. Disposition is, like essence and spirit, thus linked to Heaven, and the authors have now defined disposition, essence, and spirit as the basis on which the sage must act.

However, the authors are not claiming that the sage should follow Heaven in the sense of seeking to separate the spirit from the form. Although Heaven and, thus, the spirit, essence, and disposition are the marked terms here, there is no call for a transcendence of the Earth:

He takes Heaven as his father, Earth as his mother, yin and yang as his regulators, and the four seasons as his principles. Heaven is still by means of purity, Earth is settled by means of pacifying. As for the myriad things, if they lose these, they die; if they take these as their model, they live. (7.1b)

The entire cosmos should be the basis for the actions of the sage. Or, to put it in other terms, the sage must follow the entire cosmos as aligned and oriented by the primordial spirits.

The questions that then arise are how the sage can do so and what the implications of this are:

Now, stillness and vastness are where divine illumination rests. Emptiness and lack of differentiation are where the Way dwells. Therefore, someone who seeks it on the outside will lose it within; one who holds fast to it on the inside will lose it on the outside. This is like the root and the branches. If you trace to the root and pull it, the thousand branches and the ten thousand leaves will all follow. (7.1b)

Precisely because spirits performed the initial alignment of the cosmos, and since spirit for humans is associated with Heaven, it is through the stillness associated with Heaven that the adept can gain divine illumination and thus align himself with the cosmos. And, by the same token, it is through emptiness that one can get closer to the Way, since the Way is associated with the initial period before differentiation. The significance of this is made clearer when we refer back to the opening cosmogony of the chapter. The concern there was with the movement from spirit to form, and the implication was that form is differentiated and less refined than spirit. The sage is simply one who has become more refined.

To develop this argument further, the text explains that at the birth of humans: "Essence and spirit are what one receives from Heaven; form and frame are what one is endowed with from Earth." If all life comes from the mating of Heaven and Earth, then man contains within himself this same duality.

Thus it is said: "The one generates the two, the two generate the three, and the three generate the myriad things." The myriad things carry the *yin* on their back and embrace the *yang*. They rub the *qi* so as to become harmonized. (7.1b)

The text is recapitulating the fundamental claims made thus far: the cosmos is monistic and divides into two. The two then mate and generate the rest of the cosmos. The emphasis is on the nature of the resulting things: the entire cosmos is composed of yin and yang elements.

As a consequence, the embryo inherently includes both elements.

Therefore it is said: In the first month there is fat, in the second month blood, in the third month tissue, in the fourth month flesh, in the fifth month tendons, in the sixth month bones, in the seventh month it is completed, in the eighth month there is movement, in the ninth month it grows more active, and in the tenth month it is born. (7.1b)

In contrast to the account of the birth of humans in the *Shiwen* (see Chapter 5), there is no claim here that the spirit flows into the form; rather, birth is a process of *qi* gradually becoming a form. The resulting individual is inherently both spirit and form. Unlike the origins narrative of the *Shiwen*, the cosmology is not structured to emphasize the importance of liberating oneself from one's form.

The text continues to describe the process of formation: "When the form and frame are thereby complete, the five repositories thereupon take form" (7.1b). The five repositories are the lungs, kidneys, gall bladder, liver, and spleen. As we shall see, they are the places where *qi* is both stored and circulated. Each of these is linked to a particular sense organ:

Thus, the lungs control the eyes, the kidneys control the nose, the gall bladder controls the mouth, and the liver controls the ears. On the outside are the expressions, on the inside are the internals. Opening and closing, expanding and contracting, each has its alignment (*jing*) and regulation (*ji*). (7.1b–2a)[12]

A fundamental alignment naturally emerges with the formation of the human body. And this alignment is inherently linked to the alignment given Heaven and Earth by the primordial spirits:

----

12. On *jing ji*, cf. 1.3a.

Therefore, the head is round like Heaven, the feet are square like Earth. Heaven has four seasons, five phases, nine points, and 366 days. Humans also have four limbs, five repositories, nine orifices, and 366 joints. Heaven has wind, rain, cold, and heat; humans also have taking, giving, happiness, and anger. Therefore the gall bladder is clouds, the lungs are *qi*, the liver is wind, the kidneys are the rain, and the spleen is thunder. They thereby form a triad with Heaven and Earth, but the heart is the master. (7.2a)

Humans, in this cosmology, are the partners of Heaven and Earth. Not only are all these composed of the same substance, but all are formed by the same alignment. Accordingly, the internal forms of humans match both their external forms as well as the larger forms of the cosmos: the five repositories are linked both to the five senses and to natural phenomena.

Given this linkage of microcosm and macrocosm, with each having the same normative alignment, the concern of the text is how both the human body and the cosmos can be kept properly aligned.

Thus, the ears and eyes are the sun and moon; blood and *qi* are wind and rain. . . . If the sun and moon were to lose their courses, there will be eclipses and no light. If the wind and the rain were to be untimely, there would be ruin, destructions, and disasters. If the five stars were to lose their courses, the regions and kingdoms would receive calamities. Now, the way of Heaven and Earth is of utmost vastness with greatness, but it must still modulate its arrayed brilliance, and it must still cherish its divine illumination. How can the ears and eyes of humans last long and labor without rest? How can the essence and spirit last long, hasten on, and not stop? (7.2a–b)

Even Heaven and Earth maintain the proper alignment through modulation. Without this, nothing in the natural world would function properly.

This point about wind and rain deserves further comment. Control over the winds and rain was a power widely ascribed to spirits. In the "Jingshen," however, wind and rains are simply part of the natural movement of the universe as initially aligned by spirits. In other words, spirits do, in an ultimate sense, control the wind and rain, but only because they were the ones who aligned the cosmos so that the wind and rains would come at the proper time. Moreover, the spirits themselves became the cosmos they aligned, and it is their potency that maintains this cosmos. Accordingly, it is through proper modulation and cherishing that the divine illumination can be maintained.

And since humanity is a microcosm of the universe, then the same must hold true for humanity:

Therefore the blood and the *qi* are the flowering of humanity, and the five repositories are the essence of humanity. Now, when the blood and the *qi* can be concentrated by the five repositories and do not fall away in excess, then the chest and stomach will be full, and lusts and desires will be reduced. If the chest and stomach are full and lusts and desires are reduced, then the ears and eyes will be clear, and one's hearing and seeing will connect with their objects. When the ears and eyes are clear, and one's hearing and seeing connect with their objects, we call this clarity. If the five repositories can be gathered by the mind, and there is no deviation, then distracted attention will be overcome and the movements will not be corrupt. When distracted attention is overcome and the movements not corrupt, then the essence and the spirit will flourish and the *qi* will not dissipate. When the essence and the spirit flourish and the *qi* is not dissipating, then one will be patterned (*li* 理). (7.2b)

The concern here is precisely the same as that seen for the cosmos as a whole. The cosmos operates according to the alignment laid out by the initial spirits, and as long as the spirit of the cosmos flourishes, everything within the cosmos follows this proper alignment. However, if the spirit were to dissipate, then the sun and moon would lose their courses, the wind and rain would come at the wrong time. Since humans are a microcosm of this world, the problems humans face are identical. If one's essence and spirit dissipate, one ceases to be aligned. If, however, one can bring one's movements into proper alignment, the essence and spirit will flourish, and one will be patterned (*li*)—which is to say, one will be in accord with the proper alignment of things.

The consequence of being patterned is that one becomes divinized:

When one is patterned, one will be balanced. When one is balanced, one will penetrate. When one penetrates, one will be a spirit (*shen*). When one is a spirit, one will thereby see without anything not being seen, one will thereby hear without anything not being heard, and one will thereby act without anything not being completed. (7.2b)[13]

We thus arrive at the claim of divinization in the "Jingshen" chapter. Divinization is here the result of bringing oneself into accord with the proper patterns. Being a spirit, in other words, means that one is intuitively patterned and aligned. And since the alignment of the human is a microcosm of the alignment of the cosmos, in this state the adept hears, sees, and acts properly.

---

13. This claim of divinization is repeated later in the chapter at 7.5a: "The *hun* and the *po* souls are positioned in his abode, the essence and spirit are held fast to their root. Death and life are not altered by him. Therefore he is called: the ultimate spirit."

The consequence of becoming a spirit, then, is not that one gains control over natural phenomena or that one's spirit becomes separated from one's form and transcends the world. It is, rather, that one is able to see, hear, and act in accord with the alignment of the cosmos.

The argument thus far seems in some ways like a complex cosmological rewriting of arguments like those found in texts such as the "Neiye" and "Xinshu" chapters: the cosmos is monistic, spirit and essence are the most refined and most potent parts of this cosmos, and through cultivation humans can increase and concentrate their spirit and thereby come to understand the movements of the cosmos. However, the "Jingshen" is not arguing that such cultivation allows the adept to control things (*shi wu*)—the claim that, in radically different ways, both the "Neiye" and the *fangshi* made. On the contrary, the concern in the text is to place the adept within the existing patterns of the cosmos. This chapter, in other words, is headed in a very different direction from many of the texts we have been exploring.

The authors of the "Jingshen" emphasize the degree to which this trumps the claims made by earlier self-cultivation texts. If, for texts such as the "Neiye" and "Xinshu," acts of cultivation allow one to understand misfortune and fortune, cultivation here yields far more:

Now, orifices are the doors and windows of the essence and spirit, and the *qi* and will are the followers of the five repositories. If the ears and eyes are inundated with the pleasures of sounds and colors, then the five repositories will be moved and not remain settled. If the five repositories are moved and do not remain settled, then the blood and *qi* will overflow and not stop. If the blood and *qi* overflow and do not stop, then the essence and spirit will hasten to the outside and not be held fast. If the essence and spirit hasten to the outside and are not held fast, then there will be no way to understand the coming of misfortune and fortune—even though they might be as [huge as] mountains. If one were to make the ears and eyes refined (*jing*), clear, subtle, penetrating, and not seducible or desirous; if the *qi* and will are empty, still, calm, peaceful, and with few desires; if the five repositories are settled, pacified, abundantly filled, and not leaking; if the essence and spirit are held fast within to the form and frame and do not reach outside, then one could witness all that has passed before and see all the events to come. If you are still not able to do this, then what of the mere distinction between fortune and misfortune? (7.2b–3a)

The concern here, as in the "Neiye" and related texts, is to keep the spirit and essence within one's form. But in this cosmology, the yields are far greater: one gains nothing less than a full understanding of the entire cosmos, including knowledge of the past and future. The ability to discern fortune and misfortune, the authors argue, is a trifling consideration next to this.

Almost as if to underline this call for the adept to follow the proper alignment of the cosmos, the authors begin invoking the one text most clearly associated with such ideas: the "Inner Chapters" of the *Zhuangzi*. Several passages in the remainder of the chapter play on the themes—and at times explicitly invoke specific images and passages—discussed at length in Chapter 3.

Heaven and Earth revolve and penetrate each other. The myriad things are collected and become One. If you are able to understand the One, then there is nothing that is not understood; if you are not able to understand the One, then there is nothing that can be understood. It is like my being placed within this world. I am also one thing. I do not know if all under Heaven takes me as completing its things. Moreover, if there were no "me," would everything be complete? As such, I am a thing. A thing like other things; a thing in relation to other things. How am I to be compared with other things? And how did my birth add anything, and how will my death be a loss? Now, the producer of transformations made me into a clod; I do not have any means to oppose it. (7.3b–4a)

This clear allusion to the *Zhuangzi* and its call for acceptance of one's fate had powerful implications in the context of the early Han. At a time when the search for immortality had come to play an important role in cultural life—particularly at the imperial court—a call to accept one's lifespan and not seek to increase it certainly had resonance. As in the *Zhuangzi*, the mode of critique is to emphasize the necessity of viewing the cosmos as a whole, with one's life and death as simply part of that larger process:

Now, the producer of transformation's gathering and pulling out things is like a potter's stretching and straightening. He takes earth and that is all. When he makes it into basins and pots, it is still earth. There is nothing that distinguishes a completed vessel from broken shards returned to their source. (7.4a)

Despite these clear allusions to the *Zhuangzi*, there are significant differences. As we saw in Chapter 3, Zhuangzi's point in referring to a producer of transformations was to emphasize that one's current form is simply a momentary product of the flux of the cosmos: the producer of things has made this particular form and will soon make another. As such, one ought not reify anything and view it as deserving of preservation beyond its given allotment. But the argument of the authors of the "Jingshen" is slightly different: their point is that the substance of an individual is no different from the substance from which it is made—hence the statement that a completed vessel is still clay. Humans are of the same substance as the rest of the cosmos, and any one individual is simply a momentary rearrangement of that substance.

It is precisely this monistic claim that allows the adept to gain power. Not only can he see the past and know what is to come, but all under Heaven submits spontaneously to the spirit:

> The spirit is tranquil and without limit. It is not dispersed with things, and yet all under Heaven submits of its own accord. Therefore, the heart is the ruler of the form, and the spirit is the treasure of the heart. If the form is labored and does not rest, then it collapses; if the essence is used without ceasing, then it exhausts itself. Therefore the sage values and honors it; he does not dare overextend it. (7.4b)

Since spirits initially aligned and oriented the cosmos and since they then became the cosmos that they had aligned and oriented, all things (all forms) submit to spirit of their own accord. Thus, spirit is the basis for power, and that power consists of making the myriad things submit. Ironically, a generally Zhuangzian cosmology is being appropriated to argue that the sage does possess control over aspects of the cosmos. But it is a form of control very different from that advocated by other texts such as the "Neiye" and *fangshi*. Here, control is the power to bring about the order that should exist.

Thus the sage, while possessing tremendous power, inherently follows his pattern (*li*), completes his fate, and accords with Heaven:

> Therefore the sage uses nothingness to respond to something and invariably follows out his pattern; he uses emptiness to receive the substantial and invariably reaches his modulation. Quiet, contented, empty, and still, he thereby completes his fate. Therefore he has nothing that is deeply distant and nothing that is deeply intimate. He embraces virtue and blends in harmony so as to accord with Heaven. (7.5a)

But what does this mean? What is accomplished by becoming a spirit, aligning with the patterns of the cosmos, and according with Heaven? In the "Xinshu" chapters, as well as most related texts discussed in Chapter 4, the sage was clearly defined as a ruler, and becoming a spirit meant that the sage gained tremendous power to control things (*shi wu*). But for the authors of the "Jingshen," not only does the sage not gain such powers, but he is not necessarily a ruler at all:

The sage eats enough to keep his *qi* intact and dresses enough to cover his form. He accords with his disposition (*qing*) and does not seek what is superfluous. Not possessing all under Heaven does not injure his nature, and possessing all under Heaven does not add to his harmony. Possessing all under Heaven and not possessing all under Heaven are the same. (7.10a)

For the sage, there is no meaningful distinction between being this and being that. The sage is simply one who has become fully patterned on the cosmos and is thus always able to act in accord with the world. This is true regardless of what position he occupies. Although the authors present the sage as powerful, and although they appropriate much of the vocabulary of the self-divinization literature, their consistent claim is a Zhuangzian one: one's highest goal (and the inevitable product of becoming a spirit) is to accord with the patterns of the cosmos.

Thus far, the text has been discussing the sage—the figure who has cultivated himself to the extent that his spirit is joined fast to his form and he becomes patterned and aligned properly. As a result, he sees and hears clearly, knows the past and future, acts successfully, and brings things to their proper order. The text next turns to the True Man—the figure associated with ascension:

As for he who is called the True Man: his nature harmonizes with the Way. Therefore, he possesses, but it is as if he has nothing; he is full, but it is as if he is empty. He resides in the One and does not know duality. He orders what is inside and does not recognize what is outside. He makes clear the great purity, is without conscious action, returns to the uncarved block, embodies the root, and embraces the spirit so as to wander at the edges of Heaven and Earth. Far-reaching, he appears to be outside the world of dust and dirt. . . . Although Heaven and Earth cover and nurture, he is not embraced by them. (7.5a)

The True Man does not transcend Heaven and Earth: he is still covered and nurtured by them, respectively. But, unlike other humans, he is not embraced by them: he is not conditioned by their force.

The True Man harmonizes with the Way and embraces his spirit. He wanders at the edges of Heaven and Earth and is not snared by either. In short, the True Man, unlike the sage, transcends the forms and moves closer to the initial alignment of Heaven and Earth. Whereas the sage tries to refine his eyes and ears so they can see and hear clearly, the true man discards them: "One such as he corrects his liver and gall bladder and discards his ears and eyes. His mind and will are concentrated within, and he penetrates to and dwells with the One" (7.5b). The True Man's concern is the One, not an accurate perception of the world of forms.

And instead of aligning and patterning his form and the five repositories, the True Man ignores them: "His form is like rotten wood, and his mind like dead ashes. He forgets the five repositories, cuts off his form and limbs" (7.5b). One of the differences between the sage and the True Man, in other words, lies in their orientation toward the body. As we saw above, the birth of a human involves the gradual completion of a form, including the formation of the five repositories. The sage is the person who aligns his five repositories with the rest of the cosmos and holds his spirit fast to his form. He thus becomes a microcosm of the properly functioning cosmos. In contrast, the True Man is oblivious to body and form. Whereas the body is the sage's foundation for building a microcosm of the universe, for the True Man it is an irrelevance.[14]

The gnosis of the True Man is accordingly different from that of the sage: "He does not study and yet knows, does not look and yet sees, does not act and yet completes, does not put things in order and yet distinguishes" (7.5b). The sage sees everything and his actions complete everything; the True Man sees without looking and completes everything without acting.

Indeed, the True Man is unaffected by the world of forms outside himself as well:

Things cannot orient (*ying*) him. . . . Great swamps could burn, yet he would not get hot. The rivers could freeze over, yet he would not be cold. Great thunder could rip apart mountains, yet he would not be alarmed. Great winds could darken the sun, yet he would not be injured. (7.5b–6a)

Here again we encounter vocabulary from the *Zhuangzi*, in this case, from Zhuangzi's discussion of the *shen ren*—the divine man. But the authors of the "Jingshen" take this vocabulary far more literally than did Zhuangzi. For Zhuangzi these were metaphors for the divine man's lack of dependence on things; here they are meant quite literally: because the primordial spirits oriented the cosmos, which would later beget forms, one who can fully embrace the spirit is unaffected by the world of forms.

---

14. A similar claim can be found in "Quanyan," chapter fourteen of the *Huainanzi*: "He who can return to that which gave birth to him such that it is as if he does not yet have a form—this person we call the True Man. The True Man has not yet begun to separate from the Great One" (see *Huainanzi*, 14.1a).

Indeed, unlike the sage, the True Man does not bother to keep his essence and spirit linked to his form at all. Instead, his spirit is allowed to roam free:

He shares the same essence as the root of the great clarity and wanders at the borders of the minutest regions. He possesses an essence, yet does not control (*shi*) it; he possesses a spirit, yet does not move it. . . . He rests in the corners without crookedness and wanders in the wilds without form or enclosure. . . . His movements are without form; his rest without embodiment. Existence is as if non-existence, life is as if death. Leaving and entering are not differentiated. He employs ghosts and spirits (*gui shen*). Lost in the immeasurable, entering into the non-separated, so that his different forms succeed one another. Beginning and end are like a circle; no one can obtain his categories. This is the means by which the essence and spirit can ascend and draw near to the Way. Thus, it is where the True Man wanders. (7.6a–b)

The vocabulary here clearly reflects the ascension literature discussed in Chapter 5. The True Man wanders without form or enclosure, employs ghosts and spirits, and his essence and spirit ascend. But, here again, the authors appropriate the language associated with the True Man and place it within a generally Zhuangzian cosmology.

For example, the point about the True Man is not that his spirit is liberated from the form but that the spirit remains unaffected by the forms:

Thus, that the form interacts but the spirit has never been transformed is because one uses that which does not transform to respond to that which does transform. A thousand alterations and ten thousand revolutions, and yet it has not yet begun to have a limit. That which transforms returns to the formless; that which does not transform lives together with Heaven and Earth. (7.7a)

The forms are transformed, and anything that is just form returns to the formless. But that which does not transform is eternal, like Heaven and Earth—and this is the highest goal of the True Man.

Thus, the True Man does not transcend Heaven and Earth: his spirit lives together with them in the alignment initially given by the spirits. He thus never returns to the formless, and yet he is also not controlled by, or even affected by, the changing forms between Heaven and Earth. In this sense, his spirit is never bound:

When a tree dies, the vitality of its greenness leaves it. That which made the tree live is not the tree, just as that which fills the form is not the form. Therefore, that which generates life has never died, but that which it generates does die. That which transforms things has never been transformed, but that which it transformed does transform. If one regards all under Heaven lightly, then one's spirit will not be bound. (7.7a)

As with Zhuangzi, being liberated does not mean that one escapes but that one accepts one's fate. Although he "studies the teachers of no-death" (7.8b), the True Man's goal is not to avoid death but to reach the point at which the shifting of forms means nothing to him:

Life is not sufficient to make his will anxious, and death is not sufficient to darken his spirit. Whether contracting or expanding, looking down or looking up, he embraces his fate (*ming*) and yields to turns. Misfortune and fortune, benefit and harm, a thousand alterations and ten thousand revolutions—how can they worry him? Such a man as this embraces purity and holds fast to essence. Like the liberation (*jie*) of the cicada or the snake [from their outer skins], he wanders (*you*) in the great clarity. (7.8b)

The authors again employ language reminiscent of the ascension literature. At first glance, for example, liberation (*jie*) would appear to refer to the escape of the spirit from the form—exactly the claim of the *Shiwen*. But in fact the metaphor points to a snake who sloughs off parts of his form according to the proper season—accepting the order of Heaven. The authors' point is that the True Man embraces his fate and is not concerned with death—or immortality.

Ultimately, therefore, liberation for these authors carries a meaning slightly different from that of the *Shiwen* but very similar to that of the *Zhuangzi*: liberation refers not to the spirit leaving the form but to not allowing one's spirit to be concerned with forms. Instead, and again as in the *Zhuangzi*, the spirit of the True Man simply follows the proper movement of the cosmos rather than being weighed down by a false concern with forms. It is as if the language of ascension has been embraced in order to defend a point of view found in the *Zhuangzi*.

Thus, the authors build on texts like the "Neiye" and "Xinshu" to develop their understanding of the sage and on the ascension literature to develop their understanding of the True Man. But in both cases they reinterpret this previous literature within a generally Zhuangzian framework. The question then becomes Why? Why are they so concerned with re-reading this literature through Zhuangzi? And if the cosmology of this chapter is based in part on the *Zhuangzi*, then why do spirits align the cosmos? Zhuangzi certainly never talked about demiurges organizing the universe. So why are such claims being advanced here? And why do the authors use the words *jing ying* to describe the actions of these spirits? I begin with the latter question first.

As we have seen, these had become highly loaded terms by the early Han. For example, the First Emperor had claimed the ability to align (*jing*) the universe, and the terms were appropriated by the ascension literature to describe the spirit journeys of humans. In this literature, the spirit can traverse the universe, escaping the bounds of form and the restraints of this world.

The authors of the "Jingshen" chapter make a complex move within this debate. The patterns and alignment of the cosmos are set up by the primordial spirits, who then became the cosmos itself. On the one hand, this means that the cosmos *needs* spirits. In the "Jingshen," these spirits are not traversing the already existing boundaries of the universe; they are aligning those boundaries. The claim, in other words, is that the cosmos needs spirits in order to be properly aligned: the cosmos is organized by spirits, and the political order should be as well.

But, at the same time, the spirits did not align the cosmos through an act of will; rather, they aligned it properly. Thus, in contrast to the First Emperor's claim that he had aligned the cosmos according to his will, the spirits in the "Jingshen" chapter obey a normative plan: spirits, if they are truly spirits, follow certain paths. Spirits, in short, have the power to do what should be done. They do not have the power to do what they wish: wind and rain, for example, are simply part of the spontaneous cosmos, not something controlled by spirits. Thus, the spirits are not entities that impose their will through a direct control of natural phenomena; they are, rather, highly refined *qi* that spontaneously act as they ought.

Humans are then defined as microcosms of this cosmos aligned by the spirits and as having spirit within themselves. The text calls on humans to cultivate themselves so as to become increasingly divine. The authors have developed an ingenious way for arguing the absolute centrality of the specific mode of self-cultivation that they are advocating.

The authors used this framework to provide a re-reading of both the sage and the True Man. In both cases, the authors present their arguments within a generally Zhuangzian framework. Like the "Xinshu" chapters of the *Guanzi*, the "Jingshen" argues that the sage can become fully divine and gain a full understanding of the cosmos. However, unlike the "Xinshu" chapters, the "Jingshen" argues that the consequence of becoming divine is that the sage accords flawlessly with the movements of this world instead of gaining control over them.

And they provide a similar re-reading of the True Man—the figure associated with immortality and employed in the ascension literature and by the First Emperor. Instead of claiming that the True Man covets immortality, the authors argue that the highest form of transcendence is a spontaneous connection with the patterns of the cosmos. What distinguishes the True Man from the sage is that the True Man transcends the human form. He is thus able to accord not just with the patterns that affect the human form but also with the patterns of the entire cosmos. Hence he is unaffected by shifting human forms. The authors provide what might at first glance appear to be a contradiction in terms: a Zhuangzian re-reading of ascension.

The overall argument of the chapter is that by following a particular regimen of self-cultivation, one can become fully linked with the proper patterns of the universe. For the sage, this connection is forged through the form; the True Man connects directly with the One. In both cases, the authors supply a political reading of a generally Zhuangzian cosmology. For both sages and True Men, the goal is to accord with these patterns—not because they were established by ancient sage-kings or because they are dictated by imperial thearchs, but because they are the patterns that any spirit inherently follows. The more refined, the more divine, one becomes, the more one spontaneously follows these patterns. No matter what level of self-cultivation one achieves, one's goal should always be to accord with the patterns of the universe. And if one happens to be born a ruler, one should rule in accord with the patterns; but even if one is not a ruler, one should equally live one's life in accord with them.

Conclusion

As discussed in Chapter 1, Paul Wheatley argues that the notion of a pivot of the four quarters represented an early Chinese belief in the linkage of man with the cosmos. Although I questioned the application of this argument to the Bronze Age, it does hold for the cosmology presented in the *Huainanzi*. According to the *Book of Documents*, the Duke of Shao surveyed (*jing ying*) the land before the construction of the city of Luoyang in order to determine that the spirits acquiesced in this use of the site; here the spirits control natural phenomena, and humans have to appease them. In the chapters of the *Huainanzi* discussed here, the distinction between humans and gods, and consequently any possibility of conflict, is denied. Humans and gods are fully linked and differ only in degree of refinement. In the "Jingshen" chapter, humans are fully able to become spirits and thus move in accord with the patterns of the cosmos.

This cosmology was utilized to rethink the existing conceptions of divinization. The two major models involved a view of divinization either as a means of empowerment (e.g., the First Emperor's claim to be able to align the universe, or the claims of humans to be able to become spirits and gain control over nature) or as a means of escaping the concerns of this world, and having one's spirit traverse the cosmos.

These views did not go unopposed. One major critique called for subordination to the textual authority of the earlier sages. Another is found in the chapters of the *Huainanzi* analyzed here. Within the cosmologies presented in the *Huainanzi*, it is possible to gain control over natural phenomena, but a higher gnosis is possible. Control over natural phenomena is a lower stage of cultivation. Moreover, each stage is achieved through self-cultivation, not a mastery of formulas. In the highest stage, the spirit is simply connected with the proper patterns of the universe, unaffected by shifts in forms and unconcerned with controlling them. This is a Zhuangzian re-reading of ascension: the highest form of transcendence is a spontaneous connection with the patterns of the universe.

This cosmology has several political implications. First, neither sagehood nor the state of being a True Man is the prerogative of the ruler. Anyone can achieve either state through self-cultivation. Attainment of such a position would result in enormous autonomy from both the political order[15] and textual authority. Second, there is an inherent pattern to the universe that the ruler should follow whether he is striving to be a sage or a True Man. These *Huainanzi* chapters are indeed calls for theomorphic rulership, but of a radically different sort from the concepts of theomorphic rulership dominant at the Qin and Han courts.

The authors, therefore, have developed a position that provides them a means for criticizing state policy—the ruler is failing to accord with the proper patterns of the cosmos—as well as for claiming autonomy from any existing political or textual authority—anyone can, with cultivation, gain access to the patterns and thus live flawlessly in harmony with the cosmic or-

---

15. This point has been explored powerfully by Griet Vankeerbergen in her dissertation, "The *Huainanzi* and Liu An's Claim to Moral Authority."

der. Humans are thus granted extraordinary powers, but these powers entail subordination to the patterns of the cosmos. We can become spirits, and even ascend to the heavens, but all we gain is the power to do what ought to be done. The more humans refine themselves, the more they become the spirits in accord with the patterns of the cosmos. To claim that one has achieved theomorphic powers and can control natural phenomena at will or that one has mastered formulas that allow one to do this is simply self-delusion.

But even the self-deluded are not without power. The political arguments found in the *Huainanzi* did not win favor at the court of Emperor Wu. Liu An, the Prince of Huainan and the patron of the authors of the text that bears witness to his patronage, was charged with treason and eventually committed suicide. The kingdom of Huainan was incorporated into the imperial system in 122 BC.

8 The sacrifices that order the world
Divine Kingship and Human Kingship in the Western Han

Following the destruction of the kingdom of Huainan, Emperor Wu enlarged the Han empire and created a new sacrificial system. Less than a century later, however, over the course of a series of extraordinary court debates, a group of ministers succeeded in eradicating significant portions of this sacrificial system and putting in its place cults to Heaven and Earth explicitly modeled on early Western Zhou practices described in the *Shangshu*. In this chapter, I trace the history of these sacrificial systems and seek to understand what was at stake as well as the significance of the final outcome.

I begin by discussing the arguments of Dong Zhongshu, a minister at Emperor Wu's court. I then turn to the emperor's new sacrificial system in order to understand why particular sacrifices came to be imbued with such significance. This section is based on the "Fengshan shu" chapter of Sima Qian's *Shiji*, which attempts, among other things, to explicate the sacrificial system that Emperor Wu inherited and developed. A close reading of this chapter allows us a glimpse at the various meanings that had become associated with these sacrifices and puts us in a position to understand the arguments of the ministers who successfully eradicated Emperor Wu's sacrificial system. I am in particular interested in tracing the ways in which these ministers, building on the ideas of figures like Dong Zhongshu, successfully reasserted a distinction between the human and the divine realms. In short, in this chapter I focus on the shift in the Han ritual system from divine to human kingship.

In Chapter 1, I discussed the tendency among sinologists to focus on sacrifice as a gift—a *do ut des* arrangement. This reading of sacrifice has a long pedigree in anthropology; a notable example is the work of Henri Hubert and Marcel Mauss, who discussed sacrifice as a form of "communication" between the sacred and profane realms.[1] Although attacking Hubert and Mauss's model as being inapplicable to this or that culture has become something of a cottage industry of late,[2] at least a portion of their theory—that focused on the transformation of the human and divine spheres through the sacrifice—may provide a compelling way to approach aspects of early Chinese sacrificial practice.

My argument is in part inspired by Valerio Valeri's reading of Hubert and Mauss. Rather than communication and gift giving, Valeri emphasizes the agonistic elements underlying sacrifice: "All fundamental relations involved in sacrifice are permeated by the spirit of contest: not only interhuman relations, but also relations between humans and gods and between animals and humans."[3] Valeri describes Hawaiian sacrificial practice in terms of a conflict: "Thus the desacralization of nature implies the sacralization of man. Perhaps, then, it is possible to follow Kojève when he reformulates Hegel's interpretation of sacrifice by writing that in this rite 'il faut . . . supprimer une partie du divin pour sanctifier l'homme.'"[4] Hawaiian sacrificial practice, in other words, involves an agon between humans and gods, in which the king attempts to divinize himself while exorcising the gods from nature and thus making nature available for human appropriation.

---

1. Hubert and Mauss, *Sacrifice*, p. 97.

2. For critiques of the Hubert and Mauss model from the perspective of specific traditions, see, e.g., Detienne, "Culinary Practices and the Spirit of Sacrifice," pp. 14–15; and Heusch, *Sacrifice in Africa*, pp. 2–6. Heusch's critique is that Hubert and Mauss's model works only if the culture in question distinguishes between what can be termed sacred and profane realms—with the sacrifice thus serving to sacralize the profane. For early China, however, this would not rule out the model: as I have argued in this book, continuity was by no means an assumption in early China, and certain sacrificial models did indeed posit such a distinction that was then to be overcome.

3. Valeri, "Wild Victims," p. 109.

4. Valeri, *Kingship and Sacrifice*, p. 83.

The claims of imperial deification discussed in Chapter 6 can be read in terms of these provocative formulations: the formation of imperial practice in early China involved an attempt to appropriate divine powers and ultimately transform the ruler into a god. In this chapter, I trace the debates that developed from about 140 to 30 BC on the nature, efficacy, and significance of sacrifice. I analyze some of the competing sacrificial practices employed during this period, explore the concerns behind these practices, and study the historical implications of the choices made. Throughout, as we will see, the issues of agon and transformation became recurrent topics of debate, as several figures disputed imperial practices of appropriating divine powers and attempted to restore the distinction between humans and gods.

The Sacrifices of the Sage: Dong Zhongshu

Dong Zhongshu, who was active during the early part of Emperor Wu's reign, was a scholar of the *Spring and Autumn Annals*, and his life's work was to follow what Dong thought were the principles laid out by Confucius in the text. Like Lu Jia, Dong Zhongshu appropriated cosmological arguments in order both to advance his argument and to critique the court practices of the day.

My interpretation of Dong differs considerably from that of Heiner Roetz, who argues that Dong Zhongshu

discards the rational view of nature which Zhou philosophy had developed and Xunzi had brought to completion. Nature, for Xunzi a sphere with its own invariant rules and not linked with man by any sympathetic ties, becomes the arena of cosmic judgment. It supplants the "self" before which the Zhou Confucian had to justify his actions. Thus Confucianism pays for its rise to state orthodoxy tailored to the superstition of the powerful with a double regression: Ethically as well as cognitively it falls back on a level which the axial age philosophers had once overcome.[5]

I disagree with almost every one of these points. I argued in Chapter 4 that Xunzi does indeed see humans as normatively performing a crucial role in generating order in the cosmos, and in this sense, Dong Zhongshu's arguments are quite closely related to Xunzi's. Moreover, the cosmology of Dong Zhongshu hardly represents a "regression" to the superstitious of the court. Dong Zhongshu certainly did not represent state orthodoxy under Emperor

---

5. Roetz, *Confucian Ethics of the Axial Age*, p. 231. My interpretations of Dong have been aided greatly by Queen, *From Chronicle to Canon*.

Wu, and the cosmology he presented was, among other things, a critique of the views prominent at court.

These concerns can be seen clearly in one of Dong's major concerns, rain magic. As Dong's contemporary Sima Qian described him:

When the current ruler [Emperor Wu] came to the throne, [Dong Zhongshu] became minister of Jiangdu. He used the alterations of disasters and irregularities from the *Spring and Autumn Annals* to infer the means by which yin and yang interact together. Therefore, when seeking rain, he would block yang and release yin; when stopping rain, he would do the opposite. While practicing in this one state, he always obtained what he wanted.[6]

The study of the *Spring and Autumn Annals* provided Dong the ability not only to interpret omens but also to control the weather.

The cosmology that underlay this practice is fleshed out in the "Tonglei xiangdong," chapter 57 of Dong's *Chunqiu fanlu*. As have many others, Needham analyzes this chapter as an example of Chinese correlative thinking.[7] But, since it should be clear by now that correlative thinking was not an assumption in early China, we should instead read the text as a series of claims, and our goal should be to understand what the author is trying to argue.

The chapter closely corresponds to the *Shiji*'s description of Dong Zhongshu's views, and it seems reasonable to read it as a product of either Dong Zhongshu himself or one of his disciples.[8] The author argues that humans can in fact exercise tremendous power over the natural world, but this power does not mimic, or even rival, that of the *shen*—for it has nothing to do with *shen* at all. Rather, it is based on the resonance of yin and yang: since like attracts like, the author argues, yin attracts yin and yang attracts yang. Moreover, this correlative system is developed solely in terms of the interactions of Heaven and man: *shen* do not figure in the discussion at all. Since both Heaven and man are composed of yin and yang, one's ability to affect the natural world is defined by the degree to which one can control yin and yang so as to influence the yin and yang in the external world:

Heaven has yin and yang; humans also have yin and yang. When the yin *qi* of Heaven and Earth rise, the yin *qi* of humans responds to it and rises. When the yin

---

6. *Shiji*, 121.3127–28.

7. Needham, *Science and Civilisation in China*, pp. 281–84.

8. See the excellent discussion of this chapter in Queen, *From Chronicle to Canon*, pp. 220–21. Queen argues that the chapter can plausibly be ascribed to Dong Zhongshu himself.

qi of humans rises, the yin *qi* of Heaven and Earth also properly responds to it and rises. Their way is one. As for those who are clear on this, if they desire to bring (*zhi* 致) rain, they will activate the yin so as to make the yin rise; if they desire to stop the rain, they will activate the yang in order to make the yang rise.[9]

Rain is not controlled by *shen*; it is a product of the interaction of yin and yang. "Therefore, bringing (*zhi*) rain is not *shen*. Delusions about *shen* arise because [the rain's] pattern (*li*) is subtle and mysterious" (13.3b–4a). Everything can be measured in terms of yin and yang, and, moreover, this explains how humans can affect the natural world: they do not need to control or become *shen*, they simply need to understand these basic principles and undergo the self-cultivation necessary to utilize them.

Dong Zhongshu thus follows Xunzi in seeing rituals as not *shen*. But they are also not just *wen*: they do work. Dong Zhongshu is reworking rain sacrifices much as the *Xici zhuan* reworked divination. As in the *Xici zhuan*, the reworking involves a claim about the formal patterns of the cosmos: divination and sacrifice work, but they work because they link human actions to powers more primordial than the spirits.

But, for Dong Zhongshu, these powers are active agents. Thus, the movements of the phenomena (*wu*) are not spontaneous: "When things activate each other without form, then it is called spontaneous (*zi ran*). In fact, it is not spontaneous. There is something that is causing it to be so. Things certainly have substances causing them; but what is causing them is without form" (13.4a). For this author, however, the causative agent is not the *shen* but the yin and yang. Dong Zhongshu thus denies the efficacy of *shen* and instead proposes a model based on the interactions of Heaven and man, with human power deriving from self-cultivation. Humans do indeed have power over the natural world, but only because of their proper interactions with Heaven, not through any supposed ability to coerce—or achieve the powers of—*shen*.

The same principle of interaction between yin and yang explains omens: "If a thearch or a king is about to arise, auspicious omens will appear first. And when he is about to perish, inauspicious portents appear first. Things of the same category summon each other" (13.3b). Like Lu Jia, Dong Zhongshu supports omenology, but only by defining it as a product of the natural interactions of the universe.

---

9. *Chunqiu fanlu*, chap. 57, "Tonglei xiangdong," 13.3b; hereinafter cited in the text.

Accordingly, Dong is able to claim a complete understanding of the emergence of blessings, disasters, and misfortunes:

It is not only the *qi* of yin and yang that can be advanced or withdrawn according to category. Even the production of misfortunes, disasters, and blessings is also because of this. There is always something that first makes it arise, and things, responding to it by kind, are activated. (13.4a)

Dong Zhongshu uses a similar argument to explain why the sages of the past were able to understand and articulate these principles of interaction: "Therefore, if he who is keen of hearing, clear of sight, sagely, and divine (*shen*) looks and listens within, his words become clear and sagely" (13.4a). The claim here follows directly from the overall argument of the chapter: something arises, and things respond. Accordingly, a sage should rule by looking within himself. Human divinity (*shen*) thus resides not in gaining the powers of spirits: if one understands the proper processes of the cosmos, one will realize that the ability to control natural phenomena depends on cultivating oneself.

The essay closes with a story from the *Shangshu dazhuan* about an omen that preceded the rise of the Zhou dynasty.

At the time when the Zhou was about to arise, great red birds clutching seeds of grain gathered atop the king's palace. King Wu rejoiced, and the various ministers rejoiced. The Duke of Zhou said: "Aizai, aizai! Heaven is showing this to encourage us." He was afraid they would rely upon it. (13.4a)

The Duke of Zhou wanted to prevent the king and his other ministers from reading the omen as an indication that Heaven would support the king. Instead, the Duke of Zhou argued, the king needed to respond to the omen properly. One cannot rely on Heaven; rather, one must respond to its promptings. The text is thus an exhortation for human activity in the world. Not only do humans have the power to summon natural occurrences, but they in fact must do so if order is to prevail.

That Dong Zhongshu saw such advice as being directly applicable to his own time is clear from a series of memorials he submitted at the beginning of Emperor Wu's reign calling on the emperor to follow the principles laid out by Confucius in the *Spring and Autumn Annals*. The *Annals*, in Dong's reading, was authored to guide humans in following the Heavenly way.

Like Lu Jia, Dong Zhongshu was interested in defining the relationship between humans and Heaven through cosmological arguments, and also like Lu Jia, he wanted to define the proper way in which human power could be exercised in the world. The main tool that Dong Zhongshu utilized for this was the interplay of yin and yang, the two forces of the universe: "If a king desires to undertake an action, it is fitting for him to seek his clues in Heaven. The greatness of the way of Heaven resides in yin and yang."[10]

Dong Zhongshu's argument in these memorials is that statecraft—including omenology and sacrifice—should be based on yin and yang, which is also the way of Heaven.[11] For Dong, Heaven both generated and aligned the cosmos:

I have heard that Heaven is the ancestor of the myriad things. Therefore, it completely covers, embraces, and envelops them, and nothing is treated differently. It established the sun and moon, wind and rain, to harmonize them; it aligned (jing) yin and yang, hot and cold, to complete them. (Hanshu, 56.2515)

Heaven gave birth to the myriad things and then organized the cosmos to nourish them. The alignment (jing) of the cosmos, then, is a product neither of humans nor of sages: it was accomplished by Heaven. The sages used this alignment as their guide:

Therefore, the sages modeled themselves on Heaven and established the Way. They cherished extensively and without selfishness, disseminated virtue and displayed humaneness to enrich [the people], and established propriety and set up rituals to guide them. (Hanshu, 56.2515)

This argument is reminiscent of that given by Confucius, but Dong takes it a step further: the sages' modeling of themselves on Heaven was itself mandated by Heaven.

Humans receive the mandate from Heaven. They are certainly superior in the way they differ from the other forms of life. Within they possess the relations of father and son, elder and younger brother. Outside they possess the propriety of ruler and minister, upper and lower. When gathering together, they possess the arrays of seniority and age. Bright is the culture (wen) with which they meet each other; peaceful is the kindness with which they relate to each other. This is why humans are so noble. (Hanshu, 56.2516)

---

10. Hanshu, 56.2502; hereinafter cited in the text.

11. Portions of the remainder of this section are taken from my "Following the Commands of Heaven: The Notion of Ming in Early China."

What is distinctive about humans and makes them the most noble of creatures is that Heaven has mandated them to have hierarchy and distinctions. Moreover, they appropriate the rest of the natural world for their benefit:

They grow the five grains to feed themselves, silk and hemp to clothe themselves, the six domestic animals to nourish themselves; they yoke oxen and harness horses, ensnare leopards and cage tigers. This is how they obtain the numinousness of Heaven, and why they are more lofty than other things. Therefore Confucius said, "As for the nature of Heaven and Earth, man is the most lofty." (*Hanshu*, 56.2516)

The appropriation and domestication of nature is the means by which humans obtain the numinousness of Heaven. Ultimately, one can come to accord with the patterns of the world:

If one is illuminated about the nature of heaven, one understands oneself to be more noble than other things. Only if a person understands himself to be more noble than other things does he understand humaneness and propriety. Only if he understands humaneness and propriety does he value ritual and modulation. Only if he values ritual and modulation does he reside in goodness. Only if he resides in goodness will he delight in according with the patterns (*li*). Only if he delights in according with the patterns can he be called a gentleman. Therefore, Confucius said, "If you do not understand the mandate, you are without that with which to become a gentleman." This is the meaning. (*Hanshu*, 56.2516)

As with Lu Jia, there is a teleology here in which Heaven mandates that humans appropriate nature, and by doing so, humans come into accord with the patterns of the cosmos. Whereas the First Emperor, in his inscriptions, claimed the ability to pattern the cosmos, Dong Zhongshu is arguing that Heaven has mandated a set of patterns with which man must accord. And, unlike the "Jingshen" chapter of the *Huainanzi*, which makes a comparable claim, Dong presents the appropriation of nature as one of the crucial aspects of according with these patterns.

Heaven, then, set up the cosmos for the benefit of man. Nature was so made that man can appropriate it and thereby thrive. The implication is that the cosmos will be not properly ordered unless humans make it an object of appropriation. And this, indeed, is a crucial part of understanding Heaven's mandate.

And the cosmos itself requires that humans bring order to the world.

Therefore, the ruler rectifies his mind and thereby rectifies his court; he rectifies his court and thereby rectifies the hundred officials; he rectifies the hundred officials and thereby rectifies the myriad people; he rectifies the myriad people and thereby rectifies the four quarters. Once the four quarters are rectified, no one, distant or near, would dare not unite with the rectification, and there would be no bad *qi* to corrupt those within. Because of this, yin and yang will mix, and the wind and rain will be timely. The various forms of life will be harmonized, and the myriad people will prosper, the five grains will ripen, and the grasses and trees will thrive. All within Heaven and Earth will be moistened and greatly abundant and splendid. Everyone within the four seas will hear of the flourishing virtue and come to serve. All the things of blessing and all the auspicious omens that can be summoned will arrive, and the kingly way will be achieved. (*Hanshu*, 56.2503)

The ruler's rectification of himself inaugurates the ordering and harmonizing of his court, the people, and ultimately the natural world. The ruler thus controls the wind and rain, but only by properly following the mandate given to him.

Thus, by cultivating himself, the ruler brings virtue to the myriad forms on earth and gains the support of divine powers:

Humaneness, propriety, ritual, knowledge, and sincerity are the way of five constants. They are what the king must cultivate. When these five are cultivated, he will therefore receive Heaven's favor and enjoy the numinosity of the ghosts and spirits. His virtue will spread beyond the boundaries, reaching to the myriad forms of life. (*Hanshu*, 56.2505)

Heaven therefore requires a human sage to complete the process of ordering. Heaven gives the mandate, but a sage must put it into practice. This is true not only for the cosmos as a whole but also for the people:

Heaven's command is known as the mandate; if the mandate is not [used by] a sage, it will not be put into practice. One's substance is called nature; if nature is not transformed through education, it cannot be completed. Human desires are called the disposition (*qing*); if the disposition is not standardized and regulated (*du zhi*), it will not be modulated (*jie*). It is for this reason that a king above is attentive to upholding the intent of Heaven so as to accord with the mandate; below he endeavors to clarify, educate, and transform the people so as to complete their nature; and he corrects the appropriateness of the laws and standards and distinguishes the hierarchy of upper and lower in order to restrain their desires. When he has accomplished these three, then the great basis is established. (*Hanshu*, 56.2515)

Sagely action, again, is necessary for Heaven's commands to be realized.

As a consequence, the sage is granted extraordinary powers: not only does the order of the natural world depend on the sage, but even one's life span depends on his rule.

I have heard that the mandate is the command of Heaven, nature is the substance one is born with, and disposition is human desire. As for dying young or living long, being humane or licentious: once it is molded and completed, it cannot be purified or beautified. Order and disorder are generated; therefore things are unequal. Confucius said: "The virtue of a gentleman is like the wind; the virtue of a petty man is like the grass. If the wind blows above, [the grass] will invariably bend." Thus, when Yao and Shun practiced virtue, the people were humane and long-lived; and when Jie and Zhou practiced oppression, the people were licentious and died young. If what is above transforms what is below, what is below will follow what is above. This is like clay on a potter's wheel; only a potter can form it. Or like metal in a mold; only a smith can cast it. (Hanshu, 56.2501)

Both the human and the natural worlds depend on the sages' correctly utilizing and putting into practice the mandate of Heaven.

For Dong Zhongshu, as for Lu Jia, the last sage was Confucius. And for Dong Zhongshu, the crucial act of Confucius was to compile the *Spring and Autumn Annals*: "Confucius created the *Spring and Autumn Annals*, above calculating it to the Heavenly way, below making it substantive with the fundamentals of man; comparing it with antiquity, examining it with the present" (Hanshu, 26.2515). Since Confucius followed Heaven, the *Spring and Autumn Annals* matches the alignment of Heaven and Earth: "The great unity of the *Spring and Autumn Annals* is the enduring alignment (*jing*) of Heaven and Earth, the connecting propriety of the past and present" (Hanshu, 56.2523). Since the text matches the alignment of the cosmos, it can be used in omenology: hidden in the text is the key to interpreting the cosmos and thus to guiding human action. For example, Dong Zhongshu is said to have attributed a flood recorded in the *Spring and Autumn Annals* to the behavior of a court lady: "Dong Zhongshu took this to mean that the consort Ai Jiang was licentious and disorderly, acting contrary to the yin qi. Therefore there was a great flood" (Hanshu, 27A.1339). Since the cosmos is based on the interplay of yin and yang, similar things attract: yin will attract yin, and yang will attract yang.

Like Lu Jia, therefore, Dong Zhongshu is arguing that the classics—for Dong the *Spring and Autumn Annals* in particular—provide the principles for understanding omens properly. Here, too, the implication is that only scholars trained in the classics can advise the ruler, for only they can correctly interpret omens.

But why, if Confucius was such a sage, did he not found a new dynasty? The answer again lies with the mandate. Like Mencius, Dong emphasizes that Heaven confers the mandate; one cannot acquire it through human effort. "I have heard that the king who has been charged by Heaven invariably possesses something that human effort could not summon (*zhi*) and yet it arrives nonetheless. This is the tally of the receipt of the mandate" (*Hanshu*, 56.2500). Confucius, therefore, whatever his sagely qualities, could not become a ruler:

Confucius said: "The phoenix does not arrive, the River does not show forth the diagram. I am at my end!"[12] Self-pity can summon (*zhi*) these things; but because he held a low position, he was not able to summon them. (*Hanshu*, 56.2503)

If, however, Heaven grants one the position of ruler, then one has the power to summon the basis for order:

Now, Your Majesty, your noble position is as the Son of Heaven, your fortune encompasses the four seas. You reside in the position from which you can summon, you control the authority to summon, and you possess the resources that can be used to summon. Your actions are lofty, and your kindness deep. Your knowledge is bright, and your intentions splendid. You cherish the people, and are fond of the officers. You can be called a proper ruler. And yet Heaven and Earth have not yet responded, and auspicious omens have not arrived. Why is this? Because education and transformation have not been established, and the myriad people have not been rectified. (*Hanshu*, 56.2503)

Dong Zhongshu thus reasserts the Mencian argument that one's position determines one's ability to summon power. According to Dong, none of the Han rulers—those in position to bring order to the world—has succeeded in summoning the auspicious omens. Confucius modeled himself on Heaven, but Heaven did not grant him the position from which he could summon the omens; the Han rulers have been granted such a position, but they have failed to model themselves on Heaven.

The immediate solution to this problem is, by the way that Dong has set up the argument, clear: the Han rulers need to follow the principles laid out in the *Spring and Autumn Annals*. But there is a deeper problem with Dong's argument. Why, if Heaven mandates who will have power and if Heaven

---

12. The quotation is from *Lunyu*, 9/9.

needs a proper person to carry out the mandate and thereby bring order to the cosmos, did Heaven not put Confucius in power? Why wait more than two centuries and then allow the Qin and Han to take power—particularly if all that was required was simply for the ruler to follow the principles laid out by Confucius?

The question is quite similar to that posed by Mencius: Why is it that sages are not given the mandate by Heaven? But Dong's response is unique. Mencius answers this question with a simple statement of resignation—one must accept the mandate and attempt to do so without resentment. Dong instead offers an institutional response: although Confucius was not granted the kingship, he did author the *Spring and Autumn Annals* in order to guide humans in following the Heavenly way. The ruler should therefore establish a formal system in which people are trained to understand the alignment of the cosmos and to guide the ruler accordingly. This is, in a sense, an institutionalization of the degeneration implied in the *Mencius* and presented in the *Xici zhuan*. The implicit claim here appears to be that rulers at this point need trained scholars to guide them: Confucius understood the alignment of the cosmos, and scholars of the texts composed or edited by Confucius can guide the ruler properly.

Overall, Dong Zhongshu has therefore defined both divination and sacrifice as necessary, but the purpose of such acts is not to learn or influence the will of the divine. Rather, the goal is to place humanity properly within the cosmos and thereby ensure the proper functioning of that cosmos.

Dong Zhongshu was every bit as interested in influencing natural phenomena as were, for example, the masters of formulas. But his cosmological claims were designed to present a view of the relationship between humans and nature different from both the instrumental and the agonistic conceptions of the relation between humans and gods prevalent at court. Dong Zhongshu's goal was to articulate a cosmology in which the cosmos required human action—defined according to the traditions of Confucius—in order to function properly.

In this specific sense, Dong Zhongshu's cosmology, despite its incorporation of so much Han terminology, repudiates the sorts of arguments found in the *Xici zhuan* in favor of elements of earlier Confucian thought. For Dong Zhongshu, the goal for humans is not to replicate the patterns of an existing natural world but to cause the natural world to function properly—that is, to do as Heaven requires. The sages are to discover the proper patterns in the natural world and then to make the natural world work along those lines. In other words, the natural world will not necessarily function properly without human guidance.

This argument, then, supports human power. Nature needs humans in order to reach its most perfect state. Or, put differently, nature cannot reach its potentiality for order without human intervention.

Dong Zhongshu's solution to the tensions seen in Mencius is to grant humans extraordinary powers over the cosmos. He denies the potential for tension between sages and Heaven that Mencius posited. Whereas Mencius granted divine powers to man and saw a potential conflict with Heaven, Dong Zhongshu underlines the proper hierarchy of humans and Heaven. Humans must follow patterns. By doing so, they can exercise power over the world: they can control the rain and create the proper harmony in the world.

Dong Zhongshu's articulation of this position serves to deny the tensions that pervade the cosmology of Mencius. Heaven is an agent within this cosmology, but Heaven does not sometimes disrupt the moral patterns that should be guiding humanity. Heaven is equated with the patterns, and the only issue for Dong Zhongshu is whether the sages follow these Heavenly patterns and thereby bring order to the world.

Accordingly, if there is a discrepancy between the patterns of Heaven and the functioning of the natural or human worlds, the responsibility lies squarely with the ruler: it is the ruler who must impose the patterns of Heaven on the human and natural worlds. But for some reason, Heaven no longer grants the mandate to sages as it did in the time of Yao, Shun, and Yu; sages tend now to be ministers, not rulers. This may not be ideal, but, in Dong's view, it also need not result in a lack of order. It simply means that ministers must be properly trained in the classics so that they can guide rulers. In other words, the fact that rulers are not sages simply requires an institutional response.

The implication of this is that the famed notion of humans and Heaven existing in harmony—a view so often attributed to Dong Zhongshu—was not an assumption at all. Rather, it was a response to the political events of the time and an alternative to the vision proffered by Mencius almost two centuries before. And, unlike the authors of the *Huainanzi* chapters, Dong Zhongshu is proclaiming the absolute necessity of accepting traditions handed down from the sages—both sacrificial acts and the texts of Confucius.

The overall argument is thus quite similar to that of Lu Jia: like Lu Jia, Dong Zhongshu presents humans as playing a crucial role in bringing order to the cosmos, and like Lu Jia, Dong Zhongshu emphasizes the importance of following the traditions of the sages. But unlike Lu Jia, Dong Zhongshu does not borrow the language of ascension and divinization in order to make these points. On the contrary, Dong opposes such language. To a far greater degree than Lu Jia, Dong Zhongshu opposed the imperial system and its theomorphic claims.

The "Fengshan shu" Chapter of Sima Qian

Although Dong Zhongshu's recommendations for employing specialists in the classics at court were accepted by Emperor Wu, his cosmological notions and his ideas on sacrifices and omenology were not. In order to trace the development of the Han sacrificial system and to understand why particular sacrifices came to be imbued with a particular significance, we must turn to the "Fengshan shu" chapter of Sima Qian's *Shiji*.[13] Sima Qian was the court historian during the reign of Emperor Wu, and the chapter is in part a critique of the emperor's sacrificial system.

Emperor Wu played a major role in consolidating imperial rule in China. As part of his political program, the emperor decided to undertake the *feng* and *shan* sacrifices—sacrifices that symbolized the legitimacy of a dynasty. Sima Qian's chapter places this decision within the entire history of cultic activity in China. As many commentators have pointed out, Sima Qian's goal was to criticize Wu's decision.[14] However, there is much more of interest in the chapter than just this criticism. As I will try to argue, the chapter, if read carefully, gives us a unique and suggestive glimpse of some of the views at court concerning sacrifices and thus provides crucial clues for explicating the later debates that led to the partial eradication of Emperor Wu's sacrificial system.

Early in the chapter, Sima Qian quotes the "Shun dian" chapter of the *Shangshu*, which discusses the sacrificial system of Shun, one of the early sage-kings. Shun is described as sacrificing to the higher gods at his capital and sacrificing from afar to the mountains, rivers, and various spirits. He

---

13. Portions of this and the ensuing section are taken from my "Determining the Position of Heaven and Earth."

14. For a full discussion of this, see chapter 5 of my *The Ambivalence of Creation.*

then held an audience for the feudal lords. Every five years he made an inspection tour of the Five Mountains beginning with Mount Tai in the east, where he would sacrifice to Heaven, sacrifice from afar to the mountains and rivers, and meet with the feudal lords. He would then travel to the other four mountains (to the south, west, north, and center). This sacrificial system, based on a feudal political arrangement, continued, according to Sima Qian, with some variations, until the rise of an alternative system under the Qin.[15]

According to Sima Qian, Yu, Shun's successor and the founder of the Xia dynasty, continued Shun's sacrificial practice. But problems became apparent in the fourteenth generation: "Yu accorded with this. After fourteen generations, it came to the reign of Di Kongjia. He turned to licentiousness and was fond of spirits. The spirits were angered, and the two dragons left" (28.1356). The Xia fell three generations later.

A similar structure characterizes Sima Qian's presentation of the Shang dynasty. Two rulers are singled out. The first is Di Taiwu. One night a mulberry grew in his courtyard. Although this caused great alarm, his minister Yi Zhi argued: "Evil portents cannot overcome virtue." Di Taiwu then cultivated his virtue, and the mulberry died. Fourteen generations later, a decline set in. But Di Wuding arose and restored the dynasty. A bad portent appeared under Wuding as well, and Wuding was alarmed. But his minister Zu Ji said: "Cultivate virtue." Wuding did so, and his reign was thus longlasting and peaceful. Five generations later, however, Di Wuyi "treated the spirits with contempt" and was killed. The dynasty fell three generations later (28.1356).

Sima Qian sums up his argument thus far: "From this it can be seen that, at the beginning [of a dynasty] there is always reverence and respect, but later it deteriorates into disrespect and contempt" (28.1356–57). Overtly, this is a simple reference to the dynastic cycle: a dynasty begins in virtue and ends in vice. But Sima Qian has set up this claim in a specific way. Virtue is based here on the behavior of the ruler and involves, among other things, proper reverence for spirits. Virtue, Sima Qian argues, overrides even bad portents sent from the spirits. And vice, so to speak, involves improper reverence, an impropriety that can take the form of either being overly fond of the spirits or treating them with contempt.

---

15. *Shiji*, "Fengshan shu," 28.1355–56; hereinafter cited in the text.

With this as his frame, Sima Qian turns next to the rise and fall of the Zhou dynasty. He begins by quoting from the *Zhouguan*, a text that purports to explicate the ritual system of the Zhou dynasty:

The *Zhouguan* says: "When the winter solstice arrives, sacrifice to Heaven at the southern suburb in order to welcome the coming of the longer day. When the summer solstice arrives, sacrifice to the spirits of the Earth. At both use music and dancing, and the spirits can thereby be obtained and brought into ritual. The Son of Heaven sacrifices to the famous mountains and great rivers under Heaven. The Five Peaks he regards as his ministers, the Four Waterways as his feudal lords. The feudal lords sacrifice to the famous mountains and great rivers within their fiefdoms." (28.1357)

The Zhou is thus presented as continuing, with minor variations, the same ritual system as Shun.

The later decline of the Zhou is then connected to the rise of the Qin. "Fourteen generations after the Zhou conquered the Yin, the generations gradually declined, the rites and music were discarded, and the feudal lords acted on their own" (28.1358). It was in this context that Duke Xiang of Qin was enfeoffed. Sima Qian thus presents Qin as emerging in a period when the feudal lords were usurping the power of the Zhou.

The ensuing discussion is devoted to the emergence of a new sacrificial system in the Qin, a system that reached its zenith under Emperor Wu. The first step occurred soon after the enfeoffment. Since the state of Qin was in the far west, Duke Xiang created an "altar of the west," at which sacrifices to the White God, the god of the west, were held (28.1358). As Sima Qian argues elsewhere:

When Duke Xiang of Qin was enfeoffed as a lord, he made a western altar for use in sacrificing to the higher gods. The beginning of Qin's usurpation is clear to see. The *Liji* says: "The Son of Heaven makes offerings to Heaven and Earth, while the lords of the states make offerings to the famous mountains and great rivers within their domains." (15.685)

Qin's first sacrificial act, Sima Qian implies, was a usurpation of royal privilege.

Sixteen years later, Duke Wen of Qin had a dream, which his historian Dun interpreted as a sign from the higher gods. Duke Wen thereupon constructed an altar at Yong (28.1358). Sima Qian explains the rationalization for such sacrifices:

Some say that from ancient times, because the region of Yong is so high, it was a site for divine illumination. Altars were therefore erected for suburban sacrifices to the higher gods, and the sacrifices to all the spirits were amassed there. Since it was so used in the time of Huangdi, even though it was the waning of the Zhou, it could again be used for the suburban sacrifices. However, because such words cannot be read in any of the classics, scholars do not follow them. (28.1359)

Defenders of the Yong sacrifices argued that even though the Zhou had not yet fallen, the antiquity of the Yong altars made their "re-institution" by the Qin acceptable. However, Sima Qian is clearly calling into question the antiquity of the sacrificial system at Yong and casting into doubt such claims of legitimacy. But he is also pointing out that this new form of sacrificial practice was based on a particular set of claims concerning Huangdi. As I have argued elsewhere,[16] Huangdi had come to be associated during the late Warring States and early Han with centralized statecraft. And, as we saw in Chapter 6, Huangdi was the main figure invoked to legitimate the Qin—and, later, Han—sacrificial system.

Over the next several centuries, the rulers of Qin instituted sacrifices at Yong to the gods of the other three directions as well—presumably as a part of an increasing claim to universal dominance (28.1360, 1364). The most important Qin sacrifices, then, came to consist of the offerings at Yong to the four gods—the white, green, yellow, and red gods—symbolizing Qin control over the land (28.1376). During this process, the capital of Qin was moved to Yong.

Meanwhile, we are told, the Zhou continued to decline:

At the same time [as Confucius], Chang Hong used formulas (*fang*) to serve King Ling of the Zhou. None of the feudal lords paid homage at the Zhou court, and the power of the Zhou was limited. Chang Hong thereupon clarified the affairs of ghosts and spirits and hung up the head of a wildcat and shot arrows at it. The wildcat head symbolized the feudal lords' not coming to court. [Chang Hong] depended on the object in wild hopes of thereby summoning the feudal lords. The feudal lords did not follow this, and the Jin captured Chang Hong and put him to death. The talk among the Zhou of formulas and abnormalities began with Chang Hong. (28.1364)

The Zhou gradually fell under the sway of magicians overly oriented toward spirits who tried to use formulas to impose their will on the world. The

---

16. See my "Sages, Ministers, and Rebels."

Zhou thus fell into the same pattern of decadence seen in earlier dynasties. By presenting a concern with formulas and an interest in the spirit world as the defining moment of Zhou decline, Sima Qian sets the framework for his presentation of the Qin-Han imperium.

In 221 BC, Qin completed its conquest of the other states and created the first empire. The four altars at Yong continued to be the dominant sacrifices of the Qin state (28.1376). Not only did Qin maintain these sacrifices, however, but it also made attempts to take control of the significant cults of each region within the empire. As Sima Qian states: "When Qin united all under heaven, [the First Emperor] commanded the officials of sacrifices to put in order the frequently performed offerings to Heaven, Earth, the famous mountains, the great rivers, the ghosts, and the spirits" (23.1371). Unlike Shun's sacrificial tours, however, the First Emperor's tours of the lands under his control were not inspections of feudal lands; they were imperial tours of the emperor's own lands, intended to enhance the personal power of the ruler.

This attempt to secure divine support also, Sima Qian argues, helps to explain the rise to prominence of the *fangshi*. Given his framework of dynastic decline, seen most obviously in his descriptions of Kongjia of the Xia as being too fond of spirits and of the last Zhou kings as falling under the sway of figures with magical formulas, Sima Qian is painting this moment of imperial unification as equally indicative of the beginning of a fall into decadence—a fall that, as Sima Qian describes it, culminates in Emperor Wu.

Indeed, Sima Qian presents Emperor Wu's reign as marking the extreme point of this particular sacrificial system and mode of dealing with the spirits. Wu rebuilt and consolidated the empire that the First Emperor had created.[17] One of his policies for doing so was to re-create much of the commandery system of the First Emperor by annexing the territories of the feudal lords. Sima Qian points out how this policy was paralleled by his sacrificial practice. Thus, Wu worked to gain direct imperial control over

---

17. For a discussion of Sima Qian's views on Emperor Wu's consolidation of the First Emperor's creation, see chapter 5 of my *Ambivalence of Creation*. I referred in Chapter 6 of this book to Hegel's dictum that events occur twice. Thus, empire in Rome developed only after Augustus re-created what Caesar had created. In thinking about the First Emperor and Emperor Wu, Sima Qian would more likely have agreed with Marx's reformulation of Hegel: "Hegel observes somewhere that all great incidents and individuals occur, as it were, twice. He forgot to add: the first time as tragedy, the second as farce" (*The Eighteenth Brumaire of Louis Bonaparte*, p. 15).

the Five Peaks, a series of mountains with important sacrificial traditions. The king of Changshan, for example, was charged with a crime and removed, and Changshan was made into a commandery. As Sima Qian narrates: "As such, the Five Peaks were all situated in the commanderies of the Son of Heaven" (28.1387). Sima Qian clearly contrasts this policy of centralization, in which the Five Peaks were under direct imperial control, with the feudal system of sacrifices begun by Shun.

Indeed, whereas Shun inspected the territories of the feudal lords only once every five years, Emperor Wu undertook constant tours of his empire (see, e.g., 28.1389 and 1403). He did this so often, Sima Qian claims, that the officials in charge of the commanderies and kingdoms kept their roads and palaces and sacrificial sites in repair in anticipation of a visit from the emperor (28.1396). Also like the First Emperor, Wu strongly supported the *fangshi* in the hope that they could increase his access to the world of spirits and ultimately help him gain immortality. Indeed, the most important ritual innovations during his reign were taken on the advice of these masters.

One of these masters, Miu Ji, authored a memorial concerning the Great One, a deity who Miu Ji claimed to be above the five gods in power: "The most valued of the Heavenly spirits is the Great One. The assistants of the Great One are the five gods. In ancient times the Son of Heaven sacrificed to the Great One in the spring and autumn at the southeast suburb" (28.1386). Following the advice of Miu Ji, Wu established offerings to the Great One.[18]

At least in Sima Qian's presentation, it would appear that this addition to the sacrificial system was yet one more step in a long process that had begun with the Qin—a process involving ever more claims to dominance. Just as the Qin rulers had progressively added sacrifices to more gods at Yong until four were receiving cult, and just as the Han founder had added sacrifices to a fifth god, so Emperor Wu was laying claim to yet a more powerful deity. And Sima Qian is clearly presenting this cult, instituted in response to the advice of a master of formulas, in a negative light.

---

18. Beyond the attributes mentioned in the previous chapters, the Great One also appears to have had some associations with warfare. For example, when Emperor Wu was about to attack Nanyue, he first made an announcement and prayer to the Great One. A banner was made that the Grand Historian pointed at the country about to be attacked (*Shiji*, 28.1395). After Nanyue was defeated, Emperor Wu offered sacrifices of thanks to the god (*Shiji*, 28.1396). For possible paleographic precursors to these associations, see Li Ling, "An Archaeological Study of Taiyi (Grand One) Worship."

Another step in the development of the Han sacrificial system occurred when a certain Shaoweng gained an audience with the ruler because of his "formulas for ghosts and spirits." In response to Shaoweng's proposals, Emperor Wu built a palace in Ganquan to summon the Heavenly spirits. The following year, after performing the suburban sacrifices at Yong, Wu declared: "Now I have personally performed the suburban sacrifices to the higher gods, but I have not made offerings to the Hou-tu (Lord Earth)." In response, Kuan Shu, the Officer of Sacrifices who had been charged to continue the formulas of Li Shaojun, recommended that sacrifices be made at Fenyin. The emperor thereupon traveled east and personally performed the sacrifice to Hou-tu at Fenyin (28.1386–89).

Wu then performed the suburban sacrifice at Yong and returned to Ganquan. He ordered Kuan Shu and others to make an altar to the Great One at Ganquan. The altar was modeled on Miu Ji's altar. The top level was dedicated to the Great One. The next level consisted of five sides, each of which, in the appropriate direction, was dedicated to one of the five gods. The third level was dedicated to the various spirits. In 113 BC, Wu first performed the suburban sacrifice to the Great One. A beautiful glow appeared that night, and the next day yellow *qi* rose to Heaven. The Grand Historian Sima Tan (the father of Sima Qian), the Officer of Sacrifices Kuan Shu, and others argued that an altar to the Great One should be built in response (28.1394–95).

These sacrifices to the Great One at Ganquan and to Hou-tu at Fenyin would become two of the most important imperial sacrifices for Emperor Wu. As Sima Qian is at pains to point out, each stage in the development of Wu's sacrificial system was undertaken at the instigation of *fangshi*. In Sima Qian's narrative, these masters of formulas, who played such a major role at the court of the First Emperor as well, bear a strong resemblance to the figures that came to prominence at the end of the Zhou dynasty, and the two rulers seem quite comparable to the rulers who were too fond of spirits at the end of the Xia dynasty. In other words, Sima Qian has clearly constructed his narrative to emphasize the decadence of the religious activities of his sovereign, and he clearly means to imply that the end of the Han dynasty may be approaching.

But there is another side to Sima Qian's presentation that is of crucial importance for our understanding of the later debates concerning the Han sacrificial system. In Sima Qian's presentation of the rise of the Qin-Han system of sacrifices, imperial power and a certain mode of religious worship are directly interconnected. The system began with a transgression, when Duke Xiang of Qin inaugurated suburban sacrifices to the god of the west while the Zhou were still in power. The addition of sacrifices to the gods of the other three directions reflected the growth in Qin's claims. Moreover, all of this was, according to Sima Qian, justified as a restoration of the sacrificial system of Huangdi, the figure associated with centralized statecraft.

The Qin imperial state witnessed an enlargement of this mode of religious worship. The First Emperor spent much of his life traversing the lands under his control in order to perform what had been local sacrifices and to search for spirits and transcendents who could help him attain personal immortality. This trend reached its extreme with Emperor Wu, who, under the influence of *fangshi*, instituted cults to deities claimed to be even greater than those worshipped by previous rulers and embarked on lengthy inspection tours to perform personally local sacrifices. Here too, Huangdi was explicitly invoked as the exemplar. The rise of a particular mode of religious worship and the emergence of centralized state institutions are thus presented as linked.

As we shall see, this association between the Qin and Han sacrificial system and imperial control was also at the heart of the debates that would rage several decades later. The ministers examined below also viewed these two as linked, but their response was quite different from Sima Qian's. Sima Qian did not present the rise of the Yong sacrificial system as necessarily wrong, although he did portray it as new. And for him, a reliance on magicians and a fondness for spirits and portents were nothing but recurrent signs of dynastic decline. They may have been associated in this particular instance with the rise of empire, but Sima Qian's concern lies more in demonstrating the decadence of his own ruler rather than in critiquing the Qin-Han imperial system per se. The figures to whom we will now turn, however, had a different reading of these issues.

Determining the Position of Heaven and Earth: The Ritual Reforms at the End of the Western Han

By the end of Emperor Wu's reign, the Han was suffering from imperial overreach: the military campaigns that defined Wu's centralization and expansion were severely straining the resources of the Han state. A gradual decline set in and sparked a series of debates concerning Han statecraft that came to a head in the reign of Emperor Cheng (33–7 BC).[19] When Cheng came to power, two of his ministers, Kuang Heng and Zhang Tan, used the opportunity to push for a shift in Han policies. Their method of doing so was to call on the emperor to follow the precedents found in the classics. Their memorials are filled with references to the *Shijing* and the *Shangshu*, and they frequently critique the Han for not following antiquity. Their perspective is clearly quite different from that of Sima Qian.

The initial attack on the sacrificial system of Emperor Wu appeared in a memorial by Kuang Heng and Zhang Tan:

In the affairs of emperors and kings, none is greater than supporting the order of Heaven. In supporting the order of Heaven, nothing is more important than sacrifices and offerings. Therefore, sage-kings devoted their hearts and trained their thoughts to the fullest to establish their regulations. They sacrificed to Heaven in the southern suburb, in accordance with the propriety of yang. They offered to Earth in the northern suburb, in accordance with the image of yin.[20]

Kuang Heng and Zhang Tan are arguing in favor of sacrifices to Heaven and Earth, with the respective altars aligned on a south–north axis. This normative order, the memorial claims, was practiced in the past. However, the ritual system in place since the time of Emperor Wu "differs from the regulations of antiquity" (25B.1254). Kuang Heng and Zhang Tan argue that the main altars to the Great One and Hou-tu should be resited south and north of the capital of Chang'an:

In ancient times, Wen and Wu of Zhou sacrificed at Feng and Hao, and King Cheng sacrificed at the city of Luo. From this it can be seen that Heaven follows the king to where he lives and accepts his offerings. It is fitting that the offerings to the Great One at Ganquan and to Hou-tu at Hedong be moved and set up at Chang'an in accord with [the practices of] the ancient thearchs and kings. (25B.1254)

Since the Zhou kings offered sacrifices at their capitals, the Han emperors should too.

Kuang Heng and Zhang Tan have clearly shifted the emphasis of the sacrificial system. Emperor Wu modeled himself on Huangdi; Kuang Heng and Zhang Tan emphasize the Zhou kings. Emperor Wu traveled to various places in the empire to perform the sacrifices. In Kuang Heng and

---

19. By far the best discussion of these debates is Loewe, *Crisis and Conflict in Han China*, pp. 154–92.

20. *Hanshu* "Jiaosi zhi," 25B.1253–54; hereinafter cited in the text.

Zhang Tan's scheme, the deities travel to the ruler's capital. Kuang Heng and Zhang Tan are thus setting themselves in opposition to one of the basic assumptions behind the Qin-Han imperial system. At issue here is the relationship between the ruler and spirits, as well as the relationship between the ruler and his realm.

This memorial by Kuang Heng and Zhang Tan sparked a debate at court. Fifty officials defended the proposals through references to the classical texts. They began with a citation of the "Ji fa" chapter of the *Liji*:

"Burning victims on the great circular altar is to sacrifice to Heaven; burying victims at the square altar is to sacrifice to Earth." An offering in the southern suburb is the means of determining the position of Heaven. Sacrificing to Earth on the square altar, situated in the northern suburb, fixes the position of yin. The position for each of the suburban sacrifices is located to the south and north of where the sage-king resides. (25B.1254)

It is the ruler who determines the proper positions of Heaven and Earth. He does so through his establishment of the capital and through proper sacrifices:

The *Shangshu* says: "On the third day, *dingsi*, he [the Duke of Zhou] made offerings of two oxen in the suburbs." When the Duke of Zhou raised offerings, it was to announce his moving to a new city. He determined the sacrificial rites at Luo. (25B.1254)

The quotation is from the "Luogao" chapter of the *Shangshu*, which narrates the founding of the city of Luoyang by the Duke of Zhou. The Qin moved their capital to Yong in order to bring it closer to a spiritually potent area. The authors of this memorial are claiming that the proper method is for the ruler to choose his capital and then announce his decision to the higher powers. The Zhou observed proper procedures; the Qin and the Han did not.

Much of this rhetoric refers implicitly to the issues concerning empire. A call for the ruler to abandon sacrificial policies that require him to travel throughout the realm is, in essence, a call for the ruler to withdraw from the highly centralized form of imperial statecraft that had been developing since the emergence of the Qin. The authors are calling for a restoration of the Zhou system, and indeed, go so far as to argue that the Han, by following and expanding the new imperial system of the Qin, failed to receive the support of Heaven:

When enlightened kings and sagely rulers serve Heaven, it is illuminated; when they serve Earth, it is explored. When Heaven and Earth are illuminated and explored, then the divine illumination (*shen ming*) is arrayed. Heaven and Earth take the king as the master. Therefore, when the sages and kings instituted the rites of sacrificing to Heaven and Earth, they necessarily did so in the suburbs of the capital. Chang'an is where the sagely ruler dwells, and it is where august Heaven watches him. The sacrifices at Ganquan and Hedong have not been accepted by the spirits and numinous powers; it is fitting to move them to places with the correct yang and the great yin. We should oppose custom and return to the ancients, accord with the regulations of the sages, and set aright the position of Heaven as the rituals prescribe. (25B.1254)

Heaven wants to observe the ruler in his own capital, and its support comes only when the ruler has been judged adequate in his daily activities. Divine support does not come to the ruler because he seeks out the divinities, and the sacrifices of Ganquan and Fenyin have therefore not been accepted by the spirits.

Kuang Heng and Zhang Tan elaborated on this point in another memorial:

The *Shi* says: "Do not say: 'It [Heaven] is high above.' It ascends and descends in its work; it daily inspects us."[21] This is to say that Heaven's eyes looked over the place of the king. It also says: "It thereupon looked about and gazed toward the west. Here it is that it gave a settlement."[22] This is to say that Heaven considered the capital of King Wen as its dwelling. It is fitting at Chang'an to determine the southern and northern suburbs as the foundation for ten thousand generations. (25B.1255)

Absent here is any talk of the ruler seeking spiritual beings or ascending to Heaven. The ruler stays in his capital, and Heaven comes to him. The ruler, in other words, does not try to achieve spiritual powers; rather, he centers the kingdom by establishing his capital, and Heaven then judges his actions. The emphasis is shifted to the virtue of the ruler—and the memorialists are implying that the Qin and Han rulers have been found wanting.

Kuang Heng then went on to argue against the ornamentation of the Ganquan altar, claiming that it had no precedent: "one cannot obtain its models in antiquity" (25B.1256). In another memorial, Kuang Heng argued that Han ritual practice was largely a continuation of that instituted by the Qin feudal lords and was not based upon the proper rites of

---

21. *Shi*, Mao #288.
22. *Shi*, Mao #241.

antiquity (25B.1257). Implicit here is a rejection of the claim that the Qin-Han system is based on the sacrifices of Huangdi. In 31 BC, Emperor Cheng accepted these arguments. In the first significant rejection of the sacrificial system that had begun with the Qin and had been developed by Emperor Wu, Cheng instituted suburban sacrifices to Heaven south of Chang'an (25B.1257).

Kuang Heng and Zhang Tan went on to critique the numerous sacrifices set up at the instigation of the *fangshi*. Of the 683 such sacrifices, only 208, they argued, conformed to the rites of antiquity (25B.1257). They called on the emperor to discontinue the remaining 475. The emperor did so. The *Hanshu* states that only 15 of the 203 sacrifices at Yong were maintained. And many of the sacrifices instituted by Cheng's predecessors on the Han throne were abolished (25B.1257–58).

The debate, however, did not end here. Liu Xiang immediately authored a memorial calling for a restoration of Emperor Wu's sacrificial system. The sacrifices, Liu Xiang argued, were instituted in response to the spirits and thus should not be abolished: "Moreover, when Ganquan, Fenyin, and the five altars of Yong were first instituted, it was because there were spirits of the upper and lower realms interacting (*ganying*). Only then were [the altars] built. This was not done lightly" (25B.1258). In opposition to Kuang Heng and Zhang Tan's argument that Heaven should follow the king to where he lives, Liu Xiang is claiming that humans must respond to the spirits: if the spirits interact with humans at specific places, then those are the places where the sacrifices must be given. Liu Xiang's memorial ended with a warning of the dire consequences that could occur now that the sacrifices had been discontinued (25B.1258–59).

This memorial is of some interest, since it is one of the few extant documents written by a defender of the Qin-Han sacrificial system. Moreover, since Liu Xiang would have considered himself a *Ru*, the memorial shows the degree to which the debate—as well as many of the underlying issues concerning spirits and the empire—cut across divisions at the court. Liu Xiang is arguing that there are certain sacred sites where the spirits interact with humans, and Yong, Ganquan, and Fenyin are among these sites. The altars at these places, therefore, were instituted in response to the spirits. No claim is made here for the antiquity of the sacrifices or for their purported existence during the reign of Huangdi. Liu's argument is based solely on the spirits. Emperor Cheng, who blamed his lack of an heir on his abandonment of the institutions of his ancestors, concurred with Liu Xiang. Emperor Wu's sacrificial system was restored (25B.1259).

The response came from another official, Gu Yong:[23]

Your servant has heard that if you are clear about the nature of Heaven and Earth, you cannot be deluded by spirits and anomalies. If you understand the dispositions of the myriad things, you cannot be deluded by what does not fit into categories. Those who turn their back on the correct path of humaneness and propriety and do not honor the model sayings of the Five Classics, but are instead filled with reports about abnormalities, anomalies, ghosts, and spirits, widely revere formulas for sacrifices and offerings, seek to requite sacrifices that bring no fortune, go so far as to say that there exist transcendents in this world, chew and swallow immortality drugs. . . . They all deceive the people and mislead the masses, hold to the left [i.e., wrong] way, embrace falsity and fabrications so as to delude the current ruler. . . . It is for this reason that the enlightened king should resist them and not listen, and the sage would cut them off and not speak [of such things]. (25B.1260)

According to Gu Yong, accepting the arguments of Liu Xiang would give inordinate power to those figures—like the *fangshi*—who claim the ability to find sacred sites and interact with spirits. His critique is similar to Sima Qian's, but his solution is quite different: Gu Yong calls on the emperor to accept the nature of Heaven and Earth as found in the Five Classics.

Gu Yong continues: "When the First Emperor united all under Heaven, he was swayed by the way of spirits and transcendents." Gu Yong then criticizes the First Emperor for sending out people to "seek spirits and gather drugs" (25B.1260). The argument resembles Sima Qian's, but absent here is Sima Qian's framework of dynastic decline. What we see instead is simply an emphasis on the newness of this system and on the Zhou sacrificial system as the norm of antiquity.

This alternation between the two sacrificial systems continued during the reign of Emperor Ai (r. 6–1 BC), Chengdi's successor (25B.1263–64). Finally, in response to memorials from the chief minister Wang Mang, Emperor Ping (r. AD 1–5) instituted the reforms recommended by Kuang Heng (25B.1266–68). The system established under Emperor Wu was dismantled, and the rituals purportedly in place during the Zhou were reinstated.

In this new system, it is humans who create the center by establishing a capital and then properly aligning Heaven and Earth. This involves neither

---

23. For Gu Yong, see *Hanshu*, 85.3443–73. For a convenient summary of this career, see Loewe, *Biographical Dictionary*, pp. 132–33.

the exertion of a theomorphic will to align the cosmos nor an attempt to become a spirit in accord with the patterns of the universe. Rather, it supports a hierarchy of Heaven and man; humans create the center of the cosmos, and Heaven judges man's success.

The authors of these memorials referred to the Duke of Zhou's establishment of Luoyang. As in that earlier model, it is humans who align the capital and thus determine the position of Heaven. But absent in the Han is any notion of the agonistic relationship between humans and the divine powers that underlay the Zhou rituals. Now, the proper cosmic role of humans is to determine the place of Heaven, and the proper cosmic role of Heaven is to grant or deny approval. Heaven and man are ritually separated and yet interdependent, with each possessing its distinct place and its distinct duty.

Conclusion

The debates traced in this chapter concern two interrelated issues: the nature of the Han state and the proper relations between the ruler and the spirits. Each of the texts we have discussed—Dong Zhongshu's writings, Sima Qian's historical account, and the memorials of the reign of Emperor Cheng—assumed this linkage, and their critiques of the Qin-Han model played on both themes.

According to Sima Qian and Kuang Heng and his supporters, the Qin-Han sacrificial system, which they associated with the imperial state, was motivated by an attempt to gain control over sacred sites where spirits dwelled—sites whose sacrificial traditions, it was claimed, could be traced back to Huangdi. The emperor hoped that by communicating with the spirits of each region, he could gain both personal immortality and control over those regions. This system involved several related imperatives. Horizontally, it resulted in a drive on the part of each emperor to take control of more and more such sacred sites and to establish a cycle of visits. By the time of Emperor Wu, this had resulted in the emperor making the five sacred mountains into imperial commanderies, undertaking innumerable imperial tours, and adding the sites of Ganquan and Fenyin to the already important cultic area of Yong. Vertically, it meant appealing to ever more powerful deities, who, it was hoped, could exercise more control over the spirit pantheon. This, too, reached a new extreme with Emperor Wu, who offered sacrifices directly to the Great One. Here again, we see Emperor Wu attempting to accomplish through sacrificial activity something comparable to what self-divinization experts were seeking through cultivation. And, socially, it meant granting power to those figures—especially the *fangshi*—who claimed the ability to find and summon spirits for the emperor. In short, it was a system that inherently involved a never-ending attempt to gain more control over the territorial and spiritual realms.

In contrast, the system that, in very different ways and for very different purposes, both Sima Qian and Kuang Heng ascribed to the pre-Qin period, made no claim for the sacrality of the primary sites. Instead, the ruler provided a center for the kingdom by establishing his capital. No claim of significance was made for the site. If Heaven and Earth accepted the ruler, the capital became the place at which yin and yang interacted properly. The ruler then, from afar, paid homage to the spirits of each region and every five years traveled to the five mountains to meet with the feudal lords of each locality.

For Sima Qian, the distinction between these systems was far less important than the overall narrative of dynastic decline, a narrative that he utilized to critique Emperor Wu's concern with magical formulas and personal immortality. But for Kuang Heng and those associated with him, the distinction was all-important. At stake for them was an assertion of boundaries, an assertion that would result, they hoped, in a radically different (and, in their view, traditional) vision of rule. They were calling for a ritual system that granted the ruler tremendous power: it was he who established the center and determined the position of Heaven and Earth. But no further expansion of the ruler's power was built into the system: he had no need to gain direct control over local areas or to appeal to ever more numerous or ever more powerful deities. On the contrary, Kuang Heng's precise concern was to assert a strict demarcation between humans and spirits, between center and periphery. The ruler could not ascend to Heaven, could not become immortal, and hence should not seek to gain control over sacred sites to which spirits could be summoned to confer such powers. Humans were humans, spirits were spirits; each had its own domain, each had its own duties. And the ruler belonged fully to the human realm. In making this argument, Kuang Heng was building on claims made much earlier by Dong Zhongshu concerning the proper demarcation of the roles of humanity and the divine powers. In this formulation, man's proper duty was to establish a center and to determine the positions of Heaven and Earth.

In ultimately choosing to side with Kuang Heng and his followers, the emperors of the Western Han effected a fundamental shift in the orientation of the Han state. Following these reforms, claims of ascension and self-divinization ceased to be favored at court. And, indirectly, these reforms may in part have been responsible for the later popularity of millenarian movements, many of which would, in their critiques of the Han state, embrace the very notions of divinization and ascension that the reforms of Kuang Heng and others had driven out of the central court.

Conclusion

Culture and History in Early China

At the end of the Western Han, the dominant conception of the cosmos was of a world organized by humans, ritually separate from, yet correlated with, Heaven and Earth. Kuang Heng's model was a cosmological re-reading of narratives from the *Shangshu* concerning the Duke of Shao's aligning of Luoyang: the king places his capital and thus determines the positions of Heaven and Earth. Heaven, Earth, and man are harmonized when each performs its proper cosmological duty. But it is only if we know the significance these ideas possessed in the early Han that we can understand the real concerns behind the ritual reform—namely, various claims of divinization that had flourished in the early Han, or, more explicitly, theomorphic notions of kingship as well as self-cultivation practices that involved a rejection of textual authority and the precedents set by the past sages. It is thus fitting to end this study at this point, when the Han court forcefully rejected the claims of divinization—claims that had played such a crucial role in the reaction against sacrifice and divination and in the rise of empire. And it is not surprising that in rejecting these claims, figures such as Kuang Heng turned back to a particular, cosmological reading of Bronze Age rituals—since these were precisely the rituals that the divinization movements had reacted against.

Following David Keightley, I have argued that the paramount religious concern of the Shang and Western Zhou was to forge deceased humans into ancestors who could then be influenced through sacrifices and divinations. The rituals worked from the bottom up: the lower ancestors were weaker, yet more amenable to the blandishments of human ritual, whereas the higher powers were stronger but less malleable. The goal was thus to work one's way up the pantheon: the ritual specialists would appeal to the lower ancestors, who would in turn be directed to appeal to the higher ancestors, who would in turn be called on to pacify the more powerful, non-ancestral powers—including, most important, Di, or Heaven. These sacrificial practices represented an attempt to join nature spirits and the ghosts of deceased humans into a single, unified system. The deceased humans were transformed into ancestral spirits, defined by their roles in a hierarchy; nature spirits and unrelated yet nonetheless powerful deceased humans were similarly placed into this hierarchy as well.

By the fourth century BC, however, a new group of figures (usually referred to in the secondary literature as the *shi*) began gaining prominence at the courts of the time. It is clear from their recurrent critiques of sacrifice and divination that such figures felt themselves to be in competition with ritual specialists. Indeed, the authors of these texts not only rejected sacrificial models but also attempted to reverse them and thereby supersede them. Sacrificial models in early China operated by working from the recently deceased and less powerful local spirits toward more distant and more powerful deities. In contrast, the new model posited the One, the ultimate ancestor from which everything—all spirits, all natural phenomena, and all humans—were generated. This concept emerged, for the first time, in numerous fourth-century BC texts, such as the "Neiye," the *Taiyi sheng shui*, and the *Laozi*. The entire pantheon of deities—from local spirits to Heaven itself—as well as the natural phenomena they supposedly controlled, were subsumed under the One. And instead of appealing to this ultimate ancestor by working up the pantheon, proponents of the new model claimed direct access to the One and thus full power and knowledge over the cosmos.

Much of the interest in these texts lies in the different ways these systems based on the One were built. One approach, developed in the "Neiye" and taken further in texts like the "Xinshu" chapters, is self-divinization, which is achieved by, among other things, returning to and holding fast to the One: the sage gains power over the things of the universe by grasping the ancestor that generated them and continues to underlie them. Another approach, seen in the *Taiyi sheng shui*, is to gain full knowledge: rearranging the pantheon of the day into a series of lineal descendants from the One allowed the authors to claim that they alone understood the workings of the cosmos. In each of these texts, however, the authors claimed either the ability, or possession of the techniques that conferred the ability, to reach the One and thereby understand and exercise control over the cosmos without resorting to divination and sacrifice. What bothered figures like Xunzi and the authors of the *Xici zhuan* about these claims was that they denied the efficacy of time-honored rituals of the past. These authors therefore argued in support of divination and sacrifice, even while building their arguments on many of the same cosmological claims as the proponents of self-divinization and gnosis.

The debate between ritual specialists and cosmologists continued during the rise of empire in early China. Although the sacrificial system that arose with the Qin and Han empires has often been described as based on a correlative system, I have argued that it was based largely on a new variant of the sacrificial model—divinization through sacrifice rather than through cosmology. The process here was, horizontally, to take over more and more sacred spaces inhabited by local spirits and offer them cult and, vertically, to appeal to ever higher gods in the pantheon. The endless process of consolidating local cults while also appealing to higher gods was seen to aid in the process of the divinization of the ruler and ultimately lead to his ascension. The extreme was reached with Emperor Wu, whose consolidation of the empire coincided with his sacrifices to the Great One.

As Sima Qian correctly pointed out, this created a dynamic in which the ruler tried to gain more land and undertake more travels in order to appropriate more and more divine power. This new form of theomorphic kingship was critiqued by several voices in the early Han—from the authors of the *Huainanzi*, who called for a cosmological form of divinization, to figures like Dong Zhongshu, who rejected divinization and proposed correlatively defined sacrifices. Both of these were attempts to limit the theomorphic claims of the ruler through appeals to cosmological patterns.

Ultimately, Emperor Wu's system began to falter because of imperial overreach, and it was finally repealed near the end of the Western Han. The divinization claims that had so dominated court politics since the beginning of the Qin empire were rejected. Rulers were defined as humans, ritually separate from divine powers, with their own duties to perform. As a consequence, claims of ascension became associated with those groups who opposed the empire.

These points also have comparative significance. As we have seen repeatedly in this study, China, when discussed in a comparative perspective, has long been characterized as a culture that assumed continuity between the human and the divine world. In some comparisons, China is seen as the antithesis of the West; in others it is placed at a different point on an evolutionary line of development. But either way, early China is presented as a society devoid of the tensions between man and God, Zeus and Prometheus, that pervaded the Hebraic and Greek traditions, as a society that never experienced the distantiation of the world from divinity that has existed in the West. Although Weber portrayed this negatively, most China specialists have portrayed it positively: China has become the land where gods and men are linked in harmony, and where there exists a fundamental continuity of the human and the divine. China is also frequently presented as the one major civilization that never discarded primitive notions of harmony with the natural and divine worlds. Working from this same line of argument, scholars have built other comparative models for explaining China: shamanism, this-worldly optimism, bureaucratic harmony, sacrificial *do ut des*.

One of the few scholars working within a comparative framework who has rejected this approach is Heiner Roetz. Roetz attempts to read into early China the same transcendental breakthrough and "disenchantment of nature" that he sees as inherent in any rational evolution, and his picture of early China is wildly at odds with that of other scholars. But even Roetz attributes what he sees as the ultimate failure of Chinese philosophy to its inability to develop as strong a tension between human society and the world as in the West.

I have tried to break down the binaries of dualism/monism and tragic/harmonious cosmologies as they are often applied to Greece and China in two ways. First, I have tried to focus on how specific individuals in specific contexts worked through issues of the proper relationships between humans and divine powers and how the resulting debates played out historically. As we have repeatedly seen, characterizations of Greece as dualistic and China as monistic are of little use in this approach. Empedocles, for example, was monistic; question four of the *Shiwen* was dualistic. Moreover, even the term "monism" is insufficiently nuanced to cover the positions taken in these debates. Depending on one's method of positing the human and divine elements of the cosmos, one can assert discontinuity even while proclaiming a monistic cosmos. For example, Dong Zhongshu asserted a monistic cosmos in opposition to the theistic cosmology dominant at the imperial court of his day, but he also strongly distinguished humanity and Heaven and argued, also in opposition to the cults at the court, that humans could not become gods. A strong assertion of continuity was coupled with, at a different level, a strong assertion of discontinuity. And only by looking at the contemporary context can one understand the significance of these claims. To describe Dong Zhongshu as simply "monistic" fails to do justice to the many implications of his arguments.

And the point can be put in stronger terms when we look at attempts to describe several early Chinese authors as "monistic." Both the "Xinshu" chapters and Dong Zhongshu's cosmology are monistic, but these two monisms have very different implications. The authors of the "Xinshu" chapters were arguing for the continuity of human and divine powers in opposition to the discontinuities implied by sacrifice and divination; Dong Zhongshu was distinguishing Heaven and man in opposition to the claims of imperial divinity. For the authors of the "Xinshu" chapters, humans could become spirits and hence did not need divination and sacrifice; for Dong Zhongshu, humans were separate from the divine, but, precisely through such actions as sacrifices, had a crucial cosmic role to play. For the authors of the "Xinshu" chapters, the king was divine; for Dong Zhongshu, he was human. In short, the categorization of early Chinese thought as "monistic," in opposition to a "dualistic" cosmology of the West, breaks down at every level when we explore the historical contexts and implications of specific statements.

My second goal has been to place the debates analyzed in this book within a comparative framework that has greater explanatory power than that of a "monistic" cosmology or the related claims of shamanism and sacrificial *do ut des*. At first glance, this second goal, of seeking to analyze this period of early Chinese history from a larger perspective, might appear to be in conflict with the emphasis on nuance that characterizes my first goal. One of the underlying arguments of this study, however, has been that these two goals are mutually reinforcing, for it is precisely in the nuances of the debate that issues of comparative interest come to the fore. More specifically, it is through such nuances that one can recognize the tensions and concerns underlying the debates, and it is only, in turn, by recognizing these tensions and concerns that one can compare the Chinese material with that found in other cultures facing similar political and cultural problems.

It follows that comparison will be most fruitful when we compare cultures that have faced a similar set of historical circumstances. I have therefore agreed with the many scholars who have stressed the benefits of comparing early China and early Greece. Like early China, ancient Greece also witnessed, at roughly the same period, comparable social and political changes (the breakdown of an older aristocratic, Bronze Age society, and the growth of independent, competing territorial states, some of which developed imperial ambitions), as well as a series of interrelated debates concerning divinization, sacrifice, and cosmology. But I have tried to develop this comparison on different grounds.

I have advocated working toward a vocabulary that is both nuanced enough to allow for careful historical studies and yet open enough to maintain cross-cultural validity. Instead of categorizing cultures in terms of such dichotomies as "monism/dualism" or "immanence/transcendence," and instead of working from (even if only implicit) evolutionary frameworks based on "religion to philosophy" or "animism to humanism and rationalism" narratives, we should try to focus on terms that allow us to tease out the problems and tensions in each culture under analysis. In this book, I have argued that the tensions surrounding "divinization" or notions of continuity and discontinuity may result in more meaningful comparisons between Greece and China than do either the evolutionary or the essentializing frameworks. In both Greece and China, at roughly the same time, one finds comparable tensions surrounding sacrificial action, self-divinization, cosmology, and empire. The interesting issues for comparative studies are how and why the claims were made in each culture, and how and why various solutions came to be institutionalized. Posing the questions in this way has, I hope, yielded results that explain more than the other frameworks discussed in the Introduction.

In setting up this comparative framework, I have turned to anthropological discussions of kingship, sacrifice, and cosmology. Building on the work of figures like Lévi-Strauss and Sahlins, I have tried to develop a valid comparative vocabulary that helps to uncover the complexities of claims made in various cultures. In bringing this literature to bear on the early Chinese materials, I have based much of my analysis on the work of Marcel Granet. This is somewhat ironic, since Granet was one of the most influential figures in defining China as a land of continuity—one of the positions I critique in this book. However, as I argue in Chapters 4 and 6, a careful reading of

Granet yields a rather different portrait of early China: Granet's analyses become far more persuasive when they are taken out of Granet's own essentializing, evolutionary, and typological frameworks. Since I have found much of this anthropological theory—from Granet to Sahlins—helpful in conceptualizing the issues at hand, I hope that I have, at least to some small extent, returned the favor by helping to bring the Chinese material into broader anthropological concerns.

And when we treat these issues from such a historical and comparative perspective, many of the readings proposed from within either the evolutionary or essentialist frameworks cease to be fully convincing. We do not find in early China assumptions of harmony or of a continuity between humans and divine powers or of a lack of tension between humans and the divine. On the contrary, one of the crucial issues in early China was the recurring tension between those who wished to maintain a ritual separation of humans and divine powers and those who wished to destroy those separations and appropriate divine powers for themselves. Spirits were not only powers with which one harmonized; they were often powers one fought, cheated, appropriated, and tried to become or transcend. And a significant part of early Chinese history becomes fully understandable only when we acknowledge such tensions and trace the ways in which they played out.

Reference Matter

Bibliography

Unless otherwise noted, references to the early Chinese primary texts are to the *Sibu beiyao* editions. References to the dynastic histories are to the Zhonghua shuju editions (Beijing, 1959–).

Akatsuka Kiyoshi 赤塚忠. *Chūgoku kodai no shūkyō to bunka* 中国古代の宗教と文化. Tokyo: Kadokawa shoten, 1977.

Allan, Sarah. *The Shape of the Turtle: Myth, Art, and Cosmos in Early China.* Albany: State University of New York Press, 1991.

Allan, Sarah, and Crispin Williams, eds. *The Guodian Laozi: Proceedings of the International Conference, Dartmouth College, May 1998.* Berkeley: Society for the Study of Early China and University of California, Institute of East Asian Studies, 2000.

Aristotle. *Aristotle: Selections.* Trans. Terence Irwin and Gail Fine. Indianapolis: Hackett, 1995.

Arrian. *The Campaigns of Alexander.* Trans. Aubrey de Sélincourt. Rev. J. R. Hamilton. New York: Penguin Books, 1971.

Bilsky, Lester James. *The State Religion of Ancient China.* Taipei: Orient Cultural Service, 1975.

Bloom, Irene. "Practicality and Spirituality in the *Mencius.*" In *Confucian Spirituality,* ed. Tu Wei-Ming and Mary Evelyn Tucker. New York: Crossroad Press, forthcoming.

Bodde, Derk. "Myths of Ancient China." In *Mythologies of the Ancient World,* ed. Samuel N. Kramer, pp. 369–408. New York: Doubleday, 1961.

Bosworth, A. B. *Conquest and Empire: The Reign of Alexander the Great.* Cambridge, Eng.: Cambridge University Press, 1988.

Bousset, Wilhelm. *Der Himmelreise der Seele.* 1901. Reprinted—Darmstadt: Wissenschaftliche Buchgesellschaft, 1971.

Brashier, K. E. "Han Thanatology and the Division of 'Souls.'" *Early China* 21 (1996): 125–58.

Bremmer, Jan. *The Early Greek Concept of the Soul.* Princeton: Princeton University Press, 1983.

Brooks, E. Bruce, and A. Taeko Brooks. *The Original Analects: Saying of Confucius and His Successors.* New York: Columbia University Press, 1998.

Burkert, Walter. *Greek Religion.* Trans. John Raffan. Cambridge, Mass.: Harvard University Press, 1985.

———. *Homo Necans: The Anthropology of Ancient Greek Sacrifical Ritual and Myth.* Trans. Peter Bing. Berkeley: University of California Press, 1983.

———. "Orphism and Bacchic Mysteries: New Evidence and Old Problems of Interpretation." *Protocol of the 28th Colloquy of the Center for Hermeneutical Studies in Hellenistic and Modern Culture,* ed. W. Wuellner. Berkeley: Center for Hermeneutical Studies, 1977.

———. *Structure and History in Greek Mythology.* Berkeley: University of California Press, 1979.

Campany, Robert. "Xunzi and Durkheim as Theorists of Ritual Practice." In *Discourse and Practice,* ed. Frank Reynolds and David Tracy, pp. 197–231. Albany: State University of New York Press, 1992.

Chang, Kwang-chih. "Ancient China and Its Anthropological Significance." In *Archaeological Thought in America,* ed. C. C. Lamberg-Karlovsky, pp. 155–66. Cambridge, Eng.: Cambridge University Press, 1989.

———. "The Animal in Shang and Chou Bronze Art." *Harvard Journal of Asiatic Studies* 41, no. 2 (1981): 527–54.

———. *The Archaeology of Ancient China.* 4th ed. New Haven: Yale University Press, 1986.

———. *Art, Myth, and Ritual: The Path to Political Authority in Ancient China.* Cambridge, Mass.: Harvard University Press, 1983.

———. "An Essay on Cong." *Orientations* 20, no. 6 (June 1989): 37–43.

———. *Shang Civilization.* New Haven: Yale University Press, 1980.

———. "Shang Shamans." In *The Power of Culture: Studies in Chinese Cultural History,* ed. Willard J. Peterson, Andrew H. Plaks, and Ying-shih Yü, pp. 10–36. Hong Kong: Chinese University Press, 1994.

———. "T'ien kan: A Key to the History of the Shang." In *Ancient China: Studies in Early Civilization,* ed. David Roy and Tsuen-hsuin Tsien, pp. 13–42. Hong Kong: Chinese University Press, 1978.

Chang, Tsung-tung. *Der Kult der Shang-Dynastie im Spiegel der Orakelinschriften: Eine paläographische Studie zur Religion im archaischen China*. Wiesbaden: Otto Harrassowitz, 1970.

Chen Mengjia 陳 梦 家. *Liu guo jinian* 六 國 紀 年. Shanghai: Shanghai renmin chubanshe, 1956.

―――. "Shang dai de shenhua yu wushu" 商 代 的 神 化 與 巫 術. *Yanjing xuebao* 燕 京 學 報 20 (1936): 485–576.

―――. "Xi-Zhou tongqi duandai" 西 周 銅 器 斷 代. 6 pts. *Kaogu xuebao* 考 古 學 報 1955, no. 9: 137–75; 1955, no. 10: 69–142; 1956, no. 1: 65–114; 1956, no. 2: 85–94; 1956, no. 3: 105–27; 1956, no. 4: 85–122.

―――. *Yinxu buci zongshu* 殷 虛 卜 辭 綜 述. Beijing: Kexue chubanshe, 1956.

Chen Pan 陳 槃. "Zhanguo Qin Han jian fangshi kao lun" 戰 國 秦 漢 間 方 士 考 論. *Zhongyang yanjiuyuan, Lishi yuyan yanjiusuo jikan* 中 央 研 究 院 歷 史 語 言 研 究 所 集 刊 17 (1948): 7–57.

Ching, Julia. *Mysticism and Kingship in China: The Heart of Chinese Wisdom*. Cambridge, Eng.: Cambridge University Press, 1997.

Cook, Scott. "Zhuang Zi and His Carving of the Confucian Ox." *Philosophy East and West* 47, no. 4 (Oct. 1997): 521–53.

Cornford, F. M. *From Religion to Philosophy: A Study in the Origins of Western Speculation*. 1912. Reprinted—Princeton: Princeton University Press, 1991.

Creel, Herlee G. *The Origins of Statecraft in China*, vol. 1, *The Western Zhou Empire*. Chicago: University of Chicago Press, 1970.

Csikszentmihalyi, Mark. "Emulating the Yellow Emperor: The Theory and Practice of Huanglao, 180–141 B.C.E." Ph.D. diss., Stanford University, 1994.

Csikszentmihalyi, Mark, and Philip J. Ivanhoe, eds. *Religious and Philosophical Aspects of the Laozi*. Albany: State University of New York, 1999.

Culianu, Ioan. *Psychonadia I: A Survey of the Evidence Concerning the Ascension of the Soul and Its Relevance*. Leiden: Brill, 1983.

Detienne, Marcel. "Between Beasts and Gods." In *Myth, Religion and Society: Structuralist Essays by M. Detienne, L. Gernet, J.-P. Vernant, and P. Vidal-Naquet*, ed. and trans. R. L. Gordon, pp. 215–28. Cambridge, Eng.: Cambridge University Press, 1981.

―――. "Culinary Practices and the Spirit of Sacrifice." In *The Cuisine of Sacrifice Among the Greeks*, ed. Marcel Detienne and Jean-Pierre Vernant; trans. Paula Wissing, pp. 1–20. Chicago: University of Chicago Press, 1989.

Ding Sixin 丁 四 新. *Guodian Chu mu zhujian sixiang yanjiu* 郭 店 楚 墓 竹 簡 思 想 研 究. Beijing: Dongfang chubanshe, 2000.

Dodds, E. R. *The Greeks and the Irrational*. Berkeley: University of California Press, 1956.

Dong Zuobin 董作賓. "Yinxu wenzi yibian xu" 殷虛文字乙編序. *Zhongguo kaogu xuebao* 中國考古學報 4 (1949): 255–89.

Dumézil, Georges. *The Destiny of the Warrior.* Trans. Alf Hiltebeitel. Chicago: University of Chicago Press, 1970.

———. *Gods of the Ancient Northmen.* Ed. Einar Haugen. Berkeley: University of California Press, 1973.

———. *Mitra-Varuna: An Essay on Two Indo-European Representations of Sovereignty.* New York: Zone Books, 1988.

Durand, Jean-Louis. *Sacrifice et labour en Grece ancienne: Essai d'anthropologie religieuse.* Paris: Ecole française de Rome, 1986.

Durkheim, Emile, and Marcel Mauss. *Primitive Classification.* Trans., with an introduction, Rodney Needham. Chicago: University of Chicago Press, 1963.

Eisenstadt, S. N. "The Axial Age Breakthroughs—Their Characteristics and Origins." In *The Origins and Diversity of Axial Age Civilizations,* ed. S. N. Eisenstadt, pp. 1–25. Albany: State University of New York Press, 1986.

Eliade, Mircea. *Patterns in Comparative Religion.* Trans. Rosemary Sheed. New York: Meridian, 1958.

———. *The Sacred and the Profane: The Nature of Religion.* Trans. Willard R. Trask. New York: Harcourt, Brace, 1959.

———. *Shamanism: Archaic Techniques of Ecstasy.* Trans. Willard R. Trask. Princeton: Princeton University Press, 1972.

Empedocles. *Empedocles: The Extant Fragments.* Trans. M. R. Wright. New Haven: Yale University Press, 1981.

Eno, Robert. *The Confucian Creation of Heaven: Philosophy and the Defense of Ritual Mastery.* New York: State University of New York Press, 1990.

———. "Cook Ding's Dao and the Limits of Philosophy." In *Essays on Skepticism, Relativism, and Ethics in the Zhuangzi,* ed. Paul Kjellberg and Philip J. Ivanhoe, pp. 127–51. Albany: State University of New York Press, 1996.

———. "Was There a High God Ti in Shang Religion?" *Early China* 15 (1990): 1–26.

Falkenhausen, Lothar von. "Issues in Western Zhou Studies: A Review Article." *Early China* 18 (1993): 145–71.

———. "Sources of Taoism: Reflections on Archaeological Indicators of Religious Change in Eastern Zhou China." *Taoist Resources* 5, no. 2 (Dec. 1994): 1–12.

———. *Suspended Music: Chime Bells in the Culture of Bronze Age China.* Berkeley: University of California Press, 1993.

Fredricksmeyer, E. "Three Notes on Alexander's Deification." *American Journal of Ancient History* 1979, no. 4: 1–9.

Fung Yu-lan. *A History of Chinese Philosophy.* 2 vols. Trans. Derk Bodde. Princeton: Princeton University Press, 1952.

Gernet, Jacques, with Jean-Paul Vernant. "Social History and the Evolution of Ideas in China and Greece from the Sixth to the Second Centuries B.C." In Jean-Paul Vernant, *Myth and Society in Ancient Greece*, pp. 71–91. London: Methuen, 1980.

Ginzburg, Carlo. *Ecstasies: Deciphering the Witch's Sabbath.* Trans. Raymond Rosenthal. New York: Penguin Books, 1991.

Goldin, Paul Rakita. *Rituals of the Way: The Philosophy of Xunzi.* Chicago: Open Court Press, 1999.

Graf, Fritz. "Dionysian and Orphic Eschatology." In *Masks of Dionysus*, ed. Thomas H. Carpenter and Christopher A. Faraone, pp. 239–58. Ithaca: Cornell University Press, 1993.

Graham, A. C. "The Background of the Mencian Theory of Human Nature." In idem, *Studies in Chinese Philosophy and Philosophical Literature*, pp. 7–66. Singapore: Institute of East Asian Philosophies, 1986 (1967).

———. *Disputers of the Tao: Philosophical Argument in Ancient China.* La Salle, Ill.: Open Court, 1989.

———. "Introduction." In idem, trans., *Chuang-tzu: The Seven Inner Chapters and Other Writings from the Book Chuang-tzu*, pp. 15–19. London: George Allen and Unwin, 1981.

———. *Yin-Yang and the Nature of Correlative Thinking.* Singapore: Institute of East Asian Philosophies, 1986.

Graham, A. C., trans. *Chuang Tzu: The Inner Chapters.* London: George Allen and Unwin, 1981.

Granet, Marcel. *Chinese Civilization.* New York: Alfred A. Knopf, 1930.

———. *La civilisation chinoise.* Paris: Editions Albin Michel, 1929.

———. *Danses et légendes de la Chine ancienne.* 2 vols. Paris: Libraries Felix Alcan, 1926.

———. *La pensée chinoise.* Paris: La Renaissance du Livre, 1934.

Gu Jiegang 顧頡剛 et al., eds. *Gushibian* 古史辨. 1926–41. Shanghai: Guji chubanshe, 1982.

Guan Feng 關鋒. *Zhuangzi zhexue taolunji* 莊子哲學討論集. Beijing: Zhonghua shuju, 1962.

Guo Moruo 郭沫若. *Liang-Zhou jinwenci daxi tulu kaoshi* 兩周金文辭大系圖錄考釋. 2nd rev. ed. Beijing: Kexue chubanshe, 1958.

Guo Moruo 郭沫若 and Hu Houxuan 胡厚宣. *Jiaguwen heji* 甲骨文合集. Beijing: Zhonghua shuju, 1979–1982.

Guo Yi 郭沂. *Guodian zhujian yu xian-Qin xueshu sixiang* 郭店竹簡與先秦學術思想. Shanghai: Shanghai jiaoyu chubanshe, 2001.

Guodian chumu zhujian 郭店楚墓竹簡. Beijing: Wenwu, 1998.

Guthrie, W. K. C. *Orpheus and Greek Religion: A Study of the Orphic Movement*. Princeton: Princeton University Press, 1993 (1952).

Hall, David L., and Roger T. Ames. *Anticipating China: Thinking Through the Narratives of Chinese and Western Culture*. Albany: State University of New York Press, 1995.

———. *Thinking from the Han: Self, Truth, and Transcendence in Chinese and Western Culture*. Albany: State University of New York Press, 1995.

Hamilton, J. R. *Alexander the Great*. Pittsburgh: University of Pittsburgh, 1974.

Hansen, Chad. "A Tao of Tao in Chuang-tzu." In *Experimental Essays on Chuang-tzu*, ed. Victor Mair, pp. 24–55. Honolulu: University of Hawaii Press, 1983.

Harper, Donald. "A Chinese Demonography of the Third Century B.C." *Harvard Journal of Asiatic Studies* 45, no. 2 (Dec. 1985): 459–98.

———. *Early Chinese Medical Literature: The Mawangdui Medical Manuscripts*. London: Kegan Paul International, 1980.

———. "Warring States, Ch'in and Han Periods." In "Chinese Religions: The State of the Field," ed. Daniel Overmeyer. *Journal of Asian Studies* 51, no. 1 (1995): 152–60.

Hawkes, David. *The Songs of the South: An Ancient Chinese Anthology of Poems by Qu Yuan and Other Poets*. New York: Penguin, 1985.

He Lingxu 賀凌虛. "Lu Jia de zhengzhi sixiang" 陸賈的政治思想. *Si yu yan* 思與言 6, no. 6 (1969): 30–35.

Hegel, Georg Wilhelm Friedrich. *The Philosophy of History*. Trans. J. Sibree. 1899. Reprinted—New York: Dover Publications, 1956.

Henderson, John B. *The Development and Decline of Chinese Cosmology*. New York: Columbia University Press, 1984.

Heusch, Luc de. *Sacrifice in Africa: A Structuralist Approach*. Bloomington: Indiana University Press, 1985.

Hölderlin, Friedrich. *Hymns and Fragments*. Trans, with an introduction, Richard Sieburth. Princeton, Princeton University Press, 1984.

Holzman, Donald. "Immortality-Seeking in Early Chinese Poetry." In *The Power of Culture: Studies in Chinese Cultural History*, ed. Willard J. Peterson, Andrew H. Plaks, and Ying-shih Yü, pp. 103–18. Hong Kong: Chinese University Press, 1994.

Homer. *The Iliad of Homer*. Translation by Richmond Lattimore. Chicago: University of Chicago Press, 1951.

Horiike Nobuo 堀池信夫. "Kandai no shinsen yōsei-setsu, igaku to chishikijin" 漢代の神仙養生説医学と知識人. In *Chūgoku kodai yōsei shisō no sōgōteki kenkyū* 中国古代養生思想の総合的研究, ed. Sakade Yoshinobu 坂出祥伸, pp. 296–321. Tokyo: Hirakawa, 1988.

Hsü Cho-yun. *Ancient China in Transition: An Analysis of Social Mobility, 722–222 B.C.* Stanford: Stanford University Press, 1965.

Hsü Cho-yun and Katheryn Linduff. *Western Chou Civilization.* New Haven: Yale University Press, 1988.

Hu Houxuan 胡厚宣. "Yin buci zhong de shangdi he wangdi" 殷卜辭中的上帝和王帝. *Lishi yanjiu* 歷史研究 1959, no. 9: 23–50; no. 10: 89–110.

Hubert, Henri, and Mauss, Marcel. *Sacrifice: Its Nature and Functions.* Trans. W. D. Halls. Chicago: University of Chicago Press, 1981 (1964).

Ishida Hidemi 石田秀実. "Chūgoku kodai ni okeru seishin shippei kan" 中国古代における精神疾病観. *Nihon Chūgoku gakkai hō* 日本中国学会報 33 (1981): 29–42.

Itō Michiharu 伊藤道治. *Chūgoku kodai kokka no shihai kōzō* 中国古代国家の支配構造. Tokyo: Sōbunsha, 1987.

———. *Chūgoku kodai ōchō no keisei* 中国古代王朝の形成. Tokyo: Sōbunsha, 1975.

Ivanhoe, Philip J. "A Happy Symmetry: Xunzi's Ethical Thought." *Journal of the American Academy of Religion,* 59, no. 2 (Summer 1991): 309–22.

———. "A Question of Faith—A New Interpretation of Mencius 2B:13." *Early China* 13 (1988): 133–65.

———. "Was Zhuangzi a Relativist?" *Essays on Skepticism, Relativism, and Ethics in the Zhuangzi,* ed. Paul Kjellberg and Philip J. Ivanhoe, pp. 196–214. Albany: State University of New York Press, 1996.

Jaspers, Karl. *The Origin and Goal of History.* Trans. Michael Bullock. New Haven: Yale University Press, 1953.

———. *Socrates, Buddha, Confucius, Jesus: The Paradigmatic Individuals.* Ed. Hannah Arendt; trans. Ralph Manheim. New York: Harcourt, Brace, and Company, 1962.

"Jingmen Guodian yi hao Chu mu" 荊門郭店一號楚墓. *Wenwu* 文物 1997, no. 7: 35–48.

Kahn, Charles H. "Religion and Natural Philosophy in Empedocles' Doctrine of the Soul." In *The Pre-Socratics: A Collection of Critical Essays,* ed. Alexander P. D. Mourelatos, pp. 426–56. Princeton: Princeton University Press, 1974.

———. "Was Euthyphro the Author of the Derveni Papyrus?" In *Studies on the Derveni Papyrus,* ed. André Laks and Glenn W. Most, pp. 55–63. Oxford: Clarendon Press, 1997.

Kalinowski, Marc. *Cosmologie et divination dans la China ancienne.* Paris: Ecole française d'Extrême-Orient, 1991.

Kanaya Osamu 金谷治. *Rōsō teki sekai: Enanji no shisō* 老荘的世界淮南子の思想. Kyoto: Heirakuji shoden, 1959.

————. "Senshin ni okeru hōshisō no tenkai" 先秦における法思想の展開. *Shūkan Tōyōgaku* 集刊東洋学 47 (1982): 1–10.

————. *Shin Kan shisō shi kenkyū* 秦漢思想史研究. Tokyo: Maruzen, 1961.

Kant, Immanuel. *Critique of Pure Reason.* Trans. Norman Kemp Smith. New York: St. Martin's Press, 1965.

————. *Prolegomena to Any Future Metaphysics.* Trans. Lewis White Beck. Indianapolis: Bobbs-Merrill Educational Publishing, 1950.

Karlgren, Bernhard. "The Book of Documents." *Bulletin of the Museum of Far Eastern Antiquities* 22 (1950).

————. *The Book of Odes.* Stockholm: Museum of Far Eastern Antiquities, 1950.

Katō Jōken 加藤常賢. *Kanji no kigen* 漢字の起源. Tokyo: Kadokawa shoten, 1970.

Keightley, David N. *The Ancestral Landscape: Time, Space, and Community in Late Shang China (ca. 1200–1045 B.C.).* Berkeley: Institute of East Asian Studies, 2000.

————. "Clean Hands and Shining Helmets: Heroic Action in Early Chinese and Greek Culture." In *Religion and the Authority of the Past,* ed. Tobin Siebers. Ann Arbor: University of Michigan Press, 1993.

————. "The Making of the Ancestors: Late Shang Religion and Its Legacy." *Cahiers d'Extrême-Asie,* forthcoming.

————. "Religion and the Rise of Urbanism." *Journal of the American Oriental Society* 93, no. 4 (Oct.–Dec. 1973): 527–38.

————. "The Religious Commitment: Shang Theology and the Genesis of Chinese Political Culture." *History of Religions* 17, no. 3/4 (Feb.–May 1978): 211–25.

————. "Shamanism, Death, and the Ancestors: Religious Mediation in Neolithic and Shang China (ca. 5000–1000 B.C.)." *Asiatische Studien* 52, no. 3 (1998): 763–831.

————. "Shamanism in *Guoyu?* A Tale of the *xi* and *wu.*" Berkeley: University of California, Center for Chinese Studies, Regional Seminar, 1989. Unpublished manuscript.

————. "The Shang State as Seen in the Oracle Bone Inscriptions." *Early China* 5 (1979–80): 25–34.

————. *Sources of Shang History: The Oracle-Bone Inscriptions of Bronze Age China.* Berkeley: University of California Press, 1978.

Kern, Martin. *The Stele Inscriptions of Ch'in Shih-huang.* New Haven: American Oriental Society, 2000.

Kingsley, Peter. *Ancient Philosophy, Mystery, and Magic: Empedocles and Pythagorean Tradition.* Oxford: Clarendon Press, 1995.

————. "Greeks, Shamans, and Magi." *Studia Iranica* 23 (1994): 187–97.

Kline, T. C., III, and Philip J. Ivanhoe, eds. *Virtue, Nature, and Moral Agency in the Xunzi.* Indianapolis: Hackett, 2000.

Kroll, Paul. "Yuan You." In *Religions of China in Practice*, ed. Donald S. Lopez, Jr., pp. 156–65. Princeton: Princeton University Press, 1996.

Ku Mei-kao. *A Chinese Mirror for Magistrates*. Canberra: Australian National University, 1988.

Lau, D. C., trans. *Mencius*. New York: Penguin Books, 1970.

Lau, D.C., and Roger T. Ames, trans. *Yuan Dao: Tracing Dao to Its Source*. New York: Ballantine Books, 1998.

Le Blanc, Charles. "From Ontology to Cosmogony: Notes on *Chuang Tzu* and *Huai-nan Tzu*." In *Chinese Ideas About Nature and Society: Studies in Honour of Derk Bodde*, ed. Charles Le Blanc and Susan Blader, pp. 117–29. Hong Kong: Hong Kong University Press, 1987.

———. *Huai-Nan Tzu: Philosophical Synthesis in Early Han Thought*. Hong Kong: Hong Kong University Press, 1985.

Lévi-Strauss, Claude. *The Elementary Structures of Kinship*. Trans. James Harle Bell, John Richard von Sturmer, and Rodney Needham. Boston: Beacon Press, 1969.

———. *From Honey to Ashes: Introduction to a Science of Mythology*, vol. 2. Trans. John Weightman and Doreen Weightman. New York: Harper and Row, 1966.

———. *The Savage Mind*. Chicago: University of Chicago Press, 1966.

———. *Totemism*. Trans. Rodney Needham. Boston: Beacon Press, 1963.

Lewis, Mark Edward. *Writing and Authority in Early China*. Albany: State University of New York Press, 1999.

Li Ling 李零. "An Archaeological Study of Taiyi (Grand One) Worship." *Early Medieval China* 2 (1995–96): 1–39.

———. "Chutu faxian yu gushu niandai de zai renshi" 出土發現與古書年代的再認識. *Jiuzhou xuekan* 九州學科 3, no. 1 (1988): 105–36.

———. "Daojia yu 'Boshu'" 道教與帛書. In *Daojia wenhua yanjiu* 道家文化研究, vol. 3, ed. Chen Guying 陳鼓應, pp. 386–94. Shanghai: Guji chubanshe, 1993.

———. "Formulaic Structure of Chu Divinatory Bamboo Slips." Trans. William G. Boltz. *Early China* 15 (1990): 71–86.

———. *Zhongguo fangshu kao* 中國方術考. Beijing: Renmin Zhongguo chubanshe, 1993.

Li Xiaoding 李孝定. *Jiagu wenzi jishi* 甲骨文字集釋. 13 vols. Taibei: Zhongyang yanjiuyuan, Lishi yuyan yanjiusuo, 1965.

Li Xueqin 李學勤. "Ping Chen Mengjia *Yinxu buci zongshu*" 評陳夢家殷虛卜辭綜述. *Kaogu* 考古 1957, no. 3: 119–30.

———. "Xiaotun nandi jiagu yu jiagu fenqi" 小屯南地甲骨與甲骨分期. *Wenwu* 文物 1981, no. 5: 27–33.

Li Xueqin 李學勤 and Peng Yushang 彭裕商. *Yinxu jiagu fenqi yanjiu* 殷墟甲骨分期研究. Shanghai: Guji chubanshe, 1996.

Liao Mingchun 繆名春. "Lun Boshu *Xici* yu jinben *Xici* de guanxi" 論帛書繫辭與今本繫辭的關係. *Daojia wenhua yanjiu* 道家文化研究 1993, no. 3: 133–43.

Lin Yun 林澐. "Xiaotun nandi fajue yu Yinxu jiagu duandai" 小屯南地發掘與殷虛甲骨斷代. *Guwenzi yanjiu* 古文字研究 1984, no. 9: 111–54.

Lincoln, Bruce. *Death, War, and Sacrifice: Studies in Ideology and Practice.* Chicago: University of Chicago Press, 1991.

———. *Theorizing Myth: Narrative, Ideology, and Scholarship.* Chicago: University of Chicago Press, 1999.

Linforth, I. M. *The Arts of Orpheus.* Berkeley: University of California Press, 1941.

Loewe, Michael. *A Biographical Dictionary of the Qin, Former Han and Xin Periods (221 BC–AD 24).* Leiden: Brill, 2000.

———. *Crisis and Conflict in Han China 104 BC to 9 AD.* London: George Allen and Unwin, 1974.

Luo Genze 羅根澤. *Guanzi tanyuan* 管子探源. Shanghai: Zhonghua shuju, 1931.

———. "Lu Jia *Xinyu* kaozheng" 陸賈新語考證. In Gu Jiegang et al., eds., *Gushibian* (q.v.), 4: 198–202.

Luo Xizhang 羅西章. "Shaanxi Fufeng faxian Xi-Zhou Liwang Hu gui" 陝西扶風發現西周厲王㝬簋. *Wenwu* 文物 1979, no. 4: 89–91.

Ma Chengyuan 馬承源. "He zun mingwen chushi" 何尊銘文初釋. *Wenwu* 文物 1976, no. 1: 64–65.

Machle, Edward J. *Nature and Heaven in the Xunzi: A Study of the Tian Lun.* Albany: State University of New York Press, 1993.

Mair, Victor. "Old Sinitic *Myag*, Old Persian *Magus*, and English 'Magician.'" *Early China* 15 (1990): 27–47.

Major, John. *Heaven and Earth in Early Han Thought: Chapters Three, Four, and Five of the Huainanzi.* Albany: State University of New York Press, 1993.

Marx, Karl. *The Eighteenth Brumaire of Louis Bonaparte.* New York: International Publishers, 1963.

Mawangdui Hanmu boshu 馬王堆漢墓帛書, vols. 1 and 4. Beijing: Wenwu chubanshe, 1980, 1985.

Meuli, Karl. "Scythia." *Hermes* 70 (1935): 121–76.

Mote, Frederick. *Intellectual Foundations of China.* 2d ed. New York: McGraw-Hill, 1989.

Needham, Joseph. *Science and Civilisation in China,* vol. 2, *History of Scientific Thought.* Cambridge, Eng.: Cambridge University Press, 1956.

———. *Science and Civilisation in China,* vol. 3, *Mathematics and the Sciences of the Heavens and the Earth.* Cambridge, Eng.: Cambridge University Press, 1959.

Ngo Van Xuyet. *Divination, magie et politique dans la China ancienne.* Paris: Presse Universitaires de France, 1976.

Ning Chen. "The Concept of Fate in *Mencius*." *Philosophy East and West* 47, no. 4 (1997): 495–520.

———. "Confucius' View of Fate (*Ming*)." *Journal of Chinese Philosophy* 24 (1997): 323–59.

Nivison, David S. "An Interpretation of the 'Shao gao.'" *Early China* 20 (1995): 177–93.

Nyberg, H. S. *Die Religionen des alten Iran*. Leipzig: J. C. Hinrichs, 1938.

Nylan, Michael. "A Problematic Model: The Han 'Orthodox Synthesis,' Then and Now." In *Imagining Boundaries: Changing Confucian Doctrines, Texts, and Hermeneutics*," ed. Kai-wing Chow, On-cho Ng, and John B. Henderson, pp. 17–56. Albany: State University of New York Press, 1999.

Panagiotou, S. "Empedocles on His Own Divinity." *Mnemosyne* 36 (1983): 276–85.

Pankenier, David W. "The Cosmo-Political Background of Heaven's Mandate." *Early China* 20 (1995): 121–76.

Paper, Jordan. *The Spirits Are Drunk: Comparative Approaches to Chinese Religion*. Albany: State University of New York Press, 1995.

Peerenboom, R. P. *Law and Morality in Ancient China: The Silk Manuscripts of Huang-Lao*. Albany: State University of New York Press, 1993.

Pepin, Jean. *Idées grecques sur l'homme et sur le dieu*. Paris: Société d'Edition "Les Belles Lettres," 1971.

Peterson, Willard J. "Making Connections: 'Commentary on the Attached Verbalizations' of the *Book of Change*." *Harvard Journal of Asiatic Studies* 42, no. 1 (June 1982): 67–116.

Pindar. *Pindar's Victory Songs*. Trans. Frank J. Nisetich. Baltimore: Johns Hopkins University Press, 1980.

Plato. *Euthyphro, Apology, Crito, Phaedo, Phaedrus*. Trans. Harold North Fowler. Cambridge, Mass.: Harvard University Press, 1914.

———. *Plato's Timaeus*. Trans. Francis Cornford. New York: Macmillan, 1959.

Plutarch. *Plutarch's Lives*. Trans. Bernadotte Perrin. 11 vols. Cambridge, Mass.: Harvard University Press, 1914–26.

Pollini, J. "Man or God: Divine Assimilation and Imitation in the Late Republic and Early Principate." In *Between Republic and Empire: Interpretations of Augustus and His Principate*, ed. Kurt A. Raaflaub and Mark Toher, pp. 334–57. Berkeley: University of California Press, 1990.

Poo Mu-chou. *In Search of Personal Welfare: A View of Ancient Chinese Religion*. Albany: State University of New York, 1998.

Puett, Michael. *The Ambivalence of Creation: Debates Concerning Innovation and Artifice in Early China*. Stanford: Stanford University Press, 2001.

———. "The Ascension of the Spirit: Toward a Cultural History of Self-Divinization Movements in Early China." *Cahiers d'Extrême-Asie*, forthcoming.

———. "Determining the Position of Heaven and Earth: Debates over State Sacrifices in the Western Han Dynasty." In *Confucian Spirituality*, ed. Tu Wei-Ming and Mary Evelyn Tucker. New York: Crossroad Press, forthcoming.

———. "The Ethics of Responding Properly: The Notion of *Qing* in Early Chinese Thought." In *Emotions in Chinese Culture*, ed. Halvor Eifring, forthcoming.

———. "Following the Commands of Heaven: The Notion of *Ming* in Early China." In *Heaven's Will and Life's Lot: Destiny and Determinism in Chinese Culture*, ed. Christopher Lupke, forthcoming.

———. "Humans and Gods: The Theme of Self-Divinization in Early China and Early Greece." In *Thinking Through Comparisons: Ancient Greece and China*, ed. Stephen Durrant and Steven Shankman. Albany: State University of New York Press, forthcoming.

———. "'Nothing Can Overcome Heaven': The Notion of Spirit in the *Zhuangzi*." In *Essays on Zhuangzi*, ed. Scott Cook.

———. "Sages, Ministers, and Rebels: Narratives from Early China Concerning the Initial Creation of the State." *Harvard Journal of Asiatic Studies* 58, no. 2 (Dec. 1998): 425–79.

Qiu Xigui 裘錫圭. "Jixia Daojia jingqi shuo de yanjiu" 稷下道家精氣說的研究. *Daojia wenhua yanjiu* 道家文化研究 1992, no. 2: 167–92.

———. "Lun Li zu buci de shidai" 論歷組卜辭的時代. *Guwenzi yanjiu* 古文字研究 1981, no. 6: 262–320.

———. "Mawangdui yishu shidu suoyi" 馬王堆醫書釋讀瑣議. In idem, *Guwenzi lunji* 古文字論集, pp. 525–36. Beijing Zhonghua shuju, 1992.

Queen, Sarah. *From Chronicle to Canon: The Hermeneutics of the Spring and Autumn Annals, According to Tung Chung-shu*. Cambridge, Eng.: Cambridge University Press, 1996.

Raphals, Lisa. *Knowing Words: Wisdom and Cunning in the Classical Traditions of China and Greece*. Ithaca: Cornell University Press, 1992.

Redfield, James. *Nature and Culture in the Iliad: The Tragedy of Hector*. Chicago: University of Chicago Press, 1975.

Rickett, W. Allyn, trans. *Guanzi: Political, Economic, and Philosophical Essays from Early China*, vol. 2. Princteon: Princeton University Press, 1998.

Robinet, Isabelle. *Taoism: Growth of a Religion*. Trans. Phyllis Brooks. Stanford: Stanford University Press, 1997.

Roetz, Heiner. *Confucian Ethics of the Axial Age: A Reconstruction Under the Aspect of the Breakthrough Toward Conventional Thinking*. Albany: State University of New York, 1993.

Rosen, Stanley. *Hermeneutics as Politics*. Oxford: Oxford University Press, 1987.

Roth, Harold D. *Original Tao: Inward Training and the Foundations of Chinese Mysticism*. New York: Columbia University Press, 1999.

———. "Psychology and Self-Cultivation in Early Taoistic Thought." *Harvard Journal of Asiatic Studies* 51, no. 2 (1991): 599–650.

———. "Redaction Criticism and the Early History of Taoism." *Early China* 19 (1994): 1–46.

———. "Some Methodological Issues in the Study of the Guodian *Laozi* Parallels." In *The Guodian Laozi: Proceedings of the International Conference, Dartmouth College, May 1998*, ed. Sarah Allan and Crispin Williams, pp. 71–88. Berkeley: Society for the Study of Early China and University of California, Institute of East Asian Studies, 2000.

———. *The Textual History of the Huai-nan Tzu.* Ann Arbor: AAS Monograph Series, 1992.

———. "The Yellow Emperor's Guru: A Narrative Analysis from *Chuang Tzu* 11." *Taoist Resources* 7, no. 1 (Apr. 1997): 43–60.

Sahlins, Marshall. "Foreword." In Gregory Schrempp, *Magical Arrows: The Maori, the Greeks, and the Folklore of the Universe*, pp. ix–xiii. Madison: University of Wisconsin Press, 1992.

———. *How "Natives" Think: About Captain Cook, for Example.* Chicago: University of Chicago Press, 1995.

———. *Islands of History.* Chicago: University of Chicago Press, 1985.

———. "The Return of the Event, Again, with Reflections on the Beginnings of the Great Fijian War of 1843 to 1855 Between the Kingdoms of Bau and Rewa." In *Clio in Oceania: Toward a Historical Anthropology*, ed. Aletta Biersack, pp. 37–99. Washington: Smithsonian Institution Press, 1991.

Saiki Tetsurō 斎木哲郎. "Kōrō shisō no saikentō—Kan no Kōso shūdan to Rōshi no kankei o chūshin toshite" 黄老思想の再検討漢の高祖集団と老子の関係を中心として. *Tōhō shūkyō* 東方宗教 62, no. 10 (1983): 19–36.

Schrempp, Gregory. *Magical Arrows: The Maori, the Greeks, and the Folklore of the Universe.* Madison: University of Wisconsin Press, 1992.

Schwartz, Benjmain I. "The Age of Transcendence." Special issue: Wisdom, Revelation, and Doubt: Perspectives on the First Millennium B.C. *Daedalus*, Spring 1975, pp. 1–7.

———. "Transcendence in Ancient China." Special issue: Wisdom, Revelation, and Doubt: Perspectives on the First Millennium B.C. *Daedalus*, Spring 1975, pp. 57–68.

———. *The World of Thought in Ancient China.* Cambridge, Mass.: Harvard University Press, 1985.

Scott, Michael W. "Auhenua: Land, Lineage, and Ontology in Arosi (Solomon Islands)." Ph.D. diss., University of Chicago, Department of Anthropology, 2001.

Seidel, Anna. "Traces of Han Religion in Funeral Texts Found in Tombs." *Dōkyō to shūkyō bunka*, ed. Akizuki Kan'ei, pp. 21–57. Tokyo: Hirakawa shuppansha, 1987.

Shaughnessy, Edward L. "The Duke of Zhou's Retirement in the East and the Beginnings of the Minister-Monarch Debate in Chinese Political Philosophy." In idem, *Before Confucius: Studies in the Creation of the Chinese Classics*, pp. 101–36. Albany: State University of New York Press, 1997.

———. "Extra-Lineage Cult in the Shang Dynasty: A Surrejoinder." *Early China* 11–12 (1985–87): 182–94.

———. "A First Reading of the Mawangdui *Yijing* Manuscript." *Early China* 19 (1994): 57–66.

———. "'New' Evidence on the Zhou Conquest." *Early China* 6 (1980–81): 57–81.

———. "Recent Approaches to Oracle-Bone Periodization: A Review." *Early China* 8 (1982–83): 1–13.

———. *Sources of Western Zhou History: Inscribed Bronze Vessels*. Berkeley: University of California Press, 1991.

———. "Zhouyuan Oracle-Bone Inscriptions: Entering the Research Stage? A Review of *Xi-Zhou jiagu tanlun*." *Early China* 11–12 (1985–87): 146–63.

Shibata Kiyotsugu 柴田清継. "*Kanshi* shihen ni okeru shin to dō" 管子四篇における神と道. *Nihon Chūgoku gakkai hō* 日本中国学会報 36 (1984): 12–24.

Shima Kunio 島邦男. *Inkyo bokuji kenkyū* 殷虚卜辞研究. Tokyo: Kyuko shoin, 1958.

———. *Inkyo bokuji sōrui* 殷虚卜辞綜類. 2nd rev. ed. Tokyo: Kyuko shoin, 1971.

Shirakawa Shizuka 白川静. *Kinbun tsūshaku* 金文通釈. 56 vols. Kobe: Hakutsuru bijutsukan, 1962–.

Shirokogoroff, Sergei Mikhailovich. *Psychomental Complex of the Tungus*. London: Kegan Paul, 1935.

Si Xiuwu 司修武. *Huang-Lao xueshuo yu Han chu zhengzhi pingyi* 黃老學說與漢初政治平議. Taibei: Xuesheng shuju, 1993.

Sivin, Nathan. *Medicine, Philosophy, and Religion in Ancient China*. Aldershot: Variorum, 1995.

———. "On the Word Taoism as a Source of Perplexity, with Special Reference to the Relations of Science and Religion in Traditional China." *History of Religions* 17 (1978): 303–30.

———. *Science in Ancient China: Researches and Reflections*. Aldershot: Variorum, 1995.

———. "State, Cosmos, and Body in the Last Three Centuries B.C." *Harvard Journal of Asiatic Studies* 55, no. 1 (1995): 5–37.

Slingerland, Ted. "The Conception of *Ming* in Early Confucian Thought." *Philosophy East and West* 46, no. 4 (1996): 567–81.

Smith, Jonathan Z. *To Take Place: Toward Theory in Ritual.* Chicago: University of Chicago Press, 1987.

———. "The Wobbling Pivot." In idem, *Map Is Not Territory: Studies in the History of Religions.* Chicago: University of Chicago Press, 1978.

Smith, Kidder. "Sima Tan and the Invention of Daoism, 'Legalism,' et cetera." *Journal of Asian Studies*, forthcoming.

Smith, William Robertson. *Lectures on the Religion of the Semites.* 2d ed. London: A. and C. Black, 1894.

Tang Lan 唐 蘭. "He zun mingwen jieshi" 何 尊 銘 文 解 釋. *Wenwu* 文 物 1976, no. 1: 60–63.

Taylor, Lily Ross. *The Divinity of the Roman Emperor.* Middletown, Conn.: American Philological Association, 1931.

Thucydides. *The History of the Peloponnesian War.* Trans. Rex Warner. New York: Penguin Classics, 1972.

Tylor, Edward. *Primitive Culture.* New York: Holt, 1889.

Valeri, Valerio. "Constitutive History: Genealogy and Narrative in Hawaiian Kingship." In *Culture Through Time*, ed. E. Ohnuki-Tierney, pp. 154–92. Stanford: Stanford University Press, 1991.

———. *Kingship and Sacrifice: Ritual and Society in Ancient Hawaii.* Chicago: University of Chicago Press, 1985.

———. "The Transformation of a Transformation: A Structural Essay on an Aspect of Hawaiian History (1809–1819)." *Social Analysis* 10 (1982): 3–41.

———. "Wild Victims: Hunting as Sacrifice and Sacrifice as Hunting in Huaulu." *History of Religions* 34, no. 2 (Nov. 1994): 101–31.

Vankeerbergen, Griet. "The *Huainanzi* and Liu An's Claim to Moral Authority." Ph.D. diss., Princeton University, 1996.

Vernant, Jean-Pierre. "At Man's Table: Hesiod's Foundation Myth of Sacrifice." In *The Cuisine of Sacrifice Among the Greeks*, ed. Marcel Detienne and Jean-Pierre Vernant; trans. Paula Wissing, pp. 21–86. Chicago: University of Chicago Press, 1989.

———. "The Myth of Prometheus in Hesiod." In idem, *Myth and Society in Ancient Greece*, trans. Janet Lloyd, pp. 168–85. New Jersey: Humanities Press, 1980.

———. "Sacrificial and Alimentary Codes in Hesiod's Myth of Prometheus." In *Myth, Religion and Society: Structuralist Essays by M. Detienne, L. Gernet, J.-P. Vernant, and P. Vidal-Naquet*, ed. and trans. R. L. Gordon, pp. 57–79. Cambridge, Eng.: Cambridge University Press, 1981.

Waley, Arthur. *The Nine Songs: A Study of Shamanism in Ancient China.* London: Allen and Unwin, 1955.

Wang Aihe. *Cosmology and Political Culture in Early China.* Cambridge, Eng.: Cambridge University Press, 2000.

Wang Baoxuan 王葆玹. "Boshu *Xici* yu Zhanguo Qin Han Daojia *Yi* xue" 帛書繫辭與戰國秦漢道家易學. *Daojia wenhua yanjiu* 道家文化研究 1993, no. 3: 73–88.

Wang Yuxin 王宇信. *Xi-Zhou jiagu tanlun* 西周甲骨探論. Beijing: Zhongguo shehui kexue chubanshe, 1984.

Waters, Geoffrey R. *Three Elegies of Ch'u: An Introduction to the Traditional Interpretation of the Ch'u Tz'u.* Madison: University of Wisconsin Press, 1985.

Watson, Burton. *Ssu-ma Ch'ien: The Grand Historian of China.* New York: Columbia University Press, 1958.

Watson, Burton, trans. *Chuang Tzu: Basic Writings.* New York: Columbia University Press, 1964.

———. *Records of the Grand Historian: Translated from the Shiji of Ssu-ma Ch'ien.* 2 vols. New York: Columbia University Press, 1961.

Weber, Max. *Economy and Society: An Outline of Interpretive Sociology.* Ed. Guenther Roth and Claus Wittich. 2 vols. Berkeley: University of California Press, 1978.

———. *The Religion of China.* Trans. Hans H. Gerth. New York: Free Press, 1951.

Weinstock, Stefan. *Divus Julius.* Oxford: Clarendon Press, 1971.

West, M. L. *The Orphic Poems.* Oxford: Clarendon Press, 1983.

Wheatley, Paul. *The Pivot of the Four Quarters: A Preliminary Enquiry into the Origins and Character of the Ancient Chinese City.* Chicago: Aldine, 1971.

Widengren, G. "Henrik Samuel Nyberg and Iranian Studies in the Light of Personal Reminiscences." *Acta Iranica* 2 (1975): 419–56.

Wu Guang 吳光. *Huang-Lao zhi xue tonglun* 黄老之學通論. Hangzhou: Zhejiang renmin chubanshe, 1985.

Wu Hung. "Art in a Ritual Context." *Early China* 17 (1992): 111–44.

Xu Fuguan 徐復觀. *Liang Han sixiang shi* 兩漢思想史. Taibei: Taiwan xuesheng shuju, 1979.

Yang Jingshuang 楊景鷚. "Fangxiangshi yu danuo" 方相氏與大儺. *Zhongyang yanjiuyuan, Lishi yuyan yanjiusuo jikan* 中央研究院歷史語言研究所集刊 31 (1960): 123–65.

Yang Kuan 楊寬. *Qin Shihuang* 秦始皇. Shanghai: Renmin chubanshe, 1956.

———. *Zhanguo shi* 戰國史. 2d ed. Shanghai: Renmin chubanshe, 1980.

———. "Zhongguo shanggushi daolun" 中國上古史導論. In Gu Jiegang et al., eds., *Gushibian* (q.v.), 7a: 189–93.

Yates, Robin. *Five Lost Classics: Tao, Huanglao, and Yin-Yang in Han China.* New York: Ballantine Books, 1997.

Yavetz, Zwi. *Julius Caesar and His Public Image.* London: Thames and Hudson, 1983.

Yearley, Lee H. "Toward a Typology of Religious Thought: A Chinese Example." *Journal of Religion* 55, no. 4 (Oct. 1975): 426–43.

———. "Zhuangzi's Understanding of Skillfulness and the Ultimate Spiritual State." In *Essays on Skepticism, Relativism, and Ethics in the Zhuangzi*, ed. Paul Kjellberg and Philip J. Ivanhoe, pp. 152–82. Albany: State University of New York Press, 1996.

Yu, Pauline; Peter Bol; Stephen Owen; and Willard Peterson, eds. *Ways With Words: Writing About Reading Texts from Early China*. Berkeley: University of California Press, 2000.

Yu Ying-Shih. "Life and Immortality in the Mind of Han China." *Harvard Journal of Asiatic Studies* 25 (1964–65): 80–122.

———. "'O Soul, Come Back!' A Study in the Changing Conceptions of the Soul and Afterlife in Pre-Buddhist China." *Harvard Journal of Asiatic Studies* 47, no. 2 (Dec. 1987): 363–95.

Zanker, Paul. *The Power of Images in the Age of Augustus*. Trans. Alan Shapiro. Ann Arbor: University of Michigan Press, 1988.

Zhang Dake 張大可. *Shiji yanjiu* 史記研究. Lanzhou: Gansu renmin chubanshe, 1985.

Zhang Zhenglang 張政烺. "He zun mingwen jieshi buyi" 何尊銘文解釋補遺. *Wenwu* 文物 1976, no. 1: 66.

Zhongguo shehui kexueyuan, Kaogu yanjiusuo 中國社會科學院考古研究所. *Xiaotun nandi jiagu* 小屯南地甲骨. 2 vols. Shanghai: Zhonghua, 1980, 1983.

Index

Agriculture: and decline of shamanism, 36–37; human control over nature, 42–43; and invocation of ancestors, 46; origins, 70; sacrifices involved, 70, 71–72

Ai, Emperor, 312

Aidoneus, 91

Alexander, 235–36, 247n

Alignment, see *Jing ying* (alignment and orientation)

Ames, Roger T., 17–18, 21, 22, 23, 147–48, 152, 158

Analects, see *Lunyu*

Analytical thinking: contrast with correlative thinking, 16–17

Ancestors: ascension, 219; construction of pantheon, 44–46, 52, 67, 77, 78, 198, 317–18; curses, 46; divination to, 46–47; hierarchy, 46, 47–48, 49, 52–54, 198; invocation in *bin* rituals, 34, 47–48, 49; links to living humans, 13, 150; power, 46, 47; relationships with descendants, 68;

relationships with sages, 198–99; sacrifices to, 45, 46, 52–54, 62, 73, 238, 318; temple names, 45, 45n, 52; worship of in Shang, 38–39, 44–46, 150; in Zhou period, 59–68 *passim*. *See also* Spirits

Animals, *see* Sacrifices; Totemism

Apollo, 88

Aristotle, 87

Ascension: of ancestors, 219; critiques of beliefs, 246–47, 254–55; of Greek gods, 222–24; of Huangdi, 243–44, 257; of kings, 236, 241–42; means, 201, 216; political implications, 261, 264–65; surveys of cosmos, 219–20, 221. *See also* Immortality; Liberation; True Man

Ascension narratives: cosmologies, 221; Greek, 203–4, 222–24; Han texts, 204; historical context, 223–24; language, 219–20, 281, 282; relationship to shamanism, 202; scholarly views of, 201, 202; *Shiwen*, 219; similarities

Immortality: lack of interest in, 277;
  means of attaining, 239–45 *passim*,
  257; rulers' interest in, 239–40, 241,
  243, 313; types, 244–45. *See also* Ascension; Divinization
India: Axial Period, 11; Greek conquests,
  235; separation of human and divine,
  13; Vedic soma sacrifices, 52

Jade *cong*, 35
Jakobson, Roman, 147
Jaspers, Karl, 11, 17, 19
Ji Xian, 122–23, 125, 130
Jian Wu, 124
Jiang Yuan, 68–75 *passim*
Jing, see Essence
"Jingshen," see *Huainanzi*, "Jingshen"
Jing ying (alignment and orientation): in
  ascension narratives, 219–20, 221; by
  Great One, 162, 163–64; by Heaven,
  293; of Heaven and Earth, 212, 273–
  75; of human body, 273–75; by hu-
  mans, 262–63, 312–13; by ruler, 225,
  241, 283, 294; by spirits, 1, 2–3, 271,
  283; in *Spring and Autumn Annals*,
  296; surveys before construction, 2,
  271, 284

Kamehameha, 233
Kang, King, 59
Kant, Immanuel, 157
Katharmoi, 92
Keightley, David N., 36–40, 45–54 *passim*, 73, 77, 78, 102, 103, 105, 317
Kings: advised to transcend world, 222;
  capitals, 2, 32–33, 309, 314; criticism
  of, 252–53; dynastic cycles, 301; hereditary, 137–38; ordering of world,
  294–95, 299; powers over nature,
  225, 241–42; relationship with

Heaven, 101–2, 198, 210, 310; relations with spirits, 50; roles in ancient China, 56; "stranger," 228–30,
  233; true nature of, 178–79; universal
  rulership, 172
Kingship: criticism of, 264, 269; development in China, 159, 227–28, 230,
  236; dualistic conception, 226–28,
  233; origins, 228–30. *See also* Empires;
  Theomorphic kingship
Kingsley, Peter, 84
Kinship structures, 156, 158
Kuan Shu, 306
Kuang Heng, 308–17 *passim*

Laozi, 141, 264; comparison to *Taiyi
  sheng shui*, 165–67; cosmogony, 165;
  cosmology, 165–70 *passim*, 318; divinization claims, 167; on harmonization of humans and nature, 149;
  on sages, 166–67, 198–99
Lévi-Strauss, Claude, 146–59 *passim*, 183,
  200
Li, King, 64–65
Li Hei, 167–69, 214
Li Shaojun, 243, 244
Lian Shu, 124–25
Liberation: from bonds, 213; in Daoism,
  204; from form, 211–17 *passim*, 242,
  257, 267; meaning in *Huainanzi*, 282;
  in "Neiye," 168–69; of sages, 171;
  techniques, 218; Zhuangzi on, 133,
  136, 217, 257, 267. *See also* Ascension;
  Transcendence
Liezi, 123, 124, 130
Liji, "Ji fa," 96–97, 309
Ling, King, 246–47, 256, 303
Liu An, 286
Liu Xiang, 311
Livy, 228

Naturalism: of Laozi, 167; of Mencius,
140–43, 144; of Zhuangzi, 140–43,
144
Nature: control by spirits, 262, 265–66,
274; creation by Great One, 161–62;
harmony in, 175; morality of, 141;
patterns of, 183–84, 196; spirits of,
48, 50, 53, 96–97, 318; in Zhou cosmology, 56
—, relationship with humans: agriculture, 42–43; evolution of, 19–20;
human control, 78, 186, 256, 262–63,
266, 292, 294–95; kings' control, 225,
240; linked through *qi*, 249; music
as means of regulating nature, 175;
role of culture, 188; sages' power
over, 252; sages' understanding of,
162–63, 249–52; settlements, 41–42,
59
Needham, Joseph, 14, 15, 164, 290
"Neiye," see *Guanzi*, "Neiye"
Nestis, 91
Nicomachean Ethics (Aristotle), 87
Numa, 227, 229, 231–32
Nyberg, H. S., 85

Omenology, 254, 291, 292, 293, 296
Oracle-bone inscriptions, 34, 38–49
passim, 55
Orientation, see *Jing ying* (alignment
and orientation)
The Origin and Goal of History (Jaspers),
11
Orphics, 89–90

Pankenier, David W., 55–57, 60
Paper, Jordan, 202
Patterns (*li*), 183, 184, 188
Pensée chinoise, La (Granet), 8–9, 146,
227

Pericles, 234–35
Persia: ascension literature, 203. *See also*
Scythia
Peterson, Willard J., 190, 193
Phaedrus (Plato), 222–23
Philosophy: Chinese, 8, 141–42, 151–52,
205–6; Greek, 83–84, 87
Pindar, 88, 90
Ping, Emperor, 312
Ping Yi, 262
Pivot, 189, 190, 199–200, 263, 284
Plato, 93, 119, 203, 222–23
Plutarch, 228, 231–33
Polygenetic systems, 153, 156–57, 160,
196
Polynesia: cosmologies, 230; emergence
of state, 229–30; kingship, 233;
monogenesis, 156, 196–97; polygene-
sis, 153, 196. *See also* Fiji
Poo Mu-chou, 51, 103
Primitive cultures: *axis mundi*, 32, 33, 35;
correlative thinking, 155–56; totem-
ism, 152–54, 156
Prolegomena to Any Future Metaphysics
(Kant), 157
Prometheus, 73, 74, 75
Protestantism: contrasted to Confu-
cianism, 6–7; Weber on, 5–6n
Punishments: creation of, 106; in Qin
empire, 264
Pythagoras, 84

Qi: cosmology based on, 80; cycles of,
207, 209–10; of Heaven and earth,
207; in humans, 114–15, 125, 130, 271;
as link between humans and nature,
249; meaning, 109; Mencius on, 134;
relationship to essence, 109, 111; relationship to form, 265; utilization of,
112–13

Harvard-Yenching Institute Monograph Series
(titles now in print)